Global Perspectives
on the
COLLAPSE
of
Complex Systems

Edited by Jim A. Railey and
Richard Martin Reycraft

MAXWELL MUSEUM OF ANTHROPOLOGY
Anthropological Papers No. 8

Cover
Water buffalo on their way past the Kadalekalu Ganesha temple on the ridge above Hampi,
with the gopura of the Virupaksha temple beyond. Vijayanagara, Karnataka, India.
Photograph by John Gollings

Technical Editor
June-el Piper

Layout and Design
Donna Carpio

ISBN 978-0-912535-15-9

Library of Congress Cataloging-in-Publication Data

Global perspectives on the collapse of complex systems / edited by Jim A. Railey and Richard Martin Reycraft.
    p. cm. -- (Anthropological papers / Maxwell Museum of Anthropology ; no. 8)
  Includes bibliographical references and index.
  ISBN 978-0-912535-15-9
    1. Social archaeology. 2. Social systems--History. 3. Social change--History. 4. Social evolution.
5. Ethnoarchaeology. 6. Civilization, Ancient. 7. Prehistoric peoples. 8. Historic sites. 9. Excavations
(Archaeology) I. Railey, Jimmy A., 1956- II. Reycraft, Richard Martin.
  CC72.4.G57 2008
  930.1--dc22
                                        2008030125

Dedicated to James B. Petersen

1 9 5 4 – 2 0 0 5

Colleague, role model, friend

Contents

Figures

Tables

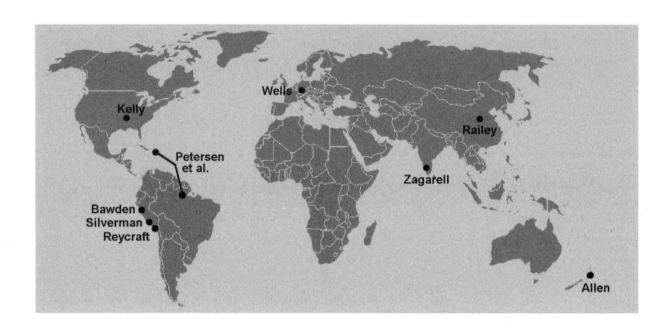

Map of world showing general location of study areas

1

Introduction

Jim A. Railey and Richard Martin Reycraft

Few topics are at once so fascinating yet potentially worrisome as the collapse of human societies. The ruins of great monuments that symbolize once-powerful states and other complex polities have long inspired awe and romanticized notions about the people who built them. The power of these sites' attraction today is testified by the many thousands who make long and expensive journeys to view such wonders as the pyramids of Egypt or the ancient Maya, the various ruins of ancient Rome, the terra-cotta army of Qin Shihuang's tomb in China, Angkor Wat in Cambodia, and many other sites that have become tourist destinations and fodder for the popular imagination. Yet these stunning monuments confront us with a dark message as well: even the most advanced (for their time, at least) and confident societies are vulnerable to total disintegration, and this message has unsettling implications for the future of today's increasingly global society. Even the collapse of a relatively peripheral state (e.g., Afghanistan) can have reverberating effects in other parts of the world.

Regardless of its unsettling implications, the collapse or transformation of complex systems is indeed part and parcel with the evolution of human societies and has been a persistent and recurrent theme of the human experience. It is thus a most worthy subject for investigation by archaeologists and historians. Yet archaeological interest in collapse has run hot and cold over the years, subject, in part, to the prevailing theoretical perspectives used to explain social evolution and change. In the study of sociopolitical evolution, interest in collapse has taken a back seat to interest in the rise of complexity and the emergence of new organizational forms. Before the 1980s, the anthropological study of collapse was primarily the domain of Marxist scholars (e.g., Friedman 1975, 1982; Friedman and Rowlands 1978), who generally acted as the spoilers in opposition to the systems and managerial theorists who held sway at that time.

Soon afterward, Renfrew (1984, first published in 1979) sought to bring collapse into the realm of systems theory and was among the first archaeologists in recent decades to offer a general, theoretical model of collapse. We return to aspects of Renfrew's model later in this discussion.

Largely by happenstance, 1988 proved to be a banner year in the study of sociopolitical collapse, as two major works on the subject were published (Tainter 1988; Yoffee and Cowgill 1988). Like Renfrew before him, Tainter offered an encompassing theory of collapse, although his thesis—spelled out in a book rather than a chapter—was more penetrating and thoroughly constructed than Renfew's chapter-length essay. Yoffee and Cowgill's effort was an edited volume that encompassed a diversity of views and ideas on the nature and causes of collapse. The effect of these two 1988 publications on the study of collapse is, to an extent, readily apparent in the pages of this volume, although some authors take explicit issue with ideas expressed in these earlier works.

Since 1988, interest in sociopolitical collapse has continued, but research results have been relegated mostly to specific case studies such as the ancient Maya (Demerest et al. 2004; Gill 2000; Webster 2002), the Bronze Age Aegean (Drews 1993), the Anasazi of the American Southwest (e.g., Stuart 2000), or the Mississippian chiefdoms of the southeastern United States (e.g., Anderson 1990; Pauketat 1992, 1994). During the 1990s, the expanding interest in "chiefdoms" (whether or not this term was used) was often accompanied by an awareness of the inherent instability of complex, prestate societies. In his edited volume on chiefdoms, Timothy Earle (1991a, 1991b) focused attention not only on how chiefdoms form, but also on characteristics of their organizational structures that made them inherently vulnerable to collapse.

Jared Diamond (2005) recently published a book that presents a serious effort to research and explain the causes of collapse and arrive at a general theory. Although he focuses to a large extent on the effects of environmental degradation, Diamond touches on many of the factors explored in this volume.

These on-going efforts enrich our understanding of collapse and identify powerful phenomena (such as natural disasters, disease, overextension, corruption, clashes of radically different cultures, environmental change and degradation, or warfare) that act as triggers of collapse events. More important, these studies reveal that collapse is a complex phenomenon whose root causes lie in social, political, and economic processes, as well as context-specific, historical and environmental circumstances. To orient the reader, this chapter explores some of the dimensions and causes of collapse and transformation, and it draws heavily upon—and benefits greatly from—previous efforts to characterize and explain these phenomena.

COLLAPSE AND COMPLEXITY

The very notion of collapse presupposes the existence of some level of complexity. Defining complexity is a task that could easily consume an entire volume in itself. For this discussion, we define *complexity* as an expansion of sociopolitical organization, which may involve scalar increases in population, formalized leadership, polity growth, territorial expansion, numbers and interconnections of decision-making units, and/or some development of specialized roles (e.g., shaman-priests, traders, warriors, engineers). Many of these attributes can be found at various levels of sociopolitical complexity, and although the study of collapse has traditionally focused on *states,* it is equally relevant to many prestate systems, including chiefdoms and even transegalitarian societies that might not have extended beyond the territory of a single village.

Accordingly, the study of collapse has focused on the loss—usually rapid and catastrophic—of material indicators of complexity. This, in turn, necessitates that we come to some agreement of what we mean when we use the term. Renfrew (1984:367–369) emphasized the sudden, catastrophic nature of collapse and listed four general features of system collapse, which are summarized here in Table 1. Note that Renfrew's features refer to the collapse of early *states,* although collapse can also occur in *prestate* complex societies (which, in fact, involves most of the case studies presented in this book). In his essay, Renfrew acknowledges that collapse may occur in prestate societies, with a specific reference to "the sudden decline of the Anasazi town sites in the southwestern United States in the thirteenth century AD" (1984:372). Moreover, not all of Renfrew's features will be found in the collapse of early states; for example, not all early states were literate, many did not have coinage, and not all cases of collapse

necessarily involve population reduction. Nevertheless, Renfew's list of features prompts of vivid picture of what is involved in the process of collapse, and many of these features will be found in cases of collapse among both state and prestate societies. Of particular interest are the specific combinations of features that occur in a given case of collapse, and the underlying factors that led to the disintegration of particular polities or systems.

Yoffee (1988) does not specifically define the term, but he does offer the important observation that the same processes and conditions used to explain the emergence and maintenance of complexity could also create conditions leading to collapse. Accordingly, the study of collapse requires a reorientation of how we think about the ingredients of complexity.

> The concern with rise, to the near exclusion of collapse, in evolutionary studies, has had important theoretical implications: social change has been perceived as a process of mutually supportive interactions that produce an irreversible succession of "emergent" levels of holistic sociocultural integration.... Collapse, on the other hand, requires that "levels" be broken down into institutional groupings of partly overlapping and partly opposing fields of action that lend the possibility of instability, as well as stability, to overarching societal institutions (Yoffee 1988:1–2).

Unlike Yoffee, Tainter is much more direct in offering a definition.

> The process of collapse . . . is a matter of rapid, substantial decline in an established level of complexity. A society that has collapsed is suddenly smaller, less differentiated and heterogenous, and characterized by fewer specialized parts; it displays less control over the behavior of its members. It is able at the same time to command smaller surpluses, to offer fewer benefits and inducements to membership; and it is less capable of providing subsistence and defensive security for a regional population (Tainter 1988:38).

Both Yoffee and Tainter stress that, for collapse to occur, a condition of complexity must have previously emerged. Collapse, then, involves two essential dimensions: (1) rapidity and (2) fragmentation, and/or reduction in scale,

Table 1. Renfrew's (1984:367–369) General Features of System Collapse

General Feature	Specific Features
Collapse of central administrative organization	a. Disappearance or reduction in numbers of levels of central-place hierarchy b. Complete fragmentation or disappearance of military organization into (at most) small, independent units c. Abandonment of palaces and central storage facilities. d. Eclipse of temples as major religious centers (often surviving, modified, as local shrines) e. Effective loss of literacy for secular and religious purposes f. Abandonment of public building works
Disappearance of the traditional elite class	a. Cessation of rich, traditional burials (although different forms of rich burial frequently reemerge after a couple of centuries) b. Abandonment of rich residences, or reuse in impoverished style by "squatters" c. Cessation in the use of costly assemblages of luxury goods, although individual items may survive
Collapse of centralized economy	a. Cessation of large-scale redistribution or market exchange b. Coinage (where applicable) no longer issued or exchanged commercially, although individual pieces survive as valuables c. External trade very markedly reduced, and traditional trade routes disappear d. Volume of internal exchange markedly reduced e. Cessation of craft-specialist manufacture f. Cessation of specialized or organized agricultural production, with farming instead on a local, "homestead" basis with diversified crop spectrum and mixed farming
Settlement shift and population decline	a. Abandonment of many settlements b. Shift to dispersed pattern of smaller settlements c. Frequent subsequent choice of defensible locations—the "flight to the hills" d. Marked reduction in population density

of a complex sociopolitical entity. Population decline has also been cited as another dimension of collapse (e.g., Tainter 1999:1020), although evidence for population continuity or even increases has been observed in some post-collapse situations (e.g., Blanton 1983:186; Graffam 1992:887; both cited in Tainter 1999:1020). Contrary to assumptions held by some, however, collapse does *not* necessarily imply regional abandonment, or replacement of local populations by outsiders, although any of these phenomena may occur in the process of collapse and transformation.

COLLAPSE OF A POLITY (OR SOCIETY) AND COLLAPSE OF A CIVILIZATION (OR CULTURE)

As the title of Yoffee and Cowgill's (1988) book implies, collapse involves both states and civilizations. Tainter, however, sees the collapse of *civilizations* as a misnomer.

Collapse is fundamentally a matter of the sociopolitical sphere. It may and frequently does have consequences in such areas as art, architecture, and literature but, contrary to widespread belief, these are not its essence. It is incorrect to speak of a civilization collapsing, though this is commonly done. A civilization (that is, a great tradition of art, architecture, and literature) is the cultural system of a complex society (Tainter 1988:41).

What is called civilization is an epiphenomenon or product of complexity. . . . Civilization emerges with socio-political complexity, exists because of it, and disappears when complexity disappears. Civilizations do not collapse; specific political structures do (Tainter 1999:989–990).

It is certainly the case, however, that the collapse of a complex polity does not necessarily bring down its associated civilization. Such has been the case throughout China's history. Distinctive elements of Chinese civilization—including its written script, bureaucratic staffing based on the examination system, architectural styles, and various art forms—survived repeated collapses, fragmentation, and reorganization of political structures. Even outside invaders—namely the Mongols of the thirteenth century and the Manchus of the seventeenth, adopted most or all of the trappings of Chinese civilization and culture once their conquests were secured.

CAUSES OF COLLAPSE

The causes of collapse can be broadly split into two main divisions, internal and external. Internal factors relate to the structure and workings of a sociopolitical system itself, and discussions of internal causes of collapse most typically refer to economic overextension in one form or another. In this chapter we highlight corruption as another important factor in the weakening and collapse of societies and present a somewhat extended discussion of this topic as it is not commonly cited in explanations of collapse.

External causes, on the other hand, involve a variety of factors that are not the result of a social system's internal structure or dynamics but rather are attributable to "natural" or "foreign" cultural forces or events. These include natural disasters. Disease is another contributor to sociopolitical collapse, and the origin of devastating epidemics often has both natural and cultural causes. The disastrous effects on Native American populations of diseases introduced by Old World invaders and immigrants is the most obvious example. Invasions or pressure from outside groups may also lead to the collapse of a complex system and/or civilization. It can, however, often prove difficult to successfully disentangle external from internal causes, as internal weaknesses in a system may make it especially vulnerable to external pressures.

The internal-external dichotomy is not so clean when one considers such factors as environmental degradation. True, the behaviors that lead to environmental destruction emanate from within human societies themselves, but the effects—and whether or not they lead or contribute to the collapse of a complex system—often depend on context-specific characteristics of the natural environment. Accordingly, environmental degradation here is considered under its own category of explanations because the causal factors lie astride the division between internal and external factors.

Internal Factors

Economic Overextension and Diminishing Returns

The notion of economic overextension and diminishing returns has been a recurrent theme in explanations of collapse. Renfrew (1984) pursued this line in his essay on collapse, couching it in a feedback-loop model popular among systems theorists of the time, and emphasizing the bioevolutionary analogy of overspecialization. It was Tainter (1988), however, who used this argument to its fullest potential, and in doing so offered perhaps the most ambitious and penetrating explanation of sociopolitical collapse. In *The Collapse of Complex Societies*, Tainter advocated that collapse is the result of diminishing returns brought on by investments that eventually result in economic overextension. Essentially, Tainter argues that initial investments in complexity are cheap and easy to sustain. To maintain itself over the long run, however, a complex society must continually invest in complexity, and such investments become increasingly costly over time, and a society eventually encounters diminishing returns. As a result, the system experiences mounting stresses that fray the edges of the sociopolitical fabric, and eventually the entire polity disintegrates. External factors (such as environmental catastrophes or stresses, or invasions by barbarians) may act as catalysts in the final demise of a society, but the ultimate causes of the collapse are traceable to diminishing returns.

Tainter's is the quintessential argument that the root causes leading to collapse are essentially *internal* (note that this is also implied by Yoffee [1988:1–2]). In a somewhat different vein, Adams makes the same argument.

> An essential—perhaps almost a diagnostic—feature of large-scale, complex but pre-industrial societies . . . was that short-term and long-term success were antithetical. Political stabilization and economic maximization were achieved only with a progressive weakening of the capacity to adapt to unforeseen challenges and changes (1978:333).

Millon (1988) makes essentially the same argument (and cites the above passage from Adams) in exploring the collapse of Teotihuacan. So does Earle, in his volume on chiefdoms (1991a); specifically, he draws a dichotomy (somewhat oversimplified, to be sure) between wealth-financed and staple-financed systems, arguing that the former are less stable than the latter. This was, Earle argues, largely because wealth-financed systems are dependent to a large extent on the acquisition of foreign prestige items.

In making his case, Earle's explanation echoes Tainter's.

> The growth in a wealth financed system can rarely be sustained because of problems of inflation, depletion, and overextension. For whatever particular reason, wealth financed systems are inherently unstable, and periodic collapses occur commonly (Earle 1991b:97).

Like Tainter, then, Earle argues that inflationary spirals among chiefdom-level societies often led to collapse, with the collapse itself often followed by reorganization and reemergence of complexity. According to Earle, among chiefdoms this often results in cycles of growth and collapse. Note the similarities to the gumsa-gumlao cycles described by Friedman (1975; see also Friedman and Rowlands 1978), and the process of chiefly cycling among southern Atlantic Coast Mississippian groups described by Anderson (1990).

Under the prevailing notion that it is internal factors that bring about collapse, external factors—such as environmental disasters or barbarian invasions—cannot by themselves bring about the wholesale collapse of a complex society. As the argument goes, such forces may finally break a sociopolitical system and usher it to its ultimate demise, but only if that society is already strained to the limit by the side effects of diminishing returns or other internal pressures. We revisit this basic premise of Tainter's diminishing-returns theory of collapse below.

Corruption and Repression:
Lessons from the Modern World

Another internal source of pressure that can threaten a polity's viability—and render it vulnerable to collapse—stems from behavioral flaws within the political system itself, specifically corruption and abuse by the ruling class. The modern world indeed offers repeated examples of polities that fail largely as a result of abuse or incompetence on the part of rulers. Archaeologists are understandably hesitant to pursue such lines of explanation, in part because the historical detail necessary to demonstrate such specific behavioral patterns are lacking in the archaeological record, especially when it comes to nonliterate societies. Getting at the past through the modern world is also fraught with potential hazards, as it could be argued that present-day geopolitical conditions are so radically different from those of the ancient past (or even among more recent, but premodern, complex societies) that any lessons to be gained would be illusory. Moreover, in today's oversensitized political climate many archaeologists probably eschew dealing with the modern world simply to avoid unintended distractions or debates.

Whether or not one accepts humanity's current state as a window on the past might depend in part on one's sentiments vis-a-vis the old, formalist-substantivist debate (LeClair and Schneider 1968). Assuming a substantivist position, one could argue that such comparisons are indeed useful. Looking at premodern complex systems, we can see that some of the services provided by sociopolitical leaders may indeed be analogous to those found in more modern systems. Take the garden magician of the Trobriand Islanders, for example (Austen 1936; Malinowski 1922). Although this individual's ostensible role was to perform magic aimed at ensuring a bountiful yam harvest, in doing so he also had an opportunity to keep tabs on productivity levels and thus anticipate the amount of chiefly tribute to be expected. Such a role is obviously similar to that of tax assessors in more-complex state systems.

Similar analogies could easily be piled up. But in terms of the study of collapse, the important point is that, when the balance between services provided and payment extracted is tipped too far in the direction of the latter, or expected services can no longer be provided (for whatever reason), a sociopolitical system becomes acutely prone to failure and disintegration. One of the easiest ways for this imbalance to arise is through greed, corruption, and incompetence on the part of rulers.

For the moment, then, let us assume that the process of collapse may have some similar threads that run through both modern and premodern sociopolitical systems, and that corruption and incompetence present a road to collapse that has been trodden for millennia. Accordingly, consider a recent essay by Rotberg (2002), who identified several important signposts of collapse observed among present-day failed states. Rotberg highlights *corruption* as one of the instigators of a nation's descent into the sociopolitical abyss. As the old saying goes, absolute power corrupts absolutely, and the dangers of corruption and cronyism are always lurking in the machinery of a hierarchical, highly centralized complex system. Patronizing particular ethnic groups, clans, classes, or kin is a common expression of corrupt systems, and these behaviors are clearly evident in historically recent and current cases, such as the hyper-abusive rule of Saddam Hussein in Iraq, Robert Mugabe's Botswana, and the collapse of Somalia (Rotberg 2002:129). History is replete with similar examples, and it does not seem an unwarranted leap to assume that the temptation toward favoritism was an ever-present threat to the viability of complex human societies, even comparatively small-scale ones.

As Rotberg explains, once a ruling elite ceases to operate for the benefit of the entire system and becomes entrenched in a pattern of corruption, the descent toward sociopolitical failure and collapse tends to snowball. As elite organizations provide fewer and fewer services,

> people feel preyed upon by the regime and its agents. . . . Security, the most important political good, vanishes. Citizens, especially those who have known more prosperous and democratic times, increasingly feel that they exist solely to satisfy the power lust and . . . greed of those in power (Rotberg 2002:129).

Although the above passage was written to characterize failure in modern, underdeveloped states, a similar process could have occurred in any ancient society where an elite organization existed. In the modern world, failed states may become vulnerable to total collapse and fragmentation or, with welfare-like handouts from wealthier nations or global organizations, may limp along for an extended period of time in their severely weakened condition. In recent years, terrorist organizations have been able to gain considerable toeholds in weakened states, Afghanistan being the obvious example. In the most extreme cases— rare in the modern world—states may descend into total collapse, which according to Rotberg (2002:133–134) is

> typified by an absence of authority. Indeed, a collapsed state is a shell of a polity. Somalia is the model of a collapsed state: a geographical expression only, with borders but with no effective way to exert authority within those borders. Substate actors have taken over. The central government has been divided up, replaced by a functioning, unrecognized state called Somaliland in the north and a less well defined, putative state called Punt in the northeast. In the rump of the old Somalia, a transitional national government has emerged thanks to outside support. But it has so far been unable to project its power even locally against the several warlords who control sections of Mogadishu and large swaths of the countryside. Private entrepreneurialism has displaced the central provision of political goods. Yet life somehow continues, even under conditions of unhealthy, dangerous chaos.

Such state "shells" exist in today's world in large part because of the modern-day sanctity ascribed to the territorial "integrity" of present-day national boundaries. In prestate and ancient worlds, there was little regard for such geopolitical protocol, nor were there any global organizations to prop up failed polities. Weakened ancient polities (many fragile to begin with, especially in the case of prestate entities with elite organizations, such as chiefdoms) were much more vulnerable to total collapse and fragmentation, and predation by rival polities in the geopolitical neighborhood. The ancient equivalent of substate actors may have included local leaders or lineage heads, or even regional leaders installed by the formerly more-powerful, central polity. Such individuals may move outside the collapsed sociopolitical system and begin to supply political goods—including security, management of economic activity, and orchestration of ceremonies—that were once provided by the now-weakened, larger polity. As paramount elites sense the increasing desperation of their positions of authority, they may respond with intensified repression. Such tactics may or may not prolong their hold on power, but the long-term effect is typically to further weaken any support elites might still enjoy among their subjects, helping to seal their ultimate fate—and that of their polity.

External Factors

Arguments and models advocating internal causes offer compelling explanations of collapse. Processes such as inflationary spirals and diminishing returns certainly appear to be relevant to many cases of sociopolitical disintegration—and these processes are easily intertwined with unhealthy tendencies toward greed, corruption, favoritism, and ineptitude. But not everyone agrees that all cases of collapse can be explained by internal factors and conditions. Causes that are external to the functioning of the sociopolitical system itself have long been advanced by many scholars to explain the demise of this or that polity or system. These include attacks from barbarians and other intruders, climate change, episodic natural disasters, and resource depletion (although the latter relates to both the potential of the natural environment and the behavioral patterns inherent in the specific culture or sociopolitical system).

In advocating his diminishing-returns theory, Tainter (1988:39–90) dismisses each of these factors as insufficient, by themselves, to cause the collapse of a complex society. Yet one is still left wondering if a sudden invasion by barbarians or a catastrophic natural disaster might not actually trigger the downfall of a polity or regional system, even an otherwise "healthy" one.

Moreover, how does one really distinguish a "healthy" system from one that is already beginning to succumb to the strains of diminishing returns? Do not all complex sociopolitical systems face challenges that must be constantly managed, and might not an unfortunate invasion or natural disaster shake up even the most carefully orchestrated balance between elite power or privileges and services to commoners, and between resource availability and extraction?

Bronson points out the temptation of tautological reasoning when seeking out internal causes of sociopolitical collapse.

> As I too am a believer in social phenomena caused by positive feedback, I do not doubt that states have often fallen for internal reasons. Yet I am uncomfortable with the partial circularity of the logic behind such explanations. How do we know that the symptoms we observe are those of decline? Because the state in question eventually falls. And how do we know that these symptoms of decline are causative agents? Either because we think we see them getting worse as the end approaches or because we have defined them that way. . . . The internal causes we are prone to cite bear a resemblance to self-justifying prophecies even if, unlike Jeremiah and his many successors, we do not always ascribe the fall of states entirely to sin (1988:197–198).

Barbarians

Bronson examines one of the exogenous factors that has been attributed to the fall of states and civilizations since scholarly interest in the subject began: the role of barbarians. Defining a barbarian as "simply a member of a political unit that is in direct contact with a state but that is not itself a state" (1988:200), Bronson underscored barbarians' attraction to the material wealth of nearby states as a recurrent source of pressure on states, both ancient and modern.[1] He noted certain key advantages that barbarian groups may enjoy at the expense of their state-organized enemies, or at least organizational features that make it difficult for states to effectively conquer them. Some reside in mountainous terrain within which it is difficult for state-organized militaries to operate successfully. It is much cheaper for barbarians to mobilize militarily than it is for states, and the risks of going to war are considerably lower for the non-state hordes. Some barbarians are especially skilled and effective warriors (although many

are not). Acephalous societies are especially difficult to conquer, as "there is no one who can offer an authoritative surrender" (Bronson 1988:205).

Bronson goes on to argue that the potential success of barbarian groups may relate to geography: specifically, the proximity to states (or productive areas where states could have developed) of expansive, mountainous homelands that have hosted large barbarian populations. He points to three examples in making his case. The first is India, where states and a high civilization have existed since ancient times, but where individual state polities historically were short-lived and susceptible to repeated predation from barbarians residing in the vast mountains of present-day western Pakistan and Afghanistan.

The second and third examples Bronson cites are in Southeast Asia—the Deli Plain around Medan in northern Sumatra, and the Central Plain around Manila in Luzon. Soils are exceptionally fertile in these areas, and they are both located along major trade routes and have good harbors—conditions that could have easily supported at least small-scale state polities. Yet only one such polity may have emerged in the Deli Plain (Kota Cina, in the thirteenth to fourteenth centuries), and there is no evidence of an indigenous, pre-Spanish state polity in the Manila area. The reason, according to Bronson, is that both areas are severely circumscribed, being surrounded by extensive mountainous terrain inhabited by large barbarian populations. In these cases, the mere presence of barbarians was enough to preclude successful state development.

Even in cases where a state is ultimately brought down by barbarian enemies, our scholarly tendency to focus on large-scale processes at the expense of more stochastic factors, along with moralistic notions that are part of our intellectual and cultural heritage, prompt us to cite internal decay of a state as responsible for its downfall. This is evident even in today's world, where terrorist attacks have led to widespread questioning of— or even laying the blame squarely on—the moral health or policies of the state-level societies targeted by terrorists. The fact that the values of the targeted state are often much closer to those of their critics—whereas modern terrorists tend to espouse premodern values that are antithetical to those same critics' sentiments—underscores how deeply rooted this notion is among large segments of the educated public in modern, state-level societies. Yet in recounting the potential advantages that some barbarian groups enjoy under certain sets of circumstances, Bronson at least entertains the possibility that predation by such groups could have brought down even "healthy" states.

Natural Disasters

Another possible external source of collapse is natural disasters. Devastating droughts, floods, volcanic eruptions, massive landslides, and earthquakes (and their potential side effects, including mudslides and tsunamis) have all been credited with wiping out individual settlements and have been implicated in the downfall of entire states or polities.

It is important to understand that not all extreme natural events produce social cataclysm. The specific characteristics of extreme natural events, such as their temporal duration, frequency of repetition, speed of onset (time between initial effects and peak effects), and spatial dispersion (distributional pattern of damage effects), interact with the socioecological characteristics of specific societies to produce cataclysms. Important social variables in this mix include resource distribution (concentrated and intensive or dispersed and extensive), capital investment facilities (irrigation technology, dams or river channels, etc.), level of technological development, population density and distribution, wealth, and level of sociopolitical complexity (Hoffman and Oliver-Smith 1999; Reycraft and Bawden 2000).

The impact severity of a disaster may be the result of a long history of ecological, political, and economic choices by a society. These choices result in specific patterns of political ecology—that is, how a society and its political system modifies and manages the local natural environment—that may either exacerbate or mitigate the destructive effects of natural disaster. As a result of their political ecological histories, some polities may be more vulnerable to a specific type of natural disaster. For example, the Tiwanaku Empire was an indigenous state that flourished in the Andean altiplano (high plateau) for approximately 500 years, between AD 600 and 1100. During this period, the Tiwanaku state expanded from its altiplano base to occupy both the eastern and western slopes of the Andean sierra. Each slope of the Andean sierra contains multiple resource zones that produce a variety of elevation-dependent crops. Resource production in the eastern and western sierras is dependent on the Amazon and Pacific Coastal weather systems, respectively, which are independent of each other. Tiwanaku resource extraction was thus extremely diverse, and although particular areas could be impacted by natural disaster, the system in general was very low-risk, which likely resulted in the polity's long period of political stability. As the Tiwanaku developed, however, the altiplano core region became heavily dependent on a highly specialized technology—raised field agriculture fed by the waters of Lake Titicaca. Increasingly successful yields from this technology fostered greater investments and population increases over time. When an extended drought hit the altiplano around 1040, the population-dense core region had become too dependent on this technology. Titicaca lake levels dropped dramatically, stranding the raised fields. The Tiwanaku Empire collapsed shortly thereafter, as large populations in the core shifted to more secure sierra locations (Kolata 2000).

The role of natural disasters in the collapse of complex systems also depends on the *scale* of both the disaster and the political system it affects. When the geographic extent of a cataclysm approaches or surpasses the territorial boundaries of a polity, severe hardship and sociopolitical collapse are likely as the society will be unable to draw resources from unaffected regions. For example, the mudslide that buried the (American) Northwest Coast village of Ozette in 1750 (see Ames and Maschner 1999:111) or the tsunamis that wiped out (or at least caused the abandonment of) coastal Maori villages in New Zealand in the mid-fifteenth century (Goff and McFadgen 2001) were far more disastrous to the single-village polities involved than the much more catastrophic (in terms of loss of human life) burial of Pompeii under volcanic ash was to the Roman Empire.

The devastating tsunami of December 2004 jolted a worldwide focus on the incredible degree and scope of destruction wrought by the massive waves that crashed into sleepy villages and seaside resorts around coastal South Asia. Those news images also alert us to the potential impact tsunamis may have had on past societies along the world's coastlines, especially in tectonically active areas prone to earthquakes and volcanic activity. As devastating as it was, the 2004 tsunami did not threaten the actual sociopolitical survival of the nations involved because each affected nation encompasses a large land mass, most of which was not directly affected by the destructive waves, and also because each of those nations is today integrated into a global network that includes massive outpourings and rapid mobilization of direct aid in the wake of such disasters. But coastal villages and seafaring or otherwise coastal-oriented polities hundreds or thousands of years ago could not depend on such outside support.

Perhaps the best-known scenario involving a tsunami-triggered collapse involves the ancient Minoans. Around 1630 BC, the small island of Thera, a mere 64 miles (103 km) north of the Minoan heartland of Crete, was blown apart by a massive volcanic eruption. Volcanic tephra and pyroclastic flows completely buried the Minoan mercantile center of Akrotiri and resulted in the complete abandonment of the island. Regional effects included dispersed ash falls as far away as the Levant, the Anatolian peninsula, and the Nile delta (McCoy and Heiken 2000). Seismic activity was felt throughout the Aegean region. This event also sent giant tsunamis racing out across the Aegean Sea, particularly to the west and south. Tsunami-generated deposits in Minoan archaeological stettings on Crete (Francaviglia and Di Sabatino 1990; Pichler and Schierling 1977; Vallianou 1996) indicate that massive waves directly affected Minoan centers on Crete.

Some researchers (e.g., Marinatos 1939; Chadwick 1976) have proposed that this event directly resulted in the collapse of Minoan civilization (both on Crete and in the entire Aegean region). Others dismiss the Thera eruption as a factor in the Minoan collapse. Tainter (1988:54) suspects that Minoans on nearby Crete "most likely stopped to watch the eruption . . ., made whatever preparations were called for, and when it was all over went about their business." This speculation seems little short of incredible considering the potential destruction such a disaster would have had on a seafaring culture. Indeed, it seems that Minoan culture, with its emphasis on maritime trade, its multiple seaports, and its administrative nodes situated so close to the sea, would have been particularly vulnerable to this type of cataclysm. Based on the wealth encountered at Akrotiri (Doumas 1983), Thera appears to have been a major economic partner in the Minoan maritime network. There can be no doubt that the eruption immediately dissolved this relationship. Tsunami waves would also have destroyed most of the Minoan port facilities and any fleets docked in the Aegean. Seismic activity would also have been very strong, likely resulting in partial collapse of many Minoan administrative centers (Marinatos 1939).

Amazingly, Minoan culture did not collapse immediately following this event. The Minoans patched up their palaces, repaired what was left of their fleets, and continued to exchange, albeit in a much diminished capacity, for a few more generations. So, can we blame the Thera eruption for the Minoan collapse? It certainly significantly disrupted their maritime network, destroyed fleets and facilities, and removed a major trade link. In short, it initiated a rapid decline that resulted in a later collapse. We should also bear in mind that, unlike the 2004 South Asian victims, the Minoans would have received no international aid in the wake of such a disaster, but would have had to pick up the pieces on their own.

Episodic climatic events have also been shown to play a hand in the collapse of complex societies. In Chapter 8, Reycraft presents evidence that the disastrous effects of an extreme El Niño event resulted in the collapse of a chiefdom-level polity of the Chiribaya in southern coastal Peru. The polity involved a symbiotic network which included procurement of marine resources along the coast and inland irrigation farming fed by a system of canals that ran along the steep sides of a valley. The El Niño event disrupted the availability of marine resources, and torrential rains resulted in landslides that breached the irrigation canals, wiping out the local agricultural capabilities. Although the local Chiribaya chiefdom may have been experiencing diminishing returns from its economic strategies, there is nothing in the archaeological evidence to suggest that it was already in trouble; in other words, this may be a case where the multi-pronged front of a natural disaster was sufficient to bring down an otherwise "healthy" complex system.

Not all extreme natural events are immediately cataclysmic. Longer-term changes in climate, especially reduced precipitation levels or changes in the seasonality of precipitation patterns, can have cumulative effects that are catastrophic for human societies. The late prehistoric societies of the American Southwest present the obvious case in point, where a prolonged drought and, perhaps more important, a change in precipitation seasonality had dire effects on the region's native peoples around AD 1300. The puebloan societies of the Four Corners region—renowned for the well-known ruins at such places as Chaco Canyon and Mesa Verde—thrived on a maize-based agricultural economy for several centuries before an extreme drought and altered precipitation patterns forced abandonment of this vast region, apparently in a matter of decades (Stuart 2000).

Disease

Epidemics could be considered together with other natural disasters, but the role of disease in the collapse of complex societies has historically involved both natural and cultural agency. The effects of Eurasian diseases that accompanied European explorers over the past several centuries, including population crashes among indigenous peoples ranging from Australia to the New World, are well known. In many cases, the inadvertent introduction of diseases to which native peoples had no natural immunity was an unintended component of a broader arsenal brought to bear on indigenous societies.

Consider the example of Inka Empire. In AD 1525 the Inka were at the apex of their political and military development. The Inka emperor, Huayna Capac, was in the process of completing the military conquest of the Ecuadorian region, thus expanding an empire that stretched south from Quito to central Chile. By this point in time, all serious military contenders to Inka supremacy in South America had been vanquished. Although Europeans had visited Central America, they had not yet traveled to South America. In sum, the Inka appeared invincible: they had a continental-scale empire; they maintained a vast, well-disciplined army; they had no competitors; and they were a wealthy and strong people. Nevertheless, in 1532 a small band of Spaniards, led by Francisco Pizarro, managed to capture the Inka emperor, and by 1536 the empire itself was effectively under Spanish control. We must ask ourselves, as the Inka undoubtedly also did, how could such an event occur? How could a motley band of Spanish privateers have defeated the Inka with their army of tens of thousands? Could better technology (horse and harquebus) have made up for such a tremendous disadvantage? Were the Spanish, as they themselves believed, blessed by God? Were the Inka a backward, weak, morally and militarily undisciplined people? Of course the answer to all of these questions is no. While horse and harquebus did have advantages in close combat, there were simply too few Spaniards to overthrow such a vast empire by themselves.

But the Spanish did have a secret weapon (of which they were completely unaware): their diseases had spread through the Andes well in advance of their military expeditions. In 1525 a plague of widespread proportion, likely smallpox, decimated the Inka Empire. This plague claimed a spectacular victim, Huayna Capac, the Inka emperor himself (Conrad and Demarest 1984). His death was a surprise, succession to the throne had not been determined, and a ferocious and bitter civil war between his two sons, Huascar and Atauhualpa, began. Huascar had the better claim to the throne, and he was based in Cusco, the Inka capital. However, Atauhualpa was based in Quito. There he could count on the support of battle-hardened Inka and Canari troops from the Ecuadorian frontier. The war tore apart an empire already damaged by plague. Factional, administrative, and economic problems that were roiling just beneath the surface of Inka organizational control erupted openly during the civil war. Ultimately, Atauhualpa defeated and killed Huascar, and as he moved south to Cuzco, he was captured by Pizarro and his men. This was an unintentional but very timely window for invasion on the Spaniards' part. No wonder they believed God was on their side.

The effects were even more direct in what is the present-day southeastern United States, where introduced diseases did most of the work in snuffing out the late prehistoric chiefdoms of the Mississippian culture. Here, unlike the conquests of the Inka and Aztec, the entrada of the Spanish conquistadors in the mid-sixteenth century was little short of a disastrous failure. Although many Mississippian chiefdoms had already collapsed, and it is likely that introduced diseases were already starting to ravage Mississippian populations before the expedition of Hernando de Soto explored the region in 1540, there were nonetheless a host of Mississippian chiefdoms still surviving at this time, some quite populous and encompassing numerous towns and villages spread over large regions (see Hudson et al. 1985). Yet during the century and a half between the Soto expedition and the journey of Marquette and Joliet down the Mississippi River in the 1670s, the vast majority of these societies had collapsed, mortality rates had led to a dramatic regional population crash, and only a few chiefdom-level societies (such as the Natchez) remained. Most of the surviving remnants of the once-great Mississippian chiefdoms reorganized themselves into more segmentary societies, forming confederacies to counter the progressive incursion of European immigrants and their descendants from the East Coast into the interior of the Southeast.

Clash of Cultures

The ravages of Eurasian diseases on the New World and other geographically marginalized peoples in the preceding half millennium alert us to the more general role of cultural clashes in the processes of collapse and transformation. Culture clash leading to the collapse and destruction of indigenous complex societies may date as far back as Neolithic times, when populations of farmers spread from centers of domestication and replaced complex societies of indigenous hunter-gatherers in their wake.

The expansion of ancient empires toppled many indigenous chiefdoms and other complex systems. But the most dramatic examples in human history, and the ones involving a clash of cultures that had evolved in isolation from each other for millennia, stem from the exploration and colonization of far-flung lands by Europeans beginning with earnest in the sixteenth century. The technological capacity, communication systems, and military capabilities of the Europeans were far more sophisticated than those of even the most complex societies they encountered, such as the Aztec and Inka of the New World. The advantages thus conveyed on Europeans were such that the complex indigenous societies they encountered collapsed quickly, with their populations exterminated, greatly reduced, and otherwise marginalized or enslaved by the newly established European colonies and derivative states. Granted, there were some momentary setbacks for the

Europeans, notably the Pueblo Revolt against the Spanish colonists in New Mexico in 1680, the Plains Indians' victory over General Custer and his troops at the 1876 battle of the Little Bighorn in Montana, and the victory of Shaka's Zulu army over British forces in 1879 at the battle of Isandlwana in present-day South Africa. In Chapter 9, Petersen and his colleagues examine the potential role played by the clash of cultures in the collapse of Caribbean and Amazonian complex societies.

Warfare

Hostility and warfare have likely been part of the human condition since our ancestors became human. Warfare of course does not lead inevitably to the collapse of a society or even the conquest of one polity by another. But warfare has played a direct role in the downfall and subjugation of many societies, and the critical factor here relates to inequities in military technologies and capabilities. Again, the obvious case here is the hemisphere-wide collapse of the New World's native societies, whose military capabilities and technologies were no match for the iron weaponry, firearms, and cavalry warfare of their invading European enemies.

But warfare has been credited with a leading role in the collapse of ancient societies as well. Drews (1993) has argued that the collapse of Bronze Age polities in the eastern Mediterranean ca. 1200 BC was a result of changes in warfare tactics. Specifically, Drews contends that Late Bronze Age armies of the "civilized" states (i.e., New Kingdom Egypt, Mycenaen and Minoan Greece, the Hittites, and various polities in Syria and the Levant) focused on chariot warfare, with chariot-mounted archers delivering the main punch in battle, while infantry and cavalry served only a supporting role. According to Drews, this was the Late Bronze Age *modus operandi* for doing battle, both between "civilized" armies and against the surrounding barbarians who generally lacked chariots.

Beginning around 1200 BC, however, Drews argues that the barbarians figured out how to neutralize the great chariot forces, primarily by attacking in massive hordes that included fleet-footed "runners" who launched javelins to take out the chariot horse teams, and whose hit-and-run tactics enabled them to evade the chariot-mounted archers. In addition to the javelin-armed runners, in the Late Bronze Age barbarian groups in southern Europe developed new forms of slashing and cutting swords (particularly the Naue Type II sword), which were more effective and lethal than the thrusting swords employed by the armies of the eastern Mediterranean states. These changes in barbarian military tactics and capabilities were,

according to Drews, the decisive factor in weakening and, ultimately, bringing down the Late Bronze Age states of the eastern Mediterranean. Moreover, their successor states transformed their own militaries in response to this new reality by shifting the focus from chariot warfare to massed infantries equipped with the new sword types and javelins, with chariots now relegated to a supporting role on the battlefield.

In the New World, the arrival of the recurved bow in the American Southwest around AD 1300–1400 conferred on its adopters a decided advantage against any enemies still using the traditional self-bow. The arrival of this new type of bow—which delivered an arrow with considerably more force, velocity, and potential distance than the earlier and simpler self-bow—appears to correlate with evidence suggesting an escalation of warfare and defensive concerns during the Pueblo III and Pueblo IV periods (LeBlanc 1999). Although LeBlanc argues that it was primarily climatic factors (i.e., reduced precipitation) that contributed to levels of competition, violence, and warfare in the Southwest, he suggests that new military capabilities, enabled by introduction of the recurved bow, exacerbated these conditions after ca. 1300.

Environmental Degradation

Although the natural environment can be thought of as an external factor in the workings of a human sociopolitical system, resource utilization and overexploitation can easily result in environmental degradation, which in turn can have serious impacts on the functioning of human societies. This is patently obvious in today's world, where such effects are well-studied and constitute a central part of the highly charged political discourse.

Today, deforestation ranks among the world's greatest environmental concerns. But the deleterious effects of obliterating natural forest cover have plagued human societies in the past and in some cases appear to have been a major factor in the downfall of complex systems. Easter Island (Rapa Nui) presents a stark example (see Kirch 1984:268; Stevenson and Cristino 1986; Casanova 1998; Sevenson and Ayres 2000; Diamond 2005:79–119). When human settlement first reached this most remote of Pacific Islands ca. AD 800–900, Easter Island was covered in a rich forest, including a now-extinct species of giant palm (Dransfield et al. 1984; Flenley and King 1984). The wood resources were sufficient for constructing ocean-going canoes with harpooning platforms for hunting porpoises (the main meat source during the early centuries following settlement of the island), and for providing the timbers and rope necessary to haul and erect the great *ahu* platforms and *moai* statues for which the island is so well known. In addition, Easter's forests provided fuelwood for cooking, heating, and cremation (the main mortuary practice throughout most of Easter's prehistory), fruits and nuts that supplemented a diet based primarily on domesticated species, and an abundance of now-extinct native bird species (Ayres 1985; Steadman et al. 1994).

By ca. 1600, Easter had been deforested, and the effects were apparently disastrous. The dwindling numbers of trees—and eventually their wholesale disappearance—led to degradation of the island's soils, severely impacting crop productivity. Timbers for erecting the great monuments were also no longer available. Large canoes could no longer be constructed, after which porpoise dropped out of the diet. Starvation ensued, and population levels began to drop. The complex, stratified sociopolitical order, which had united the island's population peak of perhaps 15,000 people under one huge polity, collapsed. The resulting crisis of faith led to toppling and destruction of the moai. Easter's society fragmented into warring factions and cannibalism became prevalent, accelerating the demographic crash. By the time the island was first encountered by Europeans in the eighteenth century, Easter was inhabited by perhaps only 2,000 people, living on a terrain stripped of trees and littered with toppled monuments constructed during the island's much more lavish past.

Sometimes the effects of environmental degradation, and whether or not it triggers a "natural" disaster, depend on the nature of the local or regional environment. The site of Ozette, on the Olympic Peninsula in present-day Washington state, marks the remains of a coastal village of the Makah people that was buried under a catastrophic mudslide around AD 1750 (see Ames and Maschner 1999:111). The mudslide was probably triggered by deforestation of the steep hillside behind the village. Because the Ozette site was probably a single-village polity typical of late prehistoric Northwest Coast societies, this "natural" catastrophe may well have caused the "collapse" of this particular society. Had the village not been situated so close to such a steep slope, denuding of the surrounding forest would not have had such disastrous effects.

POST-COLLAPSE OUTCOMES

To fully understand the collapse of complex systems, it is also essential to examine *post*-collapse societies and modes of reorganization. Following collapse, a complex polity may fragment into smaller units that resemble their larger precursor, or it "may decompose to some of the constituent building blocks (e.g., states, ethnic groups, villages) out of which it was created" (Tainter 1988:38). In outlining general features of the aftermath of collapse, Renfrew (1984:368–369) suggests a return to something resembling earlier sociopolitical and economic conditions is common. Fragmentation of redundant, organizational building blocks is often assumed to be the case with chiefdoms, which typically involve multiple local centers that are essentially copies of the paramount center in terms of organizational structure and functions. Because they lack the complex, specialized bureaucratic organs that make up state-level organizations, chiefdoms often accomplish polity growth by "stacking" kin-based organizations into larger structures, such as the conical clans described by Sahlins (1958) and Friedman (1975). Because of this essential redundancy among its loosely coalesced pieces, chiefdoms are seen as especially susceptible to fragmentation into their component parts. The apparently recurring, cross-cultural phenomenon of chiefdom cycling is one outcome of this kind of organizational structure (Anderson 1990; Earle 1991a; Friedman 1975; Pauketat 1992).

But perhaps more often than not, especially in the case of large, regional, state-level societies, collapse is followed by substantial transformation, in which the post-collapse outcome bears little resemblance to pre-collapse conditions and polities. For example, petty states may form after the collapse of an empire, tribal organizations may emerge in the wake of a state's or chiefdom's collapse, or a complex alliance of transegalitarian societies may collapse into a mosaic of smaller, local groups. In this volume, Zagarell (Chapter 3) describes a post-collapse outcome that differs substantially from the sociopolitical milieu that preceded the emergence of a regional state in South India. Railey (Chapter 4) describes a collapse that involved a spatial displacement of the geopolitical center of gravity in Shang China, with the post-collapse outcome involving a rapidly unfolding florescence that, overall, outshined its pre-collapse predecessor in various cultural markers, such as artistic achievements and mortuary ritual.

TRANSFORMATION VERSUS COLLAPSE

Although the collapse of complex systems has always held a special fascination for archaeologists and historians, it is clear that not all cases of substantial—even rapid—sociopolitical reorganization involve wholesale collapse. In some cases, complex systems may be *transformed* (either rapidly or gradually) without a complete breakdown of economic structures, loss of complexity, political fragmentation, and demographic reduction or displacement. Thus, *transformation* can occur independently of collapse and reorganization.

Whether a given sociopolitical system collapses or more gradually transforms into something else may depend in part on the inherent flexibility—or inflexibility—of the system itself in the face of changing conditions and historical circumstances. As noted above, those who advocate internal stresses as the root causes of collapse see complexity and long-term continuity among preindustrial societies as antithetical. Under this perspective, increasing complexity is synonymous with increasing rigidity such that complex systems are unable to adapt to changing conditions and circumstances (e.g., Adams 1978:333, quoted above).

But it is also conceivable that certain complex systems may be more inherently flexible than others, or at least at certain points in their own evolutionary histories, and may thus be better equipped to deal with, and adapt to, unforeseen challenges brought on by changing conditions. This does not mean that such societies gained this advantage through any special gift of foresight or enlightenment; rather, such positive survival prospects may have accrued through the essentially inadvertent emergence and coalescence of cultural marker traits and organizational characteristics over the course of a system's evolutionary history. It is also acknowledged that societies enjoying such an advantage at Point A in history may not enjoy the same advantages under different conditions at Point B, and a society that is able to transform itself at one point may be much more prone to collapse at another. The point is that the nature of human organizational and cultural variability is such that some societies may prove more able than others at adapting to changing circumstances by transforming themselves, thus avoiding wholesale collapse.

The Roman state is perhaps the best example of political resiliency and transformation in history.[2] Rome emerged as one of many cultures in the Italian peninsula during the Early Iron Age. By 575 BC, Rome had become a small urban center under Etruscan influence. The mid-sixth-century BC Roman state was monarchical, ruled by an Etruscan dynasty. The Roman king was assisted by his council of nobles (Senate) and a people's assembly. His military, judicial, and religious authority was symbolized in the *fasces,* a small bundle of rods enclosing an axe.

The Roman Republic

According to Roman tradition, the nobles revolted in 509 BC and defeated their king. Rome became a republic. Two elected rulers, called consuls, were elected by the popular assembly. The Senate advised the consuls and maintained the power of veto over their actions. The Roman magistrate grew with Roman military might, and specialized political offices, such as praetors, censors, questors, aediles, and promagistrates, were created to maintain the expanding state. Although greater democratic influences emerged between the fifth and fourth centuries BC (e.g., the tribal assembly, centuriate, and plebian council), the Senate eclipsed these bodies and became the primary executive power during the mid-second century BC. By then, Rome was a de facto oligarchy. Factional rivalries in the Senate eventually led to political support of military factions led by prominent generals (e.g., Caesar, Pompey) who used military support to push themselves into power. These leaders formed temporary alliances (e.g., the triumvirates) to rule Rome, which eventually fell in upon themselves. In 49 BC, civil war erupted between two triumvirate leaders, Caesar and Pompey. Caesar, the victor, had the Senate declare him "Dictator for Life" in 46 BC, but two years later he was assassinated by members of an opposing faction who feared the reemergence of a monarchy.

The Princeps

Caesar's assassination led to a war between the republican faction and Caesar's successors, the triumvirate of Antony, Octavian, and Lepidus. The triumvirate triumphed, only to wage war upon itself. Octavian defeated the combined forces of Antony and Cleopatra at Actum in 31 BC. In 27 BC he adopted the title of Augustus, the first Roman emperor. The Roman state had transformed again, from an oligarchical republic to a "principate." The Roman principate was an imperial system in which the emperor (the "princeps") was considered the first citizen of Rome. In this capacity he consolidated within himself many previously independent Senatorial offices (the proconsulship, tribunate, censorship, pontifex maximus, etc.) and became the primary executive authority. Nevertheless, he was not considered a monarch because the Senate retained some influence over his policies and retained the right to approve his successor. This right was vulnerable, however, because the emperors' designated heirs inevitably controlled large armies. The emperors expanded the imperial bureaucracy, the military, and the state infrastructure in order to maintain an expanding empire. The costs of these expansions resulted in increased taxation, which gradually led to economic downturns.

The Autocracy

By AD 235, economic downturns and inept emperors led Rome into a forty-year period of military mutiny and political disintegration. Multiple coups d'etat and military mutinies, coupled with barbarian invasions, resulted in a rotation of new emperors, 26 in all, most of whom were assassinated within a year or two of their ascension. The military coups completely bypassed Senate authority, which withered into obscurity. Independent states broke away in the western (Gaul, Spain, and Britain) and eastern (Palmyra, Egypt, and Asia Minor) parts of the empire. Just as total political collapse seemed imminent, the empire was restored by the Emperor Aurelian in 275. The systemic reorganizations initiated by Aurelian and his successors, such as Diocletian and Constantine the Great, completely excluded the Senate from civil and military administration. Emperors now ruled as complete autocrats, their nomination sealed by the gods and the military. As evidence of such, they adopted the diadem, a symbol of autocracy since the ancient Hellenistic kings.

The Byzantine State

In 324–330, the Emperor Constantine the Great established the city of Constantinople in Asia Minor. His sons initiated an informal split of the Empire into eastern and western halves ruled by co-emperors residing in Italy and Constantinople, respectively. This informal split became formal in 395 when each part of the empire adopted separate legislation. After multiple barbarian intrusions and de facto control of the western half by barbarian "Masters of Soldiers," the western empire finally dissolved completely in 476, when the barbarian king Odovacar became King of Italy. The eastern, or Byzantine, empire continued until it was conquered by the Turks in 1453.

While the political transformations of the Roman state are impressive, the cultural changes to Roman civilization that accompanied these changes are equally dramatic. After the conversion of Constantine the Great, the Roman empire became increasingly associated with Christianity. The reorganized imperial bureaucracy led to the creation of new political, religious, and military titles, such as dukes, counts, and vicars, which preceded the development of the medieval state. The Roman army replaced the metal breastplate, short sword, broad shield, and javelin with a leather jacket, chain mail, long sword, small round shield, and lance. Late Roman art reflected only few influences from its Classic past, became increasingly medieval in nature and design, and was strongly influenced by Christianity. Finally, the Byzantine state, which still considered itself the Roman empire, was ruled by divinely sanctioned, autocratic kings. The state religion was Eastern Orthodox Christianity, and the official language was Greek. It is safe to say that a Roman magistrate from the Republican period transposed by some magic to Byzantine Constantinople would not know that he was still in the Roman Empire and might not even be able to ask where he was in a language that could be understood by the imperial capital's citizens.

Like collapse, transformation may result in the slow death of a sociopolitical system, out of which emerges a polity, or multiple polities, that bears little resemblance to that from which it (or they) emerged. Among those who have voiced the argument that Rome, in fact, did not collapse was Bowerstock, who instead recognized that Rome underwent "transformation, reformation, and relocation" (1988:171). As a result of this transformation, the Roman Empire *eventually* fragmented and a mosaic of very different social and political systems emerged in its wake, with the Vatican remaining as the modern-day political vestige of this once far-flung empire.

Whether one chooses to interpret a particular case study as an episode of collapse or as a much less traumatic cultural and/or sociopolitical transformation may essentially boil down to one's own conceptual inclinations, which are often influenced by theoretical currents of the moment (and the same holds true for interpreting the available evidence in terms of internal vs. external factors). Archaeological case studies—even extremely well-documented ones—are subject to the formulation of different explanatory scenarios, even competing ones that may be equally plausible given current evidence. The differences may come down to semantics or differing conceptualizations, including one's own working definition of "collapse," and the appropriate scale at which patterns must be apparent before one points to them as a case of collapse. The issue may also boil down to the factors, conditions, and cultural markers that a particular researcher chooses to focus on.

THIS VOLUME

To update our understanding of collapse and transformation of complex systems, this volume highlights case studies from around the globe. This book is a spin-off of a symposium of the same title, presented at the 2000 Society for American Archaeology (SAA) meetings in Philadelphia, organized by the volume editors. Not all of the participants in the symposium chose to include their papers to this volume. The ensuing chapters begin with case studies set in Eurasia and Oceania and then proceed to those from the New World.

With its global scope, this volume introduces these region-specific studies to a wider audience and highlights their relevance to broader, theoretical concerns. The contributions reflect a healthy diversity of ideas that collectively enhance our understanding of collapse and transformation. Also, unlike most previous approaches to collapse, many of the case studies presented here deal with the collapse and transformation of *prestate* societies. As such, this volume pushes the study of collapse and transformation into new directions and pursues more general inquiries into the operation of complex systems, the evolution of human societies, and the general condition of the human species and its prospects for the future.

NOTES

1. Note that, under Bronson's definition, it can be argued that barbarians are present even in today's world. Take, for example, the "tribal" groups of western Pakistan and most or all of Afghanistan, who have remained essentially beyond the control of those nations' central governments since the time when states first formed around them. It is no accident that many global terrorists have gravitated toward these groups and taken up residence among them. From these non-state territories, terrorist groups have harassed the United States and other modern states, whose response to these attacks is proving difficult, costly, and disruptive.

2. Reference sources for this general discussion of Roman history include Sinnigen and Boak (1977) and Ostrogorsky (1969).

REFERENCES

Adams, Robert McC.
1978 Strategies of Maximization, Stability, and Resilience in Mesopotamian Society, Settlement, and Agriculture. *Proceedings of the American Philosophical Society* 122:329–335.

Ames, Kenneth M., and Herbert D. G. Maschner
1999 *Peoples of the Northwest Coast: Their Archaeology and Prehistory.* London: Thames and Hudson.

Anderson, David G.
1990 Stability and Change in Chiefdom-Level Societies: an Examination of Mississippian Political Evolution on the South Atlantic Coast. In *Lamar Archaeology: Mississippian Chiefdoms in the Deep South*, edited by Mark Williams and Gary Shapiro, pp.187–213. Tuscaloosa: University of Alabama Press.

Austen, Leo
1936 The Trobriand Islanders of Papua. *Australian Geographer* 3(2):10–22.

Ayres, William
1985 Easter Island Subsistence. *Journal de la Société des Océanistes* 80:103–124.

Blanton, R. E.
1983 The Urban Decline at Monte Albán. In *The Cloud People: Divergent Evolution of Zapotec and Mixtec Civilization*, edited by Kent V. Flannery and Joyce Marcus, p. 186. New York: Academic Press.

Bowerstock, G. W.
1988 The Dissolution of the Roman Empire. In *The Collapse of Ancient States and Civilizations*, edited by Norman Yoffee and George L. Cowgill, pp. 165–175. Tucson: University of Arizona Press.

Bronson, Bennet
1988 The Role of Barbarians in the Fall of States. In *The Collapse of Ancient States and Civilizations*, edited by Norman Yoffee and George L. Cowgill, pp. 196–218. Tucson: University of Arizona Press.

Casanova, Patricia Vargas, ed.
1998 *Easter Island and East Polynesia Prehistory.* Santiago: University of Chile.

Chadwick, John
1976 *The Mycenaean World.* Cambridge: Cambridge University Press.

Demerest, Arthur, Prudence Rice, and Don Rice, eds.
2004 *The Terminal Classic in the Maya Lowland.* Boulder: University of Colorado Press.

Diamond, Jared
2005 *Collapse: How Societies Choose to Fall or Succeed.* New York: Viking.

Doumas, C. G.
1983 *Thera Pompeii of the Ancient Aegean: Excavations at Akotiri, 1967–79.* London: Thames and Hudson.

Dransfield, J., J. R. Flenley, S. M. King, D. D. Harkness and S. Rapu
1984 A Recently Extinct Palm from Easter Island. *Nature* 312:750–752.

Drews, Robert
1993 *The End of the Bronze Age: Changes in Warfare and the Catastrophe ca. 1200 B.C.* Princeton: University of Princeton Press.

Earle, Timothy
1991a The Evolution of Chiefdoms. In *Chiefdoms: Power, Economy, and Ideology*, edited by Timothy Earle, pp. 1–15. Cambridge: Cambridge University Press.

1991b Property Rights and the Evolution of Chiefdoms. In *Chiefdoms: Power, Economy, and Ideology*, edited by Timothy Earle, pp. 71–99. Cambridge: Cambridge

University Press.

Flenley, J. R., and Sarah King

1984 Late Quaternary Pollen Records from Easter Island. *Nature* 307:47–50.

Francaviglia, V., and B. Di Sabitino

1990 Statistical Studies on Santorini Pumice Falls. In *Thera and the Aegean World*, vol. 3: *Chronology,* edited by D. A. Hardey, pp. 29–52. London: The Thera Society.

Friedman, Jonathan

1975 Tribes, States, and Transformations. In *Marxist Analyses and Social Anthropology*, edited by Maurice Bloch, pp. 161–202. New York: Tavistock.

1982 Catastrophe and Continuity in Social Evolution. In *Theory and Explanation in Archaeology: The Southampton Conference,* edited by Colin Renfrew, Michael J. Rowlands, and Barbara Abbott Segraves, pp. 175–196. New York: Academic Press.

Friedman, Jonathan, and Michael J. Rowlands

1978 Notes towards an Epigenetic Model of the Evolution of "Civilisation." In *The Evolution of Social Systems,* edited by Jonathan Friedman and M. J. Rowlands, pp. 201–276. Pittsburgh: University of Pittsburgh Press.

Gill, Richard

2000 *The Great Maya Drought.* Albuquerque: University of New Mexico Press.

Goff, J. R., and B. G. McFadgen

2001 Catastrophic Seismic-Related Events and Their Impact on Prehistoric Human Occupation in Coastal New Zealand. *Antiquity* 75:155–162.

Graffam, G.

1992 Beyond State Collapse: Rural History, Raised Fields, and Pastoralism in the South Andes. *American Anthropologist* 94:882–904.

Hoffman, S. M., and A. Oliver-Smith

1999 Anthropology and the Angry Earth: An Overview. In *The Angry Earth, Disaster in Anthropological Perspective,* edited by A. Oliver-Smith and S. M. Hoffman, pp. 1–16. New York: Routledge Press.

Hudson, Charles, Marvin Smith, David Hally, Richard Polhemus, and Chester DePratter

1985 Coosa: A Chiefdom in the Sixteenth-Century Southeastern United States. *American Antiquity* 50:723–737.

Kirch, Patrick V.

1984 *The Evolution of Polynesian Chiefdoms.* Cambridge: Cambridge University Press.

Kolata, A. L.

2000 Environmental Thresholds and "Natural History" of and Andean Civilization. In *Environmental Disaster and the Archaeology of Human Response,* edited by G. Bawden and R. M. Reycraft, pp. 163–178. Maxwell Museum of Anthropology Anthropological Papers No. 7. University of New Mexico, Albuquerque

LeBlanc, Steven A.

1999 *Prehistoric Warfare in the American Southwest.* Salt Lake City: University of Utah Press.

LeClair, Edward E., Jr., and Harold K. Schneider, eds.

1968 *Economic Anthropology: Readings in Theory and Analysis.* New York: Holt, Rinehart and Winston.

Malinowski, Bronislaw

1922 *Argonauts of the Western Pacific: An Account of Native Enterprise and Adventure in the Archipelagoes of Melanesian New Guinea.* London: George Routledge and Sons.

Marinatos, S.

1939 The Volcanic Destruction of Minoan Crete. *Antiquity* 13:425–439.

McCoy, F. W., and G. Heiken

2000 The Late Bronze Age Explosive Eruption of Thera (Santorini) Greece: Regional and Local Effects. In *Volcanic Hazards and Disasters in Human Antiquity,* edited by F. W. McCoy and G. Heiken, pp. 43–70. Geological Society of America Special Paper 345. Boulder, CO.

Millon, René

1988 The Last Years of Teotihuacan Dominance. In *The Collapse of Ancient States and Civilizations,* edited by Norman Yoffee and George L. Cowgill, pp. 102–164. Tucson: University of Arizona Press.

Ostrogorski, G. C.

1969 *History of the Byzantine State.* New Brunswick, NJ: Rutgers University Press.

Pauketat, Timothy R.

1992 The Reign and Ruin of the Lords of Cahokia: A Dialectic of Dominance. In *Lords of the Southeast: Social Inequality and the Native Elites of Southeastern North America,* edited by Alex W. Barker and Timothy R. Pauketat, pp. 31–51. Archaeological Papers of the American Anthropological Association No. 3.

1994 *The Ascent of Chiefs: Cahokia and Mississippian Polities in Native North America.* Tuscaloosa: University of Alabama Press.

Pichler, H. and H. Schierling

1977 The Thera Eruption and Late Minoan IB Destruction on Crete. *Nature* 267:819–822.

Renfrew, Colin

1979 System Collapse as Social Transformation. In *Transformations: Mathematical Approaches to Culture Change,* edited by Colin Renfrew and K. L. Cooke, pp. 481–506. New York and London: Academic Press.

1984 System Collapse as Social Transformation. In *Approaches to Social Archaeology,* edited by Colin Renfrew, pp. 366–389. Cambridge, MA: Harvard University Press.

Reycraft, R. M., and G. Bawden

2000 Introduction. In *Environmental Disaster and the Archaeology of Human Response,* edited by G. Bawden and R. M. Reycraft, pp. 1–9. Maxwell Museum of

Anthropology Anthropological Papers No. 7. University of New Mexico, Albuquerque.

Rotberg, Robert I.
2002 Failed States in a World of Terror. *Foreign Affairs* 81(4):127–140.

Sahlins, Marshall D.
1958 *Social Stratification in Polynesia*. Seattle: University of Washington Press.

Sinnigen, W. D. and A. E. R. Boak
1977 *A History of Rome to A.D. 565*, sixth ed. New York: Macmillan.

Steadman, David, Patricia Vargas, and Claudio Cristino
1994 Stratigraphy, Chronology, and Cultural Context of an Early Faunal Assemblage from Easter Island. *Asian Perspectives* 33:79–96.

Stevenson, Christopher, and William Ayres, eds.
2000 *Easter Island Archaeology: Research on Early Rapanui Culture*. Los Osos, CA: Easter Island Foundation.

Stevenson, Christopher, and Claudio Cristino
1986 Residential Settlement History of the Rapa Nui Coastal Plain. *Journal of New World Archaeology* 7:29–38.

Stuart, David
2000 *Anasazi America*. Albuquerque: University of New Mexico Press.

Tainter, Joseph A.
1988 *The Collapse of Complex Societies*. Cambridge: Cambridge University Press.
1999 Post-collapse Societies. In *Companion Encyclopedia of Archaeology*, edited by Graeme Barker, pp. 988–1039. London: Routledge.

Vallianou, D.
1996 New Evidence of Earthquake Destructions in Late Minoan Crete. In *Archaeoseismology,* edited by S. Stiros and R. E. Jones, pp. 53–78. Athens Institute of Geology and Mineral Exploration and The British School at Athens, Fitch Laboratory Occasional Paper 7.

Webster, David
2002 *The Fall of the Ancient Maya*. New York: Thames and Hudson.

Yoffee, Norman
1988 Orienting Collapse. In *The Collapse of Ancient States and Civilizations*, edited by Norman Yoffee and George L. Cowgill, pp. 1–19. Tucson: University of Arizona Press.

Yoffee, Norman, and George L. Cowgill, eds.
1988 *The Collapse of Ancient States and Civilizations*. Tucson: University of Arizona Press.

2

The Collapse of Centers in Late Iron Age Europe

Peter S. Wells

COLLAPSE AND IDENTITY

THE COLLAPSE OF CIVILIZATIONS, SOCIETIES, OR CENTERS within them is always a complex phenomenon with multiple causes and results. We can approach the related issues from any number of different perspectives, including economic, social, and political. In this paper, I examine one aspect of collapse—its repercussions on identity. The ways that individuals and groups identify themselves, and the nature of changes in feelings and expressions of identity, are issues of considerable interest today in many different disciplines that can offer productive new perspectives on human behavior in the past. Identity on all levels has significant material expressions and thus lends itself well to archaeological analysis (Graves-Brown, Jones, and Gamble 1996).

THE OPPIDA OF LATE IRON AGE EUROPE

From the middle of the second till the middle of the first century BC, the cultural landscape of temperate Europe from central France to Slovakia, from the Alps to the North European Plain (Figure 1), was dominated by large fortified centers known by the Latin term *oppida* (Wells 1999:49–53). Most, but not all, were situated on the tops of hills. These settlements were enclosed by massive walls built of earth, faced on the exterior with cut stone and supported by timber beams. At many sites, substantial portions of the walls still survive as impressive monuments to the labor efforts that went into constructing these fortifications. The enclosed areas, often hundreds of acres in extent, were densely built up on some of the sites, while others yield only sparse remains of Late Iron Age settlement. Some oppida were occupied by concentrated populations in the thousands for a century or more, whereas others appear to have served as refuges in times of danger but were never substantially inhabited. Many oppida were centers of large-scale manufacturing in pottery, iron, bronze, wood, leather, textiles, glass, and other materials. Extensive and intensive commerce is evident in quantities of large ceramic wine amphorae, fine tableware pottery, and bronze vessels from the Mediterranean world—especially Roman Italy and southern Gaul; coins from different regions of temperate and Mediterranean Europe; and raw materials such as graphite from Austria or Bohemia, copper from the Austrian Alps, and amber from the shores of the Baltic Sea.

The most extensively excavated oppidum is at Manching on the Danube River in Bavaria, Germany, where about 25 acres of the nearly thousand-acre settlement have been investigated (Sievers 2003). Those excavations have revealed a dense settlement structure with extensive architectural remains of houses, workshops, and other buildings, including some that have been interpreted as ritual in purpose. The majority of oppida throughout Europe that are known from their extant walls (as many as 150 have been identified) have to some extent been investigated archaeologically, and most show remains of structures and assemblages of material culture similar to those at Manching, though the evidence is rarely as extensive. Population estimates for the oppida are difficult to make. Disposal of the dead in most parts of temperate Europe during this period did not result in large cemeteries associated with these settlement centers; hence we do not have the skeletal populations that might provide key data for demographic studies. But based on several different kinds of settlement evidence, estimates of between 3,000 and 5,000 inhabitants for the major oppida, such as Manching, Bibracte in France, and Stradonice in Bohemia, seem reasonable.

THE COLLAPSE

Between 58 and 51 BC, Julius Caesar led his Roman army in the conquest of Gaul—modern France, Belgium, and portions of Germany and the Netherlands west of the Rhine River. In his commentaries, Caesar describes the Gallic oppida as tribal capitals. Caesar's army destroyed oppidum communities of Rome's enemies; those of allies

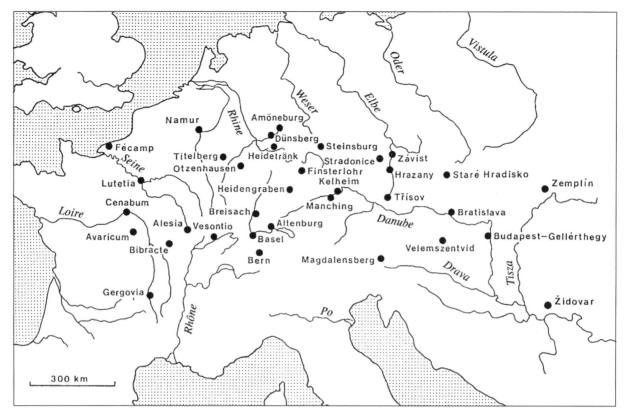

Figure 1. Map showing locations of some of the principal oppida of temperate Europe.
Note the location of the Rhine River, which formed the eastern border of Gaul for Julius Caesar
in his military campaigns of 58–51 BC. (after Wells 1993:1, Fig. 1.1).

often remained occupied for a generation or two following the conquest and then were largely abandoned in favor of new Roman towns in the river valleys (Colin 1998). Archaeological evidence is more or less consistent with Caesar's account. The excavated oppida yield evidence indicating the kind of communities (modern investigators often call them "urban" or "proto-urban") that Caesar describes (making allowance for his Roman vision of what he observed), and both the military defenses and remains of weaponry correspond to the attacks recounted by the Roman general (Duval 1994; Reddé et al. 1995).

For the end of the oppida east of the Rhine, however, we have no written sources comparable to Caesar's account of his campaigns in Gaul, and we depend completely upon the material evidence of archaeology. During the Gallic War, according to his account, Caesar made two forays across the Rhine, in the years 55 and 53 BC, but he tells nothing about peoples he encountered there. The archaeological evidence at oppida east of the Rhine that have been substantially investigated, such as Manching, Kelheim (Wells 1993), and Heidengraben (Knopf 1998),

suggests that activity there declined sharply at about the time of the Gallic War—around the middle of the final century BC. It was not until about 35 years later that Roman armies conquered the lands south of the upper Danube, in a well-documented campaign in the summer of 15 BC, led by the Roman generals Tiberius and Drusus (Zanier 1999).

The question that emerges from this situation—with implications for understanding the collapse of many other complex systems throughout human experience—is: Why did the oppida east of the Rhine decline, and what were the results for the people involved?

In Europe, research approaches to this context have tended to view the "oppidum civilization" as one distinct entity, and the post-oppidum cultural landscape as another. Each has been defined by a particular material culture assemblage, with the transition being viewed as a cultural break rather than a process. This break has been interpreted largely in terms of migration—especially immigration of peoples whom the Romans called "Germans," from regions to the north and east, southward and westward into what is now southern Germany (Rieckhoff 1995; Wells 2001). But the nature of the process of this change—the abandonment of the oppida and movement of people from the centers out into the countryside—becomes apparent if we examine the archaeological evidence in light of changes documented in arguably comparable situations on the edges of other instances of imperial expansion (e.g., Farriss 1984; Hill 1996).

In Gaul, we have not only Caesar's detailed account of the Roman attacks on, and defeat of, the tribal capitals, but also direct archaeological evidence for the battles that brought about the end of the oppida as native centers. At the oppida east of the Rhine, on the other hand, no indication of a violent end has been identified—no extensive evidence of burning or any other kind of destruction, no concentrations of weapons around entrances into the sites, where we might expect assaults to have focused, nor any extensive scatters of weapons or human bones that might

Figure 2. (above) Rim sherds and decorated pieces of pottery from the oppidum at Kelheim on the Danube River in Bavaria, Germany (from Wells 1993:44, Fig. 6.7).

indicate a final battle. At some oppida, such as Kelheim, the lack of many finds of large, useable objects adds support to the idea that the settlements were abandoned systematically, not overrun in military assaults, in which a lot of things might have been left behind.

The best general model (not yet formulated in detail, let alone systematically tested) for understanding why these sites were abandoned around the time that Caesar was waging war in Gaul (58–51 BC) is in terms of the disruption and breakdown of economic and political networks that linked the oppida east of the Rhine with those across the river in Gaul. The very similar architectural characteristics of the oppida on both sides of the Rhine, as well as the pottery (Figure 2), iron tools (Figure 3), and bronze and glass ornaments, along with the circulation of coins between regions across Europe, show that the communities based at the oppida were interconnected in economic, social, and political networks. The sizeable communities resident at the oppida (much larger than any that had existed before in those regions) could only have been sustained through regular influx of raw materials and outflow of finished trade goods. These circulation systems operated both in the territories around the individual oppida and between oppida throughout Europe. The Roman campaigns west of the Rhine in Gaul disrupted this interactive system. From Caesar's account, it is clear that tens of thousands of people were killed in battle and in reprisals carried out by the Romans, and probably many more died of starvation and disease during the war.

East of the Rhine, where direct military activity on such a large scale is not apparent, the material evidence corresponds closely to archaeological models for the breakdown of complex cultural systems (Tainter 1988).

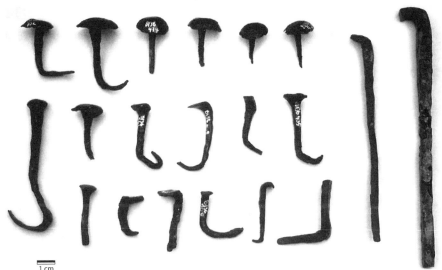

Figure 3. (right) Iron nails from the oppidum at Kelheim on the Danube River.

Along with the abandonment of the oppida (at least by the majority of their populations—some small communities probably remained in them), we have evidence for the resettlement of former oppidum populations in small communities throughout the landscape. Serial production in specialized craft industries of goods such as pottery and iron tools came to an end, replaced by manufacturing on a much smaller scale. In place of the standardized goods that characterize the oppidum settlements and the small communities that had been in their hinterlands, we find a wider range of styles in ceramics and metal ornaments, and the formation of regional groups replaces the more uniform material culture over wide areas.

MATERIAL CULTURE AS MATERIALIZATION

Objects crafted and used by people not only express and reflect ideas about social relations and identity, they also create those relations and contribute to the shaping of identity (Geertz 1983). Through practices of use, objects acquire particular meanings. Thus material culture and identity can be understood to be linked in a continuous process of creation and reaction.

The oppida of the final two centuries BC were material expressions of ideas different from anything that had existed before in temperate Europe. Settlement layout and design are carried out on the basis of a community's cultural rules; a whole complex of new rules had to be formulated to accommodate the needs of these new settlements. The most striking difference between the oppida and everything that went before in this part of the world was their sheer size, but there are other important differences as well. The scale and architecture of the walls at the oppida differed from earlier defenses. At some sites, such as Manching and Staré Hradisko in Moravia, excavation plans reveal streets and what we might call city blocks. At Staré Hradisko some streets were paved with stone. Thus we can understand the oppida as the material expression of a new way of thinking about settlement space and structure in temperate Europe. For the first time, thousands of people were moving together to live in enclosed settlements, organizing these new settlements in systematic and planned ways, and creating imposing monumental boundary walls around them.

OPPIDA AND IDENTITY

Much has been written about the origins of the oppida— why they were established during the second century BC. To summarize very briefly, their origins can best be understood in terms of the interplay between several major changes that were taking place at the time. These included the gradual expansion of Roman military, political, and economic interests, particularly into southern Gaul; substantial movements of peoples within central and northern Europe; and an increase in productivity of subsistence and industrial activities along with rapid growth in both regional and long-distance trade. Both military and commercial aspects are important for understanding the establishment and functioning of the oppida.

Although the oppida are the dominant visible remnant of Late Iron Age communities on the landscape today, and were the political and economic foci of regional groups at the time, it is important to remember that the great majority of people throughout Europe remained residents of very small village communities. These much more numerous, smaller communities formed, with the oppida, parts of an integrated cultural landscape. Large quantities of products of specialized industries based at the oppida, such as those producing fine wheel-made ceramics, bronze ornaments, and glass bracelets, are recovered at the contemporaneous small settlements.

Mass production of goods, including pottery, iron tools, and personal ornaments, largely replaced individually crafted objects when the oppida were established. This change is also apparent at some unfortified settlements of the period, such as Berching-Pollanten (Fischer, Rieckhoff-Pauli, and Spindler 1984), but not at the smallest, most typical settlements. One of the clearest indications of this change is the proliferation of the mass-produced and strikingly plain Nauheim fibula that replaced more ornate, individually crafted fibulae that were common before the middle of the second century BC (Drescher 1955). Throughout the Iron Age, fibulae—bronze or iron ornaments that worked like modern safety pins—were worn on the shoulder or chest to fasten garments, provide personal ornamentation, and communicate information about the wearer's identity. The change from individualized, ornate fibulae to mass-produced, plain objects has important implications for the way individuals perceived themselves relative to other persons (Wells 1995). This same change from complex, differentiated material culture to simpler, plainer objects is evident in other kinds of personal ornaments as well, such as belt hooks and bracelets.

Within the oppidum communities, new attitudes developed among the inhabitants, as the result of living in these much larger and densely inhabited settlements surrounded by massive walls. Another material sign of these changes is the proliferation of locks and keys on oppidum settlements for the first time, indication of changes in relationships between people living together in the new urban settings. The processes of laying out the large and complex settlements at the oppida and of constructing the walls around them required a new and more complex kind of political organization in these communities and, at the same time, created a new kind of built environment for human habitation. As Barrett (1994) has argued for prehistoric archaeology, and architects and city-planners demonstrate in modern life, constructed environments are not just expressions of a community's ideas about itself, but also agents of change that create feelings about the individual's place in society. By living inside these relatively densely populated, walled complexes, residents of the oppida developed particular feelings about who they were that distinguished them from people who lived outside. In addition to the enclosing walls and the physical structure of these urban communities, objects available to residents of the oppida also defined a special position for them. Foreign imports, including wine amphorae, ornate Roman pottery, bronze vessels, medical implements, and coins, make clear that the oppidum communities had greater access to some goods than other people had. Insofar as consumption contributes to the construction of identity, the availability of such goods played a part in the creation of the self-conception of oppidum residents. Objects associated with early writing (in Greek and Latin characters) are also largely confined to oppidum settlements (Krämer 1982).

An important qualification needs to be added. Feelings of identification with the oppidum communities and of opposition with respect to others surely varied with social status and position. Wealthy burials of this period show a striking degree of homogeneity across much of Europe (Frey 1986; Metzler et al. 1991), indicating that elites were in contact over considerable distances, and that they shared a sense of common identity on some level. Well-equipped men's graves contain long iron swords and ornate scabbards, spears, shields, Roman bronze vessels, and sometimes gold ornaments. Comparable women's graves have large quantities of bronze ring jewelry, mirrors, bronze vessels, and coins. To judge from the available evidence, nonelites tended to identify with a much more local community. Thus, when we speak of the development of a particular kind of identity at the oppida, we need to distinguish between elites and nonelites. The task of recognizing structural features on oppidum settlements associated with elites and those associated with others is still in its infancy. The archaeological character of oppidum settlements does not lend itself

easily to identifying status and wealth differences among inhabitants.

As noted above, the oppida were established at a time of considerable political and cultural stress, with military threats from Roman expansion from the south, increasing competition among regional groups in the growing trade with the Roman world (Collis 1995), and large migrations of peoples from the north. Even if we did not have the Roman written sources regarding the increasingly confrontational environment in temperate Europe during the second and final centuries BC, we still have abundant archaeological evidence for growing tensions during this period. Large quantities of valuable objects—including weapons, tools, bronze vessels, and coins—were buried in the ground and dropped into lakes and rivers in ways that indicate deliberate deposition (Brunaux 1996; Müller 1990). Though the specific reasons for making such deposits varied, the evidence strongly suggests that most are votive deposits—objects dedicated ritually to deities in the hope of winning divine favor (Bradley 1998). We know from historical contexts that the degree of such offering activity tends to increase in times of stress. Rituals that included manipulation of human bones are represented at many sites as well, including settlements, enclosures, and in bodies of water.

THE POST-OPPIDUM LANDSCAPE

The cultural landscape east of the Rhine in southern Germany after the collapse of the oppida was characterized by small communities exhibiting strikingly diverse material culture and ritual practices (Figure 4). The archaeological evidence from small settlements such as those at Eching, Paring, and Straubing-Stadtäcker enables us to see in detail how groups responded to the collapse of the complex and integrated system within which the oppida were central places, not only economically and politically, but also with respect to the creation of new identities on the part of the post-oppidum populations. When the integrated network of supply systems for foodstuffs and raw materials that had supported the oppida collapsed, individuals were forced to become more self-sufficient. They had to leave the densely inhabited, specialized centers and move out onto agriculturally productive land. The archaeological evidence shows large numbers of small settlements that were established around this time.

Because they were small and usually occupied only briefly, most of the settlements that have been studied are represented by no more than a few postholes and pits (Rieckhoff 1995). But the pottery, metal ornaments, and

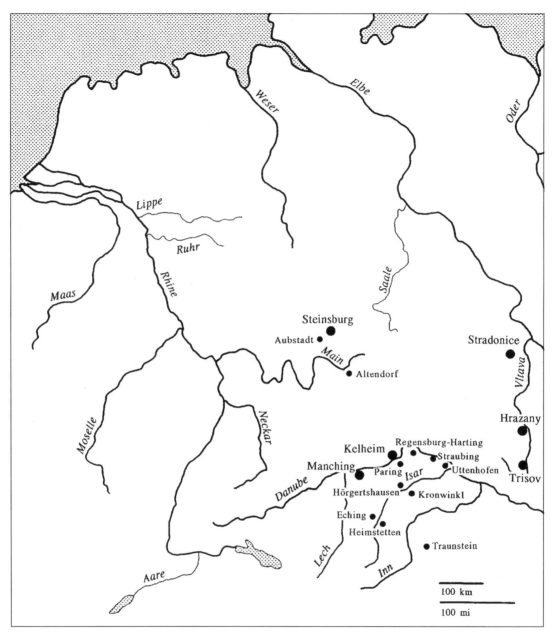

Figure 4. Map showing locations of some of the small settlements and cemeteries of the post-oppidum period (small circles) in the modern state of Bavaria, and some of the nearby oppida (large circles).

animal bones recovered provide chronological evidence and an indication of the character of the new post-oppidum communities. At Regensburg-Harting, Rieckhoff uncovered postholes and pits, along with fragments of wall plaster, which she attributes to a series of farmsteads. Pottery and fibulae indicate a date in the latter half of the first century BC. Slag fragments and furnace remains attest to small-scale forging of iron. The few iron tools recovered were individually crafted, not mass-produced as at the oppida. Almost all of the pottery (90%) is of hand-made

character, in contrast to the predominance of wheel-made pottery at the oppida (75% at Manching, for example). A mix of graphite with clay that produced a distinctive form of cooking pot is common at the oppida, but very rare at Regensburg-Harting. And Rieckhoff notes that the pottery is much more diverse at this small settlement than the assemblages of standardized wares at the centers. Finally, she notes among the animal bones a proportion of wild animals, including boar, aurochs, and red deer, much higher than at the oppida. This difference might be understood in terms of the breakdown in the provisioning systems that had supplied the oppidum populations with meat from the farms in their hinterlands. With the disruption of the supply systems, people may have needed to rely more heavily on wild resources. Coins, glass ornaments, and foreign materials such as amber, as well as Roman import vessels, are absent or very rare at these small settlements.

The people who inhabited these new communities created new varieties of material culture that expressed their new identities in the post-oppidum context. As Thomas (1996) has argued, not only do people create objects in ways that express their identities, but the process of making and using objects establishes relationships between those objects and people's identity. Pottery at the small settlements is diverse in form and in decoration, in contrast to the highly standardized ceramics at the oppida. The individually crafted quality, together with a new variety of forms and decorative patterns, of the fibulae of this period distinguish those important personal signs from the mass-produced, plainer objects from the oppida.

Rituals associated with disposal of the dead illustrate this creation of new, post-oppidum, identities particularly well. The practice of burying of the dead, common from Upper Palaeolithic times through the Middle Iron Age but abandoned in much of temperate Europe during the time of the oppida, was recreated by communities in this post-oppidum period. But unlike the situation during the Middle Iron Age, when strikingly uniform burial practices are evident across much of Europe, in this new situation, practice varied widely. Some burials contain cremations, others inhumations. Some, as at Hörgertshausen, had complex mounds erected over the burials, and fences around the mounds. Others were flat graves with no enclosures. The categories of objects placed in the graves are similar to those in earlier cemeteries—fibulae, belts, knives, and pottery—but the forms of individual objects, and the combinations in which they occur in burials, vary widely. In graves at Altendorf, Aubstadt, Hörgertshausen, Kronwinkl, Traunstein, and Uttenhofen, cremation is predominant (but not universal), and the bronze personal ornaments show marked differences from those common at the time of the oppida. These include fibulae of the type with an arched bow and that known as Beltz J, together with specific new forms of belt hooks. At Heimstetten and in other burials further west and south, inhumation is the dominant practice, and different styles of fibulae, belt hooks, and other ornaments are characteristic.

In this pattern of variability in material culture and ritual expression after the collapse of the oppida, we can discern the creation of new, regional styles and practices. For example, in much of eastern Bavaria, many burials of this period are characterized by cremation and the inclusion of personal ornaments resembling those common in regions to the north and east (Rieckhoff 1995; Völling 1995). In southern and western Bavaria, on the other hand, many communities adopted the practice of inhumation and created new ornament forms, many of them based on earlier styles of the region, and some that are similar to forms used by peoples who inhabited regions to the south in the foothills of the Alps (Keller 1984). Further west, ceramic styles represent yet a different regional expression in the post-oppidum context (Wieland 1996).

CONCLUSION

After the collapse of the oppida around the middle of the first century BC, people sought to reestablish themselves under different economic, social, and political circumstances in small communities in the countryside. Much of the landscape was, of course, already occupied by the farms and villages that had formed a part of the integrated Late Iron Age cultural landscape, of which the oppidum centers were a part. Both the newcomers to the rural environments and the existing communities were profoundly affected by the disintegration of economic and political systems, though in somewhat different ways. In the process of reorganizing their economies and communities, people created new forms of material culture and new practices. The creation of new ceramics and metal ornaments is characterized particularly by the formation of strongly regional patterns in manufactured goods. At the same time, products for which the small communities had depended upon the oppidum workshops—glass ornaments, bronze jewelry, graphite-clay pottery—disappeared from use, or became scarce.

In the strongly regional patterning of material culture that is apparent after the middle of the final century BC, many communities reached back into their pasts to recreate, on the basis of memory or curation of old objects, styles and practices. When the Roman legions under the command of the generals Tiberius and Drusus converged on the region between the Danube River and the Alps in their summer campaign of the year 15 BC, they encountered a landscape of these small communities, disarticulated from the strong links that had existed between rural settlements and the oppida. Unable to offer any larger-scale, organized resistance, these communities were conquered within a single summer, in a Roman effort apparently so easy that it was barely mentioned in the historical texts of the time.

Despite (or perhaps because of) the relative ease of the military conquest by Rome, the indigenous peoples were able to maintain much of their material culture and their ritual practices during the centuries of Roman occupation (Wells 1999). The persistence of those traditions, and of the meanings behind the material culture created and used by these groups, emphasizes the processual nature of the changes that resulted from the collapse of the oppida. The collapse of the centers and the disintegration of the economic and political networks of which they were a part constituted a change in the ways that people and their actions were linked together regionally and interregionally. In response to the collapse, and in order to rebuild their sense of themselves as individuals and members of their social groups, people reached back into their traditional pasts for the forms, practices, and meanings with which to create new communities and identities.

REFERENCES CITED

Barrett, J.
1994 *Fragments of Antiquity.* Oxford: Blackwell.

Bradley, R.
1998 *The Passage of Arms: An Archaeological Analysis of Prehistoric Hoard and Votive Deposits,* second ed. Oxford: Oxbow Books.

Brunaux, J.-L.
1996 *Les religions gauloises: Rituels celtiques de la Gaule indépendante.* Paris: Editions Errance.

Caesar, Julius.
1986 *The Gallic War,* translated by H. J. Edwards. Cambridge: Harvard University Press.

Colin, A.
1998 *Chronologie des oppida de la Gaule non méditerranéenne.* Paris: La Maison des Sciences de l'Homme.

Collis, J.
1995 The First Towns. In *The Celtic World,* edited by M. Green, pp. 159–175. London: Routledge.

Drescher, H.
1955 Die Herstellung von Fibelspiralen. *Germania* 33:340–349.

Duval, A., ed.
1994 *Vercingétorix et Alésia.* Paris: Réunion des Musées Nationaux.

Farriss, N. M.
1984 *Maya Society under Colonial Rule.* Princeton: Princeton University Press.

Fischer, T., S. Rieckhoff-Pauli, and K. Spindler
1984 Grabungen in der spätkeltischen Siedlung im Sulztal bei Berching-Pollanten. *Germania* 62:311–372.

Frey, O.-H.
1986 Einige Überlegungen zu den Beziehungen zwischen Kelten und Germanen in der Spätlatènezeit. *Marburger Studien zur Vor- und Frühgeschichte* 7:45–79.

Geertz, C.
1983 *Local Knowledge.* New York: Basic Books.

Graves-Brown, P., S. Jones, and C. Gamble, eds.
1996 *Cultural Identity and Archaeology.* London: Routledge.

Hill, J. D., ed.
1996 *History, Power, and Identity: Ethnogenesis in the Americas, 1492–1992.* Iowa City: University of Iowa Press.

Keller, E.
1984 *Die frühkaiserzeitlichen Körpergräber von Heimstetten bei München und die verwandten Funde aus Südbayern.* Munich: C.H. Beck.

Knopf, T.
1998 Zum Abschluss der archäologischen Untersuchungen im Oppidum Heidengraben. *Archäologische Ausgrabungen in Baden-Württemberg* 1998:108–113.

Krämer, W.
1982 Graffiti auf Spätlatènekeramik aus Manching. *Germania* 60:489–499.

Metzler, J., R. Waringo, R. Bis, and N. Metzler-Zens
1991 *Clemency et les tombes de l'aristocratie en Gaule Belgique.* Luxembourg: Musée National d'Histoire et d'Art.

Müller, F.
1990 *Der Massenfund von der Tiefenau bei Bern.* Basel: Schweizerische Gesellschaft für Ur- und Frühgeschichte.

Reddé, M., S. von Schnurbein, P. Barral, J. Bénard, V. Brouquier-Reddé, R. Goguey, H. Joly, H.-J. Köhler, and C. Petit
1995 Fouilles et recherches nouvelles sur les travaux de César devant Alésia (1991–1994). *Bericht der Römisch-Germanischen Kommission* 76:73–158.

Rieckhoff, S.
1995 *Süddeutschland im Spannungsfeld von Kelten, Germanen und Römern.* Trier: Rheinisches Landesmuseum.

Sievers, S.
2003 *Manching: Die Keltenstadt.* Stuttgart: Konrad Theiss.

Tainter, J. A.
1988 *The Collapse of Complex Societies.* Cambridge: Cambridge University Press.

Thomas, J.
1996 *Time, Culture and Identity.* New York: Routledge.

Völling, T.
1995 *Frühgermanische Gräber von Aubstadt im Grabfeldgau (Unterfranken).* Kallmünz: Michael Lassleben.

Wells, P. S.
1993 *Settlement, Economy, and Cultural Change at the End of the European Iron Age: Excavations at Kelheim in Bavaria, 1987–1991.* Ann Arbor: International Monographs in Prehistory.
1995 Manufactured Objects and the Construction of Identities in Late La Tène Europe. *EIRENE* 31:129–150.
1999 *The Barbarians Speak: How the Conquered Peoples Shaped Roman Europe.* Princeton: Princeton University Press.
2001 *Beyond Celts, Germans and Scythians: Archaeology and Identity in Iron Age Europe.* London: Duckworth.

Wieland, G.
1996 *Die Spätlatènezeit in Württemberg.* Stuttgart: Konrad Theiss.

Zanier, W.
1999 Der Alpenfeldzug 15 v. Chr. und die Eroberung Vindelikiens. *Bayerische Vorgeschichtsblätter* 64:99–132.

3

Collapse of Civilization and the Potential for Multilinear Evolution

Allen Zagarell

THE PROBLEM THIS VOLUME IS CONFRONTING IS THE COLLAPSE of complex systems. Certainly, as noted by multiple scholars, such collapse does occur (see especially Tainter 1988 and Yoffee and Cowgill 1988, who represent part of a longer tradition). However, a difficulty arises as to how one goes about analyzing such collapse. Most frequently collapses are handled in one of two, largely contradictory, forms. Some see collapse as a set of largely unique historical events, which can be compared only in the most general sense. On the other hand, collapse is sometimes viewed as a consequence of cross-cultural, social-organizational processes and structures, and that similar forms (for example, chiefdoms or states) can be torn from their historical and geographic contexts and compared directly with one another. In the second case, complex societies can, theoretically, be compared as systems. Yet although states and complex chiefdoms are, indeed, often *described* as systems (see, for example, Flannery 1972b), most scholars, rather than analyzing the nature of the system(s) (either in general or as historically specific and historically determined systems), simply define/typologize these entities into existence. These definitions often depend on a series of non-dynamic traits ("laundry lists," including the appearance of centralized government, monumental architecture, etc., in the case of states) that enable what at first blush appear to be rather disparate sorts of societies to be placed into the same category, thus facilitating highly generalized comparisons.

As someone who attempts to use Marxist modes of analysis to understand social dynamics, I should note that the diametrically opposed approaches briefly described above are, in my view, largely unproductive and in direct opposition to methodologies necessary to analyze social transformations. The delineation of trait characteristics of a social or economic system neither defines that system nor explicates it. It is not obvious to me that a generalized listing of "causes" or "consequences" of social collapse provides useful insights. Rather, I am of the opinion that it is more productive to examine the systemic dynamics of particular modes of production, and then the interaction of multiple coexisting (historically determined) modes making up the social formation. For example, Marxists root the boom-bust economic cycles of industry in capitalist countries in the production system (see Marx 1890), although the actual effect of these cycles is influenced by the historical relationship of forces within a particular society. If one is analyzing a system, I am arguing, the emphasis should be on the forces that produce and, over time, either reproduce or fail to reproduce the *particular* and characteristic social relations of *specific* societies. In other words, what we should look for is social reproduction, imperfect social reproduction, and social breakdown.

In regards to my processual archaeological colleagues, this is not another way of looking at the ecological conditions. Although Marx emphasized the underlying resource base and technologies that support the relations of production characteristic of particular societies, he did so in a manner sharply opposed to the way many processual archaeologists use such "core" elements. The technologies and resource base of the society, which fit into the "forces of production," are closely integrated with the social-organizational systemic dynamics. The relation between the society and these "core" elements is a reciprocal one. The social-organizational structure is influenced by the resource/technology base and, in turn, influences how those resources and technologies are actually employed. Moreover, I see no reason to assume that social configurations are to be understood as beneficial, or beneficial to all sections of their populations. This suggests differential reactions to the same stimulus by different sections of the population, and it is these differential reactions and relations that require a closer look.

Perhaps most significantly for this discussion, Marx and most Marxist scholars position the possibly multidirectional, evolutionary pathways of societies in the interplay of the structural demands of dominant modes of production (for example, see the highly generalized, idealized discussion of capitalism in *Capital*) and the peculiar historical circumstances of particular societies (note the emphasis on agency in the Eighteenth Brumaire of Louis Napoleon Bonaparte; Marx 1964). The role of history in influencing evolution is highlighted by the correspondence between Marx and Vera Zasulitch, discussing the pathway to capitalism and socialism in nineteenth-century Russia. Zasulitch, having read Marx's study of the road to capitalism in Western Europe, assumed that a similar sequence of events would be necessary for the transition in Russia. Marx made it clear to her that that was not his position (note Hobsbawm 1965). In a somewhat similar position to that taken by Fried (1967) many years later, Marx suggested that primary transitions and secondary ones might follow very different pathways. In fact, Marx seems to be suggesting that so-called secondary transitions may differ considerably from one another. He told Zasulitch that, in his view, the developments that characterized the Western European transition were not required in Russia. Indeed, he noted that the peculiar path of the historical process in Western Europe had led to the disappearance of certain groupings and institutions of the preexisting society. But those same groups and institutions still existed in Eastern Europe alongside the world capitalism which had come to pass in Western Europe. Therefore, the historical conditions for change and development in the two regions differed considerably. Given that capitalism already existed in Western Europe, the Russian transformation could be expected to differ from the western experience (Hobsbawm 1965). This vision of the indeterminacy of development is also implied in Gramsci's work (1971). Gramsci emphasized the role of agency and historical contingency, the lack of inevitability in the unfolding of history. Note especially his discussion of an unpredictable "war of position" in delineating the relative strengths of various classes, and the effect that has on the entire question of hegemony. Thus, agency and regional historical conditions influence the pathways of change.

I suggest in this discussion that history and process are not mutually exclusive elements, although since the advent of processual archaeology they have often been handled as such (note Flannery 1972a in his discussion of the divide between history and process and its significance for the New Archaeology). The delineation of a series of unique events does not, of course, explain history. It is simply a description of events, which in turn must be explained. On the other hand, in contrast to the ahistorical, processual mode of analysis, process cannot be understood without understanding the historical circumstances and conditions which help direct it. The social-organizational form (the

social formation, largely, but not exclusively, characterized by its dominant mode of production) and its consequent systemic demands largely create, in my view, the setting against which history develops. To a significant extent, the social formation structures the nature of oppositions, which must be worked out historically (for example, slave and slave owner, early centralized state power and merchants' relative independence, gender relations, and the structuring of ethnicity, among a multiplicity of oppositions). Although the social-organization form structures oppositions, it does not automatically predetermine the *means* by which those oppositions are resolved. Indeed, variations in social structure between several societies with similar modes of production, variations that may appear minor, can have important implications for social transformation.

Similarly, historical events, "historical accident," and even misreadings of situations by the participants can change evolutionary pathways. Note White's (1969) view that some things were largely inevitable, quite separate from the acts of individuals. Note the very different picture suggested by the work of Ulin (1995), in which class relations and historical "accident" interact. I am arguing that varied historical experiences can have important ramifications for the later "unfolding" of history. Human decisions, a key ingredient of human agency, can influence historical *and* evolutionary pathways.[1] For example, striking or not striking in industrial situations, revolting or acquiescing in moments of national crisis, even resisting, locally, in one form as opposed to another can have significant ramifications for further development. I am suggesting here that human history—indeed, social evolution—is not the sole consequence of either a completely impersonal set of forces or of unfettered human will. It is our job to delineate these varied elements and their interplay in the actual making of history. This task is never easy, often inexact, always approximate rather than certain, and always replete with the possibility for error, but it is necessary for more realistically evaluating change, including episodes of collapse.

COLLAPSE

Collapse itself can be divided into two broad forms. One form we can understand as *fundamentally cyclical*. This is, essentially, the sort of transition from gumlao to gumsao society discussed by Leach (1965; several other anthropologists have also discussed this cyclical transition, culminating in state emergence; see, among others, Webb 1971, as well as Zagarell 1986). In this case, the society periodically cycles through a series of forms. However, once it reaches a relatively complexly organized, but prestate, society, it experiences collapse. After collapsing, these societies essentially repeat the steps, leading to more complex gumsao society and renewed collapse. Theoretically, under ideal circumstances, such societies could occasionally make the transition to state-organized societies. In these cases the cyclical collapse would then stop. I have previously argued that there are systemic, structural impediments that separate state-organized society from non-state systems (Zagarell 1986). In that sense "collapse" is one stage in a cycle of stages. These collapses represent a society that continues to operate within one set of systemic relations. In contrast, transition to state-organized society is a qualitative change of systemic states.

This is essentially the argument made by Flannery (1972b), but he neither discusses the implications of this nor delineates the forms of transition between his multiple systemic states of band, tribe, chiefdom, and state. This is not to argue that the various stages of the most recent cycle reproduce all elements of previous cycles exactly. I assume that the cycles display cumulative change over time and that, below the surface, the "traditional" social relations are reproduced in an increasingly altered condition (quantitative change in the form of imperfect social reproduction), thus potentially facilitating the eventual transformation of the society. I am not suggesting that such cycles are only found in so-called chiefdoms. Cyclical collapse and resurrection have been posited for state-organized societies as well.[2] I only argue that cyclical collapse occurs largely within a specific mode of production or set of social-organizational givens. This sort of collapse presupposes that the newly constructed society tends to reproduce the essential elements of the preexisting society. Note that the cyclical concept separates this form from collapses, which are one-time accidents of history of the form discussed below.

The second form of collapse is a breakdown of the society, which *does not return to anything approximating the earlier condition.* It does not repeat a cycle. The political structure may collapse, and the social-organizational and economic relations of certain states may break down. Nevertheless, these sorts of collapses do not give rise to the social and economic relations of the previously existing, non-state-organized society. Many archaeologists and other scholars assume that these forms of breakdown return it to a simpler, less hierarchical society—in other words, a *return* to less complex forms of society, which they often classify within the conventional bands-tribe-chiefdom-state typology, thus suggesting a

collapse into a repeatable past, in which time is not an important variable. However, because the actual systems of production and social reproduction are rarely analyzed, in practice the relations of production, and the dynamics of social reproduction in these societies, may be significantly different than the previously existing regional society from which they evolved. In this case, breakdown may give rise to sets of new social relations that never previously existed. Although these societies *may* be less hierarchical than the preexisting states, they are not necessarily a throwback to the past. They constitute potentially new pathways, new systems, which can develop and transform in ways not previously observed. Conventional evolutionary typologies (e.g. Service's bands-tribes-chiefdoms-states, or the only marginally better system developed by Fried) often obscure the possibility that such breakdowns, and the new societies produced, represent the potential for *multilinear* evolution. New social relationships may be established that allow new forms of adaptation to existing social and physical environments. In this regard, note the discussions concerning the collapse of the Indus civilization (e.g., Kohl 1988; Allchin 1995). Indus society varied considerably from the neighboring Mesopotamian civilization, and the historical conditions surrounding its breakdown gave rise to a new civilization, the Gangetic, which is considerably different than that of the Indus, although they are both state-organized societies. Analysis of the role of collapse demands, I am suggesting, an analysis of the actual (not ideal) systems (social, economic, etc.) in operation at each stage in the development of a society, and during its so-called collapse.

THE NILGIRI HILLS OF SOUTH INDIA

The region I discuss here (Figure 5) was never a center of civilization. High above the plains, deep in the rugged, forested hills, the region was largely peopled by various so-called tribal groups. Ethnic communities, who claimed aboriginality, historically inhabited these hills. These communities have been historically described as tribes and are classified as tribes by the Indian government, although that designation has been contested by more recent scholarship (Walker 1986; note the discussion in Mahias 1997). The Nilgiri Hills have been regarded by cultural anthropologists as a largely isolated region. Therefore, it was thought to have had only limited, sporadic contact with the centers of South Indian civilization (e.g., see Hockings 1980). Scholars and the popular media have treated the aboriginal inhabitants of the region as unusual, displaying archaic behaviors and traits. Indeed, these local populations have occasionally been utilized to give us "insights" into "prehistoric" human behaviors and institutions (Walker 1997).

On the other hand, my own more recent work has demonstrated that this isolation was much less pervasive than previously imagined. There is now strong evidence—archaeological, documentary, and ethnographic—that there was extensive incorporation of these mountain dwellers into neighboring regional polities. By the time these people were studied, that incorporation had largely disappeared, providing the basis for the romantic (but mistaken) impression these people were always isolated. There is clear evidence of a period of integration into states followed by the regional breakdown of local state control, which was part of a wider collapse. Indeed, there is evidence of *periodic* breakdowns of overarching, regional state domination in this area. Subsequent to the last collapse, the region experienced wide-scale abandonment and a decline in the hierarchical complexity of the society. The picture I draw of these people and the effects of their incorporation will be imperfect and incomplete. The fullness of their society, the intricacies of their multiple production modes, and their histories are impossible to recreate. Nevertheless, I believe a basic picture of regional

life, its collapse, and a kind of resurrection can be pieced together from multiple documentary, archaeological, and ethnohistorical resources.

The indigenous populations largely came to be known to outsiders during the period of British dominance in South India. These populations have been studied to some considerable degree over the past 150 years. All the reports describe a series of groups, each of whom are identified with specific occupations: the hunting-gathering Irula and Kurumba, the pastoralist Toda, the craftsman Kotas, and the agricultural Badagas. In practice, these groups were more flexible in their subsistence activities than the occupational identities ascribed to them would seem to indicate. Nevertheless, the model is similar to caste organization in the nearby plains. The political structure described in these reports was largely egalitarian, with assemblies and interethnic representative bodies making decisions. While there were hints of differential authority, such authority seemed very limited. Extended kinship relations, somewhat hierarchical, combined with a system of priests with limited powers, largely regulated internal affairs. Interethnic relations were regulated by a system of hierarchical relationships and bound together by interethnic obligations (what have been called "proto-

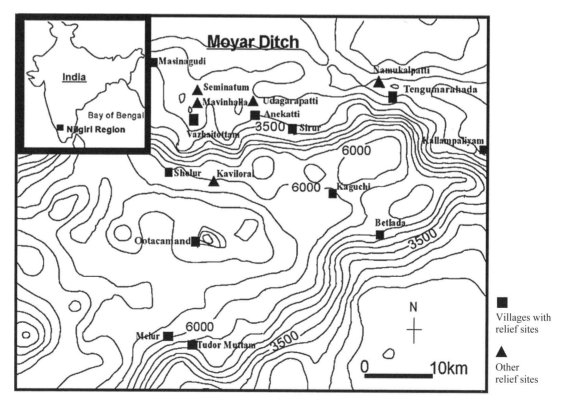

Figure 5. Sketch map of the Nilgiri Hills and hero-stone locations. Squares are villages with relief sites; triangles are other relief sites.

jajmani" relationships). Each group ensured that its own members fulfilled their intercommunity commitments. Community councils regulated individual behaviors. On the other hand, interethnic, intercommunity councils arbitrated cross-community disputes.

The system of asymmetric interethnic obligations was noted as being very similar to the jajmani (caste-organized, asymmetric obligations) relationships of the plains. However, in the plains such systems were intimately tied to unequal access to force and power (Fox 1962; for the changing conceptions of Nilgiri organization see Mahias 1997). It was unclear how such relations appeared among essentially egalitarian societies. Accumulating archaeological evidence now leaves us with good reason to believe that relationships of equality were not always characteristic of the mountains, and that these peoples were entwined in a system of state control whose center lay outside their region.

THE NILGIRIS AND STATE SOCIETY

Hints of inequalities, within kin-based communities (although not necessarily directly related to any contemporary society), can be inferred at least as early as the Megalithic. For example, there are large numbers of regional Megalithic cemeteries, some of which contained hundreds of graves. These cemeteries are often characterized by a handful of monumental graves, sometimes strategically placed, surrounded by a much larger number of more modestly sized and constructed graves (see Zagarell 1997). Further evidence of inequalities is abundant in the large number of rock art sites. Some of these sites are definitely historical and thus relevant to the discussion at hand. At many of them, carved scenes of organized warfare are typical (see Zagarell 1999). They depict highly organized armies along with military horses and elephants, both of which would have required training and upkeep. Some of the fighting human figures are considerably larger than others and wear distinctive headdresses (Zagarell 1999; for example, at Totinalai and Wananga Pallam), suggesting high status. At the rock art site of Wananga Pallam, on one of the latest paintings, which I have dated to the medieval period (Zagarell 1994), the central, elephant-mounted warrior wears a necklace (Figure 6). It appears quite reminiscent of some of the twelfth-century reliefs discussed below. At Porivorai and other newly discovered rockshelters on the northeast Nilgiri slopes, umbrellas are held above the heads of horse-mounted figures, a sign of authority and status (Figure 7). Other recent archaeological data indicate that

this region was incorporated into a broader system of state authority. For example, in the Moyar Ditch area (the area between the Nilgiri Hills and the plateau of the Karnataka Plain), high-quality statuary (including what appears to be a Pallava Vishnu figure) and temple structures imply an administrative elite reaching back to at least the ninth century AD (Figure 8). The appearance of inscriptions in the Moyar Ditch, first in Tamil and then in Kannada, suggest trading guilds and periodic change in political control of this region. By approximately the twelfth century, the Nilgiris appear to have been incorporated into the Hoysala state, reaching down from Karnataka to the north. This suggestion is supported by reports of the conquest of Kongu country, including the Nilgiris, by the general of Vishnuvardhana, and then by the statements of Balala III, who calls himself "Conqueror of the Nilagiris" and who reportedly established the administrative center of Dannaiken Kotai (Ariokiaswami 1956). This statement indicates more than a simple conquest—rather an organized control of the Nilgiri region. Indeed, Hockings (1980) suggests the intermittent appearance of gold mining enterprises during this period in the heart of the Nilgiri Mountains, very similar to mining that was taking place in the nearby Tamil Nadu regions (i.e., in Kongu; see Manimegalai 1990).

Support for an early, northern, Karnataka-based state control, not previously attested to, can be found at multiple Nilgiri sites. For example, ritual/memorial/hero-stone sites dating to the period of Hoysala rule strongly imply northern control of the Moyar Ditch. Based on a recently discovered hero-stone complex site in Karnataka (in the Bandipur animal preserve area, just north of the Moyar Ditch) in 2000, and after consultation with the Director of the Coimbatore Archaeological Museum, powerful twelfth-century Hoysala/Karnataka influence can be posited for the Moyar Ditch area. This southern Karnataka site consists of a series of finely rendered reliefs which, reportedly, were once associated with a twelfth-century temple that was subsequently uprooted and redisplayed around a tourist resort just north of the Bandipur sanctuary. The reliefs are characterized by several exceptional renditions of a four-armed god, a Vishnu figure, who is transformed into a type of hero-stone (Figure 9). On at least one of these reliefs a figure holds an umbrella over the head of this godlike figure, suggesting his authority (Figure 10). All of these godlike figures include a female, usually carrying a vase, a symbol of self-immolation, often associated with a heroic husband's death. Alongside these figures are several other reliefs of a mounted ruler or important heroic figure, with raised sword and an umbrella held over his head by another

Figure 6. Painted rock art figure riding elephant, Wananga Pallam.

Figure 7. Painted heroic figures, rock art site of Porivorai.

Figure 8. Pallava Vishnu, Thangamarahada.

figure. This high-status figure is sometimes accompanied by a woman, probably his wife, holding the symbols of her self-sacrifice (note the similar portrayal in Figure 11). In at least one picture, this hero is shown trampling an enemy underfoot. Similarly, below one of the four-armed reliefs, a battle scene is depicted. At least one of the very smallest reliefs carries a woman holding a round object in her hand, again indicating an act of sati (ritual suicide). There are also a series of other reliefs, including multiheaded gods and goddesses (perhaps a Kali figure). All these suggest a twelfth-century cult of hero worship connected with an important personality, in which a godlike figure is depicted in a form usually reserved for mortals.

Several very similar complexes were discovered during my work at other Nilgiri sites. At Vazhaitottam, in the western Moyar Ditch area of the Nilgiri Hills, there once existed a complex hero-stone site. The site itself has been destroyed. A group of large and small reliefs/statues has been piled against a tree in the village. The most exceptional is a life-sized Vishnu-like figure with four arms displayed (although only three are visible). He holds a bow and a probable club in his left arms, while his right arm rests on the pommel of his sheathed sword (Figure 12). A tiny woman with a vessel (probably containing oil, as pictured in many hero-stones) stands by his left side, likely indicating her ritual suicide. The lower tier, below his feet, is a battle scene, perhaps representing his death in battle, as is often found on hero-stones. On one side is a worshipping male figure; just below this is a flattened area which may have supported an inscription, but I was unable to discern any clear writing. This relief is an almost exact replica of one of the Bandipur reliefs, indicating how close these sites are to one another. A very similar relief depicts a much smaller, cruder, four-armed god with a raised disk, bow, probable club, and a hand on a sword. One of the reliefs also contains a mounted warrior accompanied by a wife committing ritual suicide, clearly matching the Bandipur complex (Figure 11). A grouping of multi-tiered hero-stones not far from this find may or may not be connected with these reliefs.

Figure 9. Relief originally from Bandipur Park, South Karnataka.

Figure 10. Mounted heroic figure with umbrella, originally from Bandipur.

Figure 11. Mounted heroic figure with wife committing sati (ritual suicide), Vazhaitottam.

Another complex of hero-stones and reliefs similar to those described above can be found in the nearby village of Annekatti, at Chamarayya Kotai, in the middle section of the Moyar Ditch. The Chamarayya Kotai site may be even more significant than the Vazhaitottam finds. The complex was part of a more obviously complicated ritual site. The site includes the heroic, four-handed godlike figure, now lying face down in the mud, with a bow, a probable club, a disk, and a sword, exactly in tune with the Bandipur and Vazhaitottam finds. Nearby, and likely in situ, are the heroic horseman reliefs, another relief with a woman with a vessel, as well as several other variously themed depictions. These carvings are situated immediately north of a series of stone dolmens, in connection with another dolmen. This single dolmen, probably the focus of the complex, faces east, and it contains a hero-stone and a poorly preserved, uninterpretable Kannada inscription. Somewhat disturbing in this regard is that the relief depicts Saivite worship, which I would have guessed was later in date. Nevertheless, this grouping constitutes a complex set of displayed reliefs of high quality in the tradition of the Bandipur finds, suggesting northern control of this section of the Moyar Ditch.

The site of Namukalpatti represents further potential evidence for the range of Karnataka-based control of the entire stretch of the Moyar Ditch. This site is just northwest of the village of Tangamarahada. It was clearly a place of considerable import. The site includes menhirs, dolmens, an inscription, hero-stones, and other reliefs.

Figure 12. Vazhaitottam heroic figure with sati.

The Archaeological Survey of India dates the inscription to the twelfth century. Several of the reliefs are clearly of the typical hero-stone type. They include multi-tiered depictions of the loss of life, the self-sacrificing wife, the passage to heaven, and the upper scene of paradise. Namukalpatti also includes a relief of a mounted warrior, very similar to those from the sites discussed above. Several reliefs near the crossing of the Moyar to the contemporary village of Tangamarahada were reportedly taken from Namukalpatti. They include a hero-stone and a multiheaded depiction of a goddess (Kali?), similar to reliefs at the Bandipur site. Reportedly, Namukalpatti once contained a life-sized figure which was moved near the river and is said to have been carried off during a flood. A human foot from a larger statute that can no longer be located and a Nandi figure are also found at Namukalpatti, suggesting some sort of sanctuary in the immediate vicinity. Some type of small structure, perhaps a hut similar to those regularly used by Irula and Kurumbas, once existed at the site, but its remains could only be viewed in outline.

The final bit of evidence is the establishment of Dannaiken Kotai on the extreme northeast of the Nilgiri region, under the present Bhawani Sagar reservoir. This was reportedly the administrative center for Hoysala regional rule. In 2000, I discovered the remains of a collapsed, elaborately dressed stone temple and a Kannada inscription along the edge of the Nilgiri slopes behind Dannaiken Kotai. It sits very near the present-day Irula temples, utilized by slope dwellers and ditch dwellers alike. The temple shows some similarities to the twelfth-century temple at Velankadu in Coimbatore, although these similarities remain unanalyzed. The inscription also remains untranslated and undated. Another nearby feature of considerable interest is a very extended, elevated dirt wall that seems to have directed runoff from the hills into the Dannaiken Kotai region, suggesting considerable labor mobilization. The wall is not presently dated, but it cannot have been constructed later than Vijayanagar rule, and it was perhaps built considerably earlier. I was also told of an undocumented, very large, stone defensive wall/fort that was found in the forest near the temple, but higher up in the hills. Unfortunately, I was not allowed to visit that area.

Clearer evidence in the form of inscriptions dating to the Vijayanagar period again alludes to local and regional authority figures, including regional governors and administrative heads of villages. These documents mention administrative districts in the upper reaches of the mountains (i.e., Toda Nadu). Military activity is indicated by the multiple forts distributed about the northern foothills: for example, Annekatti (Yannai Kotai; the elephant fort) in the Moyar Ditch (see Zagarell 1994 for references and Hockings 1980 for a full listing of fort sites). Some strongholds also appear in the hills themselves. In fact, the Vijayanagar regional administrative center of Dannaiken Kotai (from which Lingayat officials policed the area and controlled the entire region) was located to the east, outside but well within striking distance of the immediate area of the foothills. Members of all present-day "aboriginal" communities told me that in the past, whenever they had a dispute, they would go to Dannaiken Kotai to have it resolved. The Toda have folk stories mentioning several regional raids by soldiers from the plains, and they may include a distorted reference to Dannaiken Kotai itself. In another inscription the Moyar Ditch/northern foothills area is described as being irrigated, with Lingayats (a priestly caste) controlling either the activity or the land itself. Based on the aforementioned traditions and abandoned settlements, the foothills seem to have been much more intensively cultivated and settled by the end of the Vijayanagar period than during any preceding or subsequent period. Large numbers of abandoned agricultural villages dot the Moyar Ditch. One Moyar inscription states that the

"Okkaligas had arrived" (a reference to a farming caste). At one temple, presently maintained by the Irula (formerly a hunting-gathering, forest-dwelling community), the state is mentioned as providing monetary support for the local temple by obligating neighboring agricultural villages to provide money, labor, and materials. Indeed, some Irula communities have traditions that depict their people working as servants in the houses of the well-to-do who were once found in the northern (Moyar) foothills. Individual hero-stones of people who died committing noble acts of bravery cover the landscape, all suggesting regional elite habitation. (See Zagarell 1994 for a more inclusive discussion of the materials discussed in this paragraph.)

With the collapse of the Vijayanagar state, local traditions tell of local dynasties vying for power (Hockings 1980). A series of traditions describe continuous warfare between micro-states in the Nilgiri vicinity. Lingayat folklore details regional battles between neighboring rulers (Zagarell 1994), and their eventual abandonment of the foothills and migration into the mountain heartland. I assume the irrigation systems in the northern foothills area mentioned above were being neglected during this chaotic period. Many of the settlements were certainly abandoned. Indeed, there is an Irula tradition that some sort of epidemic struck the local populations, after which the Okkaligas totally abandoned the region. The Irula were supposedly resistant to the epidemic and were able to remain. The continuous conflict and probable breakdown of the irrigation systems may be involved in a possible malaria epidemic, a definite economic breakdown, and the consequent decline in population levels. By the time the region was occupied by the British, it was largely empty and was described as isolated and essentially untouched by time, the home of egalitarian "tribes."

REGIONAL ORGANIZATION AND STATE INCORPORATION

How was the region organized during its period of state incorporation? What modes of production were predominant during that period? An answer to these questions can only be based on the very limited documentary evidence and the reports of contemporary populations. The upland "tribal" communities likely had a strongly corporate character, similar to that which characterized them when they were described ethnographically. Individuals lived in their own communities, either villages or hamlets. There was, until recently, no evidence of village land being alienated through sales of plots to outsiders. However, I was recently informed by the Director of the Coimbatore Museum that documents (palm leaves) from the thirteenth century do describe such sales. Reportedly, one of them documents sale of land from one ethnic community to another, suggesting some level of commodity relations, which in turn suggests some level of inequality. Pastureland was available to all community members. It was particularly important for the Toda buffalo pastoralists, and perhaps also for the groups with humped cattle, a type of cattle frequently pictured in the rock art. Given the castelike rules for social interaction, there could not have been a great deal of free movement of populations from one village to another for resettlement (although local stories demonstrate that was sometimes possible). This corresponds to community descriptions of their pre-British circumstances. Based on the stories told by ethnic communities, some villages were treated as units for administrative tasks. Moreover, villages (rather than individuals) were assessed taxes. The community leadership then apparently determined each individual's tax burden. On the other hand, not all villages have memories of state taxation, suggesting the possibility that not all communities were treated equally. Some stories mention state officials collecting the taxes, albeit in the presence of the local community heads. Other stories indicate that community representatives brought taxes to Dannaiken Kotai, indicating voluntary collection and payment. In no case is there a suggestion of long-term, direct supervision of the communities by administrators who resided in the villages. Corporate community responsibility for tasks is also demonstrated in the community council structure, which oversees the fulfillment of jajmani-like tasks. In this case the various ethnic communities largely direct themselves.

Based on information from interviews, and in contrast to the collective/corporate nature of the villages, most actual production was familial, though utilizing communal agricultural lands, forests, or pasture. All families of a community farmed their own land, or herded their own cattle, perhaps laying away surplus, thereby creating the potential for stratification. However, in the case of the Toda pastoralists, it has been suggested that, alongside individually possessed and ritual-communal herds, they maintained a public-communal herd for the payment of state tribute (Zagarell 1994).

The limited memories of state incorporation among local communities, combined with the limited descriptions of the indirect form of that incorporation, suggest that direct state intervention in village life was relatively rare. The limited memory of state intervention implies such intervention must have been rarely experienced and thus was viewed largely as an external force. Therefore, village

and community life must have been relatively autonomous. If communities abided by their imposed obligations, it is easy to imagine that they experienced little contact with state authorities. Reports of periodic raids by armies from the plain, in Toda and Irula folklore, point to what would happen if they did not fulfill those obligations but also suggest that direct administrative controls were nonexistent. Therefore, state incorporation may have been perceived as largely inconsequential to daily life in the hills. Nevertheless, state intervention significantly directed regional and local forms of organization and adaptation.

Despite high levels of community autonomy, state incorporation altered community histories. State taxation must have had some effect on the centralization of power in these communities, encouraging the emergence of community representatives who could interact with the state. The proliferation of local hero-stones in the upper mountain plateau, some of very high quality, implies highly skilled artisans. But others made with considerably less skill than those characteristic of the foothills argue for the existence of locals who made claims to elite status (Zagarell 2002), and communities taking on the attributes of hierarchy and authority. Why then were there so few memories of social stratification in the hills when the British first occupied them? It should be noted that memories of the past have clearly faded. For example, rock art along the northeastern edge of the Nilgiris, discovered during the 2000 season, indicates a proliferation of humped cattle in the area sometime in the past. Such cattle are not part of Nilgiri traditional history, although they are part of the more narrow tradition of neighboring Irula hill communities. This may mean that in the past Nilgiri life differed considerably from the current ethnographic picture. Another potential factor in the seemingly limited memories of a state-organized past is the fact that the hero-stone reliefs appear to have been largely limited to the representatives of one ethnic group. This group largely consisted of communities with ties to Karnataka, suggesting that some communities may have been more internally stratified than others, even if the stratification was limited. One particular Kota community also claimed (as part of their folklore) that they had once held a high level of local authority, which they eventually lost to a Badaga group. Interestingly, a few crude hero-stones are found in connection with certain Kota communities as well. Nevertheless, despite indications of past state controls and social hierarchy, only a few memories exist of earlier external domination. I have previously argued that, based on Lingayat tales, the state was actively eliminating powerful individuals who emerged in these hill communities, protecting themselves from possible competitors (Zagarell 1994, 1995). This periodic intervention must have limited the emergence of potentially centralizing community leaders based on a system of stratification, although other factors must have come into play.

This form of indirect control is thought to be typical of South Indian medieval society. It has been delineated by Stein (1977) and Fox (1977) and described as an example of a segmentary state. The concept of the segmentary state was first developed by Southall (1956) to describe a form of state found among certain African societies. More recently, Southall (1988) compared African and South Asian segmentary states and noted broad similarities, despite dissimilarities in scale. Segmentary states are polities characterized by weak control of peripheral constituent regions. These states demonstrate a relative lack of direct intervention in the affairs of their constituent groups, although they may extract wealth from subordinated communities.

Given the existence of states dominating the hills area, the establishment of proto-jajmani relationships does not seem anomalous. It was not uncommon for South Indian states to resettle communities into areas with low population densities, and to encourage jajmani-like "cooperative" relationships between communities. Despite local Nilgiri beliefs that such communities were "always" in the hills, it is likely that some of them were either resettled there or at least reorganized by intervening states. Indeed, it is difficult to imagine how the Kota craft-community could have settled in a nonrandom, widely dispersed settlement pattern, designed to make them available to a wide number of potential clients, in non-jajmani, aboriginal circumstances. Although it is impossible to pinpoint the development of this "cooperative" jajmani relationship among the Nilgiri communities, it now seems more likely that it somehow reflects state control, and state intervention, rather than representing a prelude to the emergence of state-like relationships.

CONCLUSIONS

The collapse of the Vijayanagar state and its successor mini-states did not lead to a reproduction of the previously existing relationships. One might manage to force these communities into the band/tribe/chiefdom/state paradigm,

but it is difficult to imagine what insights that might provide. Despite the lack of centralized leaders, these communities do not reflect stereotypical visions of tribal communities, nor do they have many of the classic characteristics of chiefly organized communities. The collapse destroyed much of the structure of administrative hierarchy that facilitated organized regional life and cooperation. State intervention and control (however indirect) supported the emergence of autonomous villages. Indeed, one could argue that egalitarianism on the village level is a consequence of state intervention. Note a somewhat similar argument made for the U.S. Southwest by McGuire and Saitta (1996), emphasizing the interplay between egalitarianism and hierarchy (albeit in a non-state setting). Nevertheless, state intervention, as I have argued, had created a hierarchical set of interacting communities, linked by mutual but asymmetric obligations to one another. Moreover, I have argued that the state acted to limit internal stratification and centralized power within the constituent communities. Therefore, the collapse of regional control seems to have left a residue of autonomous villages and economically intertwined, asymmetrically related, local ethnic communities, but a system of weak authority. Regional interaction nevertheless occurred at a relatively sophisticated level, despite the absence of that authority. Thus, collapse in this local case may have created regionally complex, community ranked, but village-based egalitarian relationships, which had never existed before.

Despite my introductory words concerning Marx, accident, history, and multilineal evolution, in relatively modern conditions such a small region, regardless of its peculiarities, can be easily overwhelmed by neighbors and integrated into broader systems. However, in less modern and more provincial conditions, the opportunities for independent development may have been more plentiful. I am suggesting that, in the pathways of human development and collapse, the roads taken may be more varied than those that appear in some currently utilized models. I am arguing that a focus on the interactions between structural demands and the "accidents of history," and on human decisions and actions, gives us a richer view of development. The grouping of disparate societies and systems under the same headings often obscures the richness and variety of human adaptations under unique cultural and historical circumstances.

NOTES

I would like to thank the Fulbright Commission, the Smithsonian Institution, and the American Institute for Indian Studies for funding various aspects of my research during the years 1983, 1984, 1988, and 1991. I would also like to thank the National Endowment for the Humanities and the American Institute for Indian Studies for supporting my work in 2000. I am grateful to Western Michigan University for providing me with equipment and several research grants and for putting at my disposal computer facilities adequate to handle my data. Most of all, I would like to thank my Indian colleagues and friends who helped me carry out my work within the Nilgiris. These include Dr. Gururajarao, Professor of Archaeology at Mysore Univerity, Dr. K.V. Ramesh, and Dr. Pungandran. Special thanks go to my friend Professor Basavalinham of Udhagmandalam College. I would also like to thank Mr. Kuruvilla, Mr. Vergheez, and a multitude of local people who came to my aid (such as Kavita Mahalingam of Vachanpaliyam), and particularly the people of Karikur during my 2000 project.

1. Note the seemingly minor differences in the forms of slavery practiced by the Athenians and the Spartans, which had implications for the social-organizational histories of both these city-states and for the long-term evolution of classical Greece.

2. Some have argued that similar cyclical structures can be found among certain state-organized societies. This is, for all intents and purposes, the argument employed by Wittfogel (1957) and, to some extent, Marx, when discussing so-called hydraulic societies (or Marx and Engel's so-called Asiatic mode of production; see Hobsbawm 1965; Krader 1975; Junge 1980, among many others). Of course, other scholars also see cycles of civilization but do not root them in production modes.

REFERENCES

Allchin, F. R.
   1995 *The Archaeology of Early Historic South Asia.* Cambridge: Cambridge University Press.
Ariokiaswami, M.
   1956 *The Kongu Country.* Madras, India: University of Madras.
Flannery, Kent
   1972a Culture History vs. Cultural Process: A Debate in American Archaeology. In *Contemporary Archaeology,* edited by M. P. Leone, pp. 67–111. Carbondale: Southern Illinois University Press.
   1972b The Cultural Evolution of Civilizations. *Annual Review of Ecology and Systematics* 3:399–426.
Fox, Richard
   1962 *Caste Dominance and Coercion in the Nilgiris.* Papers of the Michigan Academy of Science, Arts, and Letters 48.
Fox, Richard, ed.
   1977 *Realm and Region.* Occasional Papers No. 14. Durham: Duke University Press.
Fried, M.
   1967 *The Evolution of Political Society.* McGraw-Hill.
Gramsci, Antonio
   1971 *Selections from the Prison Notebooks.* New York: International Publishers.
Hobsbawm, Eric
   1965 *Pre-Capitalist Economic Formations, by Karl Marx,* edited and with an Introduction by E. J. Hobsbawm. New York: International Publishers.
Hockings, Paul
   1980 *Ancient Hindu Refugees: Badaga Social History, 1550–1975.* New Delhi: Vikas.

Junge, Peter
   1980 *Asiatische Produktionsweise und Staatsentstehung.* Bremen: Selbst-Verlag aus dem Übersee/Museum Bremen.
Kohl, Philip L.
   1988 Sumer and Indus Valley Civilization Compared: Towards an Historical Understanding of the Evolution of Early States. In *Familie, Staat und Gesellschaftsformation...,* edited by J. Hermann and J. Kohn, pp. 344–356. Berlin: Akademie der Wissenschaften DDR.
Krader, Lawrence
   1975 *The Asiatic Mode of Production.* Assen, The Netherlands: VanGorcum.
Leach, Edmund
   1965 *Political Systems of Highland Burma.* Boston: Beacon Press.
Mahias, Marie-Claude
   1997 The Construction of the Nilgiris as a "Tribal Sanctuary." In *Blue Mountains Revisited: Cultural Studies on the Nilgiri Hills,* edited by P. Hockings. Delhi: Oxford University Press.
Manimegalai, S.
   1990 *Trade and Industy in Kongu.* Ph.D. dissertation, Department of History, Bhartiar University, Vellalar College for Women, Erode, India.
Marx, Karl
   1890 *Capital: A Critical Analysis of Capitalist Production,* translated by Samuel Moore and Edward Aveling and edited by Fredrick Engels, Vol. I. Moscow: Foreign Language Publishing House. (no date for this edition)

1964 *The Eighteenth Brumaire of Louis Napoleon Bonaparte.* New York: International Publishers.

McGuire, Randall, and Dean Saitta

1996 "Although They Have Petty Captains . . .": The Dialectics of Prehispanic Western Pueblo Social Organization. *American Antiquity* 61:197–216.

Southall, Aidan

1956 *Alur Society: A Study in Processes and Types of Domination.* Cambridge: H. Heffer.

1988 *The Segmentary State in Africa and Asia.* Comparative Studies in Society and History 30. New York: Cambridge University Press.

Stein, Burton

1977 The Segmentary State in South Indian History. In *Realm and Region,* edited by R. Fox, pp. 3–51. Occasional Papers No. 14. Durham: Duke University Press.

1989 *Vijayanagara: The New Cambridge History of India,* Vol. 12. Cambridge: Cambridge University Press.

Tainter, Joseph A.

1988 *The Collapse of Complex Societies.* Cambridge: Cambridge University Press.

Ulin, C. Robert

1995 Invention and Representation as Cultural Capital. *American Anthropologist* 97(3):519–527.

Walker, Anthony

1986 *The Toda of South India: A New Look.* New Delhi: Hindustan.

1997 The Western Romance with the Toda. In *Blue Mountains Revisited: Cultural Studies on the Nilgiri Hills,* edited by P. Hockings, pp. 106–135. Delhi: Oxford University Press.

Webb, M.

1971 The Abolition of the Taboo System in Hawaii. In *Readings in a Culture Area,* edited by A. Howard, pp. 261–279. Scranton, PA: Chandler.

Wittfogel, Karl A.

1967 *Oriental Despotism.* New Haven: Yale University Press.

White, Leslie

1969 *The Science of Culture: A Study of Man and Civilization.* New York: Farrar, Straus and Giroux.

Yoffee, Norman, and George L. Cowgill, eds.

1988 *The Collapse of Ancient Civilizations.* Tucson: University of Arizona Press.

Zagarell, Allen

1986 Structural Discontinuity: A Critical Factor in the Emergence of Primary and Secondary States. *Dialectical Anthropology* 10(3–4):155–177. Elsevier.

1994 State and Community in the Nilgiri Mountains. *Michigan Academician* 26(1):183–204.

1995 Heirarchy and Heterarchy: The Unity of Opposites. In *Heterarchy and the Analysis of Complex Societies,* edited by Robert M. Ehrenreich, Carole L. Crumley, and Janet E. Levy, pp. 87–100. Washington, DC: American Anthropological Association.

1997 The Megalithic Graves of the Nilgiri Hills and Moyar Ditch. In *Blue Mountains Revisited: Cultural Studies on the Nilgiri Hills,* edited by P. Hockings, pp. 27–73. Delhi: Oxford University Press.

1999 Tradition, Community and Nilgiri Rock Art. In *Material Symbols: Culture and Economy in Prehistory,* edited by J. Robb, pp. 188–204. Center for Archaeological Investigations Occasional Paper No. 26. Carbondale: Southern Illinois University.

2002 Gender and Social Organization in the Reliefs of the Nilgiri Hills. In *Hunters and Foragers,* edited by Kathleen D. Morrison and Laura Junker, pp. 77–104. Cambridge: Cambridge University Press.

4

What Happened in the Shang Dynasty?

Collapse and Florescence in the Early Bronze Age of North-Central China

Jim A. Railey

IN THIS CHAPTER, I EXPLORE AN EPISODE OF COLLAPSE AND florescence that occurred in the early Bronze Age of north China, during the historic interval identified as the Shang Dynasty (Figure 13). Throughout this time of uprooting and reestablishment, the underlying cultural markers and ideology—that is, the civilization—not only survived, after the collapse it experienced an elaboration in material culture (and, perhaps, organizational structure) that in many ways surpassed in complexity that which came before. Although the material icons and many of the cultural expressions are unique to ancient China, some of the processes that may have been involved are familiar: namely, peer-polity interaction, core-periphery relations, and the inflationary tendencies and

diminishing returns often inherent in the exchange and circulation of prestige goods.

That this episode occurred in the middle of a historically framed dynasty—the Shang—underscores the contextual vagaries of collapse. Moreover, this unusual situation may help explain why scholars—both Chinese and non-Chinese—have thus far failed to identify this interval as one involving collapse, despite the archaeological evidence being rather apparent for several decades now. Moreover, recent archaeological evidence, including the results of my own survey work in north-central China, underscores the regional magnitude of this particular episode of collapse and transformation, and my findings serve as a catalyst for the present discussion.

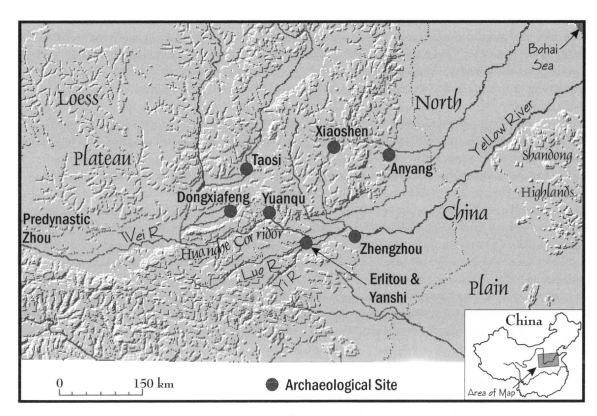

Figure 13. North-central China, showing locations of sites mentioned in the text.

HISTORICAL CONTEXT

The Shang Dynasty is the earliest archaeologically verified period recounted in traditional Chinese histories. It is also the earliest manifestation in East Asia that virtually all interested scholars agree represents a state-level society.[1] From both archaeological and textual records, the Shang has traditionally been divided into two periods, the Erligang or Early Shang (ca. 1600–1300 BC) and a subsequent period variously referred to as the Yinxu, Anyang, or Late Shang (ca. 1300–1100 BC). Recently, the notion of a Middle Shang period has gained considerable currency among Chinese archaeologists (see Tang 1999), especially following the discovery of a large walled settlement at Anyang that immediately predates the well-documented Late Shang occupation there (Tang and Liu 2000). But as for annalistic accounts of the Shang Dynasty, only those relating to the Late Shang period, in fact, have been verified by epigraphic sources, thanks to the archaeological discovery of the inscribed "oracle bones" at Anyang in the 1920s (see Chang 1980:42–45). The oracle bones corroborate the surviving ancient annals concerning the Late Shang, even though the annals themselves were written long after the fall of the Shang Dynasty (for a discussion of the relevant ancient texts, see Chang 1980:3–19). The Erligang and Middle Shang periods, like the Erlitou period (ca. 2000–1600 BC) that precedes them, equate chronologically with earlier rulers and events also documented in the ancient annals, but there is as yet no archaeological substantiation of these accounts (see Thorp 1991).

It seems likely that the annals covering at least the Erligang and Middle Shang periods are, in fact, based on actual individuals, places, and developments dating from those periods. But as one traces the annals back in time, into the Shang's predecessor, the Xia Dynasty, documented history gradually blurs into legends of superhuman heroes, some of whom correspond chronologically to late Neolithic times (Allan 1984). It is thus not at all clear where, exactly, mythology grades into history in the annals of ancient China. Archaeology plays a crucial role in reconstructing events, developments, and processes—and even the political geography—of the early Bronze Age in north-central China. Yet the implications of the archaeological record remain matters of heated debate among scholars interested in the Shang Dynasty, and especially the Early Shang, or Erligang, period.

Among Chinese scholars, much of the discussion and debate over the Early Shang focuses on two archaeologically known Erligang walled settlements, located at the present-day cities of Zhengzhou and Yanshi in west-central Henan Province (see Chang 1980:263–288, 1986:331–339; Henan Provinical Antiquities Institute 1993). Much ink has been spilled over the possible identities of these walled settlements with respect to the sequence of Early Shang "capitals" recorded in the ancient annals (e.g., Chang 1980:270–272, 1983, 1987, 1995; Zou 1979, 1980; see also discussion by Huber 1988). Such interests spring largely from the historiographical orientation of archaeology in China, where archaeology is a subdiscipline of history rather than anthropology (see von Faulkenhausen 1993). Nevertheless, discussions and debates surrounding the identities of Zhengzhou and Yanshi have proven rather fruitless, primarily because ambiguities inherent in the ancient texts make it impossible, at present, to confidently equate place names in the annals with specific archaeological sites.

Contemporary with Zhengzhou and Yanshi are two smaller walled settlements located in the mountainous region to the west. These sites, Dongxiafeng (Institute of Archaeology et al. 1988) and Yuanqu (National Museum of Chinese History and Shanxi Provincial Institute 1997; National Museum of Chinese History et al. 1996; Railey 1999), figure less prominently in the historiographic debates that swirl mainly around Zhengzhou and Yanshi, but they are nonetheless important because all four walled settlements were abandoned at roughly the same time (ca. 1300 BC). These walled cities and towns required considerable labor investment to build and maintain, and they hosted concentrated populations. Therefore, their collective abandonment must have been a momentous historical event. Moreover, there is evidence to suggest that not only were the four walled settlements given up, but their surrounding hinterlands along the lower Yellow River valley were largely evacuated as well, and this apparent depopulation underscores the dramatic collapse in the middle of the Shang Dynasty.

In this paper, I steer clear of the debates surrounding the identification of archaeological sites vis-a-vis the ancient annals and focus instead on the possible reasons why these four walled centers were suddenly abandoned at the end of the Erligang period. Drawing on theoretical models from anthropological archaeology, I explore the potential conditions and processes that led to this dramatic collapse, and the relationship of this historical episode with the subsequent emergence, to the north, of the Middle and Late Shang centers at Anyang.

ENVIRONMENTAL SETTING

The geographic stage for the present discussion centers on north-central China, specifically the lower Yellow River Valley and surroundings in northern Henan Province, and adjacent margins of Shanxi and Hebei provinces (Figure 13). The climate of this region is temperate, with hot summers and cold winters. Precipitation varies along an east-west gradient, with wetter, more humid conditions in the east giving way to a progressively drier climate to the west. Although the natural vegetation of this region was essentially wiped out centuries ago, paleobotanical evidence and relic forests (surviving in remote mountain recesses) suggest the area was covered with a deciduous forest that thinned out and eventually disappeared toward the drier west and yielded to vertically zoned biotic regimes in the higher mountain ranges (Li 1983).

Physiographically, north-central China encompasses two contrasting landscapes. To the east, the North China Plain (or Central Plain) is a vast, flat, alluvial surface studded here and there with older hills and mountains, and bounded on the east by the Shangdong Highlands and Bohai Sea. This plain has experienced rapid alluviation since ancient times, and some early Bronze Age sites lie buried beneath the present-day surface. West of the North China Plain is an intermontane region featuring a jumbled agglomeration of mountain ranges, tectonic basins, and river valleys. The Yellow River, or Huanghe, cuts through this intermontane area, and along some stretches it flows within narrow gorges that impede travel and communication. South of this "Huanghe Corridor" (Barnes 1993), several tributaries (such as the Yi-Luo River) break up the mountainous landscape and provide wider thoroughfares through the region than does the Yellow River itself.

Much of north-central China is blanketed with a mantle of loess. These eolian silts not only provide very fertile soils for agriculture but are also an excellent medium for the rammed-earth, or *hangtu,* technique that was employed for the raising of city walls, and is still used today in the construction of rural vernacular architecture. Loess is also well suited for the excavation of subterranean features, such as pithouses and underground storage silos, which were common in early Bronze Age settlements and reflect the persistence of a Neolithic lifeway among the peasant population of this time.[2]

CULTURAL AND POLITICAL DIMENSIONS

The term "Shang" is used interchangeably to denote a polity, a time period, a region, and a civilization. Elements of Shang culture, including bronze vessel styles and other artifact forms, and iconographic elements such as the distinctive *taotie* motif (Figure 14), occur over a broad area of China. But the distribution of these material markers was probably as much the result of interaction, exchange, and emulation between independent political units as it was circulation within unified polities. Indeed, most scholars agree that the Shang *polity* was a much smaller geographic entity than the broader *civilization* of which it was the centerpiece. Yet beyond this broad consensus, ideas vary as to the precise geopolitical dimensions and organizational structure of the Shang polity. Moreover, because of the oracle bones, most speculation surrounding Shang political organization has focused on the *Late* Shang polity; the absence of primary epigraphic evidence predating the Anyang florescence has inhibited similar explorations into the organizational makeup of pre-Anyang polities. These discussions of Late Shang political structure not only are relevant for an understanding of the Shang world following the

Figure 14. The *taotie* motif, a symbolic icon of Shang culture.

collapse in question but also are useful to the extent that they provide hints as to what sort of political structures (Shang or otherwise) and geopolitical networks may have preceded the Anyang-based polity.

In one of the more systematic and thoughtful analyses of the Late Shang geopolitical realm, Keightley (1983) examined oracle bone inscriptions from Anyang. He looked specifically at inscriptions describing the kinds of activities carried out by the Shang king, where those activities were carried out, names of places or rulers outside Anyang, and indicators of the political relationships between the Shang and the other places and rulers mentioned in the inscriptions. Although many of his conclusions were admittedly tentative, Keightley suggested several features of the late Shang state and its geopolitical context that are relevant to the present discussion.

One feature highlighted by Keightley is the very rudimentary, ad-hoc level of state formation at which the Late Shang polity apparently operated. The Shang do not appear to have possessed a complex bureaucracy, and the king himself seems to have made frequent travels and put in personal appearances at places other than Anyang. These travels and kingly activities included hunting expeditions, inspection of agricultural fields, and performance of sacrifices, divination, or other ritual. There are also records of the king simply having passed through, or traveled to and/or from, particular places. These itinerant activities, and the apparent hesitancy of the Shang king to delegate authority, suggested to Keightley that the polity lacked a well-integrated administration at the regional level. In this respect at least, to Keightley the Shang "state" closely resembled a complex chiefdom. Similarly, Trigger (1999:50) noted that the Late Shang state was strongly kin-based, similar to the conical clans of some Polynesian chiefdoms (cf. Friedman and Rowlands 1978; Kirchoff 1955; Peebles and Kus 1977; Sahlins 1958, 1963).

Consistent with this lack of a well-integrated, regional administration is Keightley's image of the Shang polity as territorially intermittent, or what he terms a "political-religious force-field" (1983:529).

> One has the sense, in short, of the state as a thin network of pathways and encampments; the king and information and resources traveled along the pathways, but the network was laid over a hinterland that rarely saw or felt the king's presence and authority. State power would have been generally intermittent and, in areas like [Shaanxi and Shanxi], rather transitory (Keightley 1983:548).

Keightley further suggests that participation in state activities beyond the Shang political core, as well as compliance by "provincial" leaders and populations, was perhaps situational, transient, and subject to geopolitical circumstances of the moment. Many "subjects" of the Shang state may, in fact, have been little more than temporal allies (Keightley 1983:545).

Another suggestion that emerged from Keightley's study was the possibility that Anyang was not a royal "capital" in the conventional sense, but rather a cult center (perhaps one of several). Keightley further speculates that this apparently dispersed polity may not have had a "capital" per se, or at least perhaps not until the last Shang phase (Anyang V), when references to the Da Yi Shang (the "Great Settlement of Shang")—apparently a place other than Anyang—first appear in the inscriptions. Although much speculation swirls around Da Yi Shang, its location remains a mystery.

The appearance of textual references to Da Yi Shang alerts us to possible diachronic changes in Late Shang political organization, and Keightley (1983:555–558) points to inscription evidence indicating that, toward the end of the Late Shang, the polity perhaps became more tightly integrated and territorially smaller and more compact. In tandem with this hypothesized change is Keightley's suggestion that the last of the Shang kings enjoyed a greater degree of coercive authority than their predecessors at Anyang, and they presided over a polity with more complex, formalized institutions. For example, Keightley (1983:556) notes that in the Anyang V oracle bones (as opposed to those of the earlier Anyang phases) there is no record of divining about mustering warriors for military campaigns, even though Period V references to military activities are extensive. The possible implication here is that raising men for battle was no longer for the Shang kings a concern worthy of divination.

In a more recent exploration into Shang political organization, Trigger (1999) conducted a comparative study of ancient civilizations in an attempt to determine if the Late Shang polity more closely resembled a city-state or a larger, territorial state. The results of his analysis were somewhat mixed and inconclusive, but the evidence Trigger presents appears to weigh in on the side of the Late Shang approximating a territorial state. This evidence includes the dispersed layout of Anyang, frequent travels by the king and his court, textual references suggesting frontier colonization, and relocations and numbers of "capital" cities.

Comparisons with other ancient state systems may be useful with respect to the Shang. Of special interest are

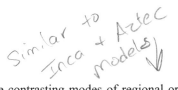
Similar to Aztec + Inca models

the contrasting modes of regional organization observed between the Inca and Aztec states (cf. Moseley 1992; Weaver 1993). The Inca created a far-flung, well-integrated empire, in the process absorbing and enculturating disparate ethnic groups. The Aztec also ranged over a large region and perhaps were equally successful at conquest warfare. But unlike the Inca, the Aztec displayed little interest in bringing their conquered foes under a regionally administered empire. Instead, the Aztec went to war and pursued conquest of their enemies primarily for the purpose of acquiring sacrificial victims. For the Aztec, turning enemies into fellow citizens would have deprived them of sources of raw material for the human sacrifices so central to their religion. Instead, polities conquered by the Aztec became tributary states that were forced to periodically support Aztec military adventurism (by providing food, shelter, and passage through their territory, but not troops and warriors). Otherwise, these "conquered" polities ran their own, indigenous affairs. One present-day legacy of the Aztec disinterest in creating a multi-regional administration and absorbing their enemies is the effective extinction of the Nahuatl language, as opposed to the Quechua language of the Inca, which is still widely spoken in the Andes and serves as testimony to the Inca administrative success at empire building.

Of course, we cannot expect the Shang polity to correspond precisely to either the Inca or Aztec models, and at any rate the evidence with respect to the Shang remains sketchy and vague in contrast to the much clearer historical documentation available for the New World empires. Nevertheless, in some important respects at least, the evidence suggests the Late Shang more closely resembled the Aztec in their geopolitical behavior. Of particular interest here is the practice of human sacrifice, which is clearly evident from both the oracle bone inscriptions and archaeological evidence, especially in the royal tombs at Anyang. Although it is doubtful that human sacrifice among the Shang ever equaled the scale and frequency with which it was practiced among the Aztec, this custom does exhibit a long historical pedigree in ancient China, going back at least to late Neolithic times (ca. 2800–2000 BC). Moreover, in ancient China human sacrifice was carried out in various contexts, not only including high-status mortuary ritual but also apparently as part of ceremonies associated with the construction and dedication of defensive walls and other architectural works (see Chang 1986:255, 287, 374).

The apparent Shang view of their neighbors as ethnic "others," and the time-honored practice of paying tribute between what appear to have otherwise been independent polities, also more closely resembles the Aztec model, as opposed to that of the Inca. The loosely knit organizational structure of the Late Shang state, and the shifting relationships between them and other polities in the region, further suggest that the Shang state fell well short of the administrative integration achieved by the Inca. The Shang indeed may have resembled the Aztec in their role as the most prominent among many regional states with which they coexisted and traded, and coerced and waged war against. At this point we are confronted with a most intriguing question surrounding the greater Shang world, and that is the degree of ethnic diversity that prevailed across north-central China during the early Bronze Age. This is a question of relevance not only to our understanding of the Late Shang state, but also to the much murkier geopolitical conditions of pre-Anyang times. Given the apparent multi-ethnic conditions that prevailed in Late Shang times, we can assume rather safely that a similar ethnic and geopolitical mosaic (or an even more heterogeneous one) characterized north-central China prior to the ascendancy of Anyang.

SOCIOPOLITICAL AND ECONOMIC MODELS

Given the inherent ambiguities in the ancient annals themselves, and the perpetual impasse from the endless debates over which site equates to which place name in the historical annals (which, again, were written long after the end of the Shang Dynasty), it is perhaps more productive at this time to pursue an alternative approach to the pre-Anyang early Bronze Age of north-central China. The approach pursued here makes use of generalized models drawn from anthropological archaeology and other social sciences. Although I acknowledge that process and evolution cannot be divorced from the history of a particular region, in the absence of historical documents that can be reconciled clearly with the archaeological record, for the moment at least the more generalized models must take precedence. In other words, rather than trying to force the pre-Shang Anyang archaeological record to fit historical annals that were written centuries later, and whose messages were probably as much political and nationalistic as they were the objective telling of history, I take the archaeological record as the starting point and use available theoretical tools to seek an explanation of the mid-Shang collapse.

Because the phenomenon examined here is regional in nature, I highlight two geopolitical models, peer-polity interaction and world-systems theory. These models are useful for conceptualizing the processes involved in the evolution of complex societies throughout the world, but their application to ancient China has been limited at best. In focusing on these models, I am not implying that they can explain fully the mid-Shang collapse and Anyang florescence that followed, nor are the models themselves foolproof. Rather, I offer them as explanatory threads to be woven together with the local archaeological record and historical annals, with the result being a plausible scenario of what happened in the Shang Dynasty.

Peer-Polity Interaction

The peer-polity interaction model (Renfrew and Cherry 1986; see also Price 1977) describes processes through which a regional cluster of polities (usually chiefdoms and early states) share a number of structural homologies. These include close similarities in economic organization, political structure, ideological systems, iconographic symbols, ritual practices, and often a common language. As the name of the model implies, however, peer polities are not politically united, and they frequently engage in interpolity warfare as well as trade and other forms of interaction. The peer-polity model predicts that, where one polity can be identified, polities of similar size, organizational scale, and cultural attributes will occur in the vicinity, and that sociopolitical change will proceed more or less simultaneously among these polities because of the close nature of their interactions. Where such features are shared within a cluster of early state-level polities, or "early state modules," we can speak of the entire cluster as a single *civilization* (Renfrew 1986:2). Citing cross-cultural data, Renfrew (1986:2) observes that the size range of early state modules clustered around 1,500 km², with an average distance of about 40 km between the central places of neighboring polities.

Elites within a peer-polity cluster typically share certain symbolic icons and esoteric religious knowledge, or what Earle (1991) refers to as an "international style." This elite exchange network serves as an important justification for acquiring and maintaining power within peer polities, and it constitutes a significant component of the political economy (Earle 1991; Helms 1979). The processes through which these various features are shared within a peer-polity cluster are essentially forms of biased transmission (Boyd and Richerson 1985) involving selection, diffusion, sharing, and modification of marker traits within a cultural tradition. One such process is referred to as *symbolic entrainment*, which "entails the tendency for a developed symbolic system to be adopted when it comes into contact with a less-developed one with

which it does not strikingly conflict" (Renfrew 1986:8) and can include the transmission of political behaviors along with their material markers. Another process is *competitive emulation*, wherein "neighboring polities are spurred to ever greater displays of wealth or power in an effort to achieve higher inter-polity status," (Renfrew 1986:8) and can perpetuate the spread of distinctive symbolic systems, and associated marker traits. The peer-polity model has also been used to help explain the spread and expansion of languages and ethnic groups (Renfrew 1986:10, 1987), in which the language of dominant groups and polity clusters may expand at the expense of less-advantaged groups' native tongues.

The peer-polity model challenges a traditional view that sociopolitical evolution necessarily passes through a stage involving city-states before territorial states can develop. This traditional view was shared by, among others, Morton Fried, who offered the following scenario concerning the earliest states in ancient China.

> If a pristine state arose in the area now designated as China, . . . it would have been in an area of hamlets and occasional migratory bands with little or no cohesion and certainly no tribes in the sense of . . . reticulated networks. . . .

> The stratified local community that has gone into state formation looks very much like a city-state and utilizes its less well-organized surroundings as a source of manpower and raw materials (Fried 1983:475, 480–481).

Unfortunately for him, Fried's scenario (with respect to China or anywhere else where early states emerged) receives little empirical support, either from the ethnographic record or from archaeology. There is, in fact, abundant evidence for stratified, territorial chiefdoms across north-central China in the late Neolithic, prior to emergence of states in the region (see Liu 1996).

Although certainly relevant to many (if not most) situations involving chiefdoms and early states, the peer-polity model may not be appropriate in every case. Trigger (1999:46), for example, points out that a number of ethnohistorically documented chiefdoms and states embraced territories much larger than the 1,500 km² cited in Renfrew's early state module. With respect to the Late Shang, Keightley (1983) postulates that something resembling Renfrew's early state module does not emerge until Period V, when the Shang state appears to have become a more compact, territorially contracted polity. It

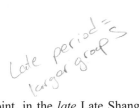

Late period = larger group

is at this point, in the *late* Late Shang (i.e., Anyang V), that he tentatively suggested a "shift from an advanced tribal to at least an incipient dynastic state" (Keightley 1983:556). Thus, as discussed earlier, the Late Shang state prior to Anyang V may have actually been a larger, albeit less-well-integrated, polity.

Given these caveats, it is perhaps best to view peer-polity interaction along a branching matrix of evolutionary possibilities rather than as an inevitable step in the emergence and development of complex societies. Peer-polity interaction may well be relevant to at least certain periods in north-central China. But we should remain alert to alternatives to the peer-polity model whereby one settlement or polity may get a leg up on its neighbors, setting the stage for predatory expansion and unequal relations, even in prestate geopolitical circumstances.

World-Systems Theory

The existence of geopolitical disparity and dominance lead us to a consideration of *world-systems*. World-systems include regions usually larger than those covered by peer-polity clusters and involve different kinds of interactions. World-systems theory (Wallerstein 1974) essentially describes core-periphery relations that emerge out of political and economic interaction between differentially advantaged polities. Cores and peripheries develop as a result of "competition between various geographically localized populations of unequal power . . . [and the] differentiation, division of labor, and interdependence among these same units" (Schneider 1991:20).

As a result of historically contingent, evolutionary processes, one area gains an "accidental edge related to past history and current environmental resources and geography" (Schneider 1991:46). This slight edge, once established, may be transformed into a significant disparity in wealth and geopolitical power through the operation of a regional "world economy" (Schneider 1991:46; Wallerstein 1974:403). Over time, changing historical circumstances lead to geographical shifts in the locations, configurations, and scales of cores and peripheries.

Although the initial focus of world-systems theory concerned the emergence and development of the capitalist world (Wallerstein 1974), more recent efforts have sought to expand this framework to the kinds of precapitalist societies of interest to most archaeologists (e.g., Champion 1989; Chase-Dunn and Hall 1991). An important focus of this effort has been on trade in "preciosities," or prestige-goods (e.g., Frankenstein and Rowlands 1978; Schneider 1991), the importance of which Wallerstein downplayed

in his model; he saw trade in foodstuffs as critical to the operation of world-systems. Regardless, the movement of prestige goods (and the raw materials used to manufacture these items) within extensive exchange networks is well documented for prestate societies, and in pursuit of the underlying geopolitical contexts and socioeconomic processes associated with such exchange, archaeologists have expanded the application of the world-systems model (e.g., Champion 1989; Peregrine 1992).[3]

For many pre- and early state situations, conceptualizing core-periphery relations may not necessarily involve the rather direct forms of economic exploitation described by Wallerstein for more developed state systems. Rather, many early-stage "cores" may simply consist of technologically, economically, and/or sociopolitically precocious polities, or even peer-polity clusters whose members are larger in scale than peripheral polities outside the core. Innovations and cultural patterns developed within these cores may diffuse (through biased transmission, including symbolic entrainment and competitive emulation) to these peripheral, smaller-scale polities who may already share, or selectively adopt elements of, the core's cultural tradition. In such cases, "peripheral" polities may not be exploited directly by "core" polities; core polities may, in fact, be competing among themselves too intensely to directly impose political hegemony onto the peripheries. But developments even in this kind of "fragmented" core may indirectly affect its peripheries, or vice versa; for example, economic and sociopolitical events or trends in either area could accelerate or curtail the regional flow of raw materials or finished prestige goods, with ripplelike consequences throughout the region. Eventually, "fragmented cores" may undergo political unification and subsequently extend their economic and political influence or authority more directly over smaller-scale societies on the peripheries. Cores may also collapse and, in effect, clear the geopolitical slate, giving rise to new, historical-evolutionary possibilities.

Consistent with its original formulation, world-systems theory is most applicable to cases involving fully developed, expansionist states with economic systems, infrastructures, and militaries capable of exploiting large regions. In state systems, trade and exchange expand as the importance of prestige goods and commodities escalates. The demand for nonlocal resources leads to one typical pattern in which "core areas accumulated precious metals while exporting manufactures, whereas peripheral areas gave up these metals (and often slaves) against an inflow of finished goods" (Schneider 1991:25). Depending on historical circumstances, this demand for nonlocal resources by the core may lead to actual colonization and political expansion, less direct forms of domination, and/or an escalation of political competition within and between peripheral polities. Such processes may stimulate sociopolitical change outside the core, leading to the formation in peripheral areas of "secondary" complex polities (Fried 1967:240–242; Kristiansen 1991) and/or the establishment of state outposts (Algaze 1993). Elites within peripheral polities may seek to monopolize economic control over local resources (especially metal ores and mineral resources), or to promote their strategic positions within trade networks. Alliances may form in opposition to core expansion but just as likely are strategies involving core exploitation of competition between peripheral polities and "buying off" local elites (through disbursement of wealth and privileges, military support in their internal political conflicts, or marriage into the royal house of the core polity). These latter strategies often prove less costly than more direct military conquest and colonization, and even conquest itself often involves a good deal of collaboration with certain elements within the targeted polity. At any rate, in any given historical context, we can expect core-periphery relations to involve a complex dynamic played out among the forces of domination, resistance, and opportunism.

Core-periphery relations may also lead to a prolific expansion of ideological and symbolic systems associated with the core civilization. Symbolic entrainment and competitive emulation lead to the widespread dissemination of core icons, including prestige goods and symbols adopted by peripheral elites seeking to legitimize their positions of power. Such goods derive value not only by virtue of their material rarity or high production costs, but also by the fact that they symbolize a "higher power" that is both exotic and mysterious, and associated with the dominant core civilization and its ideology. By gaining control over access to, and use of, such symbols, elites in peripheral polities may succeed in identifying themselves with the ideological basis for power in the dominant civilization, although this ideology and the specific use of associated prestige goods may be altered within the recipient society.

This whole process is subject directly to the forces of biased transmission (Boyd and Richerson 1985), and so the extent to which "foreign" ideologies, symbols, and other marker traits are adopted may depend in part on the cultural and linguistic "distance" between center and periphery. Moreover, relying on foreign symbols and ideology may accelerate the enculturation of secondary polities (or at least their elites), bringing them more easily

under the influence and domination of—and eventual assimilation within—an expanding state or civilization. The threat of domination and assimilation, however, may depend on the degree of political hegemony at the geopolitical core; if the core is fragmented into several early state modules, then peripheral polities may enjoy significantly greater flexibility in negotiating political arrangements than when the core is occupied by a unified, predatory state. A world-systems approach thus requires an appreciation for the sociopolitical processes involving fragmentation and collapse (Renfrew 1979; Tainter 1988; Yoffee and Cowgill 1988), as well as coalescence and expansion.

COLLAPSE AND FLORESCENCE IN THE SHANG PERIOD

Fitted with appropriate theoretical lenses, let us now turn our attention to the case study at hand. To set the stage for events that happened in the Shang period itself, first it is useful to consider evolutionary-historical developments that preceded the period in order to understand the changing geopolitical mosaic of the region in the centuries leading up to the emergence of the Shang, and which led to the development of the Erligang regional system.

Setting the Stage

The Longshan and Erlitou Periods (ca. 2800–1600 BC)

Prior to state formation in the early Bronze Age, complex chiefdoms emerged across north-central China during the late Neolithic Longshan period, dating to roughly 2800–2000 BC (see Liu 1994, 1996). Prior to this time, the most complex societies in ancient China emerged *outside* the area where the earliest states would eventually crystallize, in culturally distinct enclaves to the northeast, east, and south. By the Longshan period, however, there is widespread evidence for social complexity and inequality across north-central China, as well as in the earlier "centers." This evidence includes settlement hierarchies, marked differences in burial treatment, elaborate ceramic vessels used for ceremonial purposes, and large-scale public works featuring the construction of pounded-earth (hangtu) walls that enclosed either entire settlements or elite compounds (the latter sometimes set on low, hangtu platforms). High-cost prestige goods are common, and at least some of these (most notably, distinctive jade forms) were reserved for sociopolitical elites, suggesting the development of shared elite traditions and wealth-financed economies (cf. D'Altroy and Earle 1985; Earle

1991; Kristiansen 1991). Oracle bones are present by this time and were presumably used for divination rituals as part of ancestor-worship cults similar to those of the Late Shang, although to date none of the recovered specimens contains any recognizable inscriptions. There is evidence to suggest household-level ritual involving both animal and human sacrifice (Liu 1994:311–312), and human sacrifice is evident in various contexts, including bodies tossed unceremoniously into wells and storage pits, and beneath, and within, hangtu walls (see Chang 1986:255, 287, 374).

In a regional study of the Longshan period, Liu (1996) identified settlements and settlement hierarchies of varying scale across the region. Interestingly, the largest settlements at this time are not located in the Yi-Luo Valley or western Central Plain, where the earliest states would emerge in the subsequent early Bronze Age. Rather, they are found within the intermontane basins and valleys to the west, in an area that would later become peripheral to the Shang core. At 300 hectares, the Taosi site, in the Fen River valley of southern Shanxi (see Chang 1986:275–277), is the largest known Neolithic site in China and may have been the center of the largest and most centralized Longshan polity (see Figure 13). Taosi has a huge cemetery, from which more than 1,000 graves have been excavated, and variation in size, complexity, and contents of the individual tombs suggests a three-tiered, pyramidal social hierarchy. Another large center, Xiaojiaokou, covering 240 hectares, is situated to the south, in the rugged Huanghe Corridor (Liu 1996:253–254). In other, more tightly confined intermontane valleys, such as the Yuanqu Basin, Longshan centers were considerably smaller, on the order of 30 hectares (Railey 1999:596). Toward the Central Plain to the east, settlement data suggests sociopolitical centers and polities also were smaller than those centered at Taosi and Xiaojiaokou (Liu 1994, 1996). In the Qin River and Yi-Luo valleys, for example, the largest Longshan sites are 75–80 hectares. In the alluvial expanses of the Central Plain itself, centers are smaller still, ranging from 5 to 50 hectares. Most of the Longshan walled settlements and enclosures are located in the Central Plain, and they are also quite small (1–20 ha). Liu (1996:272–273) suggests that the pattern of smaller Longshan centers and polities in the Central Plain indicates an intense level of conflict between local chiefdoms, and that this conflict precluded larger-scale integration here during this period. In short, the Longshan period of north-central China appears to have involved peer-polity interaction, but with local peer-polity clusters varying considerably in scale.

The subsequent early Bronze Age in north-central China begins with the Erlitou period (ca. 2000–1600 BC). By this time, west-central Henan becomes the center stage of sociopolitical developments across the region. The early years of this period may have witnessed intense peer-polity competition and rapidly shifting centers of power in the western Central Plain, followed by the emergence of a preeminent polity at the site of Erlitou in the Yi-Luo Valley (cf. Li 1980; Liu 1996:273–276; Shelach 1994:270–271; Zhao 1986, 1987). By the late Erlitou period, the Erlitou settlement itself had grown to 375 hectares, larger than any known Longshan site (Liu 1996:273; Zhao 1987), and it is distinguished by its ceremonial enclosures (referred to by Chinese archaeologists as "palaces"), richly furnished elite graves, and a wealth of prestige goods, including the earliest known bronze vessels in China.

Surrounding Erlitou is a constellation of contemporary sites whose distribution suggests a regional polity minimally covering an area in western Henan between the present-day cities of Luoyang, Zhengzhou, and Dengfeng (Shelach 1994:270–271; Zhao 1987). Two other regional enclaves, possibly including proto-Shang ethnic groups and clearly involving regional polities similar in scale to Erlitou's, emerged at roughly the same time in the Xiaqiyuan culture of northern Henan and southern Hebei (Zhao 1986; Zou 1980), and in the Shangqiu area of eastern Henan (Chang 1987, 1995). Another enclave, the Xiawanggang, emerged in southern Henan at this time (Thorp 1991:7; Zhao 1987). Further to the east, the Yueshi culture emerges out of late Longshan complexes of the Shandong Peninsula (Chang 1986:369–371).

Meanwhile, in the intermontane area and Huanghe Corridor to the west, the extremely large settlements and centralized polities centered around the Taosi and Xiaojiaokou sites apparently collapsed, or were at least scaled down considerably, following the major shifts among regional centers of power around 2000 BC (cf. Liu 1996). Why these exceptionally large, complex chiefdoms disintegrated is not entirely clear, but it may be that they encountered growth limits within their circumscribed basins and valleys and could not sustain the inflation-prone tribute demands typical of many chiefdom societies. In other words, diminishing marginal returns (cf. Tainter 1988) may have caught up with these large, but unsustainable, polities.

Still, some new regional polities emerged in these mountain valleys and basins to the west, albeit scaled down somewhat from their Longshan predecessors. One such polity is located in the Linfen Basin, where it succeeded the Taosi culture, and is marked by a single center that dominates a diffuse cluster of smaller settlements (Liu 1994:288). The best known regional Erlitou-period center in the intermontane area was uncovered at the site of Dongxiafeng, which dominates a local cluster of sites within a tributary valley of the Yellow River in Xia County, southern Shanxi (Institute of Archaeology et al. 1988). Dongxiafeng covers more than 100 hectares, and the Erlitou settlement is the largest component at this site, although it is not clear exactly how extensive this component is (in part because erosion has destroyed large portions of the site). Near the center of the Dongxiafeng site are two concentric, squared ditches, each about 5–8 m in width and 3 m in depth, with the outer ditch enclosing an area of approximately 25 hectares. Within this enclosed area is at least one large, irregular-shaped pit, 2–3 m in depth and 30 m in its longest dimension. Into the loess walls of these trenches and large pit were excavated many subterranean cave dwellings, or *yaodong*.

The Erlitou occupation at Dongxiafeng was apparently a rather lengthy one, and excavators have divided it into four phases. The earliest two phases exhibit certain pottery traits clearly derived from local Longshan sources, including high-neck *li* tripods, and distinctive, S-shaped, incised scroll designs reminiscent of painted motifs on a Longshan vessel from Taosi (see Chang 1986:278, Fig. 241). The S-shaped scroll occurs in low frequencies throughout the ceramic sequence at this site (including the later Erligang components). Bronze vessels are not reported from the Erlitou component at Dongxiafeng, although bronze weapons (arrowheads and a dagger) do appear by the third Erlitou period. There are

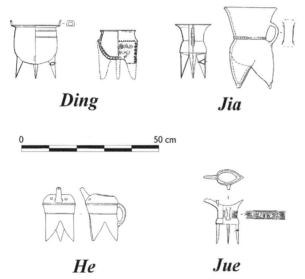

Figure 15. Distinctive vessel forms of North China's early Bronze Age. These forms occur as both ceramic and bronze vessels. Note the taotie motif on the jue vessel.

at Dongxiafeng and other sites of this period, however, ceramic versions of bronze vessel forms found at the Erlitou site, including the distinctive *jue* and *he* spouted tripods (Figure 15).

Just east of Xia County is the Yuanqu Basin, a small, tightly circumscribed depression, along the southern edge of which flows the Yellow River (Figure 16). During the Erlitou period, the Yuanqu Basin was populated by a large number of settlements, and the period features the largest number of sites here for the pre- and protohistoric time frame (Figure 17; see Railey 1999:469–607). By late Erlitou times, a major settlement and local center emerged at the Nanguan site, also known as the Yuanqu Shang Town (National Museum of Chinese History et al. 1996; Railey 1999). The Nanguan site occupies a prominent, third-terrace bluff edge that commands a sweeping vista of the Yellow River and surrounding landscape. Like Dongxiafeng, the late Erlitou settlement at Yuanqu was surrounded by a ditched enclosure and also has yet to yield bronze vessels, although ceramic counterparts of bronze ritual vessels are present. The Zhongtiao Mountains, which separate Dongxiafeng and Yuanqu, are a source of metal ores, and it is possible that these centers were supplying raw material for bronze making at Erlitou (which lacks local ore sources). If so, there is as yet no evidence that Dongxiafeng and Yuanqu were receiving finished vessels in return, or had developed their own bronze-making capabilities.

The appearance of bronze vessels and the continued diversification of ceramic forms in the Erlitou period signal, among other things, the escalating importance of increasingly codified ceremonial rituals. In historical times, these rituals involved preparation, serving, and consumption of wine and other comestibles, as sacrifices and as part of ecstatic rituals in which shaman-elites performed sacrifices to, and communicated with, ancestral spirits (cf. Chang 1989; Keightley 1978a, 1978b). The practice of divination involving the use of oracle bones continued to be a central feature of ceremonial life, and the elevation of the elites' ancestors to the status of spiritual deities (as in the *gumsa* cycles of the Kachin; see Friedman 1975) was probably a deeply rooted institution by Erlitou times, if not earlier. The proliferation of prestige goods, including finely crafted jades and bronze items, suggests both the growing importance of such materials in the expanding political economy and an intensifying level of craft and industrial specialization. Bronze vessels were cast through the rather elaborate and complex piece-mold technique, which certainly demanded considerable skill and was probably (initially, at least) a

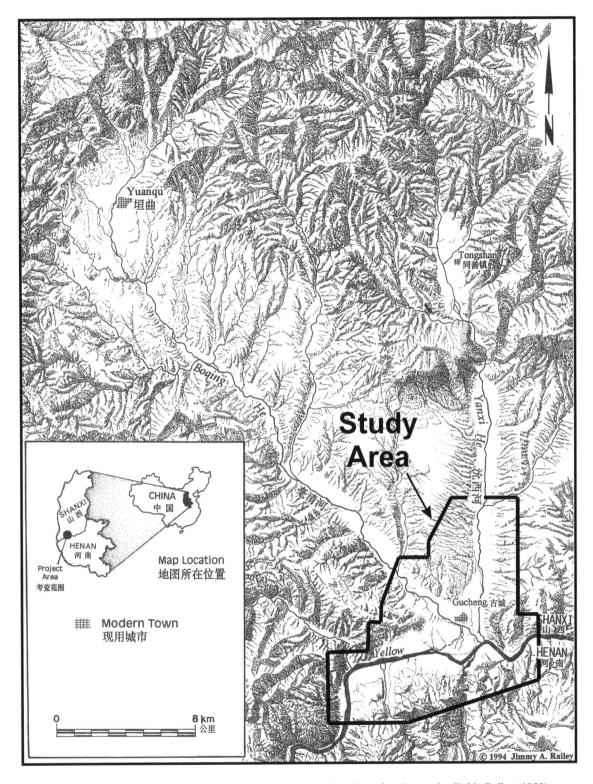

Figure 16. Physiographic map of the Yuanqu Basin, showing location of study area detailed in Railey (1999).

Figure 17. Erlitou-period sites in the southern Yuanqu Basin (adapted from Railey 1999).

closely guarded technology under elite patronage. The innovative development of this technique, apparently by Erlitou groups in the Central Plain, may have created an important source of political capital that helped tip the geopolitical balance in their favor.

The development of bronze making in north China also helped fuel expanding trade-and-exchange relations between the bronze-producing polities of the Central Plain and groups in the intermontane region, who may have supplied much of the raw material (ores) for bronze production. Local Erlitou-period polities, such as Dongxiafeng and Yuanqu, may have been built in part on the ability of local elites to manipulate and administer the extraction and export of ores. Insofar as this is true, the apparent absence of finished bronze vessels at Dongxiafeng and Yuanqu (along with the generally low frequencies of prestige goods) leaves open the question as to what these increasingly marginalized polities were receiving in return for the export of raw metals. Given that the Erlitou polity may not have exceeded the organizational capabilities of a complex chiefdom (see Liu 1994:289; Railey 1999:184–186; Shelach 1994; Thorp 1991), it is unlikely that it was exercising direct power over intermontane groups at this time. Erlitou elites, however, may have meddled in the local affairs of these groups, or shifted alliances opportunistically, in order to ensure a reliable supply of ores. At the very least, we see in the Erlitou period an expanding trade-and-exchange network linking local societies across north-central China, within a broadening sphere of economic interdependency. But along with increased trade and exchange was conflict,

which probably intensified as local elites sought to gain political advantage over their rivals. Both warfare *and* expanding economic links were undoubtedly major factors in the formation of enlarged regional polities, such as Erlitou (Liu 1996:273–276).

Walled Centers in the Yellow River Drainage

The Erligang Period (ca. 1600–1300 BC)

The Erligang period is marked by the emergence of the aforementioned walled settlements along the lower Yellow River valley. The best known are the sites of Zhengzhou and Yanshi, located in the Yellow River and Yi-Luo valleys along the western margins of the Central Plain (Figure 13). Zhengzhou and Yanshi are frequently identified by Chinese archaeologists with either of two early Shang capitals, Bo and Ao, known from later historical annals (e.g., Chang 1980:270–272; Zou 1978, 1979:183–218; see also Huber 1988). But such discussion is not limited to debates over which of these sites is which of these capitals. Maintaining that the Erligang center at Zhengzhou is the ancient Shang capital of Bo, Zou (1999) argues that Yanshi represents not Ao, but rather "Western Bo," a secondary capital of the early Shang also referred to in the ancient annals, and where Jie, the last Xia king, was exiled. Keightley (1983:525) departs even further from the Bo-Ao debate. Reckoning Shang chronology from the early king lists, he suggests that the Erligang occupation at Zhengzhou may even largely predate the beginning of the Shang Dynasty, and as such was perhaps a late capital of the Xia.

What these debates illustrate most clearly is that the purported connections between archaeological sites and historically recorded Early Shang place names are dubious at best, as is the historical veracity of the received textual accounts relating to this period. Regardless of their status vis-a-vis the historical annals, the archaeological prominence of Zhengzhou and Yanshi is sufficiently clear to demonstrate that they were important, proto-urban centers poised on the cutting edge of regional social-evolutionary developments at this time. It is also clear that, whereas peer-polity clusters may have operated in at least parts of north-central China during the Longshan and Erlitou periods, by Erligang times a core-periphery configuration, or world-system, clearly has emerged, although it remains unclear to what extent the core was unified or fragmented.

At the heart of the Erligang core is Zhengzhou, the largest known center for this period. Zhengzhou features a hangtu wall that enclosed 360 hectares, and in the northwestern portion of this enclosure a group of hangtu platforms marks a ceremonial precinct and/or elite residence district. Beyond Zhengzhou's walls was a suburban sprawl that featured a patchwork of residential areas, bronze foundries and other workshops, and cemeteries. The walled area of the Yanshi site is nearly as large as that of Zhengzhou (Figure 18) and is otherwise similar in layout, with a cluster of hangtu platforms and a south-facing main gate. Yanshi is very close to the Erlitou site, and the last occupational phase at Erlitou (Erlitou V) dates to the Erligang period, so there is some temporal overlap in the occupations at these two important sites. This raises stimulating questions concerning their historical relationships (see Thorp 1991:9–10). Given what must have been the still-lingering historical importance of the Erlitou center during at least the early portion of the Erligang period, it seems plausible that this site continued to enjoy a special status even after its eclipse by Yanshi. Perhaps Erlitou continued to be used as some sort of unwalled ceremonial center where divination rituals were carried out (see Thorp 1991:16).

Bronze vessels become increasingly common in the Erligang period and are found over a much wider area of north-central China than was the case in Erlitou times. As with their Erlitou predecessors, Erligang bronze vessels are decorated with a single frieze enclosing a scroll-type design, including the widespread taotie motif. Thorp (1985) examined bronze vessels from early

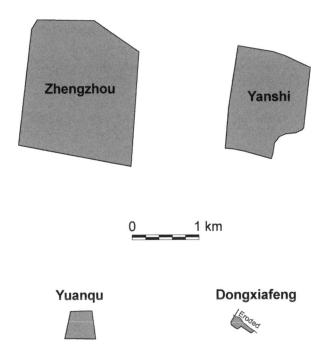

Figure 18. Size comparison of Erligang-period walled centers.

Bronze Age mortuary contexts in China and found that more or less standardized vessel forms occurred together in proscribed sets. This suggests that the vessels served specified functions in carefully orchestrated rituals carried out to communicate with ancestral spirits, similar to the use of these vessel forms in the later Shang and Zhou periods. Although shamanic ritual and ancestor worship probably had remote origins in China, perhaps going all the way back to the late Neolithic (where we also find elaborate pottery vessels and uninscribed oracle bones), these practices assumed increasingly important political functions through time, and they served an important role in the proto-bureaucratic activities associated with the Shang state (Chang 1983, 1989; Keightley 1978a, 1978b).

This is precisely the sort of theocratic, "Asiatic state" that Friedman (1975:195) suggested could evolve out of the stratification of ancestor worship, and in which certain chiefdom-like features, such as the conical clan, are retained in the early stage of state development. As a very nascent state, the Erligang polity(ies) was (were) probably not characterized by a complex, symbiotic interdependency between occupational specialists, nor by large-scale specialized craft and industrial production. Rather, it would appear that commoners were, by and large, farmers whose lifeways resembled those of their Neolithic predecessors, and who continued to turn out many of their own, everyday items, such as pottery vessels, as part of the domestic mode of production (see Railey 1999:360–400). Specialized production at this time seems to have focused on the manufacture of ceremonial bronzes and other prestige items (probably under elite patronage), along with weapons. As for the earliest state-governing officials in China, they seem not so much to have been preoccupied with mundane economic matters, but rather were focused on ritual divination and military activities (see Chang 1989; Keightley 1978a, 1978b, 1983).

At the regional level, interaction networks probably expanded during Erligang times as a result of military conquest and increased economic interdependency. Such trends likely brought local polities throughout north-central China—and beyond (Chang 1980:280–321; Thorp 1985)—more squarely within the cultural sphere of an emerging *civilization* that today is referred to as Early Shang. Although the Erligang period probably encompassed many contending polities, as well as different ethnic groups, the overarching civilization is marked by widely shared marker traits. These include architectural patterns, such as city layouts with walled fortifications, south-facing main gates, and public buildings on low, hangtu platforms. A trans-polity elite tradition is clearly in operation at this time, associated with a series of conspicuous marker traits, including prestige goods (bronze vessels, distinctive jade objects, etc.) and iconographic symbols, such as the taotie motif. The taotie motif had evolved from stylistic precursors found on late Neolithic pottery vessels and jade items (cf. Chang 1986:255, 260 [Figure 218]) and by the Erligang period already enjoyed a long historical pedigree and culturally rooted ideological significance (which remains unknown to us today [see Keightley 1978b]). These marker traits diffused throughout much of north-central China at this time, as a result of competitive emulation and symbolic entrainment (i.e., biased transmission). By adopting and maintaining control over the distribution of Shang prestige goods and symbols, elites within increasingly marginalized, peripheral polities could legitimize their own claims to rule by associating themselves with supernatural powers assumed to underlie the political and economic might of the sociopolitical center.

Of course, exchange and selective adoption of marker traits were not the only forms of interaction between polities and ethnic enclaves during the Erligang period. It is likely that interpolity warfare not only continued, but probably intensified as warfare capabilities escalated with the development of new forms of bronze weapons, and the evolution of military organization, tactics, and strategies. To what extent the early states (Shang or otherwise) used warfare as an instrument of foreign policy and predatory expansion remains unclear, but the very presence of the four walled Erligang centers clearly betrays acute concerns over defense.

In the intermontane area, Dongxiafeng (Institute of Archaeology et al. 1988) continued to serve as a major regional center in the Erligang period. Occupation of this site persisted uninterrupted from Erlitou times, but the area and population of the settlement may have contracted somewhat, and the character of this center also changed. The concentric trenches of the Erlitou period were filled in, and within this central portion of the settlement was constructed an irregular hangtu wall enclosing at least 5 hectares (a sizable ravine cutting through the central portion of the site has destroyed large segments of the wall, so its precise areal extent remains unknown). Excavations within this walled compound at Dongxiafeng uncovered regularly spaced, circular houses, suggesting rather systematic community planning. At least some of these structures were built on low, individual hangtu platforms and are quartered by cross-shaped interior walls. These features suggest a special function for these structures, which may well have been elite residences or ritual

facilities. Other notable features of the Erligang component at Dongxiafeng include sacrificial burial of multiple individuals in a bell-shaped pit, and in two well shafts.

In the neighboring Yuanqu Basin, the occupational history of the Nanguan site (i.e., Yuanqu Shang Town) parallels that of Dongxiafeng (National Museum of Chinese History and Shanxi Provincial Institute 1997; National Museum of Chinese History et al. 1996; Railey 1999). The enclosing ditch was filled in, and a hangtu wall was constructed around the site at the beginning of the Erligang period, enclosing 13.3 hectares (Figure 19). By this time, the town was divided into functionally differentiated quarters, including habitation sectors and a central elite district marked by several low, hangtu platforms. Like Dongxiafeng, the Yuanqu Shang Town is much smaller than the Central Shang centers at Zhengzhou and Yanshi, but otherwise it exhibits a generally similar blueprint, with fortification walls, a cluster of hangtu platforms, and a south-facing main gate. The local importance of the Yuanqu Shang Town is further accentuated by the abandonment and downscaling of many surrounding sites that were occupied during the preceding Erlitou period (Figure 20). This contracted settlement pattern suggests that many local residents moved into the protective confines of the walled settlement. Interestingly, available settlement evidence from the southern Yuanqu Basin does not suggest any significant population growth in the area following the early Longshan period (Railey 1999). Insofar as this is true, the evidence may indicate an increase in death rates, perhaps resulting from escalating warfare, and the export of slaves, possibly to the larger polity, or polities, centered at Zhengzhou and Yanshi.

The archaeological evidence raises important questions concerning the geopolitical relations between the small centers at Dongxiafeng and Yuanqu, on the one hand, and the larger ones at Zhengzhou and Yanshi on the other. Similarities in artifact assemblages, stylistic elements (including the taotie design on both bronze and ceramic vessels), and town/city layouts suggest widespread interaction spheres, along with a shared elite tradition or "international style." But while the political relationships between these various centers remain unknown, several alternative scenarios present themselves, all of which are equally plausible in light of present evidence.

In one scenario, we can envision a statelike polity centered at the urban sites of Zhengzhou and Yanshi. For the moment, let us assume this was indeed the early Shang state, although this remains debatable. With power consolidated in the Central Plain and Yi-Luo Valley,

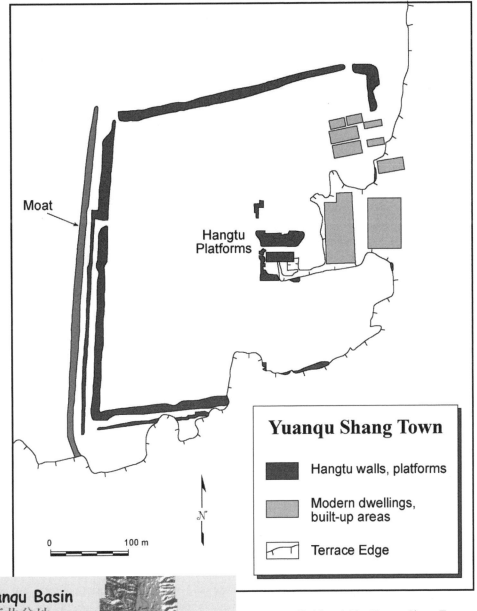

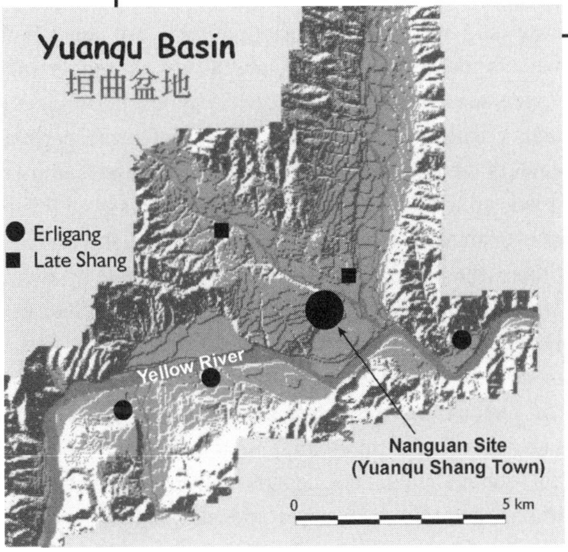

Figure 19. (above) The Yuanqu Shang Town (Nanguan site) in the southern Yuanqu Basin. This is the most recently discovered of the walled Erligang settlements.

Figure 20. (left) Distribution of Erligang and Late Shang sites in the Yuanqu Basin. Compare with the distribution of Elitou sites in Figure 17, and note the successive, period-by-period decrease in the numbers of sites.

the smaller Dongxiafeng and Yuanqu centers may have become peripheral outposts of the early Shang state. Under this scenario, local elites may have been co-opted and empowered by the Shang kings, conquered and replaced by more "cooperative" local leaders, or governed more directly by military units under the command of leaders from the Shang state itself.

In an alternative scenario, Dongxiafeng and the Yuanqu Shang Town represent independent, local polities who interacted with the larger state, or states, to the east and adopted many elements of the early Shang civilization, in part through symbolic entrainment. In this scenario, both trade and warfare may have been carried out between the various walled centers. If the core was "fractured"—for example, if Zhengzhou and Yanshi represent independent, potentially competing polities— then independence may likewise have been a more viable option for Dongxiafeng and Yuanqu. If the core was more unified (i.e., if Zhengzhou and Yanshi were part of a single polity), Dongxiafeng and Yuanqu may have found it in their interest to likewise unite as a single polity, or at least form an alliance. However, conflict between Dongxiafeng and Yuanqu cannot be ruled out, even assuming there was indeed a large, unified state to the east; the military reach of such a unified state may still have fallen short of the intermontane area. At any rate, the construction of substantial walls at the four known Erligang centers, as well as the contracted Erligang settlement pattern at Yuanqu, suggests that concerns over defense had become particularly acute at this time.

It may also be that there was an Erligang polity resembling the dispersed, loosely administered entity that Keightley (1983; see above) suggests for the Late Shang state (prior to the Anyang V period). If so, the Erligang state may have been structured in a way that does not fit neatly into the alternative scenarios described above; that is, it may have lacked a central "capital," with itinerant kings dividing their time among, and performing ceremonies at, various centers (walled or not). On the other hand, nothing resembling the sprawling, unwalled center at Anyang is known for the Erligang period, and no walled sites similar to the Erligang centers are known for the Late Shang period in north-central China. This suggests the character of the Erligang state (or states) may have been considerably different from its (their) Late Shang successor. Accordingly, political organization in the Erligang period may have involved more tightly consolidated polities resembling city-states.

Which of these various scenarios more closely approximates Erligang-period regional history remains an open question. It is quite possible, in fact, that there was a dynamic state of geopolitical relations in the region at this time. Such relations may have changed or fluctuated between conditions, allowing local autonomy at one point and integration into a larger state or states (Shang or otherwise) at another. Such conditions were perhaps contingent in part on the relative political strength of, and nature of relations between, the large centers at Zhengzhou and Yanshi at any given moment in Erligang history.

Regardless of the overarching geopolitical circumstances, the centers at Dongxiafeng and Yuanqu were obviously in close contact with Zhengzhou and Yanshi at this time, and a likely key ingredient of this contact was the metal ores used in bronze making. If we assume that the possession and ceremonial use of bronze vessels and other items had by Erligang times become critical to the display and maintenance of political power, then maintaining access to the raw materials used in bronze making (principally copper and tin) was of fundamental concern to elites residing at Zhengzhou and Yanshi, where there were no ore sources in the immediate vicinity. Ore sources in the Zhongtiao Mountains may have assumed increasing importance with the continued development of bronze industries in the Erligang period, and insofar as this is true, the smaller centers at Dongxiafeng and Yuanqu played a crucial role in the regional system by controlling the extraction and export of metal ores from the nearby mountains. Other ore sources were available in the region, however (Chang 1980:151–153), and the extent to which Zhongtiao Mountain sources were utilized by bronze makers at Zhengzhou and Yanshi probably depended to a great extent on geopolitical circumstances and relations between the Erligang core and its western periphery. At any rate, bronze vessels make their earliest, and as yet extremely spotty, appearances in the Erligang occupations at Dongxiafeng and Yuanqu, and it seems likely that these peripheral centers were receiving finished bronze vessels and other goods from the larger centers of Zhengzhou and Yanshi in exchange for the raw ores and, possibly, slaves. Even if this is true, the organization of this exchange system still remains unknown; it could have operated whether or not Dongxiafeng and/or Yuanqu were independent polities, or colonies of a larger (Shang?) state. But regardless of the overarching geopolitical conditions (which may, in fact, have been quite fluid), it is clear that the fates of all four walled Shang centers had become inextricably linked, and this linkage becomes dramatically evident in the post-Erligang archaeological record.

Collapse and Its Aftermath

The Middle and Late Shang Periods (ca. 1300–1050 BC)

Sometime around 1300 BC, a dramatic collapse of the polity, or polities, centered at the four walled Erligang centers occurred. As noted earlier, the evidence for this dramatic turn of events has been available for some time now, although few scholars have recognized or commented directly on its historical significance in terms of a regional collapse. More than two decades ago, Keightley observed that the area of northwestern Henan, so rich in Erligang sites dating to the centuries prior to the ascendancy of Anyang, was apparently political *terra incognita* as far as the late Shang incriptions are concerned—even during the pre-Anyang V Late Shang, when the state's "territory" appears to have been more extensive than in the later decades of the period.

> The inscriptions indicate no major state elements in the northern [Henan, Zhengzhou-Luoyang] region. This accords well with the small number of Late Shang occupations that have been identified in this area (Keightley 1983:540).

Although Keightley suggested that this "hole" in the Late Shang realm may have been occupied by ethnic Xia people (a dubious possibility at best), the archaeological evidence is, in fact, more consistent with a regional abandonment at the end of the Erligang period.

Recent survey efforts in north-central China underscore the widespread abandonment of the region following the end of the Erligang period. In the Yuanqu Basin, for example, the only Late Shang remains identified by surveys and excavations include a single house at one site and few Late Shang ceramics at another site (Railey 1999). No post-Erligang remains have been identified at the Yuanqu Shang Town. The paucity of post-Erligang Shang remains in the Yuanqu Basin suggests a dramatic episode of abandonment, with the post-collapse occupants living in small, scattered hamlets or farmsteads, and perhaps even opting for a mobile, pastoral way of life.

More extensive survey work in the lower Yi-Luo Valley confirms this precipitous drop in the number of Late Shang sites (Liu et al. 2004). Here, Erlitou and "Shang" period sites are roughly equal in numbers (53 and 57 sites, respectively), but among the Shang sites there are only four Late Shang components, whereas 55 sites contained Erligang components. The numbers suggest that, here too, there was a catastrophic loss of population in the Late Shang period.

What events transpired to precipitate this dramatic collapse? This remains an open question, and the historical annals provide at best only the sketchiest of hints. We do not know, for example, if the large centers at Zhengzhou and Yanshi collapsed primarily because of internal strife and breakdown of the prevailing sociopolitical order, if they fell to hostile forces from elsewhere, or if some combination of internal and exogenous forces led to their downfall. Likewise, to what extent the populations of these early Shang centers were massacred, carried off into slavery, or fled as refugees to other regions remains unclear. We also do not know if all four centers fell because they were part of a single, unified polity.

In any event, the Erligang collapse was one outcome of changing political and economic fortunes that remain poorly understood. If the collapse was precipitated by economic conditions, we might invoke diminishing marginal returns as a decisive factor (cf. Tainter 1988; Stuart 2000). In this scenario, competitive emulation involving the production and display of expensive prestige goods, such as bronze vessels, may have created an inflationary spiral from which there was no easy escape. Yet it may also be the case that the economic and exchange network that tied these four centers together was not suffering from internal decay but was abruptly severed by some exogenous factor, such as a foreign military conquest, one or more natural disasters (e.g., earthquakes, floods, or plague), or environmental degradation in the densely populated Erligang heartland.

Regardless of what the precipitating factors were, they seem to have struck down all four centers at once, apparently because the four centers were tightly intertwined within the regional network. Insofar as the local political economies at Dongxiafeng and Yuanqu were dependent on demand for metal ores from the larger centers at Zhengzhou or Yanshi, the disintegration or conquest of even one of these larger centers may have had disastrous economic and social effects on the peripheral centers to the west. Imagine, for example, during the Erligang period the elites at Dongxiafeng and Yuanqu (whether indigenous folks or colonizers from the early Shang state) maintained negotiated arrangements with local leaders and lineage heads. The "glue" to such arrangements may well have been prestige goods manufactured in the Central Plain, which were imported and bestowed on local leaders in exchange for their cooperation in organizing the extraction and export of metal ores from the Zhongtiao Mountains (and perhaps supplying slaves for export as well). Over time, the prestige goods themselves assumed an essential role not only in the maintenance of sociopolitical relations throughout the Erligang network, but also in the performance of divination and ancestor-worship ceremonies, from the largest center down to the local village. This system could have operated for decades or even a few centuries, but even so it remained a delicate arrangement, vulnerable to disruption from any number of sources, internal or external.

Although the precise geopolitical relations between these centers by the end of the Erligang period remain unknown, it does seem clear that the local political economies of Zhengzhou, Yanshi, Dongxiafeng, and Yuanqu had become so interdependent that, once one part of the network began to crumble, the entire house of cards came tumbling down.

In the wake of this collapse, north-central China appears to have witnessed not only massive relocations of people, but also an interval of regional political fragmentation. The recently defined Middle Shang period (Tang 1999) apparently represents a rather short interval of time between the Erligang and Late Shang periods, even though Tang cites stratigraphic evidence to suggest a three-phase division of the Middle Shang. Earlier, Thorp (1985) recognized what he called a "Transitional" period between the Erligang and Late Shang, which was best represented in the middle strata at the Taixi site, north of Anyang at Gaocheng, Hebei (Taixi Archaeology Team 1979). For Tang, Taixi represents one of ten Middle Shang local "types," or style zones, distinguished by stylistic attributes in their respective ceramic and bronze assemblages. Thorp, on the other hand, made the following observation:

> The typological uniformity of vessels throughout the area containing sites of the Early Shang culture, the relative homogeneity of intact assemblages, and the considerable stylistic unity of decoration do not indicate distinctive regional traditions in the Upper Erligang Phase and the Transitional Period (Thorp 1985:16).

Regardless of whether or not one follows a "splitting" (Tang) or "lumping" (Thorp) typology with respect to regional vessel assemblages, we are left with as little clarity as to geopolitical conditions in the Middle Shang as we were for the Erligang period. Nevertheless, it seems quite likely that the post-collapse, Middle Shang period was probably characterized by a highly fragmented geopolitical landscape, with numerous small polities surrounding the now largely abandoned Erligang heartland. I say *largely* abandoned because a small, Middle Shang component

at the Zhengzhou site indicates that this largest Erligang center was not completely abandoned at this time, or else it was quickly reoccupied by "squatters" unrelated to the center's Erligang population. Likewise, very ephemeral Late Shang presences were noted above for the Yuanqu Basin and lower Yi-Luo Valley.

At the same time, developments were afoot at Anyang that set the stage for its florescence during the Late Shang. Recent investigations in the Anyang area have uncovered the remains of a Middle Shang walled settlement located several kilometers from the Late Shang Yinxu site and covering approximately 4 km^2 (Tang and Liu 2000). This recent find, larger than either Zhengzhou or Yanshi, sheds considerable new light on the origins of the Late Shang center at Anyang.

The establishment of this walled settlement was apparently so close on the heels of the Erligang collapse and abandonment that it was likely constructed at least in part by, and hosted large numbers of, refugees from the collapsed Erligang centers to the south. An examination of Erligang and Late Shang site distributions in north-central China (see Figure 13) lends support to a scenario involving a major northward movement of populations from the Yellow River valley. Likewise, the sprawling Late Shang center at Anyang appears to emerge very soon after the Middle Shang walled city was occupied, suggesting historical continuity between the two. Such evidence seems to support those who contend that the centers at Zhengzhou and Yanshi were, indeed, occupied by ethnic Shang populations. But Shang ethnogenesis remains a murky issue, and it is possible that the Late Shang state known from Anyang was formed through an amalgamation of different ethnic groups, including some displaced following the Erligang collapse. Late Shang developments in the bronze industry betray a sharp break with the past, with an unprecedented diversity and stylistic elaboration of ceremonial vessels. The Late Shang florescence in bronze making may reflect the invigorating outcome of a polyglot, cosmopolitan mix at Anyang, a development that may have been fueled in part by mass movement of refugees (ethnic Shang or otherwise) northward out of the abandoned Yellow River valley centers.

The Late Shang florescence is reflected not only in stunning achievements in bronze making, but in other features as well. The huge center at Anyang is justly renowned for its impressive royal tombs, elite residences, public buildings, and spatially zoned settlement (see Chang 1980:69–135; 1986:317–331; Institute of Archaeology 1994; Li 1977; Zou 1979). Settlement and mortuary patterns, along with textual sources, portray a complex, hierarchical society made up of royalty, nobles, commoners, and slaves. The Late Shang florescence is also marked in no small way by the development of writing, as reflected in the inscriptions on both oracle bones and bronze vessels at Anyang. Being located on the western edge of the alluvial North China Plain, Anyang, like Zhengzhou and Yanshi before it, needed to import the raw materials necessary for bronze making, and the appearance of Late Shang settlements in the mountainous areas immediately to the west (such as Xiaoshen [Shanxi Institute of Archaeology 1996]) would seem to indicate that these sites were important nodes for supplying bronze ores to Anyang; in this role they were probably similar to Dongxiafeng and Yuanqu in the preceding Erligang regional system.

The Late Shang florescence suggests an impressive cultural and sociopolitical recovery following a collapse of significant magnitude. Yet, at the same time, archaeological evidence suggests the Erligang heartland remained largely depopulated over the course of the Late Shang period, and this pre-collapse core area remained off the radar screen of the Late Shang kings and their diviners. Apparently, the post-collapse landscape of north-central China was not simply one of recovery and florescence, but also one of ruins and abandoned settlements, among which dwelled a scattered, low-density population that perhaps involved pastoral groups and other "barbarians" who operated outside the web of complex polities of the Late Shang world. The apparent persistence of this demographic "hole" in north-central China is especially enigmatic considering that the Erligang heartland features fertile valleys (including the Yellow and Yi-Luo valleys) had hosted comparatively dense populations from Neolithic times onward, and became a major population center once again in post-Shang times. Perhaps future discoveries will alter our present picture of the post-collapse Erligang heartland, but for now the evidence compels us to ask why people were discouraged from resettling this area for a period of time, and why it remained beyond the realm of the nearby Late Shang state.

One possibility is that the former Erligang heartland constituted a sort of buffer zone between hostile polities of the Late Shang period. Of particular interest here are the ethnic Zhou, who were forming their own culture and expansionist polity in the Wei River valley to the west. Although the Zhou eventually conquered the Shang in ca. 1050 BC, there is no epigraphic evidence prior to Anyang V to suggest that the Shang viewed the Zhou as an enemy, despite multiple appearances of the Zhou in pre-Anyang V oracle bone inscriptions. Nevertheless, tensions between the Shang and Zhou may have simmered for a long time before finally boiling over, and as a result the Erligang heartland, positioned between these two polities, may have remained unattractive to resettlement on a large scale.

There are, of course, other possible explanations for the apparent lack of resettlement within the former Erligang heartland. If disease or some other natural disaster had devastated the region, for example, it may have instilled a profound sense of fear in the surviving population of north-central China, prompting ideological proscriptions against resettling there. Yet many other regions of the world that experienced similar disasters did not remain unoccupied for such a long period of time, and it seems more likely that the reasons for the continued abandonment of the former Erligang heartland have much more to do with geopolitical conditions in the Middle and Late Shang world that followed the Erligang collapse.

CONCLUSION

What happened during the Shang Dynasty holds several lessons not only for the study of early Bronze Age China, but for our general understanding of collapse and transformation as well. As for the general study of collapse, the Shang case underscores one of the salient points highlighted in this book: that sociopolitical and economic collapse may occur, even on a large scale, without necessarily bringing down the entire civilization or culture of which it was a part. In the case of mid-Shang collapse, not only did the enveloping civilization survive, it experienced a florescence that in many ways eclipsed developments prior to the collapse. By Late Shang times, we see larger settlements, more impressive artistic embellishment of bronzes, and greater elaboration of mortuary facilities than what is evident in the Erligang period, not to mention the advent of writing. The florescence was accompanied by a reshuffling of geopolitical centers of gravity, apparently involving massive population movements and relocations that may have brought different ethnic groups together into a new, and stimulating, cosmopolitan mix. In the case of the Shang Dynasty, it appears quite possible that collapse was, in fact, the mother of florescence.

The Shang case also illustrates another general rule, namely that polities are especially vulnerable to collapse as they become increasingly complex and larger in scale, and their economic, political, and ideological systems become more interdependent across ever-larger regions. The very raison d'être of these systems is often dependent on economic growth involving regional integration and a geopolitical symbiosis among polities offering varying sets of resources, technological capabilities, and services. As Tainter (1988) and others (e.g., Stuart 2000) illustrate, such growth is relatively inexpensive to achieve in its early stages, but it becomes increasingly costly and prone to disruption by unexpected circumstances involving either environmental or cultural perturbations (or both). Disruption may also occur simply as a result of a system expanding beyond its capabilities. Take prestige goods, for example, which are typically used as visual symbols to prop up ideological systems and an associated social order. The manufacture and circulation of prestige goods not only typically involves delicate exchange relationships that may be easily disrupted by any number of circumstances, but wealth-based economies themselves tend to assume inflationary tendencies as increasing numbers of such goods must be produced to satisfy growing demand. Leaders will naturally attempt to satisfy this demand in order to expand the economy and thus enhance their base of power. But without fundamental organizational changes and/or technological advances, it eventually becomes impossible to continue to satisfy an ever-swelling appetite for prestige goods, at which point the entire system may come tumbling down.

In the case of the Shang Dynasty, at this point we simply do not know to what extent the regional system may have collapsed under its own weight, swelled by a growing level of demand and inability to satisfy it. Likewise, we do not know what unexpected circumstances, if any, may have triggered the Erligang collapse. The Erligang system certainly appears to have involved the sort of geographically uneven distribution of resources on the one hand, and production centers on the other, that necessitate a level of interdependency that may have been quite fragile. This is especially true with respect to bronze production, the raw materials for which were procured from peripheral, mountainous areas, while production was apparently concentrated at the large walled centers of Zhengzhou and

Yanshi, on the edge of the North China Plain. Under such arrangements, growing demand, inflation, and diminishing returns in themselves may have brought the system down, although unexpected circumstances (as yet unknown) or environmental degradation could easily have played decisive role(s) and may have exacerbated and accelerated any inflationary spiral that was already set into motion by social, ideological, and economic conditions.

As for the study of ancient China in particular, the Shang case makes an important point with respect to how the early Bronze Age in this region is studied and understood. Specifically, this case illustrates how giving primacy to the ancient texts can have a blinding effect with respect to phenomena that are clearly evident in the archaeological record, such as the mid-Shang collapse. As noted above, evidence for this collapse has, in fact, been around for quite some time now; it has long been evident that Zhengzhou, Yanshi, and Dongxiafeng were all abandoned at about the same time, with more recent work in the Yuanqu Basin revealing yet another walled settlement that was given up at about the same time. But the vast majority of researchers concerned with this period have followed an ingrained habit of forcing the archaeological record to conform to accounts in the ancient texts. Given that the ancient annals are curiously silent (or at best vague) with respect to the mid-Shang collapse, there has heretofore been no clear and straightforward recognition of this particular episode of collapse, much less any attempt to investigate its historical and evolutionary circumstances. The ancient annals themselves are frustratingly vague and imprecise with respect to many crucial details, and their transcriptions were probably motivated as much by political and nationalistic concerns as they were by the objective recounting history. The archaeological record of ancient China thus has much to teach us with respect to what really happened in the Shang Dynasty, as well as other early periods covered by the ancient annals.

NOTES

There are certainly too many people to list here whom I need to thank for the success of the Yuanqu Basin project, which formed my dissertation research and inspired this paper. My research was funded by Fulbright-Hays, the National Science Foundation, the Committee on Scholarly Communication with China, and Sigma Xi. Professors Patty Jo Watson and Robert L. Thorp at Washington University in St. Louis served as the key members of my dissertation committee, and through them I established contacts and a collaborative relationship with the National Museum of Chinese History, my host institution in China. In China, Prof. Yu Weichao, then Director of the National Museum, graciously allowed me to participate in the field excavations at the Bancun site, and to carry out the other components of my fieldwork. In the field, members of Bancun and Gucheng Archaeological Teams, including Tong Weihua, Xin Lixiang, Wang Jianxin, Cao Bingwu, Wang Rui, and many, many others are due immeasurable thanks, as is Cao Jinpo of the Mianchi County Cultural Relics Exploration Office.

1. The Erlitou period, which precedes the Shang in north-central China and which is frequently equated with the Xia Dynasty, may represent a state-level society as well. But there is still vigorous debate surrounding the level of sociopolitical organization attained during the Erlitou period, as well as the historical veracity of Xia Dynasty itself.

2. It is worth noting that the environment of north-central China differs from that of many other "cradles of civilization" in that it does not involve a river valley surrounded by unforgiving desert. Thus, the emergence of civilization in ancient China poses a prominent caveat to Carneiro's (1970) circumscription theory on the origins of the state. The implications for this are also important for understanding the geopolitical dimensions of sociopolitical evolution in China itself, which involved centers of precocious development shifting through time.

3. Some archaeologists (e.g., Pauketat 1991) object to this expanded application of the world-systems model, arguing that it is not appropriate to the scale of the prestate societies in question. However, this objection appears based on an assumption that archaeologists who employ world-systems theory are literally applying the capitalistic economic processes described by Wallerstein, which is not the case.

REFERENCES

Algaze, Guillermo
  1993 Expansionary Dynamics of Some Early Pristine States. *American Anthropologist* 95:304–333.
Allan, Sarah
  1984 The Myth of the Xia Dynasty. *Journal of the Royal Asiatic Society (of Great Britain and Ireland)* 1984:242–246.
Barnes, Gina
  1993 *China, Korea, and Japan: The Rise of Civilization in East Asia*. London: Thames and Hudson.
Boyd, Robert, and Peter J. Richerson
  1985 *Culture and the Evolutionary Process*. Chicago: University of Chicago Press.
Carneiro, Robert L.
  1970 A Theory of the Origin of the State. *Science* 169:733–738.
Champion, Timothy C., ed.
  1989 *Centre and Periphery: Comparative Studies in Archaeology*. London: Unwin Hyman.
Chang, Kwang-chih
  1980 *Shang Civilization*. New Haven: Yale University Press.
  1983 Sandai Archaeology and the Formation of States in Ancient China: Processual Aspects of the Origins of Chinese Civilization. In *The Origins of Chinese Civilization*, edited by David N. Keightley, pp. 459–521. Berkeley: University of California Press.
  1986 *The Archaeology of Ancient China,* fourth ed. New Haven: Yale University Press.

  1987 Zao Shang, Xia he Shangde Qiyuan Wenti (Origins of the Early Shang, Xia, and Shang). In *Huaxia Wenming* (Ancient Chinese Civilization), edited by Tian Changwu, pp. 408–424. Beijing: Beijing University Press.
  1989 Ancient China and Its Anthropological Significance. In *Archaeological Thought in America*, edited by C. C. Lamberg-Karlovsky, pp. 155–166. Cambridge: Cambridge University Press.
  1995 Shangcheng yu Shangwangchao de Qiyuan jiqi Zaoqi Wenhua (The Origins and the Early Culture of Shang Cities and the Shang State). In *Chung-kuo Kaokuhsu'h Lunwenchi*, pp. 285–296. Taipei: Lianjing Press.
Chase-Dunn, Christopher, and Thomas D. Hall, eds.
  1991 *Core/Periphery Relations in Precapitalist Worlds*. Boulder, CO: Westview Press.
D'Altroy, Terrence, and Timothy Earle
  1985 Staple Finance, Wealth Finance, and Storage in the Inca Political Economy. *Current Anthropology* 26:187–206.
Earle, Timothy
  1991 The Evolution of Chiefdoms. In *Chiefdoms: Power, Economy, and Ideology*, edited by Timothy Earle, pp. 1–15. Cambridge: Cambridge University Press.
Falkenhausen, Lothar von
  1993 On the Historiographical Orientation of Chinese Archaeology. *Antiquity* 67:839–849.
Frankenstein, Susan, and M. J. Rowlands
  1978 The Internal Structure and Regional Context of Early

Iron Age Society in Southwestern Germany. *Bulletin of the Institute of Archaeology* 15:73–112.

Fried, Morton H.
1967 *The Evolution of Political Society: An Essay in Political Anthropology.* New York: Random House.
1983 Tribe to State or State to Tribe in Ancient China? In *The Origins of Chinese Civilization*, edited by David N. Keightley, pp. 467–493. Berkeley: University of California Press.

Friedman, Jonathan
1975 Tribes, States, and Transformations. In *Marxist Analyses and Social Anthropology*, edited by Maurice Bloch, pp. 161–202. New York: Tavistock.

Friedman, Jonathan, and Michael J. Rowlands
1978 Notes Towards an Epigenetic Model of the Evolution of "Civilisation." In *The Evolution of Social Systems*, edited by Jonathan Friedman and M. J. Rowlands, pp. 201–276. Pittsburgh: University of Pittsburgh Press.

Helms, Mary W.
1979 *Ancient Panama: Chiefs in Search of Power.* Austin: University of Texas Press.

Henan Provincial Antiquities Institute, compiler
1993 *Zhengzhou Shangcheng de Kaogu Xin Faxian yu Yanjiu* (New Archaeological Discoveries and Researches on the Shang City Site in Zhengzhou [1985–1992]). Zhengzhou: Zhengzhou Publishing House.

Huber, Louisa G. Fitzgerald
1988 The Bo Capital and Questions Concerning Xia and Early Shang. *Early China* 13:46–47.

Institute of Archaeology, Chinese Academy of Social Sciences
1994 *Yinxu de Faxian yu Yanjiu* (Archaeological Discoveries and Research at the Yin Ruins). Beijing: Science Press.

Institute of Archaeology, Chinese Academy of Social Sciences; National Museum of Chinese History; and Shanxi Provincial Institute of Archaeology
1988 *Xiaxian Dongxiafeng* (The Donxiafeng Site in Xia County). Beijing: Wenwu Press.

Keightley, David N.
1978a The Religious Commitment: Shang Theology and the Genesis of Chinese Political Culture. *History of Religions* 18:211–225
1978b *Sources of Shang History: The Oracle-Bone Inscriptions of Bronze Age China.* Berkeley: University of California Press.
1983 The Late Shang State: When, Where, and What? In *The Origins of Chinese Civilization*, edited by David N. Keightley, pp. 523–564. Berkeley: University of California Press.

Kirchoff, Paul
1955 The Principles of Clanship in Human Society. *Davidson Anthropological Journal* 1:1–10.

Kristiansen, Kristian
1991 Chiefdoms, States, and Systems of Social Evolution. In *Chiefdoms: Power, Economy, and Ideology*, edited

by Timothy Earle, pp. 16–43. Cambridge: Cambridge University Press.

Li Chi
1977 *Anyang.* Seattle: University of Washington Press.

Li, Hui-lin
1983 The Domestication of Plants in China: Ecogeographical Considerations. In *The Origins of Chinese Civilization*, edited by David N. Keightley, pp. 21–63. Berkeley: University of California Press.

Li Yangsong
1980 Cong Henan Longshan Wenhua de jige Leixing Tan Xia Wenhua de Ruogan Wenti (Discussion of Certain Questions Concerning Xia Culture, from Several Types of Longshan Culture). In *Zhongguo Kaoguxuehui di yi ci Nianhui Lunwenji*. Beijing: Wenwu Press.

Liu, Li
1994 *Development of Chiefdom Societies in the Middle and Lower Yellow River Valley in Neolithic China: A Study of the Longshan Culture from the Perspective of Settlement Patterns.* Unpublished Ph.D. dissertation, Harvard University.
1996 Settlement Patterns, Chiefdom Variability, and the Development of Early States in North China. *Journal of Anthropological Archaeology* 15:237–288.

Liu, Li, Xingcan Chen, Yun Kuen Lee, Henry Wright, and Arlene Rosen
2004 Settlement Patterns and Development of Social Complexity in the Yiluo Region, North China. *Journal of Field Archaeology* 29(1–2):75–100.

Moseley, Michael E.
1992 *The Incas and Their Ancestors: The Archaeology of Peru.* London: Thames and Hudson.

National Museum of Chinese History, Department of Archaeology, and Shanxi Provincial Institute of Archaeology
1997 Nian Shanxi Yuanqu Gucheng Nanguan Shangdai Chengzhi Fajue Jianbao 1988–1989 (Brief Report on the 1988–1989 Excavations at the Nanguan Shang Town Site, Gucheng, Yuanqu, Shanxi). *Wenwu* 1997(10):12–29.

National Museum of Chinese History, Department of Archaeology; Shanxi Provincial Institute of Archaeology; and Yuanqu County Museum
1996 *Yuanqu Shangcheng (Yi): Niandu Kancha Baogao 1985–1986* (The Shang Period Walled Site at Yuanqu [Volume 1]: Report of Surveys, 1985–1986). Beijing: Science Press.

Pauketat, Timothy R.
1991 *The Dynamics of Pre-state Political Centralization in the North American Midcontinent.* Unpublished Ph.D. dissertation, University of Michigan.

Peebles, Christopher S., and Susan M. Kus
1977 Some Archaeological Correlates of Ranked Societies. *American Antiquity* 42:421–448.

Peregrine, Peter N.
1992 *Mississippian Evolution: A World-System Perspective.*

Madison: Prehistory Press.

Price, Barbara J.

1977 Shifts in Production and Organization: A Cluster-Interaction Model. *Current Anthropology* 18:209–233.

Railey, Jim A.

1999 *Neolithic to Early Bronze Age Sociopolitical Evolution in the Yuanqu Basin, North-Central China.* Unpublished Ph.D. dissertation, Washington University, St. Louis.

Renfrew, Colin

1979 System Collapse as Social Transformation. In *Transformations: Mathematical Approaches to Culture Change*, edited by Colin Renfrew and K. L. Cooke, pp. 481–506. New York and London: Academic Press.

1986 Introduction: Peer Polity Interaction and Socio-political Change. In *Peer Polity Interaction and Socio-political Change*, edited by Colin Renfrew and John F. Cherry, pp. 1–17. Cambridge: Cambridge University Press.

1987 *Archaeology and Language: The Puzzle of Indo-European Origins.* New York: Cambridge University Press.

Renfrew, Colin, and John F. Cherry, eds.

1986 *Peer Polity Interaction and Socio-political Change.* Cambridge: Cambridge University Press.

Sahlins, Marshall D.

1958 *Social Stratification in Polynesia.* University of Washington Press, Seattle.

1963 Poor Man, Rich Man, Big Man, Chief: Political Types in Melanesia and Polynesia. *Comparative Studies in Society and History* 5:285–303.

Schneider, Jane

1991 Was There a Precapitalist World-System? In *Core/Periphery Relations in Pre-capitalist Worlds*, edited by Christopher Chase-Dunn and Thomas D. Hall, pp. 45–66. Boulder: Westview Press. (Reprinted from *Peasant Studies* 6(1):20–29, 1977)

Shanxi Institute of Archaeology, Southeast Shanxi Work Station

1996 Changzhi Xiaochang Xiang Xiaoshen Yizhi (The Xiaoshen Site at Xiaochang, Changzhi). *Kaogu Xuebao* 1996(1):63–108.

Shelach, Gideon

1994 Social Complexity in North China during the Early Bronze Age: A Comparative Study of the Erlitou and Lower Xiajiadian Cultures. *Asian Perspectives* 33(2):261–292.

Stuart, David E.

2000 *Anasazi America: Seventeen Centuries on the Road from Center Place.* Albuquerque: University of New Mexico Press.

Tainter, Joseph A.

1988 *The Collapse of Complex Societies.* Cambridge: Cambridge University Press.

Taixi Archaeology Team

1979 Hebei Gaocheng Taixicun Shangdai Yizhi Fajue Jianbao (Brief Report on the Excavations of the Shang Site at Taixi, Gaocheng, Hebei). *Wenwu* 1979(6):33–43.

Tang Jigen

1999 Zhong Shang Wenhua Yanjiu (Middle Shang Culture Research). *Kaogu Xuebao* 1999(4):393–420.

Tang Jigen and Liu Zhongfu

2000 Anyang Yinxu Baohuqu Waiyuan Faxian Daxing Shangdai Chengzhi (A Large Shang City Site Discovered outside the Yinxu Preserve, Anyang). *Zhongguo Wenwubao* (Feb. 20):1.

Thorp, Robert L.

1985 The Growth of Early Shang Civilization: New Data from Ritual Vessels. *Harvard Journal of Asiatic Studies* 45:5–75.

1991 Erlitou and the Search for the Xia. *Early China* 16:1–38.

Trigger, Bruce G.

1999 Shang Political Organization: A Comparative Approach. *Journal of East Asian Archaeology* 1(1–4):43–62.

Wallerstein, Immanuel

1974 *The Modern World-System: Capitalist Agriculture and the Origins of the European World-Economy in the Sixteenth Century.* New York: Academic Press.

Weaver, Muriel Porter

1993 *The Aztecs, Maya, and Their Predecessors: Archaeology of Mesoamerica.* San Diego: Academic Press.

Yoffee, Norman and George L. Cowgill, eds.

1988 *The Collapse of Ancient States and Civilizations.* Tucson: University of Arizona Press.

Zhao Zhiquan

1986 Shilun Erlitou Wenhua de Yuanliu (On the Origin and Development of Erlitou Culture). *Kaogu Xuebao* 1986(1):1–19.

1987 Lun Erlitou Yizhi wei Xia Dai Wanqi Duyi (The Erlitou Site and the Late Xia Capital). *Huaxia Kaogu* 1987(2):196–204, 217.

Zou Heng

1978 Zhengzhou Shangcheng zhi Tangdu Boshuo. *Wenwu* (Cultural Relics) 1978(2):69–71.

1979 *Shang Zhou Kaogu* (Shang-Zhou Archaeology). Beijing: Wenwu Press.

1980 Shilun Zhengzhou Xin Faxian de Yin Shang Wenhua Yizhi (On the New Discovery of a Yin Period Shang Culture Site at Zhengzhou). In *Xia Shang Zhou Kaoguxue Lunwenji* (Collection of Papers on Xia-Shang-Zhou Archaeology), pp. 3–29.

1999 The Yanshi Shang City: A Secondary Capital of the Early Shang. *Journal of East Asian Archaeology* 1(1–4):195–205.

5

Hillforts and the Cycling of Maori Chiefdoms:
Do Good Fences Make Good Neighbors?

Mark W. Allen

> Before I built a wall I'd ask to know
> What I was walling in or walling out
> And to whom I was like to give offense.
>
> —Robert Frost, "Mending Wall"

WARFARE HAS LONG BEEN FINGERED AS A MAJOR CULPRIT in the collapse of complex societies. History, religions, literature, and popular media frequently invoke civil war, "barbarian" invasions, or the onslaught of a formidable military power to explain the demise of particular complex societies. In contrast, in a process detailed by Lawrence Keeley (1996), anthropology has had a marked tendency to downplay the role of conflict, violence, and warfare in both ethnographic and archaeological cases. There have of course been numerous exceptions within the field, especially among archaeologists (and this list has been growing steadily in recent years—see references in Allen and Arkush 2006). Nevertheless, many of those who have pursued the role of warfare have followed Carneiro (1970, 1981, 1990, 1991) and emphasized its ability to *forge* complex societies, rather than bring them down.

It is argued here that warfare cannot simply be regarded as either a means of developing cultural complexity or a destructive force which causes sociopolitical collapse. It certainly plays a role in both processes, but rarely in simple ways. In particular, I am interested in the role of fortifications and defensive warfare in the cycling of chiefdoms. As defined by David Anderson (1994:9–10):

> Cycling encompasses the transformations that occur when administrative or decision-making levels within the chiefdom societies occupying a given region fluctuate between one and two levels above the local community. Cycling is thus the recurrent process of the emergence, expansion, and fragmentation of complex chiefdoms amid a regional backdrop of simple chiefdoms. The adoption of a regional perspective is critical to the investigation of this process, since changes in the number of decision-making levels in the chiefdoms within a given region are rarely concurrent. That is, chiefdoms rarely form or collapse in precisely the same location or with the same periodicity; instead, these societies typically expand or contract at the expense of or because of the actions of other chiefdoms. Centers of power shift or rotate over the landscape, as first one community and then another assumes prominence.

Chiefdoms are thus inherently unstable and are often characterized by a distinct form of cultural collapse. Individual polities and their leaders come and go within a regional context of cultural complexity. Yet, in many cases, cycling nonetheless entails a pattern of overall increasing complexity through time as later chiefdoms build on the foundations of their predecessors. Then too, this overall increase may collapse in turn. Fortifications are an important topic to consider in the process of cycling as they may well dictate or at least affect the stability of complex sociopolitical formations. Unfortunately, their role is often overlooked or placed into the category of symbols of chiefly power.

This paper discusses how defensive warfare transformed Maori society in prehistoric New Zealand. One point to be made is that the development of elaborate hillforts (*pa*) in these unusually large, temperate Polynesian islands led to rapid and widespread changes in settlement patterns, economic systems, and sociopolitical organization. Fortified settlements, storage facilities, and refuges were instrumental in creating these transformations, yet once in place they also acted as a distinct impediment to integration beyond simple chiefdoms. I further argue that while fortifications may not always play the same role in other cultural areas, the Maori case ought to make archaeologists more fully consider the implications of defensive warfare, and especially the roles of fortifications. Prestate strongholds frequently changed the rules of warfare, and they could thus have a dramatic impact on the course of both cultural evolution and devolution.

The first part of the paper presents the argument that the role of fortifications is often underappreciated by archaeologists interested in cultural change. With this general problem in focus, the discussion then turns to the specific example of how Maori pa both created and limited cultural transformations in prehistoric and early historic New Zealand. Maori chiefdoms of some size and complexity did develop around pa, only to fall apart owing to the inherent autonomy provided by the hillforts themselves.

FORTIFICATIONS AND DEFENSIVE WARFARE: A BREACH IN THE ANTHROPOLOGY OF WAR?

Any experienced archaeologist is able to identify the signs of fortification in the archaeological record. Palisade postholes, escarpments, embankments, ditches, stonewalls, and other features are frequently recorded in the vast majority of cultural areas around the world. Even more common are less obvious forms of defense, such as clustered houses and the choice of higher ground for settlement locations. What has been more difficult for archaeologists to achieve, however, is the full recognition of the significance of these defensive efforts. In short, we have been slow to give fortifications their due.

Keeley (1996) has argued that anthropology often "pacifies the past" as it downplays the severity of warfare in traditional and prehistoric societies. But in the case of fortifications, it is possible that even dyed-in-the-wool theorists of warfare have underestimated the effect of this particular solution to war and conflict. Prior to the development of state societies with the key ability to besiege and conduct investitures of strong points (Keegan 1993; Kern 1999), fortifications usually had a profound effect on sociopolitical organization, economic decision-making, and ideology. These roles have not been fully appreciated. Even Keeley (1996:55–58, Table 3.2) devotes only a few pages and an appendix to fortifications in his important book. In a more recent work, Keeley (2001:335) states that

> fortifications have severe limitations: they are immobile; they can defend only the tiny areas encompassed by the lethal range of their defenders' weapons; and they are dependent

on the people, supplies, and ammunition they contain when besieged. Unless a fort's supplies are superior to those of its attackers, or a friendly mobile (i.e., unfortified) force large enough to defeat its besiegers comes to its relief, like all forts it will succumb to a siege by superior numbers.

However, it must be emphasized that sieges were extremely rare in warfare prior to the development of the logistical capabilities of the most complex chiefdoms and states. *The key point should be instead that forts commonly worked very well indeed.*

Unlike anthropologists, military thinkers have had much to say about defensive warfare. R. Brian Ferguson (1984:22) suggested nearly two decades ago that military science might prove to be a profitable field in which to forage for insights on the anthropology of war. To my knowledge, this advice has not often been followed. One exception is Karl Steinen (1992), who cites some of the U.S. Army's field manuals in his paper on Mississippian fortifications. A more recent example is the study of defensive sites in the Southwest by Wilcox et al. (2001) with the invaluable insight of a highly experienced military veteran. It could be argued that every anthropologist working on warfare would do well to pay attention to the writings of military thinkers. As Mark Twain put it, "War talk by men who have been in a war is always interesting; whereas moon talk by a poet who has not been in the moon is likely to be dull."

The two most influential works on warfare are the ancient teachings of Sun Tzu in *The Art of War* and those of the Prussian military genius Carl von Clausewitz in *On War.* Other masters of war include Jomini, Machiavelli, Mao Tse-tung, and Thucydides. These thinkers cover a long time span with considerable cultural diversity. Indeed, some may argue that they are largely irrelevant outside their cultural and chronological context. Martin van Creveld (1991), for example, believes that key parts of Clausewitz's understanding of war are not relevant to premodern warfare. In contrast, Michael Handel, a professor of strategy at the U.S. Naval War College, forcibly rejects this idea. He believes that the masters of war are timeless and universal:

> the universal logic of war still exists whether or not it is codified. In the absence of a formal strategic theory, political groups or states have had to construct one based on their historical experiences and particular strategic and geographic environments. . . . Despite the fact that each political group or state developed its

own strategic concepts, none could defy the as yet unarticulated universal logic of strategy with impunity; this in turn meant that they independently and ineluctably arrived at similar conclusions (Handel 2001:xvii).

I take the view that Handel is correct and thus argue that anthropologists and archaeologists will better understand defensive warfare if they better appreciate the perspective of warriors. Of course some anthropologists, such as Turney-High (1949), have been trained by both military and academic institutions. Few, however, have chosen to bring their experiences together, and Turney-High's take on "primitive war" is not given much credence today (Keeley 1996:10–15; LeBlanc and Rice 2001:5).

While this is not the forum to delve deeply into military science, a few basic concepts of military thinking relevant to defensive warfare need to be brought into the open. First and foremost, in the words of Clausewitz (1984:358), "the defensive form of war is intrinsically stronger than the offensive." This is not simply because defenders can build stout fortifications that resist direct attack from superior forces. A strong advantage goes to the home side since "the defender is better placed to spring surprises by the strength and direction of his own attacks" (Clausewitz 1984:361). Defenders benefit from terrain more than attackers, and attackers must approach on roads and paths that are easily observed while defenders can conceal much of their positions and movements. Attacking forces that invade the territory of defenders face several other disadvantages. The invader must besiege and assault the defender's fortresses; the theater of operations becomes hostile; the invader moves further away from sources of supply while the defender moves closer to his own; there is the threat that allies will join the defender; and the defender, being in real danger, often makes the greater effort while the efforts of the attacker may slacken (see Handel 2001: Figure 13.1).

For a more recent professional opinion, the U.S. Army also acknowledges the primacy of defense and makes a further point:

the advantages of cover and concealment, advance siting . . . shorter [lines of communication], and operations over familiar terrain among a friendly population generally favor the defender. The advantages enjoyed by the attacker are the initial choices of when and where to strike and when and where to mass; these give him the initiative. The major challenge of the defense is to overcome this initial offensive advantage and look for and create early options to the transition to the offense (U.S. Army 1993:6-19 to 6-20).

Importantly, perhaps the most deadly threat to an attacking force is not bashing itself to smithereens against strong fortifications, but the threat of complete rout and annihilation sprung by defenders who achieve surprise, seize the initiative, and most devastatingly, cut off retreat. Clausewitz (1984:370) refers to this as a "sudden powerful transition to the offensive—the 'flashing sword of vengeance.'" Fortifications, in other words, are more than just a static form of defense. They are a distinct menace to would-be attackers. This is a crucial piece for understanding how defensive warfare had a profound effect on cultural evolution.

Further evidence of the universality of this concept is Mao Tse-tung's (1963:111) famous distinction of the four phases of war: "The enemy advances, we retreat; the enemy camps, we harass; the enemy tires, we attack; the enemy retreats, we pursue." In China's more remote past, Sun Tzu (1998:111) taught, "In ancient times skilful warriors first made themselves invincible, and then watched for vulnerability in their opponents."

As for the archaeologists, very few have seriously considered the roles played by fortifications or defensive warfare in general. Exceptions include some Southwestern specialists, such as Haas (1990), LeBlanc (1999), and recent contributors to Rice and LeBlanc (2001). Larson (1972) and Steinen (1992) have stressed the effectiveness of Mississippian fortifications in the Southeast. European scholars working on Bronze and Iron Age sites are keen to recognize the economic, sociopolitical, and military roles of hillforts (Bradley 1991). Arkush (2006) is currently studying long-underappreciated pre-Inka hillforts in the northern Titicaca Basin. In Oceania, fortifications are frequently the focus of research, but seldom is their significance fully considered. In New Zealand, for example, despite more than a hundred years of research on Maori fortifications, my own work (Allen 1994, 1996, 2006) in Hawke's Bay stands nearly alone as an in-depth archaeological consideration of the economic and political roles of pa in the development of Maori chiefdoms (though several archaeologists have considered them as important symbols of group prestige and power).

Another important exception is Timothy Earle (1997), who made the case for a generalized pattern of "hillfort chiefdoms." Although archaeologists are often wary of a new "type of type" to distinguish middle-range societies (Feinman and Neitzel 1984), this is a useful distinction with considerable merit. According to Earle (1997:121), in hillfort chiefdoms, "the developmental potential for political expansion and institutionalization was evidently limited. . . . This limitation is characteristic of chiefdoms in which the *primary* basis of power is defensive military might" (emphasis original). He assigns the following traits to hillfort chiefdoms: heavily fortified settlements, the preponderance of population in the largest settlement, emphasis on military power, warfare to defend territory rather than to conquer new resources, and staple rather than wealth finance systems (Earle 1997:171). Further general characteristics derived from the Maori case are suggested later in this paper.

What these few researchers have begun to develop is the recognition that fortifications and other defensive locations had a profound effect on sociopolitical evolution and stability in a wide variety of culture areas. They made it very difficult for would-be conquerors to consolidate large groups of people. Chiefdoms could be built around multiple, allied, fortified communities, but through consensus rather than conquest.

This is another crucial point. Carneiro's (1970, 1981, 1990, 1991) chiefdom conquest model has been very influential among those with an interest in the role of warfare in cultural evolution. He argues that "War provided the impetus for the rise of chiefdoms in the first place, and under favorable circumstances, for their continued evolution into states" (Carneiro 1991:180). But this idea is stymied when it comes upon a case of effective fortifications. Strong walls often prevent the amalgamation of different populations through conquest, and they also hinder internal or consensual integration. Walls protect, but they also define, limit, and exclude as they keep inhabitants in and outsiders out. Wherever fortifications appeared, chances are they had a significant impact on the likelihood of successful warfare and the extent of sociopolitical integration beyond the local level. It is important to realize, then, that *local fortifications are almost synonymous with the lack of strong central authority* (Keegan 1993:139–152; Earle 1997:105–142).

LESSONS FROM NEW ZEALAND: THE MAORI PA

Traditional Maori society certainly stands as an example of the instability of complex sociopolitical organization in Polynesia or other cultural areas of Oceania. However, Pacific scholars have long recognized that New Zealand fostered a culture that diverged significantly from the traditional Polynesian chiefdom model espoused so often in anthropology textbooks. Maori society took instability,

competition, and warfare to extreme forms. Compared with high-volcanic-island chiefdoms in Hawai'i or the Society Islands, New Zealand political organizations were smaller, less hierarchical, and more apt to drastic fluctuation (Ballara 1998; Best 1924; Buck 1949; Firth 1929; Schwimmer 1990; van Meijl 1995). While it is true that chiefly turnover was high in the most complex Polynesian societies, the polities themselves did not usually completely fall to pieces at the end of particular rulers' reigns of power (Earle 1978; Goldman 1970; Sahlins 1958).

In New Zealand, only the most exceptional individuals could weld together thousands of people. When such chiefs died or lost *mana* (Bowden 1979; Firth 1968; Winiata 1956), their hard-won political formations frequently broke down altogether. With this in mind, the Maori case nevertheless illustrates, and perhaps epitomizes, the importance of warfare and competition for status in the cycling of Polynesian chiefdoms. As I will attempt to show, this case is also an important reminder to archaeologists to more fully consider the roles played by fortifications in both the origin and collapse of cultural complexity.

New Zealand Ecology and Culture History

This Is Polynesia?

Archaeologists and historians are occasionally asked at cocktail parties or by imaginative students which event, place, or time of the human experience they would most like to be able to experience firsthand. For Polynesian specialists, the moment the first East Polynesian canoe or canoes touched ashore on Aoteaoroa (The Land of the Long White Cloud) must rank high. After several weeks at sea these voyagers were confronted with two unbelievably large islands (that together with smaller islands amount to more than 269,000 square kilometers), shockingly cool temperatures, a dense temperate rainforest, frost, and snow-clad peaks. Perhaps the moment of greatest interest would be the one when a flightless bird over twelve feet tall, and with drumsticks that went on forever, emerged out of the dense forest. Surely, this is one of the great moments in human history. There were more than a dozen species (*Dinorthiformes*) of these "prodigious birds" called *moa* (chicken) by the Maori (Anderson 1989). New Zealand prior to the entrance of humans was practically devoid of terrestrial mammals. Without competition, birds in Aotearoa went on to fill many unusual niches—such as large and flightless! As for the first Polynesian explorers, they likely believed that they had discovered a land of veritable giants with unlimited resources. In true optimal foraging mode, they apparently more or less put down their hoes and emphasized hunting and gathering for the next several hundred years. This is a classic case of "niche shift" after the initial colonization of a new island environment (Keegan and Diamond 1987).

The following description of New Zealand ecology and colonization is necessarily brief. For a fuller analysis, consult Anderson and McGlone (1992) and McGlone et al. (1994). Allen (1996) provides a detailed assessment of the resources available in Hawke's Bay, one of the more favorable regions of the southern half of the North Island. The consensus view is that first settlement was only about AD 800 to 1100, making the New Zealand archaeological sequence one of the shortest in the world (Davidson 1984, 2001; Kirch 2000). It is usually divided into two major phases or periods: an Archaic occupation lasting several hundred years, followed by the development of Classic Maori culture.

Times were probably pretty good for the early colonists on Aotearoa. But despite the size and diversity of the islands and their birds, the resource base for supporting humans was surprisingly limited. Lying between 37 and 46 degrees south of the equator, New Zealand's temperatures are cool, and they were probably even a bit cooler a thousand years ago (Burrows and Greenland 1979). Topography is frequently rugged with many mountain and hill ranges (it should be no surprise that Sir Edmund Hillary is a New Zealander). Dense forest made overland travel exceedingly difficult. Soils were well suited for forests, but not for horticulture. As the moa and other birds became scarcer through human predation and habitat destruction (widespread forest clearance through fire), other possible subsistence resources were not all that promising. These included freshwater eels, shellfish, fish, seals, and the root of the bracken fern (a starvation food in most of Polynesia, but a major staple in New Zealand). The mammals that Polynesians usually transported and established in their new island colonies either were not introduced or did not get past the "beachhead bottleneck" (Keegan and Diamond 1987). Only the Polynesian dog and rat made a successful move to New Zealand. One can imagine that if the first colonists brought chickens and pigs along, their relative costs may have been reckoned very high given the high food value of moa. At any rate, they do not appear in the archaeological record until after European contact. The pressure only increased as human populations expanded and resources continued to dwindle. Anderson and McGlone (1992) document the degradation of the New Zealand environment and its resources after human colonization. Many species, including the moa,

were extinct within a few centuries.

In many Polynesian island groups, there is ecological and archaeological evidence that after a few generations of hitting natural resources hard (and usually causing severe extirpations and extinctions), colonists settled into the familiar Polynesian economy of animal domestication combined with intensive horticulture and arboriculture based on taro, breadfruit, coconuts, sweet potatoes, and other crops (Bellwood 1978; Jennings 1979; Kirch 1984, 2000; Oliver 1989; Rollett 1998). New Zealand, however, was not a hospitable place for the vast majority of these plants. Only the hardy and undemanding sweet potato (*kumara*) approached anything like wide usage. Even this plant was only practical in the most favorable environments that New Zealand had to offer: coastal areas with warm, friable soils and a low incidence of frost. Furthermore, sweet potatoes were apparently only important after the development of a key technological innovation: roofed, semi-subterranean storage pits (*rua*) with drainage systems to protect the crop from frosts and moisture (Allen 1994, 1996; Davidson 1984; Fox 1974). This was a critical development as it allowed tubers to be stored over the winter for both provisions and plantings for the following spring. Clearly, however, over nearly all of the South Island and the interior and southern extreme of the North Island, horticulture as an important economic activity was not an option (Anderson and McGlone 1992; Best 1925; Davidson 1984; Gorbey 1970; Leach 1984; Shawcross 1967).

Economy and Warfare in the Origin of Maori Chiefdoms

The introduction of storage pit technology and intensification of limited horticulture can be seen as key heralds of the development of Classic Maori culture from the Archaic. This transition can be placed at something like AD 1300 to 1500, or from 400 to 700 years after initial colonization. Right on the heels of these forms of subsistence intensification was another important change: the proliferation of earthwork and palisaded fortifications. Pa seem to be no older than 700 years, and apparently most were built after 1500 throughout the areas where horticulture or other highly favorable resources were located (Allen 1994, 1996; Davidson 1984, 1987, 2001; Irwin 1985; Kirch 2000; Schmidt 1996). Of more than 6,000 recorded pa, only around 100 are located on the colder South Island. The vast majority are located along coastal margins of the North Island where horticulture was feasible.

The close timing of these processes has led to the development of a dominant ecological and demographic view that limitations to horticulture in New Zealand, the difficulty of clearing temperate rain forest, and population growth resulted in fierce competition for favorable areas (Allen 1996; Kirch 2000:282–283). Warfare, so important in the rest of Polynesia, became central to Maori society (Vayda 1960, 1976). Pa were part of this process as they allowed groups to defend their gardens and other coveted resources. This line of thought is well represented in the literature (Anderson and McGlone 1992; Davidson 1984, 1987, 2001; Duff 1967; Kirch 2000; McGlone 1983; McGlone et al. 1994; Vayda 1960, 1976). Archaeological research in Hawke's Bay (Allen 1994, 1996) verifies the association of pa with favorable resources, but it discounts Vayda's (1960) original emphasis on the costs of clearing forest.

It is at this point, however, that New Zealand prehistorians usually stop. They fail to fully consider the economic and sociopolitical roles and meanings of pa as well as the consequences of the intensification of horticulture and warfare. As I have argued before,

> these processes permitted Maori leaders to develop positions of power and authority by claiming rights to productive land and by organizing large and effective *pa* to establish and protect their claims. Maori traditional history makes it clear that leaders who organized and financed *pa* owned or at least controlled them. The association between pa and chiefs (*ariki*) was very strong. With *pa*, or the promise of *pa*, chiefs offered security in the form of more dependable (and likely, more varied) food as well as security from raiders. The price of participating in this system was, primarily, decreased autonomy and increased labor. I see participation in regional polity formation, *pa* construction, and increased investment in horticulture and storage as a negotiated partnership between ambitious leaders and wary but worried groups of followers (Allen 1996:178).

Complexity, Collapse, and Stalemate in Hawke's Bay

Detailed study of pa, economic resources, and Maori oral history in Hawke's Bay reveal the difficulty inherent in trying to consolidate land and people in the face of autonomous fortifications (Allen 1994, 1996). This region was a desirable one because it contained a unique combination of limited economic resources (including access to shellfish beds, forests, and dependable water sources as well as superior garden lands). The Ngati Kahungunu people, under the leadership of their elderly

chief Rakaihikuroa, invaded central Hawke's Bay from the north. They successfully incorporated the region's prior inhabitants and their few pa through siege, direct assault, threats, and diplomacy around 1550. Rakaihikuroa centered his new chiefdom on the best resources of the region and allocated other areas to his sons and other followers. Shortly thereafter, the nascent regional polity fissioned as a result of conflict between the sons and followers of Rakaihikuroa's two wives, Ruarahanga and Papauma (Figure 21). This internal conflict brought down the attempt at regional consolidation and led to the formation of two smaller polities: Te Hika a Ruarahanga and Te Hika a Papauma (as well as four even smaller polities in isolated coastal locations). Oral history, *whakapapa* (genealogy), and radiocarbon dates all tell the same story of bloody stalemate fighting between these two groups from about 1575 to 1625. A "no-man's" border zone of about 15 km between the two polities is clearly revealed by the distribution of pa sites. Eventually, the two groups did reconcile through a famous elite marriage, but there are certainly no signs of the reemergence or development of a complex polity that stretched across the entire region.

Archaeology and oral history reveal that in Hawke's Bay fortified settlements and food stores were at the crux of the formation of chiefdoms and local groups as alarmed populations contributed their labor and surpluses to these undertakings, and in the process were bound into polities. Most frequently these groups were small-scale, consisting of local groups and simple chiefdoms. In particularly productive areas, however, more complex chiefdoms with populations in the thousands developed. These cases were limited to the most productive regions in New Zealand, and they were also inherently unstable.

For another example, Sutton (1990) describes the origin of the Pouerua chiefdom in the Bay of Islands area, but he focuses on a single polity rather than a large region. The New Zealand historian James Belich (1996:87) writes, "groups made pa, but pa also helped to make groups." I would say instead that Maori chiefs could build polities through building pa. Pa were thus an expensive and portentous response to the threat of warfare and the need to secure economic resources.

The Maori Pa

The Maori fort, or pa, was frequently a massive economic undertaking organized by leaders to provide security for people, stored foods, and to some extent desirable land (Allen 1994, 1996, 2006). Their locations

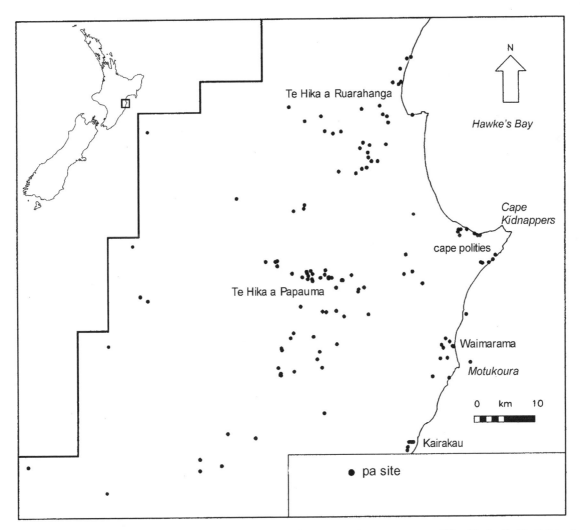

Figure 21. Distribution of pa sites in the central portion of Hawke's Bay on the eastern coast of New Zealand's North Island. Two large polities, Te Hika a Ruarahanga and Te Hika a Papauma, were separated by a buffer zone of about 15 km. Smaller coastal polities were located at Cape Kidnappers, Waimarama, and Kairakau. Isolated pa were scattered in the rugged interior regions.

on hills, ridges, promontories, and islands were selected with care to maximize tactical and sometimes strategic concerns (Figures 22 and 23). Built by specialists, they incorporated multiple lines of palisades, ditches, banks, escarpments, and raised fighting stages to augment naturally defensive positions (Best 1927; Davidson 1984, 1987; Fox 1976). Entrances were notorious for exposing attackers to flank and overhead counterattacks. To make things difficult for an attacker, pa were often subdivided with interior palisades. The highest point (*tihi*) was the place of greatest prestige and could function like a citadel or keep for last stands if attackers breached the various lines of outer defenses.

What made the pa even more formidable was the lack of effective offensive missile weapons in Maori warfare. With the advantage of gravity, defenders could hurl rocks on the heads of attackers from their walls and fighting platforms. But slings, bows, or spear throwers were not a part of Maori warfare, and attackers had a hard time inflecting casualties until they breached or scaled the defenses. As nearly all commentators note, most pa sites would be nearly impregnable unless attacked by surprise. The most authoritative descriptions of Maori warfare are those of Vayda (1960, 1976). He points out that "Direct assault seldom was successful against the strong defenses of a pa and apparently was not often tried," but that attackers sometimes did use fire, sapping, and other techniques to assault fortifications (Vayda 1960:75). Sieges were also sometimes conducted when the attackers had overwhelming numerical superiority and the logistical means, but these circumstances were not the norm (Best 1924, 1927; Vayda 1960). Thus, the

Figure 22. The central part of Otatara Pa (V21\41), the seat of the chiefdom Te Hika a Ruarahanga in Hawke's Bay. This site contains numerous terraces, house platforms, and storage pits. It housed at least several hundred people. Photograph by the author.

Figure 23. A pa of Hawke's Bay (V22\86) that functioned solely as a fortified food store in the Te Hika a Papauma polity. Ditch and bank fortifications surround a number of sweet potato storage pits. The site is approximately 120 × 50 m. Photograph by the author.

military verdict on Maori pa must be that they were highly effective defensive sites, as noted by most early European explorers in the late eighteenth and early nineteenth centuries (Salmond 1991).

Yet, the lack of missile weapons was not the sole reason that pa fortifications were effective. As a bit of an aside, it could also be noted that the Maori were fairly quick to adapt their fortification techniques to include protection from muskets during intertribal warfare in the first half of the nineteenth century (Allen 2006; Crosby 1999; Fox 1976; Vayda 1976), and eventually artillery during the New Zealand Land Wars of 1845–1872 (Belich 1986). Maori groups fighting the Crown developed highly innovative and effective earthwork defenses to cope with barrages, even when "the British fired roughly twenty times the weight of shell per square yard . . . as they did into the Somme battlefield during the initial bombardment of 24 June–1 July, 1916" (Belich 1986:295). Clearly, the design of fortifications has a long and illustrious history in New Zealand, and this tradition was more than capable of adapting to change in the technology of offensive warfare (Allen 2006).

New Zealand archaeologists have studied pa for some time now (Davidson 1984, 1987; Kirch 2000; Marshall 1987). They have been recognized as central parts of the Classic Maori settlement pattern since the 1960s (Duff 1967; Green 1963; Groube 1964). Numerous regional studies of pa have also been conducted (Allen 1994; Barber 1996; Davidson 1987; Irwin 1985; Jones 1986, 1988; Prickett 1982; Sutton 1990). For decades, chronology was a major issue that saw archaeologists attempting to seriate pa on the basis of the evolution of different forms of defense (Fox 1976; Marshall 1987). This dead-end avenue of research was finally closed off once sufficient radiocarbon dates became available by the early 1990s (Allen 1994; Schimdt 1996). But unfortunately, there has been a prevailing tendency to simply view pa as fortified villages built as a response to warfare and ecological crisis. Moreover, pa are often discussed in isolation from their social and regional context (which also makes understanding their chronology difficult). They are thus treated as elaborate settlements that afforded protection from warfare, with very little consideration of the issues involved in their construction. In sum, their political and economic aspects have been badly neglected.

One alternative view advocated by a few scholars considers the pa as more of a monument than a defensive fortification (Barber 1996; Marshall 1987; Mihaljevic 1973). In this perspective, pa are symbols of groups, territorial markers, and perhaps material embodiments of Maori cosmology. Barber (1996:877) writes, "the primal [pa] landscape may be viewed phenomenologically . . . as a temporalizing redefinition and renewal of a world in ecological crisis in the hands of restructured descent groups . . . no matter how much it was also (or became) a place of actual conflict between these groups." There is little doubt that this position has considerable merit, but then again nearly every cultural landscape constructed by humans could likewise be seen as symbolic. But does this really explain why these sites are so numerous and central to the Maori settlement pattern? I would also argue that if one wants to give primacy to symbolism, pa should be considered primarily as symbols of the power of the leaders that organized and financed their construction (see Liu and Allen 1999). As Keeley (1996:57) notes:

> few human artifacts do not acquire at least some symbolic functions and attributes, and fortifications certainly have their symbolic aspects. At the most prosaic level, they symbolize their owner's military sophistication, military power, and determination to hold occupied territory. More abstractly, they demarcate the boundary between defenders and attackers, "owners" and "usurpers." . . . In chiefdoms and states, fortifications symbolize the importance and manifest the power of a leader.

It is doubtful, though, that the symbolic message was uppermost in the minds of those who called for and built pa (Allen 2006). First and foremost, these sites were designed to protect people, land, and stored food supplies from real or potential enemies. They were also a very real means of power for ambitious chiefs because they were a key way to attract followers. People helped to build these sites in return for security and access to resources. In the process, they found themselves members of regional polities.

Pa as Impediments to Integration

The preceding discussion of Maori pa made the point that these sites were at the nexus of chiefdom formation in prehistoric New Zealand. Leaders organized and financed the construction of these sites, but only with the support of their followers, who worked much harder for the enhanced security and access to resources. Particularly ambitious leaders, however, evidently found that this solution to warfare worked all too well for several reasons. Once in place, pa made it exceedingly difficult to build larger polities as the threat level of warfare was considerably reduced. Earle (1991, 1997) has pointed out that ambitious leaders must tie followers to themselves if they are to build complex polities. One key issue of this process is how the leader can keep people from "voting with their feet" (Earle 1991:4). Groups with their own pa would not necessarily be faced with the choice of either joining a neighboring group or moving away. There may well not have been much of a security advantage to be gained by membership in a larger or more complexly organized polity. This reality would greatly reduce a leader's ability to coerce or cajole other groups into joining for protection.

The significance of the security of pa cannot be overstated. Once a group had its own fortification or set of fortifications, it could well feel more at ease about its current or potential enemies. It would still need to maintain vigilance and be wary of larger polities that could perhaps storm the walls. But it is likely that the group would feel less pressure to combine with other populations for security, a common settlement pattern shift in areas that are threatened by attack from outside the region (Rice 2001). The drawbacks for clustering in prehistoric New Zealand should be clear: lowered autonomy and a reduced economic base that was already marginal in most cases. Forts could thus allow a group to sidestep social and political integration and its high costs.

It was also very difficult for one polity to conquer and incorporate another as described by Carneiro. As discussed above, the Maori pa was a sophisticated and highly effective fortification that, more often than not, could resist direct attacks. Given a bit of familiarity with muskets and later with artillery, the Maori engineered earthwork fortifications that stand their own against the trench systems of the American Civil War or even the early twentieth century. Attacking groups needed superior numbers, but most importantly they needed the element of surprise. Maori oral history and ethnohistoric accounts from the late eighteenth and early nineteenth centuries make it clear that achieving surprise was far from impossible. Vayda (1960:75) writes that

> Maori warriors, when attacking forts, relied primarily on surprising the enemy. The warriors often were successful. Surprises are said to have been the usual cause of the fall of pa. But if the defenders remained within the pa and all attempts at surprising them failed, then the attackers either abandoned the objective or else turned to other measures. Abandoning the objective may well have been the common course.

Thus, so long as defenders were forewarned or vigilant, their pa would usually weather an attack.

The key point may well be that having a pa greatly reduced the chance that a group would be attacked at all. This is not just because a fortification was a difficult objective to attack. It must also be recognized that the pa was a very formidable latent threat. For every famous account of the successful investiture of a pa, there is likely another one attesting to the annihilation of a war party by defenders who seized the initiative and counterattacked (for examples, see references in Vayda 1960:58). Sally points and planned ambush locations could help create a highly destructive counterattack. Best provides a graphic example of this turn of events when he quotes McDonnell's 1887 account of a rout inflicted in pre-European times on Ngati-Whatua warriors after they failed in an attempt to surprise three adjacent pa:

> seeing that their attempt was hopeless, the enemy broke and fled in every direction. At once the pursuit was called by [the chief]—"show no quarter. Kill all; and the empty calabushes will be filled ere night. We will have enough dried heads to adorn every post in the fort and village, and our women shall sing to them with the flutes we will make out of their bones."
>
> The garrisons of the three forts streamed forth in pursuit, while old and infirm priests, who viewed the battle, cursed them in their flight. One such effusion was curious, "Haere! Haere! Ka tahuna e au nga hinu o to tuaroa hei turama haere i to wairua ki Te Reinga. Haere! Haere! Tenei au te haere nei!" (Run! Fly! I will melt the marrow of your back-bones whereby to light your spirits to Hades. Run! Run! I am in pursuit.)
>
> And they ran. Many brave deeds were done, but what was the use of defeated men fighting? Many of them never warded off the death blow, lest they be made prisoners and tortured. Very few escaped. Many fell into the hands of those guarding the tracks, and their varied tortures afterwards amused the people for several days, until, finally, they were eaten (McDonnell, quoted in Best 1927:171).

When a chief and his *taua* (war party) debated whether or not to attack a pa, it was not just an issue of weighing the odds of success. Such a venture could well lead to their complete and utter destruction. Offensive operations were highly risky because of the inherent strength of the defense, and its ability to turn the tables on the attackers.

It is clear that Maori chiefs who attempted to build polities solely through military conquest and subjugation of defeated enemies had a mighty tough challenge ahead of them. How many surprises could one expect to pull off within the period of a few years? Even if the chief had sufficient force to storm a pa, it would often be in the face of heavy casualties.

Conquest of a population so that it could be subjugated was very rare in New Zealand prior to European contact. Land was taken. Food was captured. If a pa was sacked, some slaves might be taken. But the usual practice when an attacking group won a major engagement was to kill nearly every man, woman, and child they could get their hands on. Though cannibalism was usually avoided in cases involving close kin, victims of fallen pa were often cooked and eaten. Mention of cannibalism is always sure to generate controversy (Arens 1979; Billman et al. 2000; Dongoske et al. 2000; Turner and Turner 1999), but as Vayda (1960:70) notes, "there is rich documentation of the importance of human flesh in the commissariat of Maori war parties." Some captives were also taken back to the attacker's community so that they could be killed and eaten by other group members.

Postmodern perspectives have challenged the severity of Maori warfare and cannibalism (Barber 1996; Belich 1996:75–81; Bowden 1984; van Meijl 1994). For example, the historian James Belich (1996:80) invokes the relative rarity of skeletal evidence of violence and the archaeological evidence of sacked pa to claim, "it seems doubtful that seventeenth- and eighteenth-century Aotearoa was more violent than Europe at the same time." This idea shows little appreciation of one thing that state societies often do well: they effectively control local violence and warfare. What he neglects to discuss is the paucity of human skeletal remains that have been studied in New Zealand (a number of which *do* clearly demonstrate lethal violence), as well as the small number of large-scale pa excavations (see Allen 2006; Davidson 1984). We cannot possibly expect archaeology to "prove" frequent warfare or cannibalism until such time as research has been directed towards answering these questions (Keeley 1996; LeBlanc 1999; Turner and Turner 1999). The "smoking gun" of these behaviors can be very elusive in the archaeological record. Such interpretations as Belich's can only be seen as part of the process of "pacifying the past," as argued by Keeley (1996). The eyewitness accounts and Maori oral history are too much in agreement and too strong to ignore—Maori warfare was extremely violent when a pa was sacked.

At any rate, there is absolutely no question that military conquest of populations was very rare in pre-European New Zealand. Pa were a key reason behind this. They raised the cost of attack by creating unacceptable casualties and risks. Their fall was a cause of bloody and desperate hand-to-hand fighting that would yield very few prisoners. This would not have been a viable strategy for ambitious Maori chiefs. *Plainly, the Carneiro model for the development of complex chiefdoms and, eventually, states through conquest warfare does not sufficiently take into account effective fortifications.* New Zealand chiefs likely included some of the most ruthless, talented, and ingenious war leaders in human history. Yet, they were typically unable to build lasting, complex political formations through conquest until the introduction of European animals, plants, and technology in the early nineteenth century (Vayda 1976). Even in the historic period, they usually sought to evict or kill enemies, not to incorporate them. Chiefs such as Rakaihikuroa of the Ngati Kahungunu could achieve spectacular victories that allowed them to build complex chiefdoms, but these formations rarely survived beyond a generation.

The Psychology of Fortifications

Psychology is unfamiliar ground for most prehistorians. In an earlier work (Liu and Allen 1999), a social psychologist and an archaeologist explored the utility of evaluating intergroup theory in psychology through the archaeological data of Maori Hawke's Bay. This brief discussion is not so ambitious. It merely seeks to recognize that fortifications do indeed have a role in the process of cultural evolution other than the material ones of physical protection and latent threat to would-be attackers. A group that builds a fortification or series of fortifications around itself is very likely to see the world differently than a group living in open settlements.

Fortification walls both exclude and include people. They provide a physical boundary between inhabitants and outsiders, members and non-members, attackers and defenders. Once in place, such a barrier would have a strong role in social perceptions of group identity and membership. Since chiefs financed and organized at least the large-scale and complex fortifications, the distinction would be all the more important—those who supported the chief were included, those who did not might not be.

One ramification of this perception would be that it would be difficult to get inhabitants to think outside the box of their own pa. Social psychology's realistic group conflict theory (epitomized in the classic experiment at Robber Cave by Sherif et al. 1961) stresses how common purposes and activities are key in the formation of intragroup and intergroup relationships (Liu and Allen 1999: Table 2). Without the need for cooperation to achieve mutual goals, ethnocentrism and distrust of outsiders will tend to predominate. Social identity theory likewise argues that once a social identity category becomes salient, differences between the in-group and the out-group are emphasized (Liu and Allen 1999: Table 1; McGarty et al. 1992; Oakes 1996).

It was noted earlier that some New Zealand archaeologists, while neglecting the association between chiefs and Maori fortifications, have rightly seen pa as important symbols of group identity (Barber 1996; Davidson 1987, 2001; Marshall 1987; Mihaljevic 1973; Sutton 1990). Pa were without question material embodiments of groups. They would have fostered within their inhabitants or occupants a sense of belonging to an in-group that was possibly in opposition to members of other groups. Then, too, fortifications made groups relatively self-sufficient. Good fences would encourage local populations not to subsume their own interests and identity for those of a larger, regional population. Only a very large, threatening, outside force was likely to dislodge groups from this localized group view. Pa *were thus more than just a physical barrier to integration; they would have likewise encouraged their builders to think locally more than regionally.*

SUMMARY AND DISCUSSION

The purpose of the above discussion was to illustrate the intertwined relationships among ecology, economy, warfare, sociopolitical integration, and fortifications in prehistoric and early historic New Zealand. Archaeological data from Hawke's Bay verify the long-standing model that ecological difficulties and population growth led to a concern with protecting key resources (but not just good garden land) starting about five hundred years ago. A concern with sociopolitical and economic processes also makes it clear that pa and polities were built around these high-quality resources as chiefs offered their followers protection from warfare and enhanced economic security. In Hawke's Bay, the most favorable economic base led to the initial development (or at least attempted development) of a large, regional chiefdom under the leadership of Rakaihikuroa. Pa warfare doomed this level of integration as the complex polity quickly

fragmented into smaller and more localized chiefdoms and independent local groups that could not be forcibly dislodged from their strongholds. Pa were utilized by leaders to build chiefdoms, but they also paradoxically ensured that attempts to consolidate large, regional polities were not likely to succeed.

Unfortunately, it is currently difficult to assess the scale of sociopolitical integration in other regions in New Zealand. Most likely, in other favorable areas of the North Island, such as Northland, the Auckland isthmus, and the Bay of Plenty (Davidson 1984; Prickett 1982), similar patterns would be found. Chiefdoms could amalgamate thousands of individuals, but in most locations the scale was much smaller.

Maori fortifications and the resources they protected were the principal means by which ambitious leaders built regional polities. The extent of integration, however, literally hit the wall. Pa prevented the level of sociopolitical complexity common in the high volcanic islands of Polynesia. The key was the inability to break the stalemate of fortifications. Leaders could extend physical and economic security, but not very far. Nor could chiefs hope to storm many holdout fortifications. They might take a few through surprise or stratagem, but not through the use of superior force.

Even the most complex political formations in New Zealand likely faced instability. Pa gave local populations the opportunity to maintain their independence. Maori chiefs, unlike their Hawaiian counterparts, were not just worried about their own rivals close to hand, or the ambitions of their enemies from other polities. They were hard pressed to forge fortified and relatively self-sufficient populations of potential followers into regional sociopolitical formations. Particular circumstances and personalities could build complex polities, but it is doubtful they could long survive. The result was continual cycling of the Maori chiefdoms from the sixteenth through the early nineteenth centuries.

It has also been argued here that the Maori case is important beyond Polynesia. Carnerio's model of the development of the chiefdom emphasizes military power in situations with social circumscription. Better-organized groups are seen as capable of conquering and assimilating other populations, leading to enhanced status and wealth for victorious leaders and populations to fill the lower ranks of society. This has been a highly influential line of thought. The strong walls of pa sites, however, would not permit such an easy regional conquest. Maori chiefs were able to build polities through consensus in the face of war, but not through forced assimilation.

Perhaps the Maori case is not unique. Prestate fortifications abound in other cultures around the world. Many commonalities exist with the southwestern United States, for example. Recent considerations of warfare and fortifications in this area also point to the difficulty of military conquest of rival populations (LeBlanc 1999; also see Rice and LeBlanc, eds. 2001). In addition, this work reminds us that offensive operations against fortifications could sometimes be successful as well, to which the many burnt sites and destroyed polities attest. It is hoped that archaeologists working in other areas will likewise reconsider the roles of fortifications in warfare and sociopolitical change.

With this end in mind, it is worth taking an additional look at Earle's model of the hillfort chiefdom. It is reasonable to consider whether the term "hillfort" is an appropriate one in the first place. In other words, must a fortification enjoy natural height and slope to be an effective defensive site? New Zealand is not the place to answer this, for the majority of pa do indeed take advantage of hills and ridges. This is not to say, however, that many flatland sites in the bends of rivers and on small islands were not also nearly impregnable. It is suggested that archaeologists working in other areas consider to what extent the model of hillforts might apply to other types of fortified sites. It may be that a fort does not have to be a hillfort to be an effective defensive stronghold.

Additional traits that are important for Maori chiefdoms and that may be appropriate for other cases include: (1) populations that are distributed in a series of smaller, confederated forts (not necessarily with the preponderance of population in the largest settlement as Earle posits); (2) a heavy reliance on stored food supplies; (3) marked boundaries between polities; (4) ideologies that stress localization, the in-group, and independence; (5) fortifications as symbols of both inhabitants and the leaders who build and control them; and (6) fortifications representing the largest economic projects or investments in a society.

CONCLUSION

This paper began with an excerpt from "Mending Wall" by Robert Frost. While it explores the nature of property boundaries and social barriers between people, it also captures the essence of the decision to build defensive walls. Fortifications are more than just a form of protection. They fundamentally alter the relationships among groups of people. Walls change social perceptions and give enhanced autonomy to their builders. As the Maori case shows, the perceived need for fortifications can lead to the development of regional polities, but once in place, they act to discourage stability and the growth of further sociopolitical complexity.

Chiefs with potential followers locked inside their fortifications were chiefs with very limited power. Fortifications could also make it very difficult for conquest-minded leaders to amalgamate groups through warfare. Moreover, it is wrong to view a fortification merely as a static defense. Pa or other types of forts were formidable threats in their own right, as they were potential staging points for highly destructive counterattacks. Their role in the evolution and devolution of complex society needs to be further considered throughout culture areas where they are common. In this volume on the collapse and transformation of complex society, the Maori case helps us to consider the role of warfare as an agent of change. Military force can be a strong source of power, but it is not limited to offense and conquest.

I would like to thank Jim Railey and Rick Reycraft for their invitation to be a part of the "I Fall to Pieces" symposium in 2000 as well as this volume. I also greatly appreciate their insightful suggestions on an earlier draft of this paper. I would also like to take this opportunity to once again thank the *tangata whenua* of Hawke's Bay (Heretaunga) for their generosity, encouragement, and financial support of my research on the pa of their ancestors. *Kia ora!* Finally, I would like to acknowledge the insights that I received from officers of the United States Army during my "tour of duty" as the cultural resource manager at the National Training Center at Fort Irwin. I especially thank the Cobra Team of OPS Group for their invitation to sit in on their seminars.

REFERENCES

Allen, Mark W.
1994 *Warfare and Economic Power in Simple Chiefdoms: The Development of Fortified Villages and Polities in Mid-Hawke's Bay, New Zealand.* Ph.D. dissertation, University of California, Los Angeles.
1996 Pathways to Economic Power in Maori Chiefdoms: Ecology and Warfare in Prehistoric Hawke's Bay. *Research in Economic Anthropology* 17:171–225.
2006 Transformations in Maori Warfare: Toa, Pa, and Pu. In *The Archaeology of Warfare: Prehistories of Raiding and Conquest,* edited by Elizabeth N. Arkush and Mark W. Allen, pp. 184–213. Gainesville: University Press of Florida.

Allen, Mark W., and Elizabeth N. Arkush
2006 Introduction: Archaeology and the Study of War. In *The Archaeology of Warfare: Prehistories of Raiding and Conquest,* edited by Elizabeth N. Arkush and Mark W. Allen, pp. 1–19. Gainesville: University Press of Florida.

Anderson, Atholl J.
1989 *Prodigious Birds: Moas and Moa-Hunting in Prehistoric New Zealand.* Cambridge: Cambridge University Press.

Anderson, Atholl J., and Matt McGlone
1992 Living on the Edge—Prehistoric Land and People in New Zealand. In *The Naïve Lands: Prehistory and Environmental Change in Australia and the South-West Pacific,* edited by John Dodson, pp. 199–241. Melbourne: Longman Cheshire.

Anderson, David G.
1994 *The Savannah River Chiefdoms: Political Change in the Late Prehistoric Southeast.* Tuscaloosa: University of Alabama Press.

Arens, William
1979 *The Man-Eating Myth: Anthropology and Anthropophagy.* Oxford: Oxford University Press.

Arkush, Elizabeth
2006 Collapse, Conflict, Conquest: The Transformation of Warfare in the Late Prehispanic Andean Highlands. In *The Archaeology of Warfare: Prehistories of Raiding and Conquest,* edited by Elizabeth N. Arkush and Mark W. Allen, pp. 286–335. Gainesville: University Press of Florida.

Ballara, Angela
1998 *Iwi: The Dynamics of Maori Tribal Organisation from c. 1769 to c. 1945.* Wellington, NZ: Victoria University Press.

Barber, Ian G.
1996 Loss, Change, and Monumental Landscaping: Towards a New Interpretation of the "Classic" Maaori Emergence. *Current Anthropology* 37:868–880.

Belich, James
1986 *The New Zealand Wars and the Victorian Interpretation of Racial Conflict.* Auckland: Auckland University Press.
1996 *Making Peoples: A History of the New Zealanders.* Auckland: Allen Lane, Penguin Press.

Bellwood, Peter
1978 *The Polynesians: Prehistory of an Island People.* New York: Thames and Hudson.

Best, Elsdon
1924 *The Maori,* 2 vols. Wellington: Harry Tombs.
1925 *Maori Agriculture.* New Zealand Dominion Museum Bulletin 9. Wellington.
1927 *The Pa Maori.* New Zealand Dominion Museum Bulletin 6. Wellington.

Billman, Brian R., Patricia M. Lambert, and Banks L. Leonard
2000 Cannibalism, Warfare, and Drought in the Mesa Verde Region during the Twelfth Century AD. *American Antiquity* 65:145–178.

Bowden, Ross
1979 Tapu and Mana: Ritual Authority and Political Power in Traditional Maori Society. *Journal of Pacific History* 14:50–61.
1984 Maori Cannibalism: An Interpretation. *Oceania* 55:81–99.

Bradley, Richard
1991 The Pattern of Change in British Prehistory. In *Chiefdoms: Power, Economy, and Ideology,* edited by Timothy K. Earle, pp. 44–70. New York: Cambridge University Press.

Buck, Peter
1949 *The Coming of the Maori,* second ed. Wellington: Whitcombe and Tombs.

Burrows, C. J., and D. E. Greenland
1979 An Analysis of the Evidence for Climatic Change in New Zealand in the Last Thousand Years: Evidence from Diverse Natural Phenomena and from Instrumental Records. *Journal of the Royal Society of New Zealand* 9:321–373.

Carneiro, Robert
1970 A Theory of the Origin of the State. *Science* 169:733–738.
1981 The Chiefdom as Precursor to the State. In *The Transition to Statehood in the New World,* edited by R. Cohen and E. Service, pp. 205–223. Cambridge: Cambridge University Press.
1990 Chiefdom-Level Warfare as Exemplified in Fiji and the Cauca Valley. In *The Anthropology of War,* edited by Jonathan Haas, pp. 190–211. New York: Cambridge University Press.
1991 The Nature of the Chiefdom as Revealed by Evidence

from the Cauca Valley of Colombia. In *Profiles in Cultural Evolution: Papers from a Conference in Honor of Elman R. Service,* edited by A. Terry Rambo and Kathleen Gillogly, pp. 167–190. Anthropological Papers of the Museum of Anthropology, University of Michigan No. 85.

Clausewitz, Carl von
1984 *On War,* edited and translated by Michael Howard and Peter Paret. Princeton: Princeton University Press.

Crosby, R. D.
1999 *The Musket Wars: A History of Inter-Iwi Conflict 1806–45.* Auckland: Reed.

Davidson, Janet
1984 *The Prehistory of New Zealand.* Auckland: Longman Paul.
1987 The Paa Maori Revisited. *Journal of the Polynesian Society* 96:7–26.
2001 Maori. In *Encyclopedia of Prehistory,* Vol. 3: East Asia and Oceania, edited by Peter N. Peregrine and Melvin Ember, pp. 222–242. New York: Kluwer Academic and Plenum.

Dongoske, Kurt E., Debra L. Martin, and T. J. Ferguson
2000 Critique on the Claim of Cannibalism at Cowboy Wash. *American Antiquity* 65:179–190.

Duff, Roger
1967 The Evolution of Maori Warfare. *New Zealand Archaeological Association Newsletter* 10:114–129.

Earle, Timothy K.
1978 *Economic and Social Organization of a Complex Chiefdom, the Halelea District, Kaua'i, Hawaii.* Museum of Anthropology, University of Michigan Anthropological Papers No. 63.
1991 The Evolution of Chiefdoms. In *Chiefdoms: Power, Economy, and Ideology,* edited by Timothy K. Earle, pp. 1–15. Cambridge: Cambridge University Press.
1997 *How Chiefs Come to Power: The Political Economy in Prehistory.* Stanford: Stanford University Press.

Ferguson, R. Brian
1984 Introduction: Studying War. In *Warfare, Culture, and Environment,* edited by R. Brian Ferguson, pp. 1–81. Orlando: Academic Press.

Feinman, Gary, and Jill Neitzel
1984 Too Many Types: An Overview of Sedentary Prestate Societies in the Americas. In *Advances in Archaeological Method and Theory,* Vol. 7, edited by Michael Schiffer, pp. 39–102. New York: Academic Press.

Firth, Raymond
1929 *Economics of the New Zealand Maori.* Wellington: A.R. Shearer, Government Printer.
1968 The Analysis of Mana: An Empirical Approach. In *Peoples and Cultures of the Pacific,* edited by Andrew P. Vayda, pp. 218–243. Garden City, NY: Natural History Press.

Fox, Aileen
1974 Prehistoric Maori Storage Pits: Problems in Interpretation. *Journal of the Polynesian Society* 83:141–154.
1976 *Prehistoric Fortifications in the North Island of New Zealand.* New Zealand Archaeological Association Monograph No. 6.

Goldman, Irving
1970 *Ancient Polynesian Society.* Chicago: University of Chicago Press.

Gorbey, K. C.
1970 Pa *Distribution in New Zealand.* M.A. thesis, Department of Anthropology, University of Auckland.

Green, Roger C.
1963 *A Review of the Prehistoric Sequence in the Auckland Province.* Publication of the Auckland Archaeological Society No. 1, and New Zealand Archaeological Society No. 2. Auckland: University of Auckland Bindery.

Groube, L. M.
1964 *Settlement Patterns in Prehistoric New Zealand.* M.A. thesis, Department of Anthropology, University of Auckland.

Handel, Michael
2001 *Masters of War: Classical Strategic Thought,* third ed. London: Frank Cass.

Haas, Jonathan
1990 Warfare and the Evolution of Tribal Polities in the Prehistoric Southwest. In *The Anthropology of War,* edited by Jonathan Haas, pp. 171–189. Cambridge: Cambridge University Press.

Irwin, Geoff
1985 *Land, Pa, and Polity.* New Zealand Archaeological Association Monograph No. 15.

Jennings, Jesse D., ed.
1979 *The Prehistory of Polynesia.* Cambridge, MA: Harvard University Press.

Jones, Kevin L.
1986 Polynesian Settlement and Horticulture in Two River Catchments of the Eastern North Island, New Zealand. *New Zealand Journal of Archaeology* 8:5–32.
1988 Horticulture and Settlement Chronology of the Waipoa River Catchment, East Coast, North Island, New Zealand. *New Zealand Journal of Archaeology* 10:19–51.

Keegan, John
1993 *A History of Warfare.* New York: Alfred A. Knopf.

Keegan, William F., and Jared M. Diamond
1987 Colonization of Islands by Humans: A Biogeographical Perspective. In *Advances in Archaeological Method and Theory,* Vol. 10, edited by Michael Schiffer, pp. 49–91. New York: Academic Press.

Keeley, Lawrence
1996 *War before Civilization.* New York: Oxford University Press.

2001 Giving War a Chance. In *Deadly Landscapes: Case Studies in Prehistoric Southwestern Warfare*, edited by Glen E. Rice and Steven A. LeBlanc, pp. 331–342. Salt Lake City: University of Utah Press.

Kern, Paul

1999 *Ancient Siege Warfare*. Bloomington: Indiana University Press.

Kirch, Patrick V.

1984 *The Evolution of the Polynesian Chiefdoms*. Cambridge: Cambridge University Press.

2000 *On the Road of the Winds: An Archaeological History of the Pacific Islands before European Contact*. Berkeley: University of California.

Larson, Lewis

1972 Functional Considerations of Warfare in the Southeast during the Mississippi Period. *American Antiquity* 37:383–392.

Leach, Helen M.

1984 *1,000 Years of Gardening in New Zealand*. Wellington: Reed.

LeBlanc, Steven A.

1999 *Prehistoric Warfare in the American Southwest*. Salt Lake City: University of Utah Press.

LeBlanc, Steven A., and Glen E. Rice

2001 Southwestern Warfare: The Value of Case Studies. In *Deadly Landscapes: Case Studies in Prehistoric Southwestern Warfare*, edited by Glen E. Rice and Steven A. LeBlanc, pp. 1–18. Salt Lake City: University of Utah Press.

Liu, James H., and Mark W. Allen

1999 Evolution of Political Complexity in Maori Hawke's Bay: Archaeological History and Its Challenge to Intergroup Theory in Psychology. *Group Dynamics: Theory, Research, and Practice* 3:64–80.

McGarty, C., J. C. Turner, M. A. Hogg, B. David, and M. S. Wetherell

1992 Group Polarization as Conformity to the Prototypical Group Member. *British Journal of Social Psychology* 31:1–20.

McGlone, Matt

1983 Polynesian Deforestation of New Zealand: A Preliminary Synthesis. *Archaeology in Oceania* 18:11–25.

McGlone, Matt, Atholl J. Anderson, and Richard N. Holdaway

1994 An Ecological Approach to the Polynesian Settlement of New Zealand. In *The Origins of the First New Zealanders*, Douglas G. Sutton, pp. 139–163. Auckland: University of Auckland Press.

Mao Tse-Tung

1963 *Selected Military Writings of Mao Tse-Tung*. Peking: Foreign Language Press.

Marshall, Yvonne

1987 *Antiquity, Form, and Function of Terracing at Pouerua Pa*. M.A. thesis, Anthropology, University of Auckland.

Mihaljevic, J. M.

1973 *The Prehistoric Polity in New Zealand: An Exercise in Theoretical Paleosociology*. M.A. thesis, Anthropology, University of Auckland.

Oakes, P. J.

1996 The Categorization Process: Cognition and the Group in the Social Psychology of Stereotyping. In *Social Groups and Identity: Developing the Legacy of Henri Taiffel*, edited by W. P. Robinson, pp. 95–119. Oxford: Butterworth-Heinemann.

Oliver, Douglas L.

1989 *Oceania: The Native Cultures of Australia and the Pacific Islands*, 2 vols. Honolulu: University of Hawaii Press.

Prickett, Nigel, ed.

1982 *The First Thousand Years: Regional Perspectives in New Zealand Archaeology*. New Zealand Archaeological Association Monograph No. 13.

Rice, Glen E.

2001 Warfare and Massing the Salt and Gila Basins. In *Deadly Landscapes: Case Studies in Prehistoric Southwestern Warfare*, edited by Glen E. Rice and Steven A. LeBlanc, pp. 289–329. Salt Lake City: University of Utah Press.

Rice, Glen E., and Steven A. LeBlanc, eds.

2001 *Deadly Landscapes: Case Studies in Prehistoric Southwestern Warfare*. Salt Lake City: University of Utah Press.

Rollett, Barry V.

1998 *Hanamiai: Prehistoric Colonization and Cultural Change in the Marquesas Islands (East Polynesia)*. Yale University Publications in Anthropology No. 84.

Sahlins, Marshall

1958 *Social Stratification in Polynesia*. Seattle: University of Washington Press.

Salmond, Anne

1991 *Two Worlds: First Meetings between Maori and Europeans, 1642–1772*. Auckland: Viking, Penguin.

Schwimmer, Eric

1990 The Maori Hapu: A Generative Model. *Journal of the Polynesian Society* 99:297–317.

Schmidt, Matthew

1996 The Commencement of Pa Construction in New Zealand Prehistory. *Journal of the Polynesian Society* 105:441–451.

Shawcross, Kathleen

1967 Fern-Root, and the Total Scheme of 18th Century Maori Food Production. *Journal of the Polynesian Society* 76:330–352.

Sherif, M., O. J. Harvey, B. J. White, W. R. Hood, and C. W. Sherif

1961 *The Robber's Cave Experiment*. Norman: University of Oklahoma Press.

Steinen, Karl

1992 Ambushes, Raids, and Palisades: Mississippian Warfare

in the Interior. *Southeastern Archaeology* 11:132–139.

Sun Tzu

1998 *The Illustrated Art of War,* translated by Thomas Cleary. Boston: Shambalah Publications.

Sutton, Douglas G.

1990 Organization and Ontology: The Origins and Operation of the Northern Maori Chiefdom, New Zealand. *Man* 25:667–692.

Turner, Christy G. II, and Jacqueline A. Turner

1999 *Man Corn: Cannibalism and Violence in the Prehistoric American Southwest.* Salt Lake City: University of Utah Press.

Turney-High, H.

1949 *Primitive War: Its Practice and Concepts.* Columbia: University of South Carolina Press. (1971 reprint edition)

U.S. Army

1993 FM 100-5: Operations. Washington, D.C.: Headquarters, Department of the Army.

van Creveld, Martin

1991 *The Transformation of War.* New York: Free Press.

van Meijl, Toon

1994 The Maori as Warrior: Ideological Implications of a Historical Image. In *European Imagery and Colonial History in the Pacific,* edited by Toon van Meijl and P. van der Grijp, pp. 49–63. Saarbrucken: Verlag fur Enwicklungspolitik Breitenbach.

1995 Maori Socio-Political Organization in Pre- and Protohistory: On the Evolution of Post-Colonial Constructs. *Oceania* 65:304–322.

Vayda, Andrew P.

1960 *Maori Warfare.* Wellington: Polynesian Society Monograph No. 2.

1976 *War in Ecological Perspective.* New York: Plenum Press.

Wilcox, David R., Gerald Robertson Jr., and J. Scott Wood

2001 Organized for War: The Perry Mesa Settlement System and Its Central Arizona Neighbors. In *Deadly Landscapes: Case Studies in Prehistoric Southwestern Warfare,* edited by Glen E. Rice and Steven A. LeBlanc, pp. 141–194. Salt Lake City: University of Utah Press.

Winiata, Maharaia

1956 Leadership in Pre-European Maori Society. *Journal of the Polynesian Society* 55:212–231.

6

Continuities and Discontinuities in Nasca Culture, Río Grande de Nazca, South Coastal Peru

Helaine Silverman

COLLAPSE IS A PLAINTIVE LEIT-MOTIF IN MODERN Western scholarship treating complex societies. What archaeologists call collapse is a post-facto perception of disorder in comparison to a more integrated and complex social, cultural, economic, and political configuration that existed at an earlier time. Archaeological and world historical literature is redolent with "rise and fall" and "origin and collapse" scenarios as a result of the attention that has been paid to great states and empires. The words "fall" and "collapse" connote cultural implosion, cultural extinction, and extreme loss of complexity. Negative cultural change may be sudden and rapid (the usual view of the Classic Maya collapse) or lengthy (as in the agonizing death throes of the Roman Empire). Regardless, the concept of catastrophic decline semantically precludes societal transformation and reorganization. Tainter (1988:193) writes that a "complex society that has collapsed is suddenly smaller, simpler . . . and less socially differentiated. Specialization decreases, . . . the flow of information drops, people trade and interact less. . . . Economic activity drops . . ., the arts . . . experience such a . . . decline that a dark age often ensues. Population levels tend to drop."

True cases of sudden ends to thriving sociopolitical enterprises are rare in the archaeological record. More common are the highly varying processes and interactions which bring about transition and restructuration in a society such that eventually the system is so altered as to be virtually unrecognizable when compared with an earlier configuration regarded as florescent or "civilizational." Renfrew (1978) uses the term "societal morphogenesis" for these transformations. He emphasizes that most cultural changes take place gradually and that perceived "sudden changes and divergences in social formations [may] not have sudden causes, but originate in a less obvious way through a conjunction of factors that are themselves changing without discontinuity" (Renfrew 1978:203–204).

Transformation occurs by means of multiple synchronic and asynchronic, gradual and rapid, lineal and nonlineal processes and events that differentially affect a society over time and result in a significant change in its complexity, organization, ideology, and behavior. Transformation typically involves changes in the distribution of power (the political structure), religion, the iconographic portrayal of beliefs, architectural forms and layout, and so forth.

Unlike "collapse" or "fall," the concept of societal morphogenesis or transformation does not have an inherent negative connotation because the evolved social formation may actually be as, or more, complex (though differently organized) than that which preceded. Also, what appears to be collapse from a truncated temporal perspective may be revealed, in the long run, to have been a short-lived stage in a longer process of transformations composed of fluctuating episodes and cycles of integration, disintegration, and reintegration.

Yoffee (1991a:44–45) has distinguished *political* collapse, which is the collapse of states, from *cultural* collapse, which is the collapse of a civilization. Jim A. Railey and Richard M. Reycraft, in their introduction to this volume, similarly contemplate the collapse of that complexity which is driven by elite political activities, while cultural traditions and fundamental belief systems may continue semi-intact. Cultural collapse precludes the possibility that another characteristic manifestation of the fallen suite of behaviors and beliefs will emerge from the decomposed predecessors. Cultural collapse must necessarily bring down the state or political apparatus of a civilization.

In the Central Andes the different names that archaeologists have given the sequential cultures (identified by pottery style) occupying a territory or region semantically suggest population replacements and major cultural discontinuities, even though this may not be the case (e.g., Mochica evolves into Chimu: see McClelland 1990 inter alia). Also, the connotation of collapse is built into the periodized Peruvian relative chronology, a scheme that is avowedly not based on cultural developmental stages (see Rowe 1962). The relative chronology recognizes a series of expansive cultural horizons and intermediate periods of regionalism. Willey (1991), in fact, has suggested that this punctuated alternation of pan-Andeanism and regional assertion was a critical dynamic in the origin and continuance of increasing cultural complexity in the Andes. But Kubler (1970), arguing a different point, has cautioned that the periods are illusory and that their analytical "hardening," as he so aptly calls it, leads us into a pernicious oversight of the existence of centers and peripheries of spatial action, and slow and fast temporal boundaries. It follows, then, that we must eschew "chronological essentialism," which "assumes that chronological units are real and discoverable" rather than analytically constructed (Ramenofsky 1998:75). This assertion, in turn, highlights the veracity of Kubler's (1970:140) methodological warning about process and historical contingency: "the composite nature of every imaginable class [i]s a bundle of durations, each having widely different systemic ages."

Why study collapse at all? The justification is stated succinctly by Yoffee (1991b:2): collapse studies "provide excellent points of entry into the social configuration of the societies that were doing the collapsing." In this chapter I consider the cultural developmental trajectory of Nasca, a constellation of "chiefdom" societies of varying size, temporality, complexity, and integration that emerged in archaeologically recognizable form on the south coast of Peru at the beginning of the first millenium AD. I document the changes in the Nasca social formation while it was recognizable as such, and I examine how and why Nasca evolved into other non-Nasca configurations through a series of archaeologically identifiable transformations.

In the presentation that follows I am influenced by Braudel's (1995) *longue durée,* which emphasizes continuity, restructuration, and transformation rather than great events. I am also influenced by Giddens's (1984) view of society as composed of a flow of social structure that is incarnated in the practices of persons. I modify Cowgill's (1991) and Yoffee's (1991a, 1991b) treatments of collapse to include complex *nonstate* social formations. And my discussion is informed by the concept of materiality, which, basically, argues that material objects play an active role in the construction of social life and in the production and reproduction of society and culture. Under this paradigm, the disappearance of key material features of social life is significant well beyond their trait-list function in defining a relative chronology or archaeological culture.

To anticipate my conclusions, I do not see a Nasca collapse so much as ongoing processes of cultural transformation and ethnogenesis on the south coast of Peru. By the end of the precolumbian period, few of the features that a thousand years earlier had defined Nasca as an archaeological culture and society still existed. In this chapter, I pick up the story with a fully emerged Early Nasca society in the Río Grande de Nazca drainage,[1] avoiding the problem of the Paracas-Nasca transition or Nasca emergence (see preliminary remarks in Silverman 1994).

THE EARLY NASCA APOGEE

In the first centuries of the first millennium AD, there was a dense Early Nasca occupation of the Río Grande de Nazca drainage (Figure 24). Hundreds of habitation sites are known (e.g., Browne 1992; Browne and Baraybar 1988; Schreiber 1999; Silverman 1993b, 2002). In addition, in the Nazca Valley proper, there arose a great ceremonial center, Cahuachi, whose earliest monumental constructions are contemporary with the earliest phase of the long Nasca pottery stylistic sequence (Orefici 1988; Silverman 1993a). During the Nasca 3 cultural apogee, more than forty semi-artificial pyramid mounds were simultaneously functioning at Cahuachi, possibly as the shrines of different groups that maintained the site through a pilgrimage system (Silverman 1990a, 1993a). Early Nasca volumetric constructions, at Cahuachi and elsewhere, were built with characteristic forms of adobes (Kroeber and Collier 1998: chap. 4) and construction fills (Silverman 1993a: chap. 6).

Lesser ceremonial centers composed of one or more platform mounds or terraced hillsides and sometimes associated with plazas and/or cemeteries also have been identified in some of the valleys of the Río Grande de Nazca drainage (Browne 1992; Browne and Baraybar 1988; Kroeber and Collier 1998; Reindel and Isla 1999; Schreiber 1999; Silverman 1993b, 2002). The Nasca also created sacred space by flattening hilltops and spurs (see, e.g., Silverman 1993b: Fig. 7) and clearing terrain at ground level, most famously on the 220 km^2 plain or pampa separating the Ingenio and Nazca valleys. There Nasca people traced immense geometrical forms, straight lines, and biomorphic figures identical to those painted on Nasca pottery (Kosok 1965; Reiche 1974 inter alia). This practice was not restricted to the pampa. The hillsides and erosional washes of the valleys surrounding the pampa also were marked with hundreds of trapezoids, quadrangles, spirals, zigzags, straight lines and combinations thereof (Reindel and Isla 1999; Silverman 1990b; Silverman and Browne 1991). Early Nasca and all subsequent geoglyphs were made by removal of surface rock to reveal a lighter-

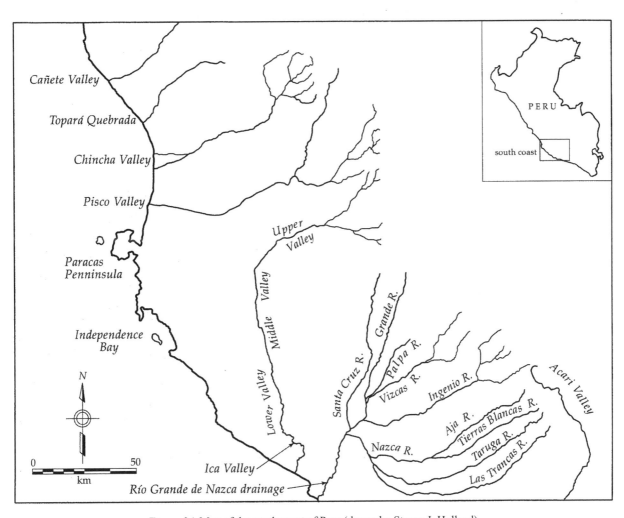

Figure 24. Map of the south coast of Peru (drawn by Steven J. Holland).

colored subsurface, with the removed rock being used to delineate the cleared area.

Early Nasca people participated in a complex religious cult, presumably integrated from Cahuachi (Silverman 1993a; Strong 1957). Religious practitioners and ritual participants dressed in imitation of the supernatural creatures of the Nasca pantheon (see, e.g., Bennett 1954: Figs. 58, 60). One of the key rituals appears to have been manipulation of decapitated human heads (see discussion in Silverman 1993a: chap. 15). These "trophy heads" and those belonging to full bodies often have frontal-occipital cranial deformation, a permanent marker of Nasca ethnic identity (Browne et al. 1993: Fig. 11).

Deities and myths were portrayed on slip-painted pottery of characteristic shapes such as double-spout-and-bridge bottles, cup bowls, drums, and panpipes. These pottery forms were used in Nasca ritual and ceremony and were widely available at habitation sites (Silverman 2002) and in burials (Carmichael 1988). Nasca pottery is iconographically elaborate and aesthetically exquisite in its manner of representation. It is regarded by most scholars as the hallmark of what can be called Nasca civilization. Its intricacy and ubiquity remain to be explained in terms of the craft system that produced it, and the relationship between the ideological system portrayed and the society that generated it.

Early Nasca was a regional society in the sense that its diagnostic material culture and behavior were exclusive within a relatively small area (the Ica Valley and the Río Grande de Nazca drainage). Foreign goods were uncommon within this heartland.[2] But Early Nasca people had significant contact with outside societies, though the mechanisms by which this was effected are not understood at present. Similarities in the style of pottery and textiles suggest that there was close interaction between Early Nasca people and those of the Pisco-Paracas region in Early Intermediate Period 1 (Nasca-Chongos) and Early Intermediate Period 3 (Nasca-Carmen) (Menzel 1971;

Peters 1991; Silverman 1997). In addition, there is said to have been strong influence in the Ica Valley from Pisco's Early Intermediate Period 2 Campana style (e.g., Massey 1992). Fancy Nasca 2 textiles from Cahuachi (Phipps 1989:269) and possibly Cabildo, in the middle Grande Valley (Sawyer 1997), have been compared to Paracas Necropolis materials. Actual Nasca 2 and, especially, Nasca 3 pots were acquired by inhabitants of the Acarí Valley to the south (Valdez 1998). Cross-knit looped textiles and a few Nasca pots linked Nasca people to others living further south along the coast, notably in the Ocoña, Camaná, and Sihuas region (see, especially, Disselhoff 1969) and as far south as Moquegua (Goldstein 2000).[3] Joerg Haeberli (personal communication 2000) suggests that cross-knit looping may have been invented on the far south coast and moved north, impacting Nasca textile art in Early Intermediate Period 1 especially; conversely, Nasca goods appear to have moved south in Early Intermediate Period 3.

THE BRIEF NASCA 4 COLLAPSE

Cahuachi ceased to function as a great civic-ceremonial and pilgrimage center after Nasca 3, as evidenced by the cessation of major construction and the rarity of Nasca 4 and later sherds on the site's surface and in excavated contexts (Rowe 1963; Silverman 1993a; Strong 1957). Thus far, only one construction at Cahuachi is known to date to Nasca 4, the Room of the Posts (Silverman 1993a:318, Figs. 13.40, 13.41). The cause of Cahuachi's demise is not understood, but Cahuachi was not alone. Other major sites occupied in Nasca 3 times declined, notably Los Molinos in the Palpa Valley (see Reindel and Isla 1999) and Site 165/Ventilla in the Ingenio Valley (Silverman 2002; see photograph of site in Silverman 1990b: Fig. 5). Browne (1992) identified so few Nasca 4 sites in Palpa that he legitimately questioned the temporal reality of the ceramic phase. Silverman's (1990b: Fig. 4) preliminary analysis of the Ingenio–middle Grande survey data similarly revealed a significant decrease in habitation sites in Nasca 4. Furthermore, fewer geoglyphs appear to have been in use during Nasca 4 than previously (Silverman 1990b:448). Nevertheless, there were Nasca 4 habitation sites; one thriving Nasca 4 community in Tierras Blancas, in the southern drainage, was excavated by Kevin Vaughn (1999). Still, in the absence of the strong role formerly played by Cahuachi, and lacking any great Nasca 4 site(s) in the Nazca drainage, we can speak of a "sociopolitical vacuum" at this time.

Silverman (1993a) has suggested that because Cahuachi did not evolve into a ceremonial city but

remained essentially an "empty" ritual center, Cahuachi was incapable of coping with increasing sociopolitical complexity and its associated tension. In contrast, Orefici (cited in *Life Magazine,* December 1999) has argued that a catastrophic earthquake and El Niño–precipitated mudslide wrecked Cahuachi and caused the decline of its cultural sphere ca. AD 350. On the other hand, Petersen (1980) claimed desertification as the proximal cause of the decline of Cahuachi and the Nasca 3 social formation. Clearly, much fieldwork remains to be conducted before the cause(s) of the recorded changes in settlement patterns can be firmly asserted.

Proulx (1968) argues that Nasca 4 was a brief phase in comparison with Nasca 3 and notes that the pottery style in the Ica and Nazca valleys diverged in shape and design, probably as a result of the demise of Cahuachi. Nevertheless, there was still significant iconographic continuity between the Nasca 3 and Nasca 4 phases in terms of the major supernatural and natural themes and overall "monumental" manner of representation, as well as vessel shapes and pottery technology (see Proulx 1968). Furthermore, in Nasca 4 an important new being was introduced in the ceramic iconography, the Horrible Bird (Proulx 1968:86). Clearly, the Nasca pottery style was still Nasca and was evolving, and its distribution at habitation sites suggests the continuing practice of localized rituals of the cosmological system represented on pottery, even in the absence of a florescent ceremonial center.

On the other hand, it is significant that cross-knit looped textiles appear to have been no longer made after Nasca 3, and embroidery declined greatly in frequency (Phipps 1989). Because of the amount of labor implicated in textile production and the conventionalized symbolic imagery depicted in these techniques, this change in textile style must have been related to the demise of Cahuachi as a place of organized cult activity.

The decline of Cahuachi may or may or may not have had an impact beyond the Río Grande de Nazca drainage. The local Early Intermediate Period 4 occupation of the Acarí Valley is not well established (see Valdez 1998). However, in contrast to previous opinion (Rowe 1963), some Nasca 4 pottery is present at two of the major sites in the valley. This reassessment has led Valdez (1998:119) to conclude that there was not a total collapse of the Acarí settlement pattern. The connection—or not—between changes in settlement pattern in Acarí and Nazca remains a subject for investigation.

Carmen society in the Pisco Valley is crossdated to Nasca 3–4 (Menzel 1971). Insofar as it is known, Carmen remained vigorous following the demise of Cahuachi. The role that Nasca people may have played in local Pisco society remains to be determined (Silverman 1997).

THE DIFFERENT CONFIGURATION OF COMPLEXITY IN NASCA 5

The apparent collapse of Nasca 4 society was resolved in Nasca 5 times (AD 526 ± 90: L-335E; see Rowe 1967: Table 1; Strong 1957: Table 4) through the interplay of endogenous and exogenous factors. In the sixth century AD, climatic conditions were unstable, with sequential droughts occurring throughout the Central Andes (Thompson et al. 1985). Probably in response to worsening aridity, a system of filtration galleries was created in the southern tributaries of the Río Grande de Nazca drainage in order to tap the supply of underground water (Silverman 1993a:327).[4] This new irrigation system was a significant subsistence-oriented technological advance. It enabled settlement in previously dry stretches in the southern drainage (Schreiber and Lancho Rojas 1995). The agricultural impact of the filtration galleries may have promoted population growth, and irrigation's organizational parameters could have contributed to the increasing differentiation of Nasca society.

Cahuachi was being used only as a locus of individual offerings and for burials placed between mounds, not on them as had been the apogee pattern (Silverman 1993a:318; Strong 1957). Even without Cahuachi, I would argue that Nasca society was as, or more, complex at this time as before, but differently organized. La Muña was a spectacular burial and civic-ceremonial site in the Palpa Valley (Reindel and Isla 1999). Smaller but significantly differentiated Nasca 5 burial sites also have been identified in the Ingenio Valley, notably at Site 81 (Silverman 1993b:114, Fig. 10). Site 165/Ventilla, in the Ingenio Valley, recovered from its Nasca 4 slump and grew to its greatest size; many smaller Nasca 5 habitation sites are known.

Actual trophy head-taking increased in Nasca 5 times (Browne et al. 1993; Silverman 1993a:221–226, 327), probably a prelude to the dramatic increase in militaristic themes on Nasca 6 pottery (Roark 1965:56). The preponderance of male victims (see Verano 1995: Table 1) suggests that battles provided the opportunity for obtaining trophy heads, though these could have been ritual battles. Decapitated heads were still being prepared in the traditional manner (see, e.g., Browne et al. 1993: Figs. 12, 13; Silverman 1993a: Figs. 15.1, 15.2) and exhibit typical Nasca cranial deformation (Browne et al. 1993: Fig. 11). However, the caching of actual Late

Nasca trophy heads (Browne et al. 1993: Fig. 10) and their iconographic display by human actors (chiefs and warriors: see de Lavalle 1986:136 top right, 167 bottom) contrasts with the Early Nasca situation in which real trophy heads were less frequent,[5] and iconographically they were usually associated with mythical beings and ritual performers (e.g., Bennett 1954: Figs. 58, 60; Proulx 1968: Plates 1, 3, 6). My sense is that Late Nasca males were deploying an individually enhancing actor/agency strategy in local settings rather than participating in a collective/communal representation of ritual and power, as had been the case at Cahuachi.

Nasca 5 society may have come into contact with or pressure from Wari, an expansive state that was forming in the adjacent highlands (see Silverman 1988). This proposition is precariously supported by a single Nasca 5 radiocarbon date (see above) and the published sixth century AD dates for Middle Horizon 1 in the Ayacucho Basin, and the coherent sequence formed by the majority of the published Middle Horizon dates (see, e.g., Isbell 1983: Table 1). This is also when Lima Interlocking designs from the central coast first appeared on Nasca pottery, suggesting a Nasca receptivity to foreign ideas.

I believe that the instability generated in the aftermath of Cahuachi's demise, the problems created by the sixth century AD droughts, the opportunities opened by the construction of the filtration galleries, and the challenges posed by Wari presence together contributed to the emergence of competitive "secular" elites; to increased social differentiation as manifested in burial patterns; to increased trophy head-taking; to settlement pattern changes; to the tripartite split in the Nasca 5 pottery style into the Conservative Monumental, Progressive Monumental, and Bizarre Innovation substyles (Blagg 1975); and to the subsequent iconographic shift to militaristic themes on pottery in Nasca 6, which likely reflected reality (Roark 1965).

Though different from the Early Nasca social formation, Nasca 5 society is still recognizably Nasca. I see evidence of dynamic experimentation along many parameters—social, political, economic, ideological. Various internal and external factors, events, and processes provided positive opportunities for innovation and personal advancement. At the same time, the changes also may have been perceived as destabilizing and disorienting. Foucault's (1972:191, 1973:312) notion of "epistemological breaks" appropriately describes the kinds of perceptual and conceptual shifts that took place rapidly in Nasca 5. Also of relevance is Jameson's concept of the "cultural dominant." "Radical breaks between periods do not generally involve complete changes of content but rather the restructuring of a certain number of elements already given: features that in an earlier period or system were subordinate now become dominant" (Jameson 1983:123). The importance of Jameson's dynamic formulation is the possibility it conceives of coexistence of features from different time periods at the same time but in a newly differing intensity and structural position. In this dialectic, time is subordinated to the embodied exercise of discourse and epistemology, forming a circle of engagement and closure. Foucault's epistemological breaks are Jameson's reprioritized cultural dominants.

THE WARI INTRUSION

Wari pottery and textiles are quite well known in the Río Grande de Nazca drainage (see, e.g., Menzel 1964). In the majority of cases, the Early Middle Horizon material comes from looted burials. There is also the great Wari pottery offering deposit at Pacheco in the Nazca Valley, which is dated by Menzel (1964) to Middle Horizon 1B. Kroeber (1944:29) ventured that "Pacheco [pottery] looks like something worked out where and when Nazca [Nasca] and Tiahuanaco [Wari] traditions were both active, with a vigorous local component added; and then the resultant high-grade style was transported into the Nazca valley." I think Pacheco represents Wari's attempt to establish itself in the drainage on ideologically bolstered terms; Pacheco was not an administrative site, but rather one at which important rituals were conducted (contra Schreiber 1999, who argues it is a failed Wari attempt at conquest). This could explain Pacheco's location near Cahuachi but Wari's reluctance or inability to locate its representatives on top of that once-great site.

Interestingly, few Early Middle Horizon habitation sites have been identified in the Río Grande de Nazca drainage (Browne 1992; Proulx 1999; Reindel and Isla 1999; Schreiber 1999; Silverman 1993b:118). Between ca. AD 550 and 750 (the time corresponding to the Early MH = MH 1A, 1B, 2A, 2B; see Isbell 1983: Table 1) people appear to have conducted activities at nondomestic sites and died but did not live there. Obviously, this is an improbable situation. The most logical explanation of the anomalous settlement pattern is that Wari intruded onto the south coast while Nasca society was still florescent, in other words, contemporary with the Nasca 5-6-7 ceramic phases and their associated habitation sites (see Silverman 1988, 1993b; Strong 1957:43; cf., e.g., Menzel 1977:52).[6] This reconstruction does not imply that there were many highlanders in the Río Grande de Nazca drainage, but they were archaeologically obvious by their distinctive material culture (pottery and textiles) and nondomestic architecture (tombs, civic sites, and other special-purpose sites, such as Pacheco). Site 459 in the Ingenio Valley (Figure 25) may be classifiable as a Wari site. Schreiber (1999) reports an "imperial Wari site" in Tierras Blancas at Pataraya. Several other candidates for Wari architectural status appear on early aerial photographs but were destroyed years before the current era of survey. At a few sites in the Ingenio–middle Grande valleys, a circumstantial case can be made for the coexistence of Late Nasca and Early Middle Horizon/Wari people on the basis of the surface association of Nasca and Wari pottery and proximity of Nasca and Wari architecture.[7]

In my reconstruction, Wari intruded into the drainage as drought conditions were being felt. Indeed, Wari's interest in the Río Grande de Nazca drainage may have been exploratory in response to the desiccating climate. Nasca people had devised the filtration galleries as a way to tap vitally needed subsurface water. Nasca settlements were flourishing. Perhaps Wari was initially seeking to establish long-distance alliances that might serve as a social safety net.

Also, Wari became interested in Nasca society just when Wari itself was coalescing as a great city and state. Perhaps Wari's emergent elites were seeking to enhance their prestige through contact with the brilliant Nasca society; various scholars see Nasca influence on Wari pottery (e.g., Knobloch 1983:284–285, 289–296, 304–308; Lumbreras 1974:152; Menzel 1964, 1977:52). Incipient Nasca elites may have welcomed the highlanders and possibly acquired their pottery and textiles as luxury goods to be socially/strategically deployed. The change in the nature of the Nasca 5 Harvester from an individual associated with plants to one who carries jagged staffs in Nasca 6 could represent a Nasca syncretism of Wari's frontal-face deity. Note, too, my previous suggestion that a tracing on the south wall of the Room of the Posts at Cahuachi is a simplified version of the rayed frontal face of the Wari staff deity/Gateway of the Sun deity at Tiwanaku (Silverman 1993a:181, Fig. 13.11). Since the Room of the Posts was entombed by Nasca 8/Loro people, that tracing cannot be more recent than Nasca 8/Loro and may be earlier.

I see the Nasca-Wari relationship as having stages and changing over time. In the Río Grande de Nazca drainage, I think there was a peaceful encounter in Nasca 5, heightening conflict in Nasca 6, and major reorganization of the local Nasca population in Nasca 7 that was provoked or organized by Wari. I argue the latter point because I

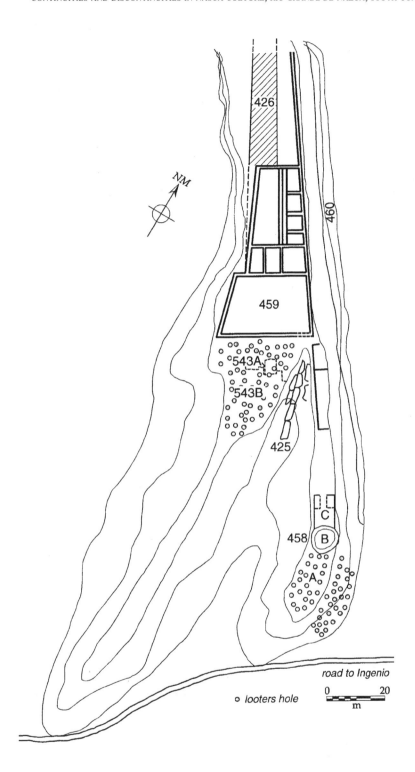

Figure 25. Sketch map of Site 459 (with surrounding sites)
in the Ingenio Valley (drawn by the author).

recorded very few Late Nasca habitation sites in Ingenio, Browne recorded few in Palpa, and Schreiber (1999) documented a virtual depopulation of the Nazca Valley in Late Nasca times. These dramatic shifts in settlement pattern suggest that the original relationship of benign Wari-Nasca mutual interest was short-lived.

Interestingly, several geoglyphs in the Ingenio Valley appear to have been used during the Early Middle Horizon, though all had been laid out earlier by Nasca people (see Silverman and Browne 1991: Table 1). Clarkson (1990) documents Middle Horizon sherds on lineal geoglyphs on and off the pampa; she believes, in fact, that the lineal geoglyphs postdate Nasca. The marking and making of sacred space by means of ground clearance is an important feature of ideological continuity of Nasca identity from earlier times, despite the upheaval caused by Wari.

COMPLEXITY, TENSIONS, AND INTERNATIONALIZATION IN LATE NASCA SOCIETY

The Late Nasca period was dynamic and exciting as well as unstable. Competitive Nasca males were jockeying for position in a new social reality they themselves were constructing. Wari offered these elites expanded opportunities for networking at the same time that Wari exacerbated societal tensions that were being manifested in increased trophy head-taking and increasing socioeconomic differentiation, as seen most notably at La Muña.

The dramatic and unequal breakup of the florescent Nasca 5 settlement pattern in Nasca 6 times resulted in significant intervalley differences and simultaneous conservative and innovative cultural manifestations. This situation strongly suggests varying local and individual/group responses to the unstable sociopolitical and climatic milieu.

Schreiber (1999: Fig. 11.8) recorded three "large towns," one each in the three southernmost tributaries of the drainage, and a handful of small and large villages. Browne (1992) observed a sharp decrease in settlement in Palpa between Nasca 6 and Nasca 7, and Reindel and Isla (1999) report no new settlements after Nasca 5. I found a progressively sharp decrease in settlement in the Ingenio–middle Grande valleys after Nasca 5. No archaeologist has reported a Late Nasca ceremonial center. Geoglyphs continued to be made or used, but probably no longer the biomorphs (concluded because the style of representation of the great figures is unproliferated; see below).

The Nasca pottery style was still recognizable as such, even though the dominant mode of iconographic representation was now proliferous (designs complicated by the attachment of multiple hooks and scrolls attached to abstracted bodies) rather than monumental (representational) as was the case in Early Nasca times. Proliferation also characterizes Late Nasca textiles, which, furthermore, were increasingly made by woven techniques rather than embroidery as had been done in Early Nasca times (Phipps 1989:298). On pottery, painted scenes of human warfare were common (e.g., Verano 1995: Fig. 11; de Lavalle 1986:167 bottom, 169 top, 174; Lothrop and Mahler 1957: Plate XIXf),[8] and trophy heads continued to be taken. Heads were still deformed in the classic form.

There was a significant attempt to represent the individual on Late Nasca pottery (cf. Roark 1965:56–57) and to mark elite status in such attributes as moustaches and goatees, insignia, elaborate headdresses, dress, feather cloaks, and earrings. This conspicuous ornamentation supports the argument that Nasca society had become significantly more differentiated, even though the landscape was balkanized.

There was interregional contact throughout the Central Andes at this time (Shady 1981, 1982, 1988). Nasca 7 people appear to have participated significantly in this exchange. Nasca 7 was the time of the greatest geographical distribution and influence of the Nasca ceramic style (see Kroeber 1944:29). Nasca 7 sherds are present in Pisco, Chincha, and Cañete to the north of Nazca (Kroeber 1937; Menzel 1971:126–128),[9] and in Acarí to the south (see Lothrop and Mahler 1957; Valdez 1989, 1990). Nasca 7 people also were in contact with their contemporaries in Ayacucho (Knobloch 1983; Kroeber 1944:29; Paulsen 1983). There was also Late Nasca contact with Late Lima people of the central coast (see Kroeber 1944: fn. 24; Patterson 1966). Evidence of Nasca 7 contact with Mochica people of the north coast is particularly strong (Proulx 1994), though perhaps it would be more correct to say that there is strong evidence of Mochica contact with Nasca 7 people since no Nasca material is known at Mochica sites, nor were there Nasca mariners, in contrast to the seaworthy Mochica. Unfortunately, archaeologists have no empirical data, at present, to show how and by whom interregional contact and exchange was organized and what the ramifications were in local Nasca society, although network and agency models (e.g., Blanton et al. 1996) will probably prove relevant.

THE END OF THE NASCA CULTURAL IDENTITY

Following the collapse of Cahuachi and the pilgrimage sphere it integrated, there was never again a single great

cultural center in the Río Grande de Nazca drainage. Yet, as we have seen, Nasca society reorganized, survived, and thrived for several centuries more. But at some point the Nasca people ceased to be Nasca. I argue that this occurred when the cosmology underwriting their rituals ceased to be expressed in coherent iconographic form on pottery, when pottery lost its vivid polychromy, when panpipes and double-spout-and-bridge bottles ceased being made, and when banded geometric designs appeared on new, heavy-walled forms. The so-called Nasca 8 phase marks the beginning of the end of the Nasca cultural identity (Silverman 1988).

Scholars have long recognized the striking difference between Nasca 8 pottery and that of the preceding Nasca phases (e.g., Gayton and Kroeber 1927:26–33; Strong 1957:40–41). Today Nasca 8 is frequently called Huaca del Loro (Strong 1957) or Loro to indicate just how different it is from Late Nasca (Carmichael 1988; Silverman 1988). Radiocarbon dates confirm the relative chronology and stylistic evaluation. Two radiocarbon dates with good contexts date Nasca 8/Loro to ca. AD 700–900 (L-335F, I-14,442: see Silverman 1993a: Table 3.1). This is consistent with the single published Nasca 7 date of AD 576–698 (Y-126: see Lothrop and Mahler 1957:47; Rowe 1967: Table 1) and the previously noted sixth century AD date for Nasca 5.

Highland presence in the drainage is notable at this time in the form of small, circular, fieldstone temples at Huaca del Loro (Paulsen 1983; compare to circular buildings at the site of Wari in Isbell et al. 1991: Figs. 3, 4, 6, 8, 17), Pacheco (Paulsen 1983: Fig. 1b), and Tres Palos II (Strong 1957:38–40, Table 1). The ritual deposit of broken Nasca 8/Loro pots in the Room of the Posts (see Silverman 1993a: Figs. 13.36, 13.39, Table 13.3)[10] was an act as outside Nasca cultural canons as the pottery that was left behind, yet reminiscent of Wari smashed pottery offerings (e.g., Anders 1990; Menzel 1964), though the Room of the Posts material can not be reconstituted into whole pots, unlike most of the Wari vessels. The ritual entombment of an Early Nasca temple is also outside Nasca canons as they are currently known. And, of course, the wood colonnade at Estaquería (see Kroeber 1944: Plate 10; Silverman 1993a:79; Strong 1957:34), which may have been constructed in very late Nasca/Nasca 8/Loro times, is a radically new concept in ceremonial architecture. Strong (1957: Table 1) also reports a smaller posted site at the appropriately named Tres Palos I, which probably dates to Nasca 8/Loro on the basis of its association with the dated Tres Palos II circular temple (field notes of William Duncan Strong curated in the Department of Anthropology at Columbia University).

Nasca 8/Loro burial patterns show significant changes from preceding Nasca phases. Most obvious is an increased frequency in multiple burials in Nasca 8/Loro times, even though they are still uncommon (Carmichael 1988:354). These multiple burials could have been influenced by the Middle Horizon practice of collective tombs (see, e.g., Reiss and Stubel 1880–1887; Pezzia 1969:127–128). A Nasca 8/Loro burial at Cahuachi (Ubbelohde-Doering 1958:82–84, Fig. 13) is similar to Wari burials in the lower Ica Valley (see Cook 1992:357) in terms of the deceased being seated on a coil—in the Nasca 8/Loro case made of a spiral basketry-like arrangement of vegetal material tied with cloth strips, in the Wari case made of worked cloth stuffed with raw cotton.

In contrast to the discontinuities I have indicated, there also appears to have been cultural continuity from earlier Nasca times, as seen in the taking of trophy heads. Ubbelohde-Doering's (1958:88–89) Morro-Grave 1 at Cahuachi contained nine trophy heads. The treatment of trophy heads may show ideological continuation of the fertility and regeneration ideology that has been argued to underwrite Nasca trophy heads (see, e.g., Silverman 1993a:222). Unfortunately, Ubbelohde-Doering does not indicate if the heads show typical Nasca cranial deformation. There is also a striking continuity in the presence of two planed, upright huarango posts in Ubbelohde-Doering's tomb and the planed huarango post among the eleven other ones in the earlier Room of the Posts at Cahuachi (Silverman 1993a: Fig. 13.2)

Schreiber's (1999) claim that Nasca people fled from the Nazca Valley south to Las Trancas to avoid Wari domination is plausible. Yet in Las Trancas they rapidly lost their Nasca identity. The Late Nasca style synthesized features of Wari pottery to become Nasca 8/Loro, a new yet epigonal style. The lateness of the Nasca 8/Loro absolute dates (no earlier than ca. AD 700) and the divergence of the Nasca 8/Loro style from Nasca strongly support the Wari having been in the Río Grande de Nazca drainage while Nasca pottery still had exquisite polychrome iconography—in other words, prior to Nasca 8/Loro.

RESTRUCTURATION OF THE DRAINAGE AFTER WARI

Thus far, no fieldwork has been conducted specifically on the period between the fall of Wari and the rise of the distinct Late Intermediate Period Poroma people. Therefore, interpretation rests largely on pottery style.

The sudden fall of the Wari Empire at the end of Middle Horizon 2B is manifested in the Río Grande de Nazca drainage by the end of the fancy Atarco pottery style with its Wari-related iconography (according to the generally accepted scenario; see Menzel 1964). The post-Wari Soisongo style of the Río Grande de Nazca drainage lacks mythical designs (see Menzel 1964). Lyon (1968:11) assessed the post-Wari situation in Ica and Nazca from the perspective of ceramic art as "an active rejection on the part of the previously subjected peoples of those symbols which they associated with their erstwhile [Wari] overlords." She argues that "with the withdrawal of the representatives of empire, there was a conscious effort made to change the decorative style." It is fascinating that the indigenous people of Ica and Nazca did not reach back in time to the pre-Wari Nasca style once they were free of Wari. This lack of Nasca archaism and revival strongly suggests that south coast society and its belief system had irrevocably changed and that the "old ways" were not remembered, understood, or appreciated. Here we would have the end of a civilization as Yoffee (1991a, 1991b) conceives it. And yet, Late Middle Horizon (post-Wari) pottery has been found on a handful of geoglyphs in the Ingenio–middle Grande region (Silverman and Browne 1991: Table 1), and Clarkson (1990: Fig. III.20) reports Middle Horizon 3-4 pottery on the geoglyph fields she surveyed, including the main pampa between the Ingenio and Nazca valleys. So some long-term cultural behavior endured, even if its meaning may have changed. Furthermore, a pattern of rows of Late Middle Horizon and Late Intermediate Period burials, sometimes placed within low-walled rectangular enclosures (see Units W, X in Silverman 1993a:78, Fig. 2.6), appears to continue a pattern of "Middle and Late Nazca tombs . . . run[ning] in somewhat lineal formation" (Strong 1957:32, possibly referring to Unit 12C at Cahuachi; see Silverman 1993a: Figs. 2.4, 5.16, 5.18).

Ubbelohde-Doering's (1958:90, 92) "cotton" graves in Las Trancas postdate Nasca 8/Loro. These burials also indicate patterns of continuity and discontinuity with earlier times. As in the Nasca 8/Loro grave at Cahuachi (Morro-Grave 1), the "cotton" mummies sit on a spiral-like basket. But these seats are different from the one in Morro-Grave 1. Also, there is a different, eastward orientation of the body. And heads are not deformed, whereas those of Nasca and Morro (Nasca 8/Loro) people were.[11]

COMPLEXITY WITHOUT CENTRALIZATION

There is no evidence to indicate that the Río Grande de Nazca drainage was politically centralized during the Late Intermediate Period (Menzel 1959). But this situation should not be read as a statement of cultural noncomplexity. To the contrary, the Late Intermediate Period settlement pattern was dense, and some Late Intermediate Period sites were quite large and agglutinated: for instance, Ciudad Perdida de Huayurí in the Santa Cruz Valley (Ojeda 1981: map) and the spectacular Cerro Colorado site at the junction of the Grande and Nazca rivers. The number, size, and nucleation of Late Intermediate Period sites, including many registered during my survey of the Ingenio and middle Grande valleys, suggest a large population at this time. At the same time, the protected location of sites such as Ciudad Perdida de Huayurí supports the notion of late prehispanic "warring tribes" as related and portrayed in Guaman Poma's (1980:60–61) "fourth age of the auca pacha runa." Perhaps defensive concerns reflect competition for scarce resources in the drainage.

Nevertheless, these same people engaged in significant interaction with other societies to judge from the quantity of fine Ica-Chincha trade wares among the indigenous Poroma style pottery (see Robinson 1957) on the surface of Late Intermediate Period habitation sites and looted cemeteries. Furthermore, there clearly were socioeconomic differences among this population as evidenced by ordinary and exceptional remains present at cemeteries.

Public space existed at many of the Late Intermediate Period sites in the Río Grande de Nazca drainage, but, until recently, ceremonial architecture per se was unreported. At a site in the Taruga Valley, Conlee (1999) has documented an area of civic-ceremonial architecture consisting of a plaza and small mound. Kauffmann Doig discovered a "Painted Temple" in Ingenio (see Kauffmann Doig and Chumpitaz 1993).[12]

Urton (1990:194–195) presents ethnohistoric evidence showing that there were two hereditary lines of curacas in the Río Grande de Nazca drainage in the late prehispanic period. The cacique principal came from the Nazca Valley and belonged to the Nasca or Nanasca family. The other cacique was from Ingenio, home of the Ylimanga line. Furthermore, Urton (1990:195, Fig. IV.13) reconstructs the existence of four parcialidades in addition to the two moieties straddling the pampa. These four groups were called Nasca, Cantad, Poromas, and Collao and were territorially manifested in the lower Nazca, upper Nazca/Tierras Blancas, Las Trancas, and Ingenio valleys, respectively. In turn, these parcialidades were composed of ayllus. Urton (1990:197) suggests that each river in the drainage had an upper and lower parcialidad, not just the ones named in the ethnohistoric source.

THE INKAS' IMPERIAL REORGANIZATION

According to the traditional chronology, the Inkas conquered the south coast of Peru in the second half of the fifteenth century (Menzel 1959). There is dramatic and uncontrovertible evidence of the Inkas in the various valleys of the south coast. In the Río Grande de Nazca drainage the Inkas established two administrative centers, one in the Nazca Valley at Paredones (see photo in Bridges 1991:49; excavations and clearing by the Instituto Nacional de Cultura have revealed imperial Inka stone masonry: see Herrera 1997) and the other in Ingenio at La Legua (Tambo de Collao; Figure 26). The Inka center in the Ica Valley may have been "Old Ica" (Menzel 1976). In Pisco, the Inkas established themselves at Lima La Vieja and Tambo Colorado; in Chincha, at La Centinela; and in Acarí they built a center at Tambo Viejo (Menzel 1959). Menzel (1959) argues convincingly that the Inkas tailored their rule and its physical manifestation to the circumstances of the late prehispanic societies of each valley. The flexibility of Inka statecraft has been well documented elsewhere (see, e.g., D'Altroy 1992).

I believe there is dramatic evidence of the actual act of Inka conquest in the Ingenio Valley. Site 207 is a large geoglyph field located at the base of the huge Late Intermediate Period Site 201 hillside settlement at La Legua, which controlled the west end of the constriction between the middle and lower Ingenio Valley. Remains of hundreds of Late Intermediate Period decorated pots, possibly broken in situ, were observed on the surface of the geoglyph field. Many of the geoglyphs are unfinished (see Silverman 1990b: Figs. 6, 17). I think that elaboration of the geoglyphs ceased suddenly as a result of the intrusion of the Inkas into the valley. The Inkas laid out their administrative center, Tambo de Collao, at the base of this hill, also facing west, and in front (north) of the geoglyph field.

Inka sherds were rarely observed on the surface of sites in the Ingenio Valley, but at Site 154 their presence is quite significant in terms of Inka administration of the valley. Here a small architectural unit (intrusive in an ordinary Late Intermediate Period habitation site) is built of angular and square fieldstones with a layout that is reminiscent of the tambos discussed by Hyslop (1984: chap. 19). A 1620 document states that an Inka road ran eastward through the Ingenio Valley to Lucanas in the highlands (Urton 1990:203).

Figure 26. Aerial photograph of Tambo de Collao in the Ingenio Valley
(courtesy of Adriana von Hagen).

THE TRANSFORMATION FROM INDIGENOUS TO COLONIAL STRUCTURES

There is evidence that as soon as the grip of the Inka state loosened, the local population of Nazca sought to revert to its local, indigenous identity and its traditional authorities. This is seen in the latest construction phase at Paredones, where typical Poroma mud brick walls overlie imperial Inka stone masonry.[13] But the native population of the Río Grande de Nazca drainage declined precipitously in the early colonial period, as it did elsewhere, through Spanish-introduced disease and direct and indirect aggression. The encomienda system, viceregal government, and Jesuit missionization all acted to alter the native economy, ecology, and sociopolitical organization. Indeed, during the first two decades of Spanish occupation the entire Ingenio Valley was sold to a single Spaniard (Urton 1990:195).

Nevertheless, for decades into the colonial period there still was a significant native presence in the Ica-Nazca region. Archival documents concerning the Jesuits make reference to various "caciques," and their names, as recorded in a series of wills bequeathing their land to the Church or contesting Jesuit claims, show native ancestry despite the deceased's conversion or birth into the Catholic faith (see Quijandría Alvarez 1961; Urton 1990:194–195). The Nanascas, for instance, survived into the 1640s. Today, only the archaeological ruins and an occasional legend have survived the centuries.

CONCLUSIONS

Collapse is a concept typically applied to the irreversible disintegration of large, interregional systems: the fall of the Roman Empire (Gibbon 1993) and the Classic Maya collapse (Culbert 1973) are the two most obvious examples. The Early Nasca world was a much smaller system of component societies ("chiefdoms" of varying size and complexity) that were integrated on the basis of shared ethnic identity, religion and ritual, economic orientation and strategy, and sociopolitics. Or, applying Stone's (1999:117) New Archaeology phrase to Early Nasca, the system was "held together by common information flow structures."

Unlike the paradigmatic cases of collapse, Nasca society was able to reorganize itself in situ after the brief Nasca 4 interlude and reemerge in recognizable Nasca form. Nasca 5 societies maintained essential cultural continuities with their Early Nasca predecessors, such as the Anthropomorphic Mythical Being, double-spout-and-

bridge bottles, panpipes, painted textiles, trophy heads, cranial deformation, and geoglyphs. But many new features developed in Nasca 5, such as the filtration galleries, individualizing and competitive ideologies manifested in multiple approaches to iconographic representation, and more elaborate burial patterns as at La Muña and Site 81. The very success of the morphogenesis of Nasca society suggests that, as important as Cahuachi had been, the component groups that had supported Cahuachi were actually stronger than the whole. Nasca 5 was a brilliant social formation in its own right.

Another apogee of settlement and cultural, sociopolitical, and economic complexity was reached in the context of factionalism in Nasca 7 times. The geographical extent of Nasca 7's interregional ties, seen most clearly in pottery, is a testament to the successful evolution of a vibrant, noncentralized arrangement of competitive, elite-run domains. The Late Nasca situation seems to parallel that described by Tammy Stone for the U.S. Southwest:

> because aggregates of individuals perceive and experiment with organizational structures in different ways depending on local conditions, very different structures may arise at different communities within a region and even within a single community. Additionally, as the experimentation results in organizational structures which have varying degrees of success, community stability (and therefore occupational length) is expected to be highly variable. Finally, the experimentation with new organizational structures results in rapid socio-cultural change and a dynamic period of shifting patterns of cooperation and competition (Stone 1999:112).

Ultimately, Wari (whether contemporary with Nasca 5-6-7 or later) was the force that ended the Nasca cultural tradition, even though Wari itself seems to have been influenced by Nasca, at least in terms of its elite pottery style. By the time the Wari Empire collapsed, ca. AD 800–900, Nasca culture—as it is known by its archaeological signatures—was no longer in existence, having evolved into the non-traditional Nasca 8/Loro society.

If Late Nasca and Wari were contemporary, then it is possible that Nasca elites were co-opted by Wari such that by the time Wari withdrew from the south coast, these elites not only had lost their power and influence, they were no longer culturally Nasca. And the common folk did not recall the way things were prior to Wari. I think

Wari irreparably severed the connection with the past on the south coast. But Wari did not break south coast society. Local communities and some traditions continued to function throughout most of the prehispanic period, and the Late Intermediate Period appears to have been a time of unprecedented population size and density and wealth. The Nazca region seems to have been resilient precisely on the basis of its agricultural villages. Arguably, the greatest expression of this local level of cultural assertion and permanence was the geoglyph phenomenon, which Urton (1990) and I (Silverman 1990a, 1990b) have interpreted as the physical manifestation of Andean social practice and social organization.

In their introduction to the inaugural issue of the *Journal of Material Culture,* Miller and Tilley (1996:9) emphasize that

> materiality is something that is . . . often present as a sign of other people's agency and not one's own. Most often, as in the landscape and buildings that surround us, the agents so signified are historical, representing the accrued labour of generations. . . . we inherit . . . the material environment of agricultural field systems, buildings and boundaries [,] . . . also our specific taxonomies and ways of interacting with that environment [, and] the way religious traditions in our area have conceptualized over millennia the gross world of material form.

This approach to the material legacy of the past is especially appropriate to discussions of the collapse of complex cultural systems for it highlights material culture not just as identificatory markers useful to archaeologists, but also as active components of systems of meanings that underwrote the social life of the civilizations that are the subject of this volume. In this paper I have argued that the abandonment of Cahuachi as a cult center of organized pilgrimage, while creating and reflecting conditions of significant change in Early Nasca social formation, nevertheless did not inhibit the continuing development of Nasca culture and society. Transformation or morphogenesis of fundamental material aspects of Nasca culture and society occurred over the following centuries such that Nasca society continued to produce and reproduce itself as Nasca. But, ca. AD 700–900, in that period of time referred to as Nasca 8/Loro, profound cultural change occurred in Nasca society, possibly the result of an interrelated suite of events (climate change, construction of filtration galleries, intrusion of Wari, increased tension in Nasca society, greater frequency of trophy head-taking and a change in its locus of signification and manipulation to the overtly human sphere, increasing socioeconomic differentiation among the population, etc.), such that most material forms of Nasca culture disappeared or were so altered as to no longer produce and reproduce society as Nasca. Although the immediately post-Wari period is not well understood in the Río Grande de Nazca drainage, settlement pattern analysis shows that the Late Intermediate Period was a time of abundant habitation sites whose inhabitants shared a material culture of pottery and textile styles, burial practices, and particular foreign goods. By processes not yet documented, there occurred an ethnogenesis over the course of the Middle Horizon such that the succeeding late prehispanic populations appear to have made no connection to the local pre-Wari past other than in their continuing elaboration of geometric and lineal geoglyphs and their use of Cahuachi and other Nasca sites as appropriate loci of burials. The *long durée* approach I have taken to the Río Grande de Nazca drainage has permitted recognition of nuanced qualities of positive (civilization, transformation) and negative (collapse, decline, decrease in complexity) culture change, enabling us to recognize ancient assertions of hegemony and counter-hegemony, domination and resistance, and agency and practice.

NOTES

1. As in previous publications, here, too, I maintain an orthographical distinction between Nasca for the archaeological culture of the Early Intermediate Period and Nazca for the geographical region. I persist in my assertion that this convention avoids ambiguity. This chapter was completed in 2002 and has not been updated since original submission.

2. Of course, obsidian (see Burger and Glascock 2000) and *Spondylus* were acquired from outside. Tropical forest wood (Silverman 1993a:167), monkeys (assumed on the basis of their iconographic representation), colored bird feathers and even birds (Orefici 1993: color figure 31) are also known.

3. I suspect strongly that Goldstein's (2000) report of Nasca pottery and textiles in Moquegua is a case of down-the-line trade from valleys of the far south coast which are located north of Moquegua, rather than constituting evidence of a direct contact between Moquegua and Nazca. Proulx (2000) and Goldstein (2000) argue that Nasca goods were manipulated as

status or prestige items by elite members of local communities of the far south coast.

4. I accept the Schreiber and Lancho Rojas (1995) dating of the inception of the filtration gallery system to Nasca 5 and I reject the contention by Barnes and Fleming (1991) that the filtration galleries are a Spanish colonial introduction.

5. The Feature 24 trophy head from Cahuachi postdates Nasca 3 (cf. DeLeonardis 2000: Table 2). The five trophy heads at Tambo Viejo (see DeLeonardis 2000: Table 2) are of debateable Nasca identity in light of Valdez's (1998) contention that there is no Nasca 3 occupation of the Acarí Valley but, rather, contact of local Acarí people with Cahuachi.

6. I note Gayton and Kroeber's (1927:30–31; see also Kroeber 1944:30–31) reasonable argument that—notwithstanding the somewhat conflated temporal placement of the Tiahuanaco, Epigonal, and Ica styles—"the non-Nazca stylistic traits in the Y material are more easily interpreted as relatively late than early. Tiahuanaco, Epigonal and Ica—the foreign styles chiefly represented in Y—have always been considered by Uhle, Tello, Means and others as later than Nazca. The situation calls for no special comment if it is assumed that the influence of these foreign styles began to invade the Nazca district after the typical native style A-X-B had begun to disintegrate. The opposite assumption would involve an explanation of why the extraneous influences first reached the Nazca area, then failed to affect it while a local Nazca style was developing, but subsequently replaced it." Tello's (1942) "Chanca" is in part highly proliferous Nasca 7 (e.g., Tello 1942: Plate 19 bottom), part Nasca 8/Wari (Tello 1942: Plate 19 top), and part Chakipampa and other Wari styles (Kroeber 1944: pl. 39).

7. McEwan (1996:181, Fig. 12) reports the excavated co-occurrence of a Nasca 6 bowl (large fragment) with Cajamarca style sherds in a midden at the great Wari site of Pikillacta near Cuzco. Gordon McEwan (personal communication, 2000) has an uncalibrated date of 1350 ± 60 BP for that midden. All of his dates suggest that construction of the site of Pikillacta began around AD 600. Cajamarca sherds are associated with Moche V pottery at San José de Moro in the Jequetepeque Valley on the north coast (Donnan and Castillo 1992). The tomb containing this association is dated to "sometime after A.D. 550" (Donnan and Castillo 1992:42). This dating strongly suppports the similar date for Nasca 6-Cajamarca-Wari at Pikillacta, thereby supporting my argument of contemporaneity between Nasca 5-6-7 and Wari.

8. Nevertheless, the hard evidence for Late Nasca warfare appears more iconographic than real because Late Nasca habitation sites are not located strategically, nor is defensive/offensive architecture described in the published literature.

Furthermore, despite the prevalence and increase of actual Nasca trophy heads in Nasca 5 and later times, few skulls show evidence of violent head injuries, although, obviously, death could result from injuries to other parts of the body (see de Lavalle 1986:174).

9. Kroeber (1944: fn. 24) indicates that Tello found Nazca B sherds at Huaca Malena in the Asia Valley, north of Cañete.

10. Recall that whole pots also were left in the Room of the Posts (Silverman 1993a: Figs. 13.12–13.35).

11. But bear in mind that not all Nasca people had deformed skulls. We also must be careful about the bias of a small sample.

12. The temple was uncovered through looting; it had been deeply buried when the area was surveyed by my team and, therefore, was not visible. I am dating the temple to the post-Wari period on the basis of the iconography of the painted images on the interior temple walls (see Kauffmann Doig and Chumpitaz 1993: Figs. 6, 10b, 14, 15) and the fact that the building form and style are thus far unknown for previous cultures.

13. Similarly, Menzel (1960) observed that the local Ica population reacted negatively to the Inka occupation as manifested by their collection and, sometimes, imitation of Epigonal (MH 4) and Chulpaca (early LIP = LIP 1–5) pottery. This antiquarianism (representing 6% of the pottery found in later LIP gravelots) revived stylistic elements of the Wari intruders, a time not in living memory. Immediately upon the end of the Inka domination there was an outright nativistic reaction. The Iqueños reverted "wholesale . . . to the local style which immediately preceded the relatively brief Inca occupation period. . . . No vessel found is free from its stylistic effects. . . . This revival coincides with an almost complete loss of features of Inca origin" (Menzel 1960:597). In language anticipating the current domination-and-resistance paradigm in archaeology (e.g., Pauketat 1998; Pauketat and Emerson 1999), Menzel (1960:599–600) observed, "It was unquestionably a reaction to the Inca occupation based on frustration rather than extreme hardship. The primary point of sensitivity at Ica involved local pride in prestige based on pottery artistry of some two to three hundred years' standing. Ica prestige did not diminish in this respect under the Inca, but it became second to foreign prestige wares, such as Inca and North Coast pottery, and a symbol of Inca domination. It is thus not the loss of prestige but rather the alteration of its symbolic associations and status which caused the reaction at Ica. It is no accident that the nativistic reaction manifested itself so emphatically in pottery, since pottery was a major symbol of local pride and independence in pre-Inca times."

REFERENCES CITED

Anders, Martha B.
1990 Maymi: Un Sitio del Horizonte Medio en el Valle de Pisco. *Gaceta Arqueológica Andina* 17:27–39.

Barnes, Monica, and David Fleming
1991 Filtration-Gallery Irrigation in the Spanish New World. *Latin American Antiquity* 2:48–68.

Bennett, Wendell C.
1954 *Ancient Arts of the Andes.* New York: Museum of Modern Art.

Blagg, Mary Margaret
1975 *The Bizarre Innovation in Nazca.* Unpublished M.A. thesis, Department of Art History, University of Texas at Austin.

Blanton, Richard E., Gary M. Feinman, Stephen A. Kowalewski, and Peter N. Peregrine
1996 A Dual-Processual Theory for the Evolution of Mesoamerican Civilization. *Current Anthropology* 37:1–14.

Braudel, Fernand
1995 *A History of Civilizations.* New York: Penguin.

Bridges, Marilyn
1991 *Planet Peru: An Aerial Journey through a Timeless Land.* New York: Aperture.

Browne, David M.
1992 Further Archaeological Reconnaissance in the Province of Palpa, Department of Ica, Peru. In *Ancient America: Contributions to New World Archaeology,* edited by Nicholas J. Saunders, pp. 77–116. Oxbow Monograph 24. Oxford.

Browne, David M., and José Pablo Baraybar
1988 An Archaeological Reconnaissance in the Province of Palpa, Department of Ica, Peru. In *Recent Studies in Pre-Columbian Archaeology,* edited by Nicholas J. Saunders and Olivier de Montmollin, pp. 299–325. BAR International Series 421. Oxford.

Browne, David, Helaine Silverman, and Rubén García
1993 A Cache of 48 Trophy Heads from Cerro Carapo, Peru. *Latin American Antiquity* 4:359–382.

Burger, Richard L., and Michael Glascock
2000 Locating the Quispisisa Obsidian Source in the Department of Ayacucho, Peru. *Latin American Antiquity* 11:258–268.

Carmichael, Patrick
1988 *Nasca Mortuary Customs: Death and Ancient Society on the South Coast of Peru.* Unpublished Ph.D. dissertation, University of Calgary.

Clarkson, Persis B.
1990 The Archaeology of the Nazca Pampa: Environmental and Cultural Parameters. In *The Lines of Nazca,* edited by Anthony F. Aveni, pp. 117–172. Philadelphia: American Philosophical Society.

Conlee, Christina
1999 Sociopolitical Complexity in the Late Intermediate Period in Nasca: New Evidence from the Site of Pajonal Alto. Paper presented at the 64th Annual Meeting of the Society for American Archaeology, Chicago.

Cook, Anita
1992 The Stone Ancestors: Idioms of Imperial Attire and Rank among Huari Figurines. *Latin American Antiquity* 3:341–364.

1994 *Wari y Tiwanaku: Entre el estilo y la imagen.* Lima: Fondo Editorial, Pontificia Universidad Católica del Perú.

1999 Asentamientos paracas en el valle bajo de Ica, Perú. *Gaceta Arqueológica Andina* 25:61–90.

Cowgill, George L.
1991 Onward and Upward with Collapse. In *The Collapse of Ancient States and Civilizations,* edited by Norman Yoffee and George L. Cowgill, pp. 244–276. Tucson: University of Arizona Press.

Culbert, T. Patrick, ed.
1973 *The Classic Maya Collapse.* Albuquerque: University of New Mexico Press.

D'Altroy, Terence N.
1992 *Provincial Power in the Inka Empire.* Washington, DC: Smithsonian Institution Press.

de Lavalle, José Antonio
1986 *Nazca.* Colección Arte y Tesoros del Perú. Lima: Banco de Crédito del Perú.

DeLeonardis, Lisa
2000 The Body Context: Interpreting Early Nasca Decapitated Burials. *Latin American Antiquity* 11:363–386.

Disselhoff, Hans
1969 Früh-Nazca im äußersten Süden Peru, Provincia de Camaná (Dep. Arequipa). *Verhandlungen des XXXVIII Internationalen Amerikanisten Kongress* 1:385–391.

Donnan, Christopher, and Luis Jaime Castillo
1992 Finding the Tomb of a Moche Priestess. *Archaeology* 45(6):38–42.

Foucault, Michel
1972 *The Archaeology of Knowledge.* New York: Harper Colophon.

1973 *The Order of Things: An Archaeology of the Human Sciences.* New York: Random House.

Gayton, Anna H., and A. L. Kroeber
1927 The Uhle Pottery Collections from Nazca. *University of California Publications in American Archaeology and Ethnology* 24(1):1–46.

Gibbon, Edward
1993 *The Decline and Fall of the Roman Empire.* New York: Knopf.

Giddens, Anthony
1984 *The Constitution of Society: Outline of a Theory of*

Structuration. Berkeley: University of California Press.

Goldstein, Paul

2000 Exotic Goods and Everyday Chiefs: Long-Distance Exchange and Indigenous Sociopolitical Development in the South-Central Andes. *Latin American Antiquity* 11:335–361.

Guaman Poma de Ayala, Felipe

1980 *El Primer Nueva Corónica y Buen Gobierno.* Critical edition by John V. Murra and Rolena Adorno. Quechua translations and analysis by Jorge L. Urioste. Mexico City: Siglo Veintiuno.

Herrera, Fernando

1997 Trabajos preliminares en Paredones en el valle de Nazca. *Tawantinsuyo* 3:119–126.

Hyslop, John

1984 *The Inka Road System.* New York: Academic Press.

Isbell, William H.

1983 Shared Ideology and Parallel Political Development: Huari and Tiwanaku. In *Investigations of the Andean Past,* edited by Daniel H. Sandweiss, pp. 186–208. Ithaca, NY: Latin American Studies Program, Cornell University.

Isbell, William H., Christine Brewster-Wray, and Lynda E. Spickard

1991 Architecture and Spatial Organization at Huari. In *Huari Administrative Structure: Prehistoric Monumental Architecture and State Government,* edited by William H. Isbell and Gordon McEwan, pp. 19–53. Washington, DC: Dumbarton Oaks.

Jameson, Fredric

1983 Postmodernism and Consumer Society. In *Postmodernism, or the Cultural Logic of Late Capitalism,* by Fredric Jameson. Durham: Duke University Press.

Kauffmann Doig, Federico, and Evaristo Chumpitaz

1993 Exploración del Templo Pintado, de El Ingenio, Nasca (Perú). *Baessler-Archiv. Beiträge zur Völkerkunde* neue folge band XLI:39–72. Berlin.

Knobloch, Patricia Jean

1983 *A Study of the Andean Huari Ceramics from the Early Intermediate Period to the Middle Horizon Epoch 1.* Unpublished Ph.D. dissertation, Department of Anthropology, SUNY-Binghamton.

Kosok, Paul

1965 *Life, Land and Water in Ancient Peru.* Brooklyn: Long Island University Press.

Kroeber, Alfred Louis

1937 *Archaeological Explorations in Peru, Part IV, Cañete Valley.* Anthropology Memoirs II(4). Chicago: Field Museum of Natural History.

1944 *Peruvian Archaeology in 1942.* Viking Fund Publications in Anthropology 4.

Kroeber, Alfred L., and Donald Collier

1998 *The Archaeology and Pottery of Nazca, Peru: Alfred*

L. Kroeber's 1926 Expedition. Walnut Creek, CA: Altamira.

Kubler, George

1970 Period, Style and Meaning in Ancient American Art. *New Literary History* 1(2):127–144.

Lothrop, S. K., and Joy Mahler

1957 *Late Nazca Burials in Chaviña, Peru.* Papers of the Peabody Museum of Archaeology and Ethnology 50(2). Cambridge: Harvard University.

Lumbreras, Luis G.

1974 *The Peoples and Cultures of Ancient Peru.* Washington DC: Smithsonian Institution.

Lyon, Patricia

1968 A Redefinition of the Pinilla Style. *Ñawpa Pacha* 6:7–14.

Massey, Sarah A.

1992 Investigaciones arqueológicas en el valle alto de Ica: Período Intermedio Temprano 1 y 2. In *Estudios de Arqueología Peruana,* edited by Duccio Bonavia, pp. 215–235. Lima: FOLMCIENCIAS.

McClelland, Donna

1990 A Maritime Passage from Moche to Chimu. In *The Northern Dynasties: Kinship and Statecraft in Chimor,* edited by Michael E. Moseley and Alana Cordy-Collins, pp. 75–106. Washington, DC: Dumbarton Oaks.

McEwan, Gordon F.

1996 Archaeological Investigations at Pikilaacta, a Wari Site in Peru. *Journal of Field Archaeology* 23:169–186.

Menzel, Dorothy

1959 The Inca Conquest of the South Coast of Peru. *Southwestern Journal of Anthropology* 15:125–142.

1960 Archaism and Revival on the South Coast of Peru. In *Men and Cultures: Selected Papers of the Fifth International Congress of Anthropological and Ethnological Sciences,* edited by Anthony F. C. Wallace, pp. 596-600. Philadelphia: University of Pennsylvania Press.

1964 Style and Time in the Middle Horizon. *Ñawpa Pacha* 2:1–105.

1971 *Estudios arqueológicos en los valles de Ica, Pisco, Chincha y Cañete.* Arqueología y Sociedad 6. Lima: Universidad Nacional Mayor de San Marcos.

1976 *Pottery, Style and Society in Ancient Peru: Art as a Mirror of History in the Ica Valley, 1350–1570.* Berkeley: University of California Press.

1977 *The Archaeology of Ancient Peru and the Work of Max Uhle.* Berkeley: R. H. Lowie Museum of Anthropology, University of California.

Miller, Daniel, and Christopher Tilley

1996 Editorial. *Journal of Material Culture* 1(1):5–14.

Ojeda, Bernardino

1981 La ciudad perdida de Huayurí. *Boletín de Lima* 16–17–18:78–82.

Orefici, Giuseppe

1988 Una expresión de arquitectura monumental Paracas-

Nasca: "el templo de escalonado de Cahuachi." In *Atti Convegno Internazionale Archeologia, Scienza e Societá nell'America Precolombiana,* pp. 191–201. Brescia: Centro Italiano Studi e Ricerche Archeologiche Precolombiane.

1993 *Nasca: Arte e Societá del Popolo dei Geoglifi.* Milan: Jaca Book.

Patterson, Thomas C.

1966 *Pattern and Process in the Early Intermediate Period Pottery of the Central Coast of Peru.* University of California Publications in Anthropology 3. Berkeley.

Pauketat, Timothy R.

1998 Refiguring the Archaeology of Greater Cahokia. *Journal of Archaeological Research* 6:45–89.

Pauketat, Timothy R., and Thomas E. Emerson

1999 Representations of Hegemony as Community at Cahokia. In *Material Symbols: Culture and Economy in Prehistory,* edited by John E. Robb, pp. 302–317. Center for Archaeological Investigations, Occasional Paper No. 26. Carbondale: Southern Illinois University.

Paulsen, Allison C.

1983 Huaca del Loro Revisited: The Nasca-Huarpa Connection. In *Investigations of the Andean Past,* edited by Daniel H. Sandweiss, pp. 98–121. Ithaca: Latin American Studies Program, Cornell University.

Peters, Ann

1991 Ecology and Society in Embroidered Images from the Paracas Necrópolis. In *Paracas Art and Architecture: Object and Context in South Coastal Peru,* edited by Anne Paul, pp. 240–314. Iowa City: University of Iowa Press.

Petersen, Georg

1980 *Evolución y Desaparición de las Altas Culturas Paracas-Cahuachi (Nasca).* Lima.

Pezzia, Alejandro

1969 *Guía al Mapa Arqueológico-Pictográfico del Departamento de Ica.* Lima: Editorial Italperu.

Phipps, Elena

1989 *Cahuachi Textiles in the W. D. Strong Collection: Cultural Transition in the Nasca Valley, Peru.* Unpublished Ph.D. dissertation, Department of Art History, Columbia University.

Proulx, Donald

1968 *Local Differences and Time Differences in Nasca Pottery.* University of California Publications in Anthropology 5. Berkeley.

1994 Stylistic Variation in Proliferous Nasca Pottery. *Andean Past* 4:91–107.

1999 Settlement Patterns and Society in South Coastal Peru. Report to the H. John Heinz III Charitable Fund.

2000 An Analysis of Nasca Pottery from the Department of Arequipa, Peru. Paper presented at the 19th Annual Northeast Conference on Andean Archaeology and Ethnohistory, Dartmouth College.

Quijandría Alvarez, Cornelio

1961 *Orígen y Fundación del Colegio e Iglesia de San Luis Gonzaga de los Jesuítas de Ica.* Ica: Tip. Cultura.

Ramenofsky, Ann F.

1998 The Illusion of Time. In *Unit Issues in Archaeology: Measuring Time, Space and Material,* edited by Ann F. Ramenofsky and Anastasia Steffen, pp. 74–84. Salt Lake City: University of Utah Press.

Reiche, Maria

1974 *Peruvian Ground Drawings.* Munich: Kunstraum München E.V.

Reindel, Markus, and Johny Isla

1999 Das Palpa-Tal: Ein Archiv der Vorgeschichte Perus. In *Nasca: Geheimnisvolle Zeichen im Alten Peru,* edited by Judith Rickenbach, pp. 177–198. Museum Rietberg Zürich.

Reiss, Wilhelm, and Alphons Stübel

1880–1887 *Peruvian Antiquities. The Necropolis of Ancón in Peru. A Series of Illustrations of the Civilisation and Industry of the Empire of the Incas. Being the Results of Excavations by W. Reiss and A. Stübel,* 3 vols. London and Berlin: A. Ascher.

Renfrew, Colin

1978 Trajectory, Discontinuity and Morphogensis: The Implications of Catastrophe Theory for Archaeology. *American Antiquity* 43:203–222.

Roark, Richard P.

1965 From Monumental to Proliferous in Nasca Pottery. *Ñawpa Pacha* 3:1–92.

Robinson, David A.

1957 *An Archaeological Survey of the Nasca Valley, Peru.* Unpublished M.A. thesis, Department of Anthropology, Stanford University.

Rowe, John H.

1962 Stages and Periods in Archaeological Interpretation. *Southwestern Journal of Anthropology* 18:40–54.

1963 Urban Settlements in Ancient Peru. *Ñawpa Pacha* 1:1–27.

1967 An Interpretation of Radiocarbon Measurements on Archaeological Samples from Peru. In *Peruvian Archaeology. Selected Readings,* edited by John H. Rowe and Dorothy Menzel, pp. 15–30. Palo Alto, CA: Peek Publications.

Sawyer, Alan

1997 *Early Nasca Needlework.* London: Laurence King.

Schreiber, Katharina

1999 Regional Approaches to the Study of Prehistoric Empires. Examples from Ayacucho and Nasca, Peru. In *Settlement Pattern Studies in the Americas: Fifty Years since Virú,* edited by Brian R. Billman and Gary M. Feinman, pp. 160–171. Washington, DC: Smithsonian Institution Press.

Schreiber, Katharina J., and Josué Lancho Rojas

1995 The Puquios of Nasca. *Latin American Antiquity* 6:229–

254.

Shady, Ruth

1981 *Intensificación de contactos entre las sociedades andinas como preludio al movimiento Huari del Horizonte Medio.* Lima: Boletín del Museo Nacional de Antropología y Arqueología 7.

1982 *La cultura Nievería y la interacción social en elmundo andino en la época Huari.* Arqueológicas 19. Lima: Museo Nacional de Antropología y Arqueología.

1988 La época Huari como interacción de las sociedades regionales. *Revista Andina* 6:67–99.

Silverman, Helaine

1988 Nasca 8: A Reassessment of Its Chronological Placement and Cultural Significance. In *Multidisciplinary Studies in Andean Anthropology,* edited by Virginia J. Vitzthum, pp. 23–32. Michigan Discussions in Anthropology 8. University of Michigan, Ann Arbor.

1990a The Early Nasca Pilgrimage Center of Cahuachi: Archaeological and Anthropological Perspectives. In *The Lines of Nazca,* edited by Anthony F. Aveni, pp. 209–244. Philadelphia: American Philosophical Society.

1990b Beyond the Pampa: The Geoglyphs of the Valleys of Nazca. *National Geographic Research* 6:435–456.

1993a *Cahuachi in the Ancient Nasca World.* Iowa City: University of Iowa Press.

1993b Patrones de asentamiento en el valle de Ingenio, cuenca del río Grande de Nazca: una propuesta preliminar. In *Gaceta Arqueológica Andina* 23:103–124.

1994 Paracas in Nazca: New Data on the Early Horizon Occupation of the Río Grande de Nazca Drainage, Peru. *Latin American Antiquity* 5:359–382.

1997 The First Field Season of Excavations at the Alto del Molino Site, Pisco Valley, Peru. *Journal of Field Archaeology* 24:441–457.

2002 *Ancient Nasca Settlement and Society.* Iowa City: University of Iowa Press.

Silverman, Helaine, and David M. Browne

1991 New Evidence for the Date of the Nazca Lines. *Antiquity* 65:208–220.

Stone, Tammy

1999 The Chaos of Collapse: Disintegration and Reintegration of Inter-regional Systems. *Antiquity* 73:110–118.

Strong, William Duncan

1957 *Paracas, Nazca and Tiahuanacoid Cultural Relationships in South Coastal Peru.* Society for American Archaeology Memoirs No. 13.

Tainter, Joseph A.

1988 *The Collapse of Complex Societies.* Cambridge: Cambridge University Press.

Tello, Julio C.

1942 *Origen y Desarrollo de las Civilizaciones Prehistóricas Andinas.* Lima.

Thompson, Lonnie G., E. Mosley-Thompson, J. F. Bolzan, and

B. R. Koci

1985 A 1500-Year Record of Tropical Precipitation in Ice Cores from the Quelccaya Ice Cap, Peru. *Science* 229:971–973.

Ubbelohde-Doering, Heinrich

1925/26 *Alt Peruanische Gefässmalerein.* Marburger Jahrbuch für Kunstwissenschaft, Band 2. Marburg: Verlag des Kunstgeschichtlichen Seminar der Universität Marburgan der Lahn.

1958 Berich üben archäologische Feldarbeiten in Perú. *Ethnos* 2–4:67–99.

Urton, Gary

1990 Andean Ritual Sweeping and the Nazca Lines. In *The Lines of Nazca,* edited by Anthony F. Aveni, pp. 173–206. Philadelphia: American Philosophical Society.

Valdez, Lidio

1989 Excavaciones arqueológicas en Gentilar (PV74-5). In *Archaeological Investigations in the Acarí Valley, Peru: A Field Report,* edited by Francis A. Riddell, pp. 42–55. Sacramento: California Institute for Peruvian Studies, and Arequipa: Universidad Católica de Santa María.

1990 *Informe de los trabajos de Campo de la Temporada de 1990 del "Proyecto Arqueológico Acarí, Yauca, Atiquipa y Chala."* Sacramento: California Institute for Peruvian Studies.

1998 *The Nasca and the Valley of Acarí: Cultural Interaction on the Peruvian South Coast during the First Four Centuries AD.* Unpublished Ph.D. dissertation, Department of Archaeology, University of Calgary, Alberta.

Vaughn, Kevin

1999 Early Intermediate Period Complexity on the South Coast of Peru: New Perspectives from Marcaya, an Early Nasca Domestic Site. Paper presented at the 64th Annual Meeting of the Society for American Archaeology, Chicago.

Verano, John

1995 Where Do They Rest? The Treatment of Human Offerings and Trophies in Ancient Peru. In *Tombs for the Living: Andean Mortuary Practices,* edited by Tom D. Dillehay, pp. 189–228. Washington, DC: Dumbarton Oaks.

Willey, Gordon R.

1991 Horizonal Integration and Regional Diversity: An Alternating Process in the Rise of Civilizations. *American Antiquity* 56:197–215.

Yoffee, Norman

1991a The Collapse of Ancient Mesopotamian States and Civilization. In *The Collapse of Ancient States and Civilizations,* edited by Norman Yoffee and George L. Cowgill, pp. 44–68. Tucson: University of Arizona Press.

1991b Orienting Collapse. In *The Collapse of Ancient States and Civilizations,* edited by Norman Yoffee and George L. Cowgill, pp. 1–19. Tucson: University of Arizona Press.

7

Collapse as Historical Process: The Moche Case

Garth Bawden

THE FOCUS OF MY STUDY IS THAT CATEGORY OF GROUP organization usually termed "early complex society" by anthropologists and "ancient civilization" by historians. Such systems usually possessed hierarchical and centralized institutions of authority sanctioned by formal ideologies that were grounded in beliefs of supernatural protection and direction. Early complex societies usually persisted for long periods of time, experiencing fluctuating fortunes. The dynamics underlying their historic trajectories, their success and failure, and most particularly for my purpose the factors leading to their end, have, at least since the time of Edward Gibbon's great treatise on the decline of the Roman Empire, represented a central interest of modern historians, philosophers, and social scientists alike. However, the nature of collapse continues to resist general scholarly agreement. In my paper I follow the dictionary and define collapse as abrupt and complete breakdown with concurrent disintegration of practical organizational effectiveness and loss of significance or meaning. It follows that, when referring to the end of a complex social system, collapse involves failure of the institutions that had ensured effective functioning of the managerial sector, political fragmentation, and dissolution of the shared traditions of belief that had provided the ideological foundations for cultural integrity. Studies of the decline of past civilizations usually utilize this transformational understanding of societal collapse and seek to identify the factors that brought about such dramatic events. However, I believe that the terminal stages of the histories of complex societies rarely conform to such a simple scenario. In this chapter I present my position, propose a structural scenario for the "end" of social complexity, and use a specific example to illustrate this process

EXISTING THEORIES OF
SOCIAL CHANGE AND COLLAPSE

Research into the nature and development of collapse in complex society falls naturally into several broad categories. Early scholars were basically essentialist in focus and sought generalities in the spiritual life history of civilizations. This category includes Oswald Spengler's (1962) notion that cultural decline is the result of weakening spiritual vitality, and Arnold Toynbee's (1962) position that decay of creative spirit ultimately led to collapse in ancient civilizations. The great American anthropologist Alfred Kroeber (1944, 1957) believed that innate high cultural values of a society stimulate the creative cycles that represent its greatest achievements. However, in his important suggestion that such life histories could incorporate several peaks of creativity through reconstitution, Kroeber (1963:39ff) differs from his two counterparts.

A more recent, internally diverse group of theories is inspired by biological evolution. Cultural evolutionary models (Fried 1960; Haas et al. 1987; Isbell 1997; Johnson and Earle 1987; Kristiansen 1991; Service 1960, 1975) owe their motivation to the notion of biological development as originally conceptualized by Herbert Spencer whereby social systems advance through a sequence of general stages of complexity by adaptation to the wider exterior environments within which they exist. The progressive specialization that accompanies increasing complexity causes them to become less able to adjust to changing circumstances. They then become vulnerable to conquest by more generalized (adaptable) competitors (Sahlins and Service 1960). By contrast, the selectionist wing of evolutionists (i.e., Dunnell 1980; Leonard and Jones 1987) rejects the universal developmental stages central to cultural evolutionary thought, allows for historical specificity in developmental traditions, and sees wide diversity among the resulting organisms (societies). A third biological approach sees the social system as an organism composed of interacting parts whose natural state is equilibrium. Disturbance of equilibrium, usually precipitated by factors external to society, brings widespread realignment among the systemic components until new balance is attained or the

101

entire organism is transformed or collapses (i.e., Flannery 1972; Renfrew 1984).

Another group of theories with which I am in overall agreement regards social change as emanating from innate internal social tension. Among these are archaeologists who espouse various versions of the dictum that collapse is associated with material contradictions inherent in past complex systems (De Marrais et al. 1996; Gilman 1981, 1984; McGuire 1992; Patterson and Gailey 1987; Zagarell 1986). A related group of studies explores the role of underlying structural mechanisms in creating and destroying social constructs (Friedman 1989; Friedman and Rowlands 1978; Godelier 1986; Kristiensen 1984). Other scholars address change deriving from internal tensions that emerge between various competing institutions of central government and that existing between central authority and the subsidiary groups who expect to receive benefit from their service to society (Eisenstadt 1969; Tainter 1988). Cessation of such benefits provokes more overt conflict that may lead to collapse. The concepts underlying most critical traditions in contemporary archaeology take this approach to the extreme. By privileging individuals with the ability to change internal group configuration through conscious manipulation of the specific beliefs and ideas that constitute cultural experience, this scenario empowers them as effective social actors (Giddens 1984), the ultimate building blocks of social construction and change.

Even though most theories of social evolution ostensibly addressed collapse, with the exception of the early twentieth century essentialists none of them was significantly concerned with the specific nature of this phenomenon. Collapse was treated as a given consequence of other, more important causal factors, its temporal parameters, and specific impacts manifestly apparent in the material record. Consequently, as a source of information on the dynamics of its related society, it has usually been afforded less interest than other stages of the evolutionary cycle and regarded in ways that diverted interest from its internal structure to its precipitating causes. Thus when collapse is viewed as the short-lived terminal chapter of the evolutionary continuum, the mechanisms that motivate society are naturally more clearly identified by studying earlier, fully functioning phases. Alternatively, if we merely view collapse as the dramatic event that demonstrates the inability of a social system to adjust to increasing stress, it is again more fruitful to explore the traits within the system that may have caused the breakdown than the event itself. Rarely has the possibility been explicitly acknowledged that collapse is not merely a transformative event. In this study of Moche society I

regard collapse as an integral manifestation of the longer evolutionary process, and thus a complex and challenging focus for research in its own right.

This brief review highlights several points that are pertinent to my discussion of collapse:

1. A central premise of essentialist and cultural evolutionary models seeks to identify universal trends in social evolution. Here general evolutionary stages are identifiable by finite sets of institutional characteristics and describe a range of complexity from simple to highly differentiated. I strongly sympathize with an opposing view that sees cultural traditions as being constructed within the contexts of their unique historic and spatial experiences and thus not subject to general developmental forces.

2. The adaptive emphasis of cultural evolutionary and systems theorists promotes a view of change as response to outside pressure. If systemic equilibrium cannot be restored by these means, profound disruption and collapse may ensue. By contrast, other scholars affirm that change and collapse chiefly emanate from innate internal tensions that provoke conflict between unequal social classes or institutions. Again, I generally take this viewpoint in my study.

3. Although essentialist concepts are now largely discredited in studies of civilization, the belief that great ideas underlie cultural vitality, reinterpreted as the motivations of groups and individuals within complex society, has risen to prominence in recent years. In accord with this approach, I examine here the role of factional ideology and individual motivation as potent forces for social construction.

4. Most of the evolutionary and Marxist theories noted above assume a fairly predictable historical course for civilization, with life stages comparable to those of a biological organism, ending in death (collapse). However, long ago Kroeber (1963:39ff) presented the concept that civilizations could avert decline through what he termed "cultural reconstitution." In this study I follow the lead of other recent scholars who take a similar course in exploring collapse as a process rather than a terminal event (Tainter 1988; the contributors to Yoffee and Cowgill 1991).

THE INTERNAL STRUCTURE OF COLLAPSE

I accept it as a given that complex societies are constructions of time and space, their particular cultural and social manifestations representing the consolidated accumulation of experience drawn from long histories of internal mediation and external relations. It follows that all aspects of their development, including their demise, possess both territorial and historical dimensions. Thus, I regard the terminal chapter of a complex society as comprising a structural evolution that encompasses the period before, during, and following the events that are usually regarded as denoting collapse. This historical process is characterized by the interplay between its temporal and spatial dimensions throughout a course that, while occasionally involving collapse as it has traditionally been understood, more frequently creates transformation and renewed vitality.

It must be clear that within the total inventory of social and political dynamics that constitute the integrative structure of a civilization prior to a period of deterioration lie the seeds of subsequent decline. Similarly this same structure provides the available resources with which society confronts the forces of disintegration. For the purposes of analysis, we can usefully identify the actual material dimensions of this underlying structural reality. On the spatial level the territorial dimensions of a society combined with its prevailing physical environment (long-term climatic conditions, topography, riverine and maritime configuration, tectonic setting) significantly affect internal and external communication, the nature of economic and political consolidation, and the potential for unified or selective response to threat. In the temporal domain, several historically derived factors are equally important in creating the context within which a society confronts stress. Most important in this respect are the modes of group organization and political authority that evolve through time as the principal integrative mechanisms of society. Overlapping and penetrating these integrative strategies are prevailing belief systems. Such collective beliefs, often deeply grounded in the mythical origins of the community, serve to both unite the wider collectivity and identify the boundaries of its constituent sub-groups. Of special importance in this respect are the nature and effectiveness of the dominant ideology that serves as official dogma promulgated by rulers as the basis for social order.

A second important point regards the very meaning of collapse. As I have already emphasized, this phenomenon has often been seen as an event precipitated by easily identifiable causes, usually external to the society, which initiate uniform and irreversible deterioration that is clearly seen in the archaeological record. However, I prefer to treat this phenomenon as a critical stage in the history of a society characterized by a series of menacing impacts and measured responses whose character is historically shaped by the material and mental factors that I detailed above. Within this scenario, the responses available to the rulers of any particular area are limited by the physical and organizational factors that prevail, together with the degree of disruptive impact. However, within this limitation, threatened leaders always have the ability to make unique decisions drawn from their range of available options. It is important to note that in this critical process the likelihood of change is exceedingly high, even if the reaction to threat is ultimately successful.

Finally, the aftermath of the process of collapse is equally complex. Infrequently there is collapse in the sense traditionally ascribed to the Classic Maya case, where the old order and its legitimizing ideological system was believed to have disappeared in the context of social and political fragmentation (Culbert 1991). However, even here there is now growing recognition that collapse was not uniform and that continuity occurred, albeit at different levels of social integration in the various Maya regions. It is therefore just as likely that the process of decline ultimately leads to transformation and recovery within a restructured society whose territorial limits may change but then remain intact within their new borders. Again, the nature of the existing circumstances and the immediately preceding history of crisis and response will dictate the shape of this ultimate outcome. If successful, the very actions that were effective in meeting the crisis may well themselves generate altered social strategies and potentials in the evolving context of a deeply changed but vital society. Moreover, in the longer term such immediately successful modifications will often incorporate the seeds of future problems, continuing the stress-response cycle that may sometime in the future threaten the stability of society again.

Two summary points should be clear from my discussion. First, I accept that civilizations as stable and long-lasting systems of sociopolitical order do come to an end. Second, I believe that their terminal phases are rarely as dramatic or final as sometimes supposed. Within this framework I regard decline as a process comprising a series of stress-response cycles that progressively modify the existing structure of society. These cycles inevitably involve rejection of important aspects of the earlier cultural tradition but also permit others to persist into subsequent periods of reconstitution. Thus there is now fairly general acceptance that the "collapse" of the western Roman Empire as traditionally marked by the deposing of Romulus Augustulus, its last emperor, was probably little noticed by the broader populace and in any case only affected a portion of the empire. In fact, this largely symbolic event merely marked the end of a single discredited institution of authority whose functions had long been exercised by others. Most other institutions continued unchanged into the succeeding period. Only after centuries of further disruption and modified reconstitution that resulted in the rise of feudal society as a new integrative system can we guardedly regard Classical civilization as having so transformed as to have effectively disappeared, although many of its specific tenets never disappeared from the Western tradition. Thus, an approach that rejects the necessity for a single culminating event of collapse and admits the probability of geographically and quantitatively differentiated transformation occurring over an extended time frame offers great potential for identifying the dynamics that drove the evolution of civilization and thus for revealing the real nature and meaning of its end.

AN EXAMPLE OF COLLAPSE AS PROCESS

Moche society flourished along the Peruvian north coastal littoral (Figure 27) from roughly AD 100 to at least the late eighth century AD (Figure 28; all dates in this chapter are AD). Until recently, the prevailing view of this archaeological culture was shaped by a characteristically evolutionary scheme that saw it evolving from the preceding Gallinazo phase around 100 with its probable geographical origins in the Moche Valley in the south of the region. In the Middle Moche period (Moche III and IV; Figure 28, ca. 300–600) this local society created a centralized political state that expanded symmetrically to the north and south from its capital, located at the Huacas del Sol and de la Luna in the Moche Valley, to militarily dominate the entire north coast. This florescent phase continued until around 600, when in the Late Moche period (Moche V; Figure 28) major collapse occurred in the face of catastrophic climatic disruption and external invasion that caused the loss of the southern half of the state and its reorganization around a new northern capital, Pampa Grande in the Lambayeque Valley (Figure 27). Although this rump state struggled on precariously for a few more generations, it could not prevent the general collapse of Moche society that occurred around 750 in the context of settlement abandonment, disappearance of state organization, and breakdown of political and ideological structure. This, of course, is a conventional scenario for externally generated collapse in complex society. However, although there is now little doubt that major environmental disruption did affect much of Peru at this time (Chapdelaine 2000; Moseley 1987; Shimada 1994; Shimada et al. 1991), closer analysis of the later Moche phase from the viewpoint suggested in the first part of

this chapter reveals that, instead of simple collapse, it is much more probable that a complex process of differential impact and response occurred throughout the region, with local strategies creating new foundations for differential transformation in various parts of the region.

I examine this process in three sections. First is the long period preceding the events usually seen to denote collapse, namely the period from about 300 to 600 (Middle period; Figure 28) when Moche civilization had fully consolidated and when it experienced its most successful and florescent phase. By examining this period of stability we can better understand the precise nature of the Moche social structure, and thus the strengths and weaknesses that shaped the subsequent leadership decisions in a time of crisis when prevailing authority was threatened. Second, I examine the developments of the period of crisis from 600 to 750 (Late period; Figure 28). This is the relatively short period of a few generations during which Moche civilization was traditionally believed to have collapsed under pressure from external political and environmental disruptions. I will show that such a simple and uniform scenario cannot be supported by the evidence and that the actual history of this crisis period was one in which local leaders responded to the disruption in diverse ways best suited to their own specific circumstances. These local responses led to further differential transformation in the eighth century and beyond. Finally, I discuss the period following 750, the later Middle Horizon period of Andean archaeological chronology (Figure 28), when Moche civilization is believed to have disappeared from the north coast region. We shall see that instead the cycle of crisis-response that we can trace from the late sixth century continued to drive the historic developments of the various north coast regions and that only in one limited and localized sense can we talk of collapse in the traditional sense.

Pre-Collapse Situation (300–600)

By contrast to earlier understanding, there is now growing acceptance that there was no unitary Moche state. Rather, a number of small, autonomous polities occupying river valleys of differing size and hydraulic capacity probably existed along the desert coast, sharing the same cultural forms and beliefs and, importantly, the same elite ideology. The only partial exception to this pattern involved the southernmost part of the region, where an extensive polity centered in the Moche Valley incorporated up to seven river valleys (Figure 29). These valleys had been dominated by north coast elites who

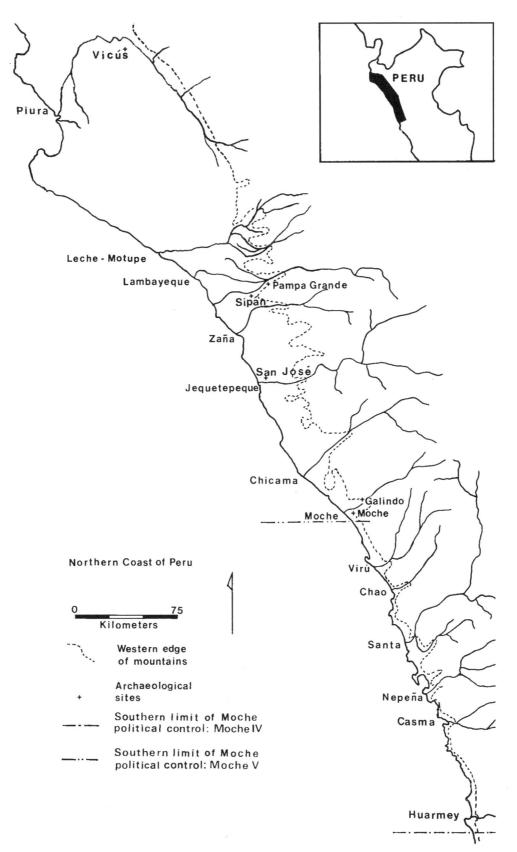

Figure 27. Map of the north coast of Peru showing river valleys, principal archaeological sites mentioned in the text, and the territorial expansion of the southern Middle Moche polity.

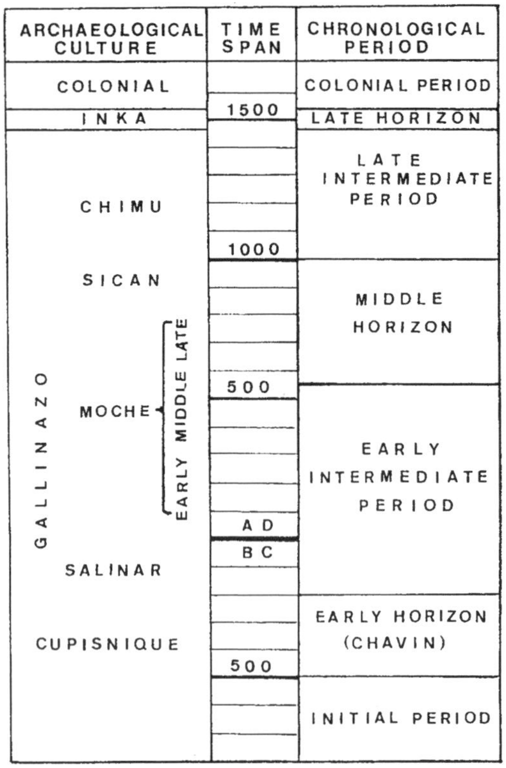

ARCHAEOLOGICAL CULTURE	TIME SPAN	CHRONOLOGICAL PERIOD
COLONIAL		COLONIAL PERIOD
INKA	1500	LATE HORIZON
CHIMU		LATE INTERMEDIATE PERIOD
SICAN	1000	
		MIDDLE HORIZON
MOCHE	500	
		EARLY INTERMEDIATE PERIOD
	AD	
SALINAR	BC	
CUPISNIQUE		EARLY HORIZON (CHAVIN)
	500	
		INITIAL PERIOD

Figure 28. Cultural chronology of the north coast of Peru.

had never adopted the Moche political system and its ideological symbolism and who continued to adhere to the Gallinazo cultural inventory until they were forcibly incorporated into the expanding southern polity. Elsewhere Gallinazo societies persisted in the northern valleys of the region throughout Moche history, their last autonomous polities only being finally conquered late in the period by the Lambayeque Valley polity in the far north. Thus Moche society never represented a monolithic entity. It was internally divided into numerous local polities and shared the north coast with neighbors who recognized a distinct political structure drawn from the same cultural and historical tradition (Figure 29).

Each Middle Moche polity comprised a sociopolitical and economic unit led by an elite group that wielded power largely through its success in manipulating traditional cultural and mythical principles through elaborate ritual. Their subjects were agriculturalists living in small villages scattered along the edges of the river valleys who were using small irrigation systems to water their fields. These people adhered to a social pattern wherein local kin-related and largely self-sufficient communities were attached to their land by traditional principles of ancestral reverence and sacred place. Here, central power loosely integrated local allegiances in an internally contradictory sociopolitical system that always held the potential for

tension between the aspirations of leaders and the needs of their subjects.

The Moche archaeological inventory that has until recently been used to characterize Moche culture as a whole—codified elite iconography, monumental architecture, elaborate metallurgy and jewelry—is more correctly described as the material symbolism of a dominant ideology of power. Specialist craftsmen who worked on behalf of the ruling elites created these fine materials and embellished them with the mythical and ritual imagery of the ruling political system. Production and distribution was tightly controlled, with the most elaborate items being used in the central locations of power to enhance the status and authority of the rulers. Other, less-elaborate examples were distributed to lower-status groups in order to diffuse the concepts of official power through all strata of society and to tie them to the prevailing social order. At the apex of Moche society, the sharing of the narratives and ceremonies of a successful power structure by the rulers of the numerous local polities through this codified iconographic system emphasized the potency of this common ideology and thereby increased their authority. By contrast, other categories of Moche material culture show little distinction from those of earlier and succeeding north coast societies. Thus, only in the restricted political sector do we see a distinctive inventory of specialized material artifacts that served to assert and bolster the prevailing political order.

The Moche institutions of political power were constantly reaffirmed by ritual manipulation of the great platform mounds that still dominate the coastal valleys. As ideological symbols located in sacred time and space, platforms replicated the mountains whose divinities provided the vital streams that supported human life. Their platform summits acted as stages where, in full public view (Moore 1996), leaders conducted rituals rooted in the mythic origins of north coastal people, which regularly manifested the tenets of their religious belief. The culminating act of this ritual was sacrifice of elite prisoners taken in ritual combat (Alva and Donnan 1993; Bawden 1996). Their blood was offered to the earth as the precious gift of life essence to ensure fertility and the cosmological balance necessary for human existence. By officiating at these rituals, leaders became the arbiters of social integration, gaining supernatural and political power from their roles. Moreover, at sites like Sipán, their burial in the great ritual structures (Alva and Donnan 1993) permanently identified them and the social order that they had headed when alive with the sacred centers of Moche social life and their embodied meaning. In this

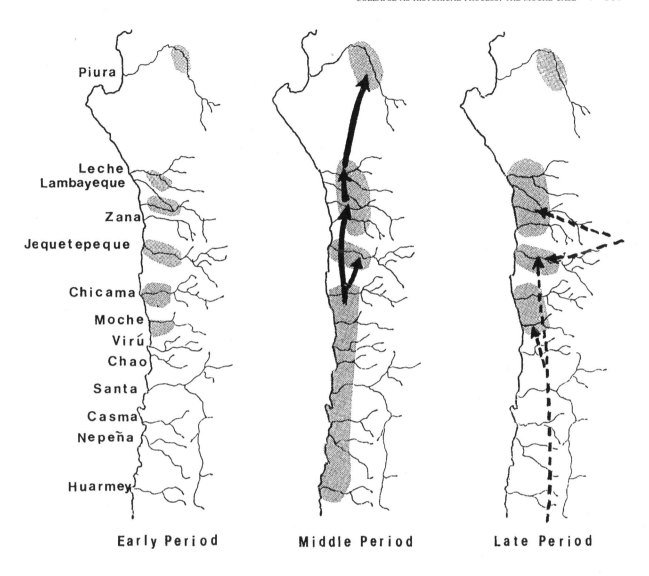

Piura

Leche
Lambayeque

Zana

Jequetepeque

Chicama

Moche

Virú

Chao

Santa

Casma

Nepeña

Huarmey

Early Period   **Middle Period**   **Late Period**

Figure 29. Maps of the north coast of Peru showing the evolution of Moche political hegemony.

Left-hand map shows emergence and consolidation of the Moche polities in the Early phase. Center map shows political expansion by the Moche Valley–based polity in the Middle period. Arrows show the now-discredited model of northern conquest by this polity. Right-hand map shows Late period Moche retreat from the southern valleys and expansion of the Lambayeque Drainage–based Pampa Grande polity to the sea. Dashed arrows show the chief sources of outside influence.

way, as mediators with the supernatural past, present, and future in the liminal space of ritual, elites themselves were the medium that ensured cosmological balance. Together, platforms and revered ancestral leaders proclaimed the supernatural sanction of their prevailing order, thereby maintaining an ideological discourse that actualized the underlying tenets of north coast social structure to provide the basis for common identity and political stability.

Moreover, the wider ceremonial cycle that included the sacrifice ceremony linked the various local Moche polities as ritual partners whose collaboration was necessary for its implementation and thus for the success

of the shared political ideology that it proclaimed. The scenes of single combat between elaborately accoutered elite warriors and the subsequent arraignment of the prisoners that are such common themes in Moche narrative art probably depict ritual warfare between representatives of the various polities, the defeated being destined for sacrifice on the great platforms. This is a distant counterpart to the modern ritual battles or *tinkuys* that still occur between Andean traditional groups with the object of asserting their individual identities while at the same time ritually connecting them with their neighbors during times of festival. In this way, ritual battle between the Moche polities and the subsequent sacrifice ceremony served to actively manifest a powerful shared ideology that transcended local territorial borders and incorporated otherwise autonomous societies into a wider collective political system. By so doing, it established a powerful support for the existing order, its ideological base, and its leaders. However, this system required active involvement of all its members and raised the possibility that if one or more were unable to participate this would not only weaken their own ideological underpinnings but also adversely affect those of their neighbors, who could no longer conduct the ritual of interpolity ritual warfare. We will see that such interdependence actually played a destructive role in the subsequent period of crisis.

Critical to the support of any social order is general acknowledgment by its adherents that it addresses their circumstances and needs. The beliefs and practices described in this section collectively played a central role in ensuring this positive connection. There are two vital requirements for the success of a dominant ideology. On the conceptual level it must persuade the majority of the populace to accept the reality and related aspirations that it espouses and thus mobilize them to actively participate in actions intended to achieve these goals. On the practical level, people must see that the dominant ideology and the sociopolitical order of which it is part bring them definite material benefits and improve their lives. The Middle Moche system appears to have succeeded in both of these areas. The symbols and practices of power overwhelmingly asserted an ideology of inclusion that incorporated all levels of society. The rulers ensured that their subjects had direct accessibility to the central tenets of official ideology through public ceremonial and the controlled distribution of items of ideological symbolism. This encouraged large-scale support by all social groups. To a large degree, the success of this ideology appears to have stemmed from its successful grounding in shared mythic and ancestral belief in a rural society largely organized by kinship principles. On the material level, it appears that the Middle Moche period was one of economic security and agricultural plenty. This was especially true for the southern polity, where there is little doubt that domination and exploitation of the southern valleys brought significant economic benefits. Thus, the society was one in which a vital ideological superstructure, strengthened through participatory ritual practice and shared cultural belief, represented the linking structure within which a group of otherwise separate north coast polities flourished during the period. Moche civilization represents the collective material and conceptual achievements of these polities.

To this juncture I have described the material remains of Middle Moche society as a single elite category of political symbolism. While it is true that at this time (but not later, as we will see) this assumption of unity appears to be valid, this does not mean that the cultural configuration of the local polities were similarly identical. Although as far as we know the people of the north coast shared a common history, they inhabited an extensive area that was internally divided by wide bands of desert. This geographical separation was quite understandably accompanied by local modifications of the wider north coast cultural tradition. Thus, the various Moche polities, while sharing salient cultural and political strategies, developed in somewhat different ways. Three of these are now clearly emerging through study of their archaeological residue, each with its own environmental, historical, and structural variation of wider Moche tradition (Figures 27 and 29). Others, such as the equally distinctive Moche occupation of the Piura Valley, remain to be fully described. In the north the huge Lambayeque Valley system was probably the location of several such polities, which included the well-known center of Sipán. The rulers of this region were able to draw on abundant water resources of a multi-river system for their agricultural base, and we can assume that they possessed a greater capacity to successfully confront the regular drought and El Niño events that afflicted the region than their counterparts in smaller valleys. To the south lay the Jequetepeque Valley, incorporating an irrigable region almost as large as that of its northern neighbor. The Moche settlements of this area lay on or near a major route connecting the coast with the highlands and were probably always in contact with their inland neighbors to an extent not matched by most other valleys, stimulating trade and affording an avenue for foreign influence to reach the coast.

Although the material manifestations of these two northern Moche regions are very similar in most respects, there are differences that suggest that their histories were distinct. For example, one of the chief stylistic markers of Moche ceramics—the so-called Moche IV phase— is present in Lambayeque but absent in Jequetepeque. Also, comparison of the prevailing narrative scenes depicted in ceramic iconography suggests some minor variations in their common political ideology. Finally, in architecture, the centrally oriented ramps of Jequetepeque Valley platforms replace the characteristic lateral ramps of the far north. However, one common aspect of the two northern valley systems is very important for understanding their social structure. While the great rituals of social integration are precisely depicted in many media, their central officiants are never given physiognomic distinguishing traits that would indicate them as recognizable individuals. Instead, narrative art indicates that participants in these rituals possessed importance through their (probably ascribed) positions and the functions that they exercised, not through their personal qualities. This approach conforms to that to be expected in a society still largely organized by principles of kinship and shared mythic belief, where the ruling group, though powerful and rich, was still structurally undifferentiated from the rest of the community. This pattern stands in dramatic contrast to the situation in the southern polity centered at the Huaca del Sol, to which I now turn.

The small, water-scarce Moche Valley was the center of an extensive Middle period polity that incorporated the seven southernmost valleys of the region, probably through coercion (Figure 29). Its capital was a large center in the lower Moche Valley dominated by the two huge platform complexes: the Huacas del Sol and de la Luna near the modern village of Moche (Figure 27). Intrusive Moche centers modeled after this chief settlement spread down the coast in a wave of expansion not seen further north. This political advance was understandably accompanied by structural developments intended to control and integrate a large and diverse territory and its initially hostile subjects. Thus the expanding polity introduced complex management and economic institutions, revealed by the large, intrusive administrative centers and their accompanying central storage-redistribution facilities and major agricultural realignment projects. The political sector would have similarly expanded to meet the need for coordinating the expanded institutions. At the apex of government, these differentiated institutions were clearly controlled by a ruling group that incorporated a level of hierarchy and personal achievement not seen elsewhere in the Moche political domain. This individualizing and hierarchical quality is most explicitly seen in the incorporation into the symbolism of central power of the renowned class of figurative ceramic vessels, which (as Donnan has confirmed) depict portraits of specific rulers at various stages of their lives and political careers. In this southern Moche polity, power and its success rested to an unmatched degree on the person rather than the functions and institutions of power as in the north.

Although the very presence of this complex sociopolitical system is a reflection of southern Moche success, it brought with it a degree of potential weakness unmatched in the northern polities. In such a relatively hierarchical system the collective bonds of traditional kinship would have been loosened to a significant degree,

together with the broadly communal power base that kinship offered. Instead the rulers reinterpreted political power as personal achievement, thereby differentiating themselves as a group from their subjects and elevating themselves as the sole arbiters of the destinies of society. In addition, the creation of new institutions for administrative and economic management in the south would have offered unprecedented opportunities to their leaders to construct their own power bases in potential opposition to each other and to the central political authority. Thus, the very success of the southern polity created potential internal tension between the upper and lower rungs of society and between different factions of the ruling elite. As long as stability persisted, the economic and psychological benefits of the territorial expansion to society as a whole would have kept these divisive forces dormant. However, with the onset of major threat in the late sixth century, the southern polity was already structurally ripe for internally generated disruption to a degree absent in its two northern counterparts.

The Period of Crisis and Its Aftermath (600–750)

In the last decades of the sixth century, north coast peoples experienced profound disruptions. Scholars have traditionally ascribed these events to climatic disaster and external invasion (see Bawden 1996 for a summary) and assumed that they caused rapid, uniform, and total collapse over the next few decades. One of the suggested external causes—Wari invasion—is now largely discredited, although the presence of a strong and possibly hostile state beyond the borders of the Moche area may have contributed to the instability that emerged at this time. However, it is now fairly clear that climatic disruption did impact the north coast at this time, its detrimental economic consequences probably posing a major challenge to the leaders of the Moche polities. Nevertheless, given the documented ability of regional administrations to recover from all such major events in the Spanish colonial and modern periods, I believe that environmental pressure alone cannot account for the subsequent major transformation of the entire regional sociopolitical structure. Rather, I suggest that existing internal sociopolitical structure was the most important factor in this process, presenting local leaders with a limited set of possible choices in the face of threat to their order. Their specific responses, shaped by the historical trajectories on the north coast, represent the active dynamics that initiated the process of relatively rapid change. Archaeology supports this position by revealing clear differences in the development of various local Moche centers subsequent to the initial crisis. It appears, then, that local leaders made distinct choices that led to quite different outcomes. The determining factor would therefore be internal circumstance and choice rather than inexorable external pressure. I will now turn to these decades of impact, and the distinct responses of various Moche polities.

The Southern Moche Polity

While in the northern areas the effects of disruption were less severe, geographical and historical factors determined that the most severe impact fell on the Moche Valley, which in the previous period had controlled a domain extending south to Huarmey (Figure 29). These extensive southern domains, presumably occupied by the descendants of conquered populations with cultural and social backgrounds that differed from their Moche masters, were abandoned (Figure 29) and the Moche Valley itself was reduced to a small remnant, vulnerable to now-hostile neighbors. At this juncture it is impossible to know if the breakdown was initiated by the internal stresses that I described above or if a series of major climatic disruptions in the late sixth century triggered the internal events. Certainly the internal and external forces overlapped chronologically and became part of the same crisis faced by the leaders of the southern Moche polity. Economically, loss of the resources of the south was exacerbated by dune inundation of agricultural land south of the river and possibly by an influx of displaced settlers from the southern valleys. Such events would have brought major hardship to the Moche Valley populace. Inability of the ruling elite to successfully evade these harmful developments appears to have discredited them in the eyes of their remaining subjects. Their extreme social and political differentiation now turned against them, and they were seen as the sole cause of disaster, no longer able to provide supernatural and material benefits to their subjects. Failure generated responses that transformed Moche Valley society.

A key element in the southern response occurred in the conceptual realm with rejection of the most important elements of the previously successful ideological system in the face of social disruption and political and economic breakdown. Most dramatic was abandonment of the largest architectural symbol of Middle Moche political ideology and power in the south—the great Huaca del Sol platform. However, this shift was accompanied by rejection of most other symbols of existing authority. Thus, production of ceramic portraits of rulers, the ultimate symbols of individualizing government in the

southern Moche Middle period, ceased together with the wide range of representational symbolism that had also characterized the earlier time, indicating an end to the powerful rituals that had served to maintain social integration.

Equally dramatic was the break-up of the remaining rump polity into two successor mini-states. Recent work at the erstwhile capital of the southern polity indicates that following abandonment of the Huaca del Sol a significant settlement remained at the site, ruled by successor leaders domiciled in the Huaca de la Luna. This reduced settlement attempted to maintain some of the traditional Moche cultural forms, albeit in rather impoverished form, and persisted until the late eighth century. However, concurrently, another new town of very different character, Galindo, was founded in the upper valley (Figure 27). This initiative is best regarded as a dramatic attempt to control the best remaining agricultural land in the Moche Valley and to impose control over a reduced and probably disillusioned and hostile population. Here most of the middle and upper valley population was clustered in a context of unprecedented social separation, with much of the population segregated on a hillside behind walled *barriados* (see Bawden 1982 for a detailed presentation). Inevitably, this resettlement would have threatened the integrity of the local groups who formed the bulk of the population. First, they were separated from their rural ancestral places, along with the kin-related community organization that prevailed in such settings, and congregated in an urban setting where these traditional life-ways were no longer possible. Moreover, the nature of the new ideological system imposed by the leaders in reaction to rejection of its predecessor would doubtless have exacerbated this alienation. The founders of Galindo rejected the architectural forms and functions of their Middle Moche antecedents and replaced central platforms with innovative architectural forms that emphasized enclosure and social separation. The accompanying portable symbolism abandoned all traditional connection and instead linked leadership to pan-Andean concepts in an effort to free it from identification with the failures of the Middle Moche system. It was reserved for the exclusive centers of elite control and symbolism. Thus both the physical centers of the new ideology and its portable symbols excluded commoners.

The new architectural complexes of Galindo with their strictly controlled access and high walls; the separation of rulers and ruled in segregated, walled compounds; the strict control of food resources; and the basic demographic shift from rural to urban (Billman 1996:292) collectively mark a radical change in the institutional structure of power at a time of threat. As a result of the profound breakdown and vulnerability of the Galindo rulers, social control changed from overtly participatory to coercive and exclusionary. The resulting sense of alienation among the commoners directed them to actively construct their own bases of social identity. This looked to the home as the focus for reconstitution of traditional identity through innovative in-house burial ritual whereby interment in internal room platforms restored ancestral place to its kin in the autonomous social setting of the household (see Bawden 2001 for explanation). At Galindo the internal social contradiction innate in the adjustments initiated by their Middle Moche predecessors reached their greatest degree in the efforts of a desperate elite to stem the tides of decline. Clearly this situation would have to be resolved or further collapse would be inevitable.

In the south, then, the radical reaction of successor leaders to the impact of the late sixth century crisis was molded by a preexisting situation that incorporated contradictory social structural elements—hierarchical, individualizing leadership contrasted with kin-focused communal principles in the bulk of the population—and competition between the leaders of the new institutions of political expansion. These potentially destructive forces were masked by the political success and economic benefits of the Middle period, but they emerged in open opposition in the crisis of 600. The ensuing disruption reached all levels of society. With the loss of most of its territory, the remaining Moche Valley state fragmented into two small successors, possibly the culmination of internal competition between opposing sectors of the Moche elite. Both rejected the ideology of their predecessors, although the Huaca de la Luna polity seems to have attempted to reorganize on more traditional cultural foundations. Its larger, upper-valley counterpart, Galindo, totally rejected traditional forms and instituted a new order based on coercive control and group separation, a new ideational foundation that was overtly alien to its subjects. It is apparent that the distinctive ideational systems of ruler and ruled—one universal and looking to maintain political authority, the other internally focused on local kinship groups and seeking to promote basic group identity—represented basically incompatible constructions of power. The exclusivity of the new ideology meant that it could not gain broad acceptance, unlike its Middle Moche predecessor, or inspire the new tenets of shared cultural cognition essential for its success. Although the new regime proved to be successful in controlling decline, in the short term

this could only persist as long as its leaders possessed the power and will to impose the accompanying drastic social reorganization and ideological transformation. With the bulk of the population increasingly alienated from their leaders, a new cycle of pressures was ultimately unavoidable. Thus, only a few generations later the new Galindo social order collapsed in the context of social and physical destruction, and the new city was abandoned together with its experimental urbanism. Concurrently the Huaca de la Luna polity appears to have progressively declined in population and in the ability of its leaders to maintain a cohesive society. By the late eighth century, Moche Valley society had reverted to the pattern of small-scale rural communities that were the building blocks of north coast society, and the already deeply transformed and fragmented Moche political structure disappeared from the southernmost portion of the north coast cultural tradition.

The Central Region: Jequetepeque

Further north in the Jequetepeque Valley, history took a different course. Although major changes also occurred here in the seventh and eighth centuries, they did not match their southern counterparts in either severity or the degree of transformation that they initiated. On the physical level, the climatic disruption that affected the entire north coast appears to have caused sand inundation in areas to the south of the river, as it had in the Moche Valley, with accompanying loss of agricultural land (Shimada 1994:121–122). However, there was no accompanying loss of an extensive political and economic hinterland with the extreme disruption that this had inflicted in the southern state. Moreover, with the easier access to nearby highland resources provided by the topography and location of the Jequetepeque Valley, the material plight of its inhabitants was probably never as grave as in the societies further south.

As mentioned above, the political structure of the Jequetepeque and more northern valleys appears never to have assumed the degree of political hierarchy attained by their Moche Valley neighbors. To a large extent this is probably explained by the fact that the southern leaders headed a large territorial conquest state that had incorporated numerous river valleys and had developed an administrative and economic structure of considerably greater complexity than that found further north. As I have noted, while espousing an ideology of inclusion, the southern Moche leaders, as part of their extensive political development, built the largest of the Moche platforms—the Huaca del Sol and its counterparts in the conquered valleys—and used their specialist ceramic craftsmen to produce a category of highly realistic portraits that focused symbolic and practical authority on them as powerful individuals to a degree never seen farther north. Indeed, it was partly because of this extreme level of differentiation and assumption of personal responsibility for the welfare of the state that the transformation was so great when they and the system that they ruled were perceived to have failed in the crisis of 600.

By contrast, the symbolism of the Jequetepeque Valley and its northern counterparts focused on the position and roles that leaders played as the heads of the institutions of social integration rather than on their individual persons. In such a system the portrait vessels of the Moche Valley would have been meaningless as symbols of power in the northern valleys and are understandably absent. This relatively greater degree of articulation between the various strata of society and its more communal focus corresponded more to the fundamental kinship orientation of north coast society, and there was less structural contradiction between the institutions of government and the organizational principles that directed the lives of the commoners. Nevertheless, the rulers of Jequetepeque depended on the presence of their southern neighbors as ritual partners, both to conduct the ritual warfare that was a central part of their ceremonial of power and as participants in the shared political structure that supported all the Moche elites in a region-wide ideological system that sanctioned their positions and social order. The fall of the southern polity and collapse of its conceptual foundations would have removed its rulers from this mutually supportive network, placing ultimately intolerable pressure on prevailing ideological practice and ultimately forcing its modification. We have seen that in the Moche Valley the entire inventory of ideological narrative symbolism was rejected and disappeared from the material record. In the Jequetepeque Valley, although the transformation was not as drastic, significant change of like quality did occur. The introduction of new narrative scenes like the burial theme, painted in the traditional style of Moche elite art and only produced in the Jequetepeque Valley, reveals this attempt to change the ideological focus from the earlier shared beliefs to new, locally focused myths and rituals of social integration.

The work of Luis Jaime Castillo at San Jose de Moro (Figure 27) is revealing another aspect of cultural change in the Jequetepeque Valley during the time of crisis. Although valley settlement remained stable, it is clear that its population experienced considerable hardship, which stimulated significant modification of in the overall sociopolitical order. Castillo has suggested

that the authority of Moche leaders of the Middle period depended significantly on their ability to firmly control the production and distribution of ideological symbolism, with different social strata acquiring the forms that fitted their specific status and role (Castillo 2001; De Marrais et al. 1996:23–27). Following the destructive events of the early seventh century, it appears that this pattern was disrupted throughout the north coast. With the forced modification of the conceptual basis of power, the ability of a unified ideological symbolism to connect all social strata would have similarly weakened. Thus, intensive symbolic production and distribution of the less potent and familiar Late Moche symbols would have lost its earlier meaning and purpose. Instead, in order to augment the power of its new ideology, leaders supplemented their new themes attached to traditional Moche media with elaborate foreign ceramic symbolism imported from the central coast—a region completely outside the Moche sphere. Here we see local rulers supplementing the traditional, though modified, structure that gave them the status of continuity, with outside ideological symbols that brought meaning that transcended Moche social conception. Leaders here introduced new concepts augmented by foreign symbols of rank as a means to modify their ideological base and retain power, but attempted to do this within the overall context of existing Moche culture.

Although as part of the region-wide pressures Moche ideological system came under significant stress in the Jequetepeque Valley, the underlying structure of belief that endowed specialist shamans with the ability to enter the supernatural to renew cosmic balance on behalf of society was probably less affected. In the south, the extreme political differentiation of leadership from its traditional social base and focus on the person of the rulers would have largely negated this structural role. However, in the more communally oriented Jequetepeque Valley society, the shamanistic quality of Moche leadership would have afforded leaders a broader power base for recovery of their status, if not of the ideological forms that had failed to avert disruption. The archaeology of the period suggests that from this position they were able to achieve social change using the existing order rather than being forced to cling to power through radical transformation.

Jequetepeque Valley leaders succeeded in averting collapse, largely ensured ideological and material continuity, and reconstituted social stability in their domain. There was no coercive and radical social reorganization, unlike in the Moche Valley, nor was there collapse a few generations later. However, the ideological changes that they initiated inevitably encouraged further innovation once the rigid control and codification that had characterized earlier symbolism and ritual had been loosened. Thus we find that the original foreign imports were later replicated in the valley, combined with more traditional Moche forms in the context of decline in quality of elite craft. Again, although response in this valley resulted in revitalization in the latest Moche period, the process of cultural modification, once precipitated, encouraged continued change into subsequent periods. While it is not possible to see any termination of the reconstituted Late Moche complex social order or the territorial integrity on which it was built, by the so-called Transitional period of the late eighth century, controlled change had progressed to the extent that it is difficult to talk of an integrated Moche cultural or ideological material inventory.

The North: The Lambayeque Complex

I draw the third and final example of the response by Moche rulers to the crisis of 600 from the northern part of the region—the Lambayeque Valley. Here, although we see similarities to both of the examples discussed previously, the precise nature of response was determined by decisions that were again shaped by the peculiar geopolitical and historical circumstances in which local leaders found themselves. In the Middle Moche period the Lambayeque Valley complex had been the location of several important centers. The best known of these is Sipán. In the interior of one of the platforms at Sipán, several elite burials contained individuals clothed in the regalia worn by the principal officiates of the sacrifice ceremony and accompanied by elaborately crafted items that depicted the activities associated with this important ritual. Nowhere in these burials is there any indication that the personal identity of the occupant was being stressed. Rather, the Sipán burials contextually connect these important people to the vital ritual roles they had performed while living and the sacred place where this performance occurred. Emphasis is on the central functions of political authority, its ideological foundation, and the elite ruling group of which the Sipán individuals were members. Thus these burials are a collective affirmation of the existing Middle period social order rather than monuments to important individuals. This practice links the conception of power with that of the Jequetepeque Valley rather than with the more differentiated Moche Valley pattern, affording it greater structural capacity to confront threat within the context of its own meaning and averting the degree of profound transformation that afflicted the contemporary southern

polity. Also lessening the impact on Lambayeque society, on the material level, direct environmental consequences of the late sixth century droughts were probably even less in the Lambayeque Valley than in the two southern zones. Again, agricultural land located near the coast was probably abandoned (Shimada 1994:128–130). However, the status of the Lambayeque complex as the largest agricultural zone on the north coast, with its large hydraulic capacity supported by several adjacent rivers, would have helped alleviate the resulting impact.

Nevertheless, the breakdown of the wider Moche elite network, resulting from the inability of its members to sustain activities central to their status as ritual partners, and the disruption of the ritual process itself would have severely affected the basis of authority that had sustained the rulers of Sipán and other local Moche centers of the Middle period. Within the context of their relatively greater residual power, local leaders addressed this challenge to their authority in a very different way than their southern counterparts. We have seen that through much of its history communities embracing the Moche political order coexisted on the north coast with others who retained allegiance to the older, Gallinazo system. In the Middle period the Moche polity centered at the Huaca del Sol expanded south and incorporated several valleys that had remained within the Gallinazo cultural sphere in that area. However, other, autonomous Gallinazo communities persisted in the lower parts of the large northern valleys, including the Lambayeque complex. In the Late period, Moche leaders incorporated these surviving Gallinazo populations into an expanded polity, established a new and elaborate capital at Pampa Grande in the upper valley using the newly conquered subjects as forced laborers to construct architectural edifices of unprecedented size, and significantly modified the traditional symbols of the revitalized political leadership.

The fact that invasion was initiated at this particular time, after the two populations had lived together without excessive conflict for centuries, highlights the perceived degree of threat felt by leaders who were now experiencing an unprecedented degree of internal weakness. In a manner not uncommon in such circumstances, Lambayeque rulers attempted to avert internal breakdown by launching foreign conflict at a time when other Moche leaders were taking very different courses: Moche Valley leaders were inflicting radical coercive control on their own subjects, and the leaders of the Jequetepeque Valley appeared most concerned with instituting reform of the existing tradition rather than making a dramatic change. Partly this decision was made possible by the greater residual strength of the

Lambayeque to mobilize a large military force. Partly it was explicit choice among a number of possible courses. Clearly leaders could have taken a similar direction to those of their fellow leaders and focused on rebuilding their society's internal structural supports. Given the relatively greater resources remaining under their control, it would seem that such action would have had a very good potential for success. Nevertheless, their actual expansive policy clearly demonstrates the importance of individual choice acting within historical and spatial circumstance in determining response to crisis.

These Lambayeque Valley developments with their major demographic and political innovations at first appear to herald an abrupt change from the past. However, closer examination reveals that they were intentionally undertaken within the context of persisting Moche tradition. Thus, some of the chief traditional institutions and symbols of authority remained as the focus of the transformed order. As was the case at San José de Moro in the Jequetepeque Valley, and contrasting with the Galindo transformations, the dominant architectural symbol of traditional Moche power and political ideology—the platform mound—was retained as the central focus of power at the new town of Pampa Grande. Indeed, this great structure and its subsidiaries stand at the center of the urban complex in a great walled precinct that arguably represents the greatest feat of construction ever accomplished by a Moche authority. Similarly, much of the Late period ceramic iconography of the valley remains solidly in the tradition of Moche material symbolism.

Lambayeque Valley rulers, like their southern counterparts, succeeded in their immediate intentions—to halt the process of decline and to reconstitute the supports of their political domains on new social and ideological principles. However, once initiated, this process carried with it long-term and probably unforeseen and unintended consequences. By initiating successful external conquest, the Lambayeque Moche leaders, like their Moche Valley predecessors centuries before, established new and broader managerial needs that could not be met by existing institutions. As Izumi Shimada describes (1994), the Gallinazo conquest and resettlement, combined with the managerial requirement of building a new city containing some of the largest structures ever built on the north coast, required a high degree of managerial specialization and institutional differentiation. Lambayeque leaders of the Late period instituted these necessary reforms, thereby creating greater political hierarchy and social complexity. However, inherent in the new urban system was an unprecedented level of internal social and ethnic differentiation, exacerbated by the need to control a resentful foreign population. Clearly, internal tension, though probably dormant for a significant period, was a real component of the new system, awaiting the next phase of weakness to emerge as a destructive force.

At Pampa Grande the ceramic evidence indicates that during the eighth century foreign influence was growing, emanating from the expanding Wari Empire. While Late Moche ceramic iconography and forms remained dominant, it is quite possible that here, as elsewhere, the weakened tradition of Moche ideology was giving way to new cultural and ideological concepts that accompanied the weakening authority of local leaders. Given the fact that a major segment of the Pampa Grande population was descended from conquered Gallinazo outsiders who were forcibly settled at the site, this loosening of central control would in all probability have encouraged previously dormant inter-group tension to be expressed through outright competition. Although at this stage of archaeological knowledge the exact details of this process cannot be clearly discerned, there is little doubt that after a few generations the potential tensions innate in the new social order encouraged further dilution of the previously strong central authority and brought a new crisis sometime in the late eighth century. Overt internal conflict at this time resulted in the burning of the central architecture of government and political ideology at Pampa Grande and rapid abandonment of much of the settlement.

Following the fall of Pampa Grande, the material styles of Moche society merged with those of Wari state ideological symbolism in new centers of social integration, such as Huaca la Mayanga (Donnan 1972), which echoed the settlement patterns of the Middle Moche period. This new period of cultural reconstitution culminated in the so-called Early Sicán phase of Lambayeque Valley history, which also incorporated many Moche artistic and architectural modes and the belief systems that they expressed. By this achievement, the successors of the latest Pampa Grande rulers initiated a new phase of reconstitution, cultural vitality, and political recovery on modified ideological foundations, replacing the rejected Late Moche system. In so doing, they successfully utilized the specific circumstances of the late eighth century that had led to the abandonment of Pampa Grande to build another society using many traditional concepts and strategies of power. As was the case in the Jequetepeque Valley, continuity matched change in the process that we quite arbitrarily use to mark the end of Moche society in the north. Again, the term "collapse" hides the true nature of transition.

The Aftermath (750–1000)

Just as the processes of the crisis period were complex and diverse, so were their ultimate outcomes in the centuries that followed. According to the archaeological record as we now see it, this later period is similar to that which preceded the disruptions, with both being characterized by processes of social evolution that appear relatively gradual. In this they contrast with the more rapid changes generated by the Moche polities in the seventh and eighth centuries. In each of the three examples the social situation that emerged, though transformed by the consequences of decisions made by Moche rulers, set the stage for subsequent social evolution. However, in one profound way the later period differed from the former. The Middle period pattern in which numerous Moche polities were connected and reinforced by sharing a common ideology, once interrupted, never returned in the pre-European era. Subsequent north coast unity occurred under the umbrella of invasion and conquest. Thus, the period of crisis, though far from bringing the collapse often attributed to it, did lead to the permanent transformation of the region-wide sociopolitical system that lay at the core of Moche civilization, giving cause and meaning to its great symbols of political belief. So, we must describe the aftermath of florescent Moche civilization, in spite of its major continuity with the past, as one of differential local development, wherein each part of the north coast differed in form and substance from its counterparts.

Only in the Moche Valley, the location of the former Middle Moche southern polity, can we see anything close to traditional collapse. Here, a relatively long period of impact and response occurred in the context of political fragmentation, internal conflict, and overall decline in the ability of leaders to maintain either effective institutions of social integration or a belief system able to connect the various component groups within society. It followed that each desperate stage of attempted reconstitution brought new pressures that ultimately brought down the social order in the middle of the eighth century and terminated the last vestiges of the Moche civilization as a coherent system. With the controlling superstructure removed, people left the abandoned Moche centers and returned to a rural life based on village agriculture, with the only evidence of any centralizing force being a new foreign religious cult originating in the powerful Wari ideological system that appears to have been centered at the Huaca del Sol, probably co-opting its historic sacredness as a fitting place for its location (Menzel 1977). Although

some Moche cultural traits appear in the new Chimú polity of the tenth century, their meaning and contexts were reinterpreted to fit an entirely new structure. There was little direct continuity with the earlier civilization.

Elsewhere, no collapse occurred in this sense, and various degrees of continuity laid the groundwork for transition to later periods. We have noted that leaders in the Jequetepeque Valley, while failing to prevent an irreversible process of ideological and social change, were able to direct this change within existing Moche social norms. They even instituted new local rituals proclaimed in traditional symbolic form to replace the broader partnerships that had supported the earlier dominant ideology. However, there was concurrently a steady increase in foreign symbols and, more significantly, syncretism of Moche and foreign symbolic motifs and forms. By the end of the ninth century there was little sign of a coherent Moche ideological inventory, although many traditional symbols continued in the newly emerging Transitional culture (Castillo and Donnan 1994). Moreover, during this same period funerary rituals and architectural forms changed, the main modification being the introduction of collective burial, replacing the prevailing Moche practice of individual burial. This shift indicates a move toward a more communal basis for society and marks a telling sign of deep change in the concepts of group integration and ideas regarding the supernatural foundations of society.

We can assume that in the Transitional period the process of gradual change initiated in the time of crisis had progressed so far that the remaining Moche ideological symbols had lost their original significance. In spite of their continuing presence in the material record, their context of meaning had changed in quality, and with it we can no longer validly talk of a continuing Moche tradition. The unbroken process of historical development of the Jequetepeque Valley tradition in the period from 600 to 900 had produced a society organized by fundamentally new principles, many of them resulting from the merging of earlier Moche tenets with new, influential concepts of foreign origin. Moche civilization in the Jequetepeque Valley had evolved out of existence even before its late tenth century incorporation into a new, multi-valley conquest state centered in its northern Lambayeque neighbor.

As I have already noted, in spite of the overthrow of the Late Moche order marked by the burning and abandonment of Pampa Grande in the late eighth century, Lambayeque Valley history embodied a great deal of continuity. Thus, in the immediately succeeding period, sites such as the Huaca la Mayanga, following Middle

Moche architectural tenets and displaying important Moche symbols (Donnan 1972), suggest that the successors of the overthrown leaders of the Pampa Grande polity were able once again to reconstitute their authority along largely traditional lines. However, incorporation in the monumental Mayanga murals of central symbols of imperial Wari political ideology shows that at this time Lambayeque leaders, like those of other polities, were becoming increasingly dependant on new, pan-Andean ideas to reinforce their failing local systems. On this immediate post–Pampa Grande base they constructed the foundations of a new, florescent civilization whose great ceremonial platform centers and iconography indicate close links with the Moche past. Here, even more perhaps than in the Jequetepeque Valley, change occurred within an overriding context of continuity. The ensuing Sicán political system that reached florescence in the tenth century reinterpreted and used central Moche sociopolitical concepts (Shimada 1990). Thus, a number of powerful polities linked by a single ideology emerged throughout the Lambayeque complex. Their leaders used the same architectural and settlement canons as had their Moche predecessors and propelled important themes of Moche ideology into the future. By 1000 these polities had expanded south, replicating the Middle Moche expansion of many centuries before, and reunited the valleys north of the Moche Valley into the Lambayeque political realm. Here, continuity and reconstitution gave a continuity to north coast civilization that transcended the disruptions of the Late Moche period.

CONCLUSIONS

While the precise configuration of the late period of Moche history is still far from clear, its outline is gradually emerging. Our conventional view of the rise of a homogenous, centralized state centered on the Moche Valley, its consistent expansion through the region in the Middle period, and its subsequent collapse in the face of the intolerable effects of climatic disruption and foreign intrusion, must be revised. Current archaeological research is revealing a much less uniform picture, one in which there is significant geographical and temporal variability within the wider context of Late Moche sociopolitical development.

It is now evident that any developmental model for Moche civilization that accepts consistent and uniform cultural evolution, or proposes purely materialist causes for its collapse, must be rejected. Even more significantly, the idea of collapse as swift, inevitable, and final must be revised. By this point there can be little doubt that environmental disruption did affect the north coast of Peru in the late sixth century, bringing with it major deleterious results, but there is no reason to believe that this was the sole reason for the major transformations that affected the numerous existing polities, each of which was impacted differently and each of which possessed its own historically and geographically determined potential for meeting the crisis. Rather, recent work shows that we should look elsewhere for the factors that were decisive in determining that related change would not be temporary or reversible. Thus, the overarching ideological system that linked the otherwise autonomous Moche leaders and provided their supernatural authority required the involvement of all in a continuing cycle of ritual practice and symbolic display. Disruption of this network, probably initiated by the profound weakening of the southern polity, would have lessened the ability of its partners to maintain their traditional ritual interaction, necessitating the modifications that are apparent in the archaeological record, and thereby eroding the ideological core of Moche political order and ultimately leading to its demise. The end of Moche civilization lay in the inherent structural qualities of the cultural and ideological belief that regional leaders constructed as the basis of their power.

However, this transition took many decades, evolving differentially through local trajectories that in many parts of the Moche area were gradual and not necessarily negative. Indeed, we have seen structural change in the Lamabayeque Valley being implemented by political reconstitution and successful imperial expansion, not the picture usually associated with decline and collapse. Over the roughly three centuries that elapsed from the onset of the late-sixth-century time of crisis it is possible to trace a process during which the belief system that comprised the conceptual core of Moche was progressively diluted by foreign ideas, ironically introduced by Late Moche leaders themselves to bolster the now-rejected traditional ritual system. Thus, by 900, even in the north, where social and political vitality continued unchecked, it is no longer possible to talk of a Moche-dominated society. The succeeding Lambayeque phase, though incorporating many important, Moche-derived qualities, reconfigured these into a new conceptual system with its own material manifestations and symbols. Clearly, to understand such a process we must look at the internal conceptions and motivations of the various Moche polities as they developed in the region in order to identify the bases for their differential strategies and degrees of success and failure in dealing with crisis.

In conclusion, it is unwise to assume that collapse as we view it in the archaeological record was necessarily rapid, uniform, or final. Its study should take into account the important factor of local variation that was an integral part of early complex society, and the equally diverse evolutionary histories that accompanied this spatial variation. Collapse is neither inevitable nor irreversible, depending as it does on the intentional decisions of leaders limited only by the historically and physically particular environments within which they act.

[handwritten margin note: change in complexity causes a collapse]

REFERENCES

Alva, W., and C. B. Donnan
  1993 *The Royal Tombs of Sipán*. Los Angeles: Fowler Museum of Cultural History.

Bawden, G.
  1982 Galindo: A Study in Cultural Transition during the Middle Horizon. In *Chan Chan: Desert Andean City*, edited by M. Moseley and K. Day, pp. 285–320. Albuquerque: University of New Mexico Press.
  1996 *The Moche*. Oxford: Blackwell Publishers.
  2001 The Symbols of Late Moche Social Transformation. In *Moche: Art and Political Representation in Ancient Peru*, edited by J. Pillsbury, pp. 285–306. Washington, DC: National Gallery of Art.

Billman, B.
  1996 *The Evolution of Prehistoric Political Organizations in the Moche Valley, Peru*. Unpublished Ph.D. dissertation, University of California, Santa Barbara. Ann Arbor: University Microfilms.

Castillo, L. J.
  2001 The Last of the Mochicas: A Perspective from the Jequetepeque Valley. In *Moche: Art and Political Representation in Ancient Peru*, edited by J. Pillsbury, pp. 307–332. Washington, DC: National Gallery of Art.

Castillo, L. J., and C. B. Donnan
  1994 La Ocupación Moche de San José de Moro, Jequetepeque. In *Moche: Propuestas y Perspectivas*, edited by S. Yceda and E, Mujica, pp. 93–146. Lima: Universidad Nacional de la Libertad.

Chapdelaine, C.
  2000 Struggling for Survival: the Urban Class of the Moche Site, North Coast of Peru. In *Environmental Disaster and the Archaeology of Human Response*, edited by G. Bawden and R. Reycraft, pp. 121–142. Anthropological Papers of the Maxwell Museum of Anthropology 7. Albuquerque.

Culbert, T. P.
  1991 The Collapse of Classic Maya Civilization. In *The Collapse of Ancient States and Civilizations*, edited by N. Yoffee and G. L. Cowgill, pp. 69–102. Tucson: University of Arizona Press.

De Marrais, E., Castillo, L. J., and T. Earle
  1996 Ideology, Materialization, and Power Strategies. *Current Anthropology* 37:15–32.

Donnan, C. B.
  1972 Moche-Huari Murals from Northern Peru. *Archaeology* 25:85–95.

Dunnell, R. C.
  1980 Evolutionary Theory and Archaeology. *Advances in Archaeological Method and Theory* 3:35–99.

Eisenstadt, S. N.
  1986 *The Origins and Diversity of Axial Age Civilizations*. Albany: State University of New York Press.

Flannery, K. V.
  1972 The Cultural Evolution of Civilizations. *Annual Review of Ecology and Systematics* 3:399–426.

Fried, M.
  1960 On the Evolution of Social Stratification and the State. In *Culture in History: Essays in Honor of Paul Radin*, edited by S. Diamond, pp. 713–731. New York: Columbia University Press.

Friedman, J.
  1989 Culture, Identity and World Process. In *Domination and Resistance*, edited by D. Miller, C. Tilley, and M. Rowlands, pp. 246–260. London: Unwin and Hyman.

Friedman, J., and M. Rowlands, eds.
  1978 *The Evolution of Social Systems*. London: Duckworth.

Giddens, A.
  1984 *The Constitution of Society*. Berkeley: University of California Press.

Gilman, A.
  1981 The Development of Social Stratification in Bronze Age Europe. *Current Anthropology* 22:1–24.
  1984 Explaining the Upper Palaeolithic Revolution. In *Marxist Perspectives in Archaeology*, edited by M. Spriggs, pp. 115–126. Cambridge: Cambridge University Press.

Godelier, M.
  1986 *The Mental and the Material: Thought, Economy and Society*. London: Verso.

Haas, J., S. Pozorski, and T. Pozorski, eds.
  1987 *The Origins and Development of the Andean State*. Cambridge: Cambridge University Press.

Isbell, W. H.
  1997 *Mummies and Mortuary Monuments: A Postprocessual Prehistory of Central Andean Social Organization*. Austin: University of Texas Press.

Johnson, A. W., and T. Earle
  1987 *The Evolution of Human Societies*. Stanford: Stanford University Press.

Kristiansen, K.

1984 Ideology and Material Culture: An Archaeological Perspective. In *Marxist Perspectives in Archaeology*, edited by M. Spriggs, pp. 72–100. Cambridge: Cambridge University Press.

1991 Chiefdoms, States and Systems of Social Evolution. In *Chiefdoms: Power, Economy and Ideology*, edited by T. Earle, pp. 16–43. Cambridge: Cambridge University Press.

Kroeber, A. L.

1944 *Configurations of Culture Growth.* Berkeley: University of California Press.

1957 *Style and Civilization.* Ithaca: Cornell University Press.

1963 *An Anthropologist Looks at History.* Berkeley: University of California Press.

Leonard, R. D., and G. T. Jones

1987 Elements of an Inclusive Evolutionary Model for Archaeology. *Journal of Anthropological Archaeology* 6:199–219.

McGuire, R. H.

1992 *A Marxist Archaeology.* New York: Academic Press.

Menzel, D.

1977 *The Archaeology of Ancient Peru and the Work of Max Uhle.* Berkeley: R. H. Lowie Museum of Anthropology, University of California.

Moore, J. D.

1996 *Architecture and Power in the Ancient Andes.* Cambridge: Cambridge University Press.

Moseley, M. E.

1987 Punctuated Equilibrium: Searching the Ancient Record for El Niño. *Quarterly Review of Archaeology* 17:19–27.

Patterson, T. C., and C. W. Gailey, eds.

1987 *Power Relations and State Formation.* Salem, WI: Sheffield.

Renfrew, A. C.

1984 *Approaches to Social Archaeology.* Cambridge: Cambridge University Press.

Sahlins, M. D., and E. R. Service, eds.

1960 *Evolution and Culture.* Ann Arbor: University of Michigan Press.

Service, E. R.

1960 The Law of Evolutionary Potential. In *Evolution and Culture*, edited by M. D. Sahlins and E. R. Service, pp. 93–122. Ann Arbor: University of Michigan Press.

1975 *Origins of the State and Civilization: The Process of Cultural Evolution.* New York: Norton.

Shimada, I.

1990 Cultural Continuities and Discontinuities on the Northern North Coast of Peru, Middle-Late Horizons. In *The Northern Dynasties: Kingship and Statecraft in Chimor,* edited by M. E. Moseley and A. Cordy-Collins, pp. 297–394. Washington, DC: Dumbarton Oaks.

1994 *Pampa Grande and the Mochica Culture.* Austin: University of Texas Press.

Shimada, I., C. B. Schaff, L. G. Thompson, and E. Moseley-Thompson

1991 Cultural Impacts of Severe Droughts in the Prehistoric Andes: Application of a 1500-Year Ice Core Precipitation Record. *World Archaeology* 22:247–270.

Spengler, O.

1962 *The Decline of the West.* New York: Modern Library. [Originally published in 1918–1922]

Tainter, J. A.

1988 *The Collapse of Complex Societies.* Cambridge: Cambridge University Press.

Toynbee, A. J.

1962 *A Study of History.* Oxford: Oxford University Press. [Originally published in 1933–1954]

Yoffee, N., and G. L. Cowgill, eds.

1991 *The Collapse of Ancient States and Civilizations.* Tucson: University of Arizona Press.

Zagarell, A.

1986 Trade, Women, Class and Society in Ancient Western Asia. *Current Anthropology* 27:415–431.

8

Sociopolitical Collapse, Niche Adaptation, and Ethnogenesis

Prehistoric Social Responses to Natural Disaster in the Far South Coast of Peru

Richard Martin Reycraft

THE CHIRIBAYA

Between approximately AD 1000 and 1350, an economically complex chiefdom flourished in the Lower Osmore drainage of south coastal Peru (Figure 30; all dates in this chapter are AD). This society is now identified as the Chiribaya, and this interval has been defined as their Classic phase (Reycraft 1998). For the Chiribaya, this phase was a time of cultural florescence, population growth, and agricultural development in which they expanded their territory to encompass the coastal valley, the coastal plain, and even portions of the lower Andes foothills (Jessup 1990; Owen 1993; Rice 1993). The Classic phase Chiribaya maintained a two-tier settlement system, and their material culture (standardized ceramics, decorated textiles, model boats, smelted copper fishing paraphernalia, and gold ceremonial pectorals and axes) indicates the presence of a differentiated socioeconomic system with elites and several varieties of economic specialists (Boytner 1992; Jessup 1990; Moseley 1992; Owen 1993).

The Chiribaya placed large quantities of decorated pottery, basketry, textiles, wood, and metal items in their elite tombs. At times they even interred human attendants with their leaders (Lozada Cerna 1998). Their seat of government, Chiribaya Alta (Figure 31), contains disproportionate quantities of elite burials and large residential structures (Buikstra 1995; Moseley 1992). At their apex, the Chiribaya elite planned and completed several large corporate labor projects within their territory. These projects include a long embankment wall at Chiribaya Alta, stone ceremonial plazas at several coastal sites, and a 9-km-long irrigation canal network carved into the rock wall facing the coastal valley.

The Chiribaya stopped producing their elite material culture by 1360. Their largest villages and most complex irrigation systems were also abandoned at this time (Jessup 1990; Satterlee 1993). Geoarchaeological analysis (Satterlee 1993) of the deep, compressed sediments that overlie most Classic phase sites indicates that the Chiribaya endured an extreme El Niño Southern Oscillation (ENSO) event during this retrenchment period. Torrential rains resulting from this "mega" Niño produced large mudflows that breached irrigation canals and buried habitations and associated agricultural fields. In this paper, I discuss the nature of this event and some Chiribaya responses to it.

El NIÑO SOUTHERN OSCILLATION

The following is a brief introduction to El Niño (for more extensive overviews of the subject see Reycraft 2000 and Caviedes 2001). The social impact of an El Niño event depends on spatiotemporal variations in intensive storm characteristics (torrential rains), their interaction with local ecological variables (soil aridity, local topography), and the technological, settlement, and demographic characteristics of cultural groups experiencing the climatic episode. Differences in the severity and distribution of destructive effects will also influence the nature and intensity of the social response to these events (Burton et al. 1978; Sheets and Grayson 1979; White 1974).

Marine Ecosystemic Effects

Severe El Niño events may mature for five months and often last longer than a year (Barber and Chavez 1983; Caviedes 1984). During an extreme ENSO event, shifting tradewinds result in a large incursion of surface tropical waters that depress the cold, nutrient-rich, coastal Humboldt current (Arntz 1986; Barber and Chavez 1983; Cane 1983; Caviedes 1984). As a result, high-density pelagic species of fish such as sardine (*S. sagax*) and anchovy (*E. ringens*), which feed on cold-current phytoplankton and zooplankton, die or migrate south to Chilean waters. These species are replaced by more solitary subtropical species such as tuna (*T. albacore*) and bonito (*S. chiliensis chiliensis*) (Alamo V. and Bouchon 1987; Arntz 1986; Barber and Chavez 1983; Caviedes

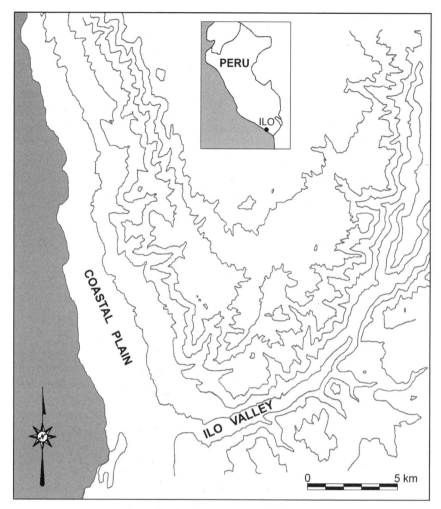

Figure 30. The Lower Osmore study region:
the Ilo Valley is the lowest portion of the Osmore drainage.

1984). Marine invertebrates experience similar effects. This species replacement results in drastically lower fishing yields. As the fish disappear, fur seals, sea lions, and guano birds, which feed on the pelagic species, also die or migrate to southern refuges (Arntz 1986; Tovar et al. 1987).

Topographic Flood Effects

The study region is one of the world's driest deserts, and under normal climatic conditions it receives virtually no annual rainfall (Schwerdtfeger 1976). The influx of tropical currents during an extreme ENSO event inundates this hyper-arid landform with torrential rains (Goldberg et al. 1987). This rainfall appears as extensive areal increases in daily background precipitation and localized, intensive torrential storm cells. During an El Niño year, the coastal regions of Peru may receive more than 50% of their normal annual precipitation in a single rainstorm. These heavy

rains result in overflowing rivers, bank erosion, flash floods, and the inundation of dwellings and cropland.

CHIRIBAYA SOCIAL ECOLOGY

The Chiribaya occupation of the Lower Osmore can be divided into coastal plain and inland valley components (Figure 30). In contrast to the spacious river valleys of north coastal Peru, the Lower Osmore is a deep, narrow ravine with sheer walls that have traditionally prevented large-scale importation of marine resources to the interior. During the Classic phase, the Chiribaya lived in several large villages along the base of the valley perimeter. A 9-km-long irrigation canal, carved into the rock face of the valley and spanning multiple *quebradas* (arroyos), fed an extensive agricultural system that linked many of these sites.

The coastal plain, a narrow belt of hyper-desert situated between the base of the Andean foothills and

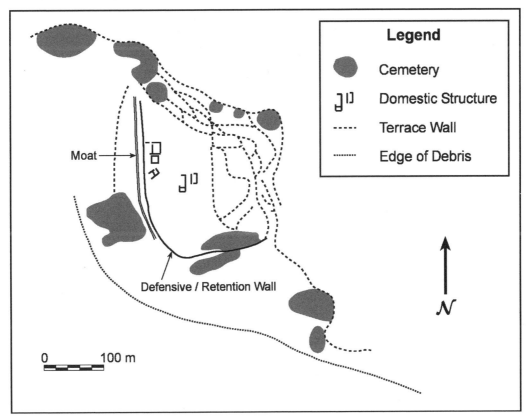

Figure 31. The Chiribaya Alta site. All of the identified structures are shown, but the site has been heavily looted and many have probably been destroyed. The site was an elite village with a few, large residences, and elite cemeteries.

the Pacific Ocean, contains a series of freshwater springs (Clement and Moseley 1989). The Chiribaya who lived adjacent to these springs were able to exploit three contiguous ecological microzones. The foothills, which are located directly above the springs, supported dense patches of fog-fed vegetation. The abundant projectile points and camelid pens found in these foothills indicate their importance for small game hunting and llama herding. Directly below this zone a series of spring-fed drainages supported short irrigation systems. Finally, below the irrigation areas, the ocean provided abundant seafood, including high-density pelagic fish, near-shore solitary species, and both sandy beach and rocky littoral shellfish (Bawden 1989; Reycraft 1998).

THE IMPACT EVENT AND THE CHIRIBAYA RESPONSE

Large portions of most Classic phase Chiribaya sites were buried beneath a thick, highly compact debris-flow deposit (Figure 32). Radiocarbon dates of cultural material found in this stratum indicate it was deposited circa 1360 (Satterlee 1993).

The debris flows in the Lower Osmore Valley breached the irrigation canal at every quebrada and buried it where it passed along agricultural terraces. Ten-meter-thick flows buried some of the higher-elevation agricultural terraces (Satterlee 1993). The El Niño impact was less severe along the coastal plain because most coastal Chiribaya settlements and agricultural fields were situated above quebradas, near freshwater springs. In most cases, the quebradas contained the debris flows until they reached the lower parts of these sites. The coastal Chiribaya were not totally fortunate, however, as most of their low-elevation irrigation canals were buried, stranding the agricultural fields below them. Astonishingly, an entire coastal Chiribaya village (which was lamentably situated below the mouth of a coastal quebrada) was buried by a large, fan-shaped debris flow (Satterlee 1993) (Figure 33).

Post-Disaster Settlement

The Chiribaya responded to this catastrophic event in a variety of ways. First and foremost, they abandoned nearly the entire valley. Approximately 77% of their valley agricultural sites were deserted after the event

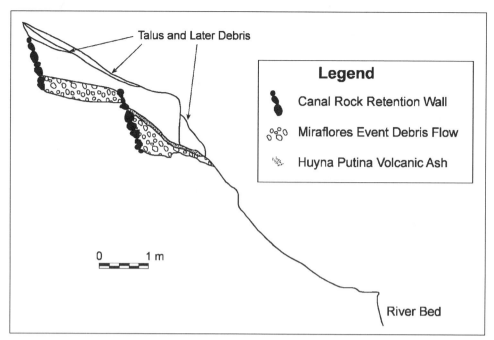

Figure 32. Classic Chiribaya phase valley irrigation canal profile (note "Miraflores" El Niño deposits). The ash is from the 1600 eruption of the Huaynaputina volcano near Arequipa Pery. It is used region-wide as a stratigraphic marker for pre-1600 deposits.

(Reycraft 2000: Fig. 38b). All of the large, Classic phase agricultural complexes were also abandoned. A few post-disaster valley settlements contained vestigial residential areas that, in some sites, were constructed atop the old agricultural terraces. The long canal network was completely destroyed by the event. The Chiribaya did not reconstruct this irrigation system. Indeed, there is no further evidence of canal construction in the Lower Osmore Valley until the Spanish colonization of the area in the sixteenth century. Perhaps the most telling abandonment was that of Chiribaya Alta. This site, which once represented the political apex of Classic phase Chribaya power, was abandoned despite the fact that it remained untouched by the debris flows.

In a stark contrast to the Osmore Valley situation, six out of seven Classic phase Chiribaya coastal settlements managed to endure the disaster (Reycraft 2000: Fig. 38b). Nevertheless, substantial portions of these villages were discarded. In most, the upper habitation and irrigation areas endured while the lower domestic and agricultural terraces were abandoned. The mid-elevation agricultural fields at one site (Carrizal Spring) were also buried; however, these terraces were reactivated by covering the hardened debris flows with organic-rich, domestic midden soil. Fossil roots and root casts found in this soil indicate that the reactivation efforts were successful.

One of the most notable transformations in the post-disaster Chiribaya social system was the appearance of a

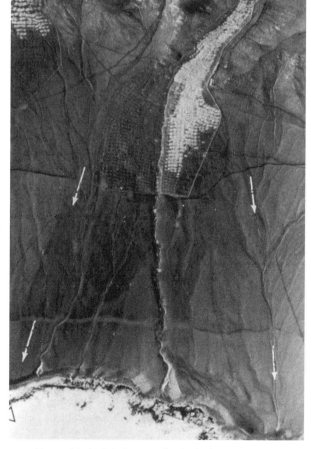

Figure 33. Aerial photograph of Miraflores quebrada (note fan-shaped El Niño event debris flow).

new suite of coastal settlements (Reycraft 2000: Fig. 38b). These settlements, named the Burro Flaco site complex (after a peculiarly named type-site), were established on the beach directly below many of the coastal spring communities. The Burro Flaco sites were specialized fishing villages. Domestic structures and middens at the type-site are full of fishing paraphernalia and marine faunal remains. Burial accouterments also contained fishhooks, harpoons, and model fishing boats. Although agricultural remains are abundant in the domestic middens at these sites, because neither irrigation sources nor agricultural fields are present, these products must also have been imported from the spring sites.

Post-Disaster Material Culture

Household Archaeology

Several post-disaster Chiribaya domestic structures were excavated at the coastal Carrizal Spring and Burro Flaco sites. The evidence indicates that the Chiribaya maintained their vernacular architectural traditions throughout the disaster. Thus, both pre- and post-disaster Chiribaya domestic architecture was constructed of cane wattle-and-daub in a rectangular or square design with modular internal room divisions (Reycraft 2000; Rice 1993).

A second type of structure was found at the Burro Flaco sites: trapezoidal rock enclosures lacking domestic features. These two types of structures were usually associated in a pattern reminiscent of the household-patio complex commonly found in both the Andean highland and Mesoamerican regions. In the latter areas, patios serve as external work areas for the inhabitants of the domestic structures. Excavation data at Burro Flaco suggest a similar function for the rock enclosures. The cane structures contained hearths, ash dumps, and domestic refuse, whereas the rock enclosures held ceramic and botanical debris, some marine fishing gear, and small storage features. The household-patio complex does not appear to have been a feature of Classic phase Chiribaya sites (Jessup 1990; Rice 1993).

Ceramic Assemblages

Pre-disaster, Classic phase Chiribaya ceramics were relatively standardized. They were manufactured with red-orange to red-brown pastes, red slips, and were often elaborately decorated in geometric combinations of black, white, orange, and brown motifs (Jessup 1990; Umire and Miranda 2001). Classic phase ceramic bowls have a semi-ovoid shape, one or two handles, and everted, straight, or

inverted mouths. Bowl rims are decorated with white dots on a black base, and the majority of bowls are decorated on the interior with motifs such as pendant three-point stars, semicircles, bands filled with alternating semicircles, or cross-ribbon bands.

Post-disaster Chiribaya ceramics are generally similar to their Classic phase predecessors. Similar pastes, slips, and, for the most part, vessel forms were used during both phases. Nonetheless, whereas up to 40% of Classic phase ceramics were elaborately decorated, the post-disaster ceramics were almost completely undecorated (1% decorated wares). A few vessel forms also changed after the El Niño event. These changes are most evident in the following types of bowls:

Chiribaya-style bowls. These vessels have similar shapes, pastes, and slips as their Classic phase processors, but they are primarily undecorated. Rarely, the interiors are decorated with simplified, vestigial Classic phase designs.

Chiriquiña-style bowls. The term Chiriquiña was coined to emphasize the expression of a foreign stylistic influence on some post-disaster Chiribaya bowls (Reycraft 1998). The influence came from the Estuquiña culture, a neighboring people who occupied the mountainous Upper Osmore region during the immediate pre- and post-disaster era. Chiriquiña became an important ceramic sub-tradition in which Estuquiña formal characteristics, such as vessel shape, rim angle, and protuberance type, were merged with Chiribaya decorative attributes and pastes (Reycraft 2005).

Textiles

Like their ceramic counterparts, pre- and post-disaster Chiribaya textiles share many formal attributes. Most are warp-faced and utilize predominantly z-spun, s-plied wool threads. The major differences between the textiles of these two phases are related to color palettes and the amount of labor invested in their production (monitored by dense weaves, dyed cloths, and complex design motifs). To emphasize some of these distinctions, I will discuss the stylistic change in Chiribaya shirts and hats. I chose these textile categories because ethnohistoric sources suggest that hats and shirts, the most visible clothing items, were considered the primary indicator of ethnicity in the ancient Andean world (Cobo 1956 [1653]).[1]

Classic phase Chiribaya shirt decoration varied from undecorated, natural brown shirts to elaborate specimens with purple, blue, red, and gold warp lateral stripes over a maroon or coffee-colored base cloth (Clark et al. 1993). Variability in Classic phase Chiribaya shirt quality and form has been assigned to both gender-sex and status-rank distinctions. Textiles from the prime site, Chiribaya Alta, are generally finer, denser, and had more elaborate dye coloring and finish techniques than those studied from other Classic Chiribaya sites (Boytner 1992). Several status and sex groups have also been identified in the Classic phase textile data. One of these groups utilized large, standardized, trapezoidal shirts with repetitive lateral warp stripes in combinations of red and purple, red and blue, and red and greenish blue (Clark et al. 1993).

Post-disaster Chiribaya shirts are decorated with warp-striping, supplemental warp-pin striping, or supplemental discontinuous warp-pin striping arranged in all-around-symmetrical, lateral-symmetrical, or shoulder/sleeve-central/torso designs. In a striking contrast to their elegantly dyed Classic phase predecessors, the post-disaster Chiribaya shirts were decorated in natural hue combinations of black, gold, and tan or over a coffee or brown base (Reycraft 2000: Figs. 43 and 44). Dyed yarns or evidence of standardization of shirt color or structure has not been found on post-disaster Chiribaya shirts.

Classic phase Chiribaya hats are tall, either cylindrical or square, and were constructed by the knotted-looping of wool fibers. These hats are decorated in monochrome relief with zigzag, diamond, and vertical line motifs (Reycraft 2000: Fig. 45). Most Classic phase Chiribaya hats are red and black; however, some are solid dark brown.

Post-disaster Chiribaya hats were manufactured of camelid wool with the looping-over-foundation technique. Known examples of post-disaster Chiribaya hats are all short and pillbox-shaped. The decorative patterns were constructed by yarn color changes within the weave structure. The most common hat designs accentuate contrasting patterns in natural, brown, black, and gold yarns. For example, excavation revealed a plain brown hat, a gold and black zigzag motif hat, and a brown hat with symmetrically arranged golden triangles (Reycraft 2000: Fig. 46).[2]

These changes in textile tradition are striking because, unlike Classic phase Chiribaya textiles, post-disaster Chiribaya shirts and hats are often strikingly similar to Estuquiña examples. Both have similar design patterning and structural form, and both utilized predominantly natural, coffee, brown, black, and gold undyed yarns (Reycraft 2005).

Mortuary Data and Prestige Goods

Although Classic phase and post-disaster Chiribaya tombs are identical in form, major differences occur in types of articles placed in burials of the two periods.

Classic phase Chiribaya tombs, especially those from Chiribaya Alta, have been heavily looted because of the quantity and quality of their mortuary articles. The prime site contains nine distinct cemeteries and abundant elite burials. These elite tombs often contain copious decorated ceramic wares, multicolored ornate textiles, fine basketry, and, at times, gold and copper prestige goods along with human attendant burials (Buikstra 1995; Lozada Cerna 1998). Singular among these prestige goods are gold ceremonial hand axes. Several of these axes are on display in local museums, all reputedly looted from Chiribaya Alta. The axes most likely functioned as status objects and symbols of office for high-ranking Chiribaya leaders.

Although current information is still limited, post-disaster Chiribaya tombs do not contain these elite burial objects. Most of the grave goods that have been found in these burials are vastly simpler versions of their Classic period counterparts. For example, the ceremonial hand axes, formerly constructed of gold, now appear with wooden or cane shafts that hold poorly smelted copper axe blades.

DISCUSSION AND CONCLUSIONS

The Chiribaya Valley–based communities were large, agriculturally specialized, and organizationally linked along an irrigation canal. Settlement systems with such attributes are particularly sensitive to the effects of intense natural disasters, particularly in arid areas where alternative resources are scarce (Burton et al. 1978; Sheets and Grayson 1979; White 1974). The most conspicuous Chiribaya disaster response, the mass abandonment of the Lower Osmore Valley, was the result of a hazardous political decision. The Chiribaya leaders provided for the vast majority of their own, and their constituents', resource needs with the construction of a single, precariously situated canal network. Although this large irrigation system may have initially been constructed by accretion, its finished worth is represented by the total labor and materials that would be required to rebuild it (Earle 1978). In a single stroke the ENSO event rendered the entire system useless.

Irrigation-dependent populations that lack alternative food sources must rapidly repair their canal system or face starvation (Earle 1978). Extreme El Niño events spread destruction across vast territories. Once the destructive effects of the El Niño event surpassed the extent of their territorial jurisdiction, the Chiribaya leaders would have been unable to draw resources and manpower from unaffected regions within their domain.

Speedy reconstruction efforts require larger work crews, and, as the irrigation system fed multiple communities, essential labor would have been required from several settlements. The conscription of large labor crews from different settlements necessitates a very coordinated level of organizational leadership. Without this authority, resource-stressed settlements would be unlikely to donate labor to rebuild distant (downstream) sections of the canal. The leaders of the Chiribaya valley settlements were faced with an immense reconstruction effort but lacked viable alternative food resources.

There is good evidence that the Chiribaya political hierarchy did not survive for long after the event. Prior to the disaster, Chiribaya leaders resided in large residential compounds and were buried in exclusive cemeteries at Chiribaya Alta. The tombs of these leaders contained elaborate burial goods, such as standardized multicolored tunics, gold ceremonial axes, gold pectorals, highly decorated ceramics, wood burial litters, and human retainers (Buikstra 1995; Lozada Cerna 1998; Reycraft 1998). After the disaster this elite material culture disappeared, and Chiribaya Alta was abandoned.

Finding themselves without their political hierarchy and their large irrigation network, the only viable option for the vast majority of the valley peoples was migration. Regional abandonment on such a large scale invariably leads to questions concerning the destination of the former inhabitants. During the period in question, Estuquiña peoples occupied the adjacent Upper Osmore region. Around the time the Lower Osmore Valley was abandoned, population swelled in the Upper Osmore, and former valley-bottom Estuquiña occupations were relocated to defensive hilltop locations. The latter activity suggests the occurrence of raiding, which often accompanies rapid population migrations into previously settled regions. Increased quantities of marine shell and fish bone found at Estuquiña sites during this period also indicate greater levels of coastal-highlands contact (Stanish 1992).

This evidence suggests the possibility of substantial coastal migration into the Upper Osmore region. However, no diagnostic Chiribaya stylistic traits appear in this region to document such an event. The lack of Chiribaya stylistic attributes in the Upper Osmore may be explained by concomitant changes in material culture that occurred in the Lower Osmore region. After the disaster, the Chiribaya ceramic assemblage lost most of its decorative embellishment and, along with the textiles assemblage, adopted selected Estuquiña stylistic motifs. Chiribaya imitation of Estuquiña textile colors and motifs and ceramic vessel form and finish attributes would, in effect,

have camouflaged the more portable material culture items employed by coastal migrants in the highland zone. In short, based on what we now know about post-disaster Chiribaya culture, we should not expect to see "diagnostic" portable Chiribaya material culture accompanying this migration. Studies by Reycraft (1998) and Stanish (1993) suggest that domestic structure form is a more practical monitor of group affiliation in the south Andean region.

In contrast to their valley brethren, the coastal spring communities were relatively small, utilized diverse resources, and were organizationally self-sufficient. Before the onset of the ENSO event, the Chiribaya coastal settlements relied on irrigation agriculture, shallow and deep sea fish, and sandy beach and rocky littoral shellfish for their primary resource needs. Camelids, deer, and several small mammals were also utilized as protein supplements. Although their primary resources would have been severely affected by the El Niño, these coastal populations did have viable alternatives. The increased levels of background precipitation that occur during an El Niño often result in a coastal bloom of fog-fed vegetation (Caviedes 1984)—an important resource for both domesticated camelids and wild species. Camelids, deer, and other wild species that utilize this vegetation would have been more abundant during the disaster. Although not plentiful, tropical fish species would also have been available throughout the El Niño event.

Another advantage for the coastal communities was organizational autonomy. Not being linked along a single irrigation canal, the coastal settlements were not as interdependent as their valley counterparts. Their irrigation systems were small, self-contained, and more easily repairable. Coastal people did not have to rely on the conscription of labor from multiple settlements for system repair because self-interested labor groups could be recruited among relatives and friends inside each community. The coastal communities were also able to shed some of their excess population through the colonization of a new environmental niche.

As noted above, the sea, which is the first resource affected by ENSO events, is also the first resource to recover from such an event (Arntz 1986; Tovar et al. 1987). As the warm El Niño currents withdraw, the cold coastal current quickly returns, and marine nutrients will rapidly return to their previous levels. Many of the fish, birds, and sea mammals that have migrated south come back with the return of the cold current. Although these species may take generations to replenish their pre-disaster numbers, sufficient quantities of marine wildlife would have been available to sustain small fishing populations.

Fishing would also have been assisted by the onset of a La Niña, the cold phase of ENSO that follows many extreme events. During La Niña, cold-water currents strongly reassert themselves and produce better-than-normal fishing conditions. Thus, after the El Niño event, favorable fishing conditions would return and fishing would have become a very important resource for stressed coastal populations.

The Burro Flaco sites represent a successful response to the stresses placed on large populations when their resources are constrained. The novel characteristic of the beachfront Burro Flaco sites is site specialization. Before the Miraflores ENSO event, fishing and agricultural peoples lived together at the Chiribaya spring and valley mouth settlements. After the event, the fisher-folk established specialized settlements directly on the beach. Intersite cooperation between these populations was necessary because the beach locations lacked a freshwater supply.

A comparison of site structure data from Burro Flaco and Carrizal Spring reveals both similarities and differences between the two sites. The Burro Flaco domestic pattern is reminiscent of a household-patio complex. This spatial arrangement has not been found at other types of Chiribaya sites (Jessup 1990; Rice 1993).

The placement of exterior patio work locations is often related to the organization of, and the necessity for, corporate labor in resource procurement and processing. Such defined exterior locations provide loci for multi-household, extended family groups to work together. The socio-spatial domestic arrangements seen at Burro Flaco, as opposed to all other Chiribaya settlements, suggest that labor was organized differently at these sites. These differences may be a reflection of the distinct corporate labor requirements of specialized marine settlements as opposed to more generalized agropastoral/fishing communities. Although marine resources were utilized at both sites, closer examination of the faunal and artifact assemblages at Burro Flaco and Carrizal Spring revealed intersite differences in resource procurement strategies. While the occupants of Carrizal Spring supplemented their carbohydrate diet with fish, shellfish, and some land mammals, the occupants of Burro Flaco, in addition utilizing these resources, also exploited sea mammals (Reycraft 1998). This discrepancy is also apparent in the tool assemblages found at both sites; several wooden and copper toggle harpoons were found at Burro Flaco, but none appeared at Carrizal Spring.

Owing to the size and intelligence of sea mammals, their exploitation frequently requires the coordination of multiple individuals in both the hunting and processing

phases. Resource procurement strategies requiring high levels of task synchronicity among multiple individuals often result in the formation of corporate labor groups. These labor groups are usually composed of related kin in the form of extended families (van den Berghe 1979). As these fishing communities matured, they apparently developed distinct corporate and social structures in response to the requirements of their specialized marine environment.

As Zagarell states in Chapter 3,

variations in social structure between several societies with similar modes of production, variations that may appear minor, can have important implications for social transformation.

Similarly, historical events, "historical accident," and even misreadings of situations by the participants can change evolutionary pathways.

While minor variations in social structure between societies with similar modes of production can have significant consequences during social upheaval, small variations in social structure that exist *within* a complex society can also have these effects. The collapse of a complex society "may give rise to sets of social relations that never previously existed. Although these societies *may* be less hierarchical than the preexisting states, they are not necessarily a throwback to the past" (Zagarell, Chapter 3, this volume). When complex societies collapse, they do not simply return to some prior, less-organizationally-complex state. Complex polities generate multiple economic modes of production, some of which are dominant, others less so. In the Chiribaya example, sociopolitical collapse was linked to a dominant, irrigation-dependent mode of production. This mode of production was all but eliminated by a cataclysmic event. New avenues of development were explored after the disaster. Primary among these was a marine fishing specialization.

The manifest Estuquiña stylistic presence in post-disaster Chiribaya material culture suggests a strong cultural influence from the adjacent sierra region. Post-disaster Chiribaya ceramic bowl forms have obvious Estuquiña stylistic attributes, and the percentage of decorated/undecorated wares in the post-disaster Chiribaya ceramic assemblage is very similar to the ratio of decorated wares found in the Estuquiña ceramic assemblage. Likewise, post-disaster Chiribaya textiles often mimic Estuquiña textiles in their form and color palette.

On the other hand, post-disaster Chiribaya architecture and tomb form are consistent with Classic phase antecedents, and no Estuquiña sites or domestic structures have been found in the Lower Osmore region. This evidence does not indicate a population replacement or an invasion by highland Estuquiña peoples. The evidence does, however, suggest that the Estuquiña did influence the stylistic choices made by post-disaster Chiribaya people. I suggest that post-disaster Chiribaya people had begun the process of changing their ethnic identification (Reycraft 2005). Exterior clothing and ritual ceramic wares, the items of material culture that have the most emblematic potential (Rice 1987: 251; Wobst 1977), show evidence of borrowing of significant Estuquiña stylistic attributes. Vernacular architecture and tomb form, more latent indicators of ethnic identification, do not. The Spanish conquest of the study area disrupted this re-identification process.

CONCLUSION

Sociopolitical collapse is a complex phenomenon that can take many forms and may occur for many reasons (Tainter 1988; Yoffee and Cowgill 1988). In the case of the Chiribaya, collapse occurred in a territorially restricted polity with precariously located, critical infrastructure, as it attempted to cope with a natural catastrophe. However, in contrast to a stereotypical view of collapse, the Chiribaya did not vanish, nor did they simply cycle back to some less-complex form of existence. They adapted. They created new social forms; they entered new environmental niches; and, somewhat like the post-*oppidum* societies described by Wells (Chapter 2), they began to create new social identities in the process.

I thank the Fulbright Foundation, the Latin American Institute, and the Southern Peru Copper Corporation for their generous support of this research.

NOTES

1. Spanish accounts attest that the Inka could identify the ethnic affiliation of individuals by observing their cap and shirt style. For this study, textile information was taken from mortuary and domestic contexts.

2. The shape and design of the latter example appear identical to an Estuquiña hat depicted by Clark (1993: Fig. 3.21b).

REFERENCES CITED

Alamo,V., and M. Bouchon
  1987 Changes in the Food and Feeding of the Sardine (*Sardinops sagax sagax*) during the Years 1980–1984 off the Peruvian Coast. *Journal of Geophysical Research* 92:14,411–14,415.

Arntz, W.
  1986 The Two Faces of El Niño 1982–83. *Meeresforsch* 31:1–46.

Barber, R. T., and F. P. Chavez
  1983 Biological Consequences of El Niño. *Science* 222:1203–1210.

Bawden, G.
  1989 Pre-Incaic Cultural Ecology of the Lower Osmore Region. In *Ecology, Settlement and History in the Osmore Drainage, Peru,* edited by D. Rice, C. Stanish, and P. Scarr, pp. 183–206. BAR International Series 545i. Oxford.

Boytner, R.
  1992 *Ilo-Tumilaca/Cabuza, Chiribaya, and Their Relationships with the Tiwanaku Culture as Can Be Seen in the Textiles from the Coastal Osmore Valley, Southern Peru.* Unpublished M.A. Thesis, Department of Anthropology, UCLA.

Buikstra, J.
  1995 Tombs for the Living . . . or . . . for the Dead: The Osmore Ancestors. In *Tombs for the Living: Andean Mortuary Practices,* edited by T. Dillehay, pp. 229–280. Washington, DC: Dumbarton Oaks.

Burton, I., R. W. Kates, and G. F. White
  1978 *Environment as Hazard.* Oxford: Oxford University Press.

Cane, M. A.
  1983 Oceanic Events during El Niño. *Science* 222 (4629):1189–1194.

Caviedes, C. N.
  1984 El Niño 1982–83. *Geographical Review* 74:267–290.
  2001 *El Niño in History: Storming through the Ages.* Gainesville: University Press of Florida.

Clark, N. R.
  1993 *The Estuquina Textile Tradition: Cultural Patterning in Late Prehistoric Fabrics from Moquegua, Far Southern Peru.* Ph.D. Dissertation, Anthropology Department, Washington University in St. Louis.

Clark, N. R., P. Palacios, and N. Juarez
  1993 Projecto Textil III, Chiribaya Baja: Cementero 1 Fardos y Textiles. Preliminary report for Projecto Contisuyu. Unpublished ms. on file, Museo Contisuyu, Moquegua, Peru.

Clement, C. O., and M. E. Moseley
  1989 Agricultural Dynamics in the Andes. In *Ecology,*

Settlement and History in the Osmore Drainage, Peru, edited by D. Rice, C. Stanish, and P. Scarr, pp. 435–456. BAR International Series 545i. Oxford.

Cobo, Bernabé
1956 *Historia del nuevo mundo,* edited by P. F. Mateos. Biblioteca de Autores Espanoles, Vol. 91–92. Madrid: Ediciones Atlas. [Originally published in 1653]

Earle, T.
1978 *Economic and Social Organization of a Complex Chiefdom: The Halelea District, Kaua'i Hawaii.* Anthropological Papers No. 63. Ann Arbor: Museum of Anthropology, University of Michigan.

Goldberg, R. A., G. Tisnado, and R. A. Scofield
1987 Characteristics of Extreme Rainfall Events in Northwestern Peru during the 1982–1983 El Niño Period. *Journal of Geophysical Research* 92:14,225–14,241.

Jessup, D.
1990 *Desarollos Generales en el Intermedio Tardio en el Valle de Ilo, Peru.* Moquegua, Peru: Informe Interno del Projecto Contisuyu, Museo Contisuyu.

Lozada Cerna, M.
1998 *The Señorio of Chiribaya: A Bio-Archaeological Study in the Osmore Drainage of Southern Peru.* Ph.D. dissertation, University of Chicago. Ann Arbor: University Microfilms.

Moseley, M. E.
1992 *The Inca and Their Ancestors.* London: Thames and Hudson.

Owen, B.
1993 *A Model of Multi-ethnicity: State Collapse, Competition, and Social Complexity from Tiwanaku to Chiribaya in the Osmore Valley, Peru.* Ph.D. dissertation, University of California, Los Angeles. Ann Arbor: University Microfilms.

Reycraft, R.M.
1998 *The Terminal Chiribaya Project: The Archaeology of Human Response to Natural Disaster in South Coastal Peru.* Ph.D. dissertation, University of New Mexico. Ann Arbor: University Microfilms.
2000 Long-Term Human Response to El Niño in South Coastal Peru, circa A.D. 1400. In *Environmental Disaster and the Archaeology of Human Response,* edited by G. Bawden and R. M. Reycraft, pp. 99–121. Maxwell Museum of Anthropology Anthropological Papers No. 7. University of New Mexico, Albuquerque.
2005 Style Change and Ethnogenesis among the Chiribaya of Far South Coastal Peru. In *Us and Them: Archaeology and Ethnicity in the Andes,* edited by R. M. Reycraft, pp. 54–73. Cotsen Institute of Archaeology Monograph 53. University of California, Los Angeles.

Rice, D. S.
1993 Late Intermediate Period Domestic Architecture and Residential Organization at La Yaral. In *Domestic Architecture, Ethnicity, and Complementarity in the South Central Andes,* edited by M. S. Aldenderfer, pp. 66–82. Iowa City: University of Iowa Press.

Rice, P. M.
1987 *Pottery Analysis: A Sourcebook.* Chicago: University of Chicago Press.

Satterlee, D.
1993 *Impact of a Fourteenth Century El Niño on an Indigenous Population near Ilo, Peru.* Ph.D. dissertation, University of Florida, Gainesville. Ann Arbor: University Microfilms.

Schwerdtfeger, W.
1976 *Climates in Central and South America.* Amsterdam: Elsevier Press.

Sheets, P. D., and D. K. Grayson, eds.
1979 *Volcanic Activity and Human Ecology.* New York: Academic Press.

Stanish, C. E.
1989 Household Archaeology: Testing Models of Zonal Complementarity in the South Central Andes. *American Anthropologist* 91:7–24.
1992 *Ancient Andean Political Economy.* Austin: University of Texas Press.

Tainter, J. A.
1988 *The Collapse of Complex Societies.* Cambridge: Cambridge University Press.

Tovar, H., V. Guillen, and D. Caberrera
1987 Reproduction and Population Levels of the Peruvian Guano Birds. *Journal of Geophysical Research* 92: 14,445–14,448

Umire, A., and A. Miranda
2001 *Chiribaya de Ilo, un aporte a su diffusion.* Lima: Consejo Nacional de Cienca y Techologia.

van den Berghe, P. L.
1979 *Human Family Systems, An Evolutionary View.* New York: Elsevier Press.

White, A. U.
1974 Natural Hazards Research: Concepts, Methods, and Policy Implications. In *Natural Hazards Local, National, Global,* edited by G. F. White, pp. 3–16. London: Oxford University Press.

Wobst, M.
1977 Stylistic Behavior and Information Exchange. In *For the Director: Research Essays in Honor of the Late James B. Griffin,* edited by C. E. Cleland, pp. 317–342. Ann Arbor: University of Michigan Press.

Yoffee, N., and G. L. Cowgill, eds.
1988 *The Collapse of Ancient Civilizations and States.* Tucson: University of Arizona Press.

9

Collapse among Amerindian Complex Societies in Amazonia and the Insular Caribbean: Endogenous or Exogenous Factors?

James B. Petersen, Michael J. Heckenberger, Eduardo Goes Neves, John G. Crock, and Robert N. Bartone

COMPLEX SOCIETIES IN AMAZONIA AND THE INSULAR Caribbean had developed long before the arrival of Europeans and other nonindigenous people in the Western Hemisphere during the late 1400s, 1500s, and thereafter. Although there is still debate about the degree of social complexity, none of the present authors question the observation that at least some Amerindian groups in both of these interrelated culture areas were socially complex at the time of colonial contact. For example, in Amazonia, the Tapajos and Omagua were sufficiently recorded by the earliest European explorers (during the 1500s) to enable us to say that they were socially complex— seemingly "chiefdoms," in modern terms (Denevan 1996; Myers 1992; Roosevelt 1987, 1989, 1999). Various chiefdoms and other complex Amerindian polities were also present in Amazonia at the time. Likewise, Columbus and other Europeans recorded socially complex groups in the insular Caribbean, often collectively known as the Taino, during the late 1400s and early 1500s. Most or all of the Taino polities were certainly chiefdoms, along with numerous other groups on the South American and Caribbean mainland, and it was the Taino who served as the basis for the definition of "chiefdom" in the first place (Oberg 1955). Speaking of both the insular and the mainland Caribbean, Robert Carneiro (1981:48) says: "The Circum-Caribbean area no doubt had the largest number of chiefdoms of any region in the world."

Most scholars would agree that these historically recorded groups in Amazonia and the insular Caribbean represented socially complex societies, many of which were chiefdoms. Not all would fully agree on the level of complexity in each case, and this matter obviously needs much more discussion, but that is not the central point of the present paper. We are certainly concerned with the timing of the development *and* collapse of social complexity, given the *assumption* of social complexity among some historical cultures, as sketched below. Yet, we are primarily interested here in whether internal, non-colonial, non-European factors were ever responsible for indigenous collapse in these two culture areas, both considered part of the South American lowlands. Did collapse of social complexity occur, and if so, what factors were responsible? Did the mix include economic, sociopolitical, environmental, and/or other factors?

We do not provide absolutely conclusive answers to any of these questions here, and the following account is occasionally speculative. This ambiguity is due in part to the nature of the archaeological record upon which it is based and the relatively limited amount of regional research accomplished to date in both regions, especially in Amazonia. We simply do not have much concrete data about continuity and change in prehistoric technology, economics, subsistence-settlement patterns, and other anthropological issues in the South American lowlands. Even the ethnographic record is woefully incomplete or altogether lacking for substantial portions of these culture areas, especially in the Caribbean, because of the early and devastating effects of contact between Amerindians and colonial peoples. The lack of archaeological research and scarce ethnohistoric data leave large gaps in the record for many cultural groups, and many others have gone completely unrecorded.

Not to be daunted, and using our collective research in both regions, we first outline the arguments for social complexity and then briefly present the relevant data for collapse, such as they are known or reconstructed, given our particular perspectives. These perspectives include three important points:

First, interpretive bias varies among the authors, ranging from healthy skepticism to strong support for these propositions. Nonetheless, we all believe that previous reconstructions in Amazonia and the insular Caribbean have not fully appreciated the available data for reconstruction of social complexity among tropical chiefdoms and other polities.

Second, we all support to various degrees the idea that the collapse of some of these tropical chiefdoms was an indigenous affair; that is, collapse was inherent in their indigenous sociopolitical systems long before contact with European and other nonindigenous peoples. We fully recognize the devastating effects of colonial contact and its overwhelming contribution to the collapse of many, many native polities, large and small, over the past 500 years—as a consequence, no chiefdoms have existed in either region for a long time.

Third, none of us believes that tropical environments were uniformly, if at all, restrictive to cultural evolution, as some strict materialist scholars have argued. Instead, many tropical environments were (and are) so rich under indigenous technologies and practices that they helped foster the evolution of social complexity in the first place. We believe that environmental conditions alone did not structure when and where complex societies would arise in these regions, although rich aquatic environments may have been the scene of the earliest and most common tropical chiefdoms.

Instead, knowing what we do of indigenous politics through oral history (as in the Upper Xingu and the Northwest Amazon culture areas, for example), we recognize the idiosyncratic character of indigenous history relative to individual leaders. This leadership and the broader "political economy" were critical in the development of complex societies regionally. Indigenous accounts suggest that a range of contingencies pertained to the developmental trajectories of complex societies in the tropical lowlands, including their formation and collapse in some cases, with emphasis here given to the latter. These contingencies are very often quite difficult to identify in the archaeological record, yet we are individually and collectively working to identify these and other archaeological signatures and thereby test attendant propositions.

Collapse may be defined in various ways, and it is sometimes strictly limited to socially complex polities (e.g., Tainter 1988; Yoffee 1988). One example, speaking of state-level polities from a structural standpoint, reports that collapse, "in general, ensues when the center is no longer able to secure resources from the periphery, usually having lost the 'legitimacy' through which it could 'disembed' goods and services of traditionally organized groups. The process of collapse entails the dissolution of these centralized institutions that had facilitated the transmission of resources and information, the settlement of intergroup disputes, and the legitimate expression of differentiated organizational components" (Yoffee 1988:13).

For our purposes, we dichotomize collapse into two broad categories: endogenous, or internal, versus exogenous, or external. We use this distinction to differentiate between those factors that were unequivocally external to the indigenous societies and those that were not necessarily so, unlike others who have used these terms differently (e.g., Kaufman 1988:223–229). *Endogenous* factors are specifically meant to include those that are internal to one or more Amerindian societies. Even in cases where one Amerindian polity adversely affected another, we consider this endogenous collapse because the collapsed polity had some integral role in the process; nor can one indigenous group be easily isolated from all others given the typical degree of social interaction among all such polities. In contrast, we use *exogenous* to describe those factors that are more clearly external, or more completely beyond the control of the Amerindian polity. We take exogenous factors to include the effects produced by contact with colonial Europeans and other nonindigenous people, as well as natural disasters.

THE DEVELOPMENT OF SOCIAL COMPLEXITY IN AMAZONIA AND THE INSULAR CARIBBEAN: A BRIEF OUTLINE

According to the evolutionary framework of Julian Steward and his contemporaries (Carneiro 1981; Lathrap 1970; Rouse 1962; Steward 1948; Steward and Faron 1959), at the time of European contact, most Amerindian groups across the South American lowlands were either "tribes" or "chiefdoms." For purposes of this discussion, we use this typical (but admittedly simple) sociopolitical classification system, as has often (but unevenly) been done over the past 40–50 years. Many other alternatives have been suggested for both categories, including division of chiefdoms into simpler and more complex forms (e.g., Arnold 1996; Earle 1987, 1997; Johnson and Earle 1987:18–24). The most significant difference between these sociopolitical categories is that *tribes*, approximately what some consider "chieftaincies," are kin-based, autonomous, domestic, and lack formalized vertical hierarchies, with low-key, if any, stratification. Achieved status and "short-lived" leadership are represented. In contrast, *chiefdoms* are more overarching than tribes in terms of size, duration, and social control, and they are clearly stratified and nonegalitarian. Status is ascribed and leadership is long-term, with potential specialists in religion, trade, and warfare, among other issues. Tribute payments up the status chain are common, and settlement hierarchy is necessarily present in chiefdoms as well (e.g., Carneiro 1981, 1998; Redmond et al. 1999:111–113; Roosevelt 1999:16–17; Spencer 1998:104–108; Whitehead 1998).

On the basis of the incomplete ethnohistoric record alone, most researchers see clear evidence that social complexity was represented in Amazonia and the insular Caribbean, along with other regions in the South American lowlands, at the time of contact. These apparently complex polities are poorly known in general, with many relevant questions remaining unanswered. First, what was the scale of this complexity, and did the polities in fact represent complex societies, including chiefdoms? Second, how widespread were complex societies in each of these two regions, and when did they arise, prehistorically and historically? Still other questions about chiefdoms and tribes pertain here, such as particular causal factors and specific origins, the relevant stimuli for differential change in social complexity, and the mix of "environment" and "culture" as primary determinants, among other issues.

Even where tropical chiefdoms have been recognized in the past, relatively little has been specifically written about their collapse in either region beyond effects attributed to European contact. This situation is due, in part, to overwhelming evidence for exogenous collapse at the hands of nonindigenous people during colonial and postcolonial times (e.g., Denevan 1996; Monteiro 1999; Morey 1979; Neves 1999; Porro 1994; Roosevelt 1993:274–276; Sued Badillo 1995; Vidal and Zucchi 1996; Whitehead 1998, 1999; Wilson 1990; Wright 1999). We feel that the magnitude of contact factors has obscured evidence of shifting polities, even of collapse, during late prehistory. It has further masked variable (but tentative) evidence for collapse predating the invasion of both regions by nonindigenous people.

Social Complexity in Amazonia

In Amazonia, diverse environments played a critical role in providing prehistoric Amerindians with different resources, subsistence and otherwise. Precolumbian human occupation of Amazonia began by 11,000 years ago, or 9000 BC, but it is poorly known in general until after ca. 2000–1000 BC. Using composite terminology, the earliest cultural period in Amazonia was the Paleoindian or early Preceramic period, a time of Pleistocene colonization by mobile hunter-gatherers. It is dated to ca. 9500–8000 BC. The second period, the Archaic, middle and late Preceramic period, or time of Early Sedentary Adaptations (Roosevelt 1989:43–45), lasted from ca. 8000 BC until about 2000/1000 BC. This period encompassed early-mid Holocene hunter-gatherers and, toward its end, incipient cultivators. The third and final period of Amerindian prehistory was the Ceramic period, 2000/1000 BC–AD

1500/1600, when ceramics, crop cultivation, and long-distance trade became widespread. Crop raising was an important determinant of sedentism and social complexity on some level, depending on the setting.

For Roosevelt (1989:45), what we have called the Ceramic period was the time of Early Horticultural Villagers and Agricultural Chiefdoms, although the latter were neither uniform nor ubiquitous. Pottery is very common at most Ceramic period sites, making them relatively easy to find. Consequently, this period is fairly well known relative to the Preceramic period in general, and individual regional polities have sometimes been recognized in archaeological studies, given adequate regional samples. These polities were often socially complex, certainly tropical chiefdoms in some settings. In particular, complex societies were dependent on intensive horticulture in Amazonia (Denevan 1996; Myers 1992; Oliver 2001; Roosevelt 1980, 1987, 1989, 1993, 1994, 1999).

Past reconstructions of prehistoric polities in Amazonia, with a few exceptions, have typically emphasized the "counterfeit paradise" quality of the entire region (e.g., Meggers 1971, 2001; Meggers and Evans 1983; cf. Moran 1993; Neves 1999; Whitehead 1996). In other words, some adamant researchers have suggested that Amazonia is more ecologically restrictive than it first appears. They point out presumably significant differences between environments—fertile floodplains, or varzea, in particular, and smaller upland tributaries without fertile floodplains, or terra firme. This difference is recognized as a critical determinant of environmental richness and poverty, particularly because of differences between floodplain and non-floodplain soils.

In this view, fertile floodplain soils are rare in Amazonia, representing only about 2% of the total region, although floodplains in general cover a larger area. Thus, rich environments for human subsistence and its intensification are correspondingly rare, since floodplain soils are supposedly necessary for plentiful crops, particularly seed crops such as maize. In this perspective, complex societies are recognizable, but they were quite rare and always the exception (Meggers 1971; Moran 1993). Other, more liberal researchers also recognize the dichotomy between varzea and terra firme as being important, and they too support the primacy of varzea environments over the terra firme. However, they suggest that social complexity was generally more common regionally than the conservatives recognize, but again they limit it largely to varzea and near-varzea settings. In other words, some scholars recognize prehistoric sociopolitical complexity in Amazonia varying in direct correlation with differences between varzea and terra firme environments (e.g., Lathrap 1970; Roosevelt 1989, 1991).

Recent research and reassessment of the importance of this dichotomy has led others to suggest that the story is more complicated than this, perhaps much more complicated (e.g., Denevan 1996; Moran 1993; Whitehead 1996). This view is supported by our individual and combined research in various portions of Amazonia. It may be that floodplain soils were not critical in some or all cases, if manioc, a highly important non-floodplain crop, provided the major portion of non-protein nutrition, rather than maize. Agricultural intensification based on the cultivation of manioc and other non-floodplain crops and fruits may have led to the rise and elaboration of social complexity, ultimately including tropical chiefdoms, when populations grew and ideological factors, specifically political capital, were affected (Heckenberger 1998; Petersen et al. 2001).

Along with manioc and other crop cultivation, the aquatic richness of Amazonia was likely a second critical variable, providing copious fish, turtles, and other foods. Local and long-distance trade may have been important too (e.g., Boomert 1987; Lathrap 1973; Myers 1982). These variables and other distinctions are very important for modeling social complexity in Amazonia, yet vigorous debate continues today (e.g., Denevan 1996; Heckenberger 1998; Heckenberger et al. 1999, 2001; Meggers 2001; Oliver 2001; Whitehead 1996). Examples from our own and others' research in Amazonia are presented below to support our case, beginning first with three areas where we currently work or have worked in the past.

In the Northwest Amazon near the border of Brazil and Colombia (Figure 34), prehistoric sites are consistently small, based on recent, extensive excavations (Neves 1998, 1999, 2001). Amerindian settlements on the Vaupes River on the uppermost Negro River were and are most often located near rivers, except where defensibility seems important. The prehistoric societies were seemingly very similar to those known historically in the same area—the ethnographic Northwest Amazon culture area—including the presence of multi-ethnic regional networks. Thus, settlements apparently were not linked hierarchically or strongly stratified, and although the prehistoric Amerindians were more socially complex on some level than those of today, they were more similar to tribes than chiefdoms. This relative lack of complexity may have been due to very depauperate soils in the area, the relatively limited nature of aquatic resources in these upland rivers, and/or the leveling effect of the multi-ethnic networks (Moran 1993:43, 47, 53).

In contrast, very large prehistoric settlements, cumulatively as large as 50–80 hectares or more in some cases, occurred much farther down the Rio Negro in central Amazonia. These sites have recently been identified on high riverbanks or "bluffs" along floodplain and non-floodplain rivers. Our Central Amazon Project (CAP) area lies almost on the equator, near the confluence of the Negro and Solimoes rivers at the beginning of the Amazon River proper. Large settlements are located on both the Negro River (non-varzea) and Solimoes River (varzea) bluffs in the CAP study area. We know precious little about Amerindians in this area after European contact because they were transformed and eradicated before they were well recorded.

The Manao (or Manoa) and other Arawakan-speaking peoples apparently lived on and near the Negro-Solimoes confluence at contact, but they were soon decimated through European slave raiding, diseases, warfare, and missionization. Some Manao likely survived locally in one form or another until the late 1700s (Metraux 1948; Porro 1992, 1994; Vidal and Zucchi 1996). Limited evidence suggests that the Manao were very similar to the socially complex Omagua who lived upstream on the Solimoes River toward Peru, as well as the Tapajos who were downstream at the confluence of the Tapajos and Amazon rivers (Denevan 1996; Meggers 1971; Metraux 1948; Myers 1992; Nimuedajú 1952; Porro 1994; Roosevelt 1999; Vidal and Zucchi 1996; Woods and McCann 1999).

Archaeological ceramics and ceramic distributions establish differential concentrations at some large settlements attributed to the Guarita phase of the Polychrome horizon/tradition and have been dated to ca. AD 800–1400, or later, in the CAP study area. Late prehistoric "elite/ceremonial" polychrome ceramics are represented adjacent to a large plaza-like area with several mounded middens at Açutuba, a huge *terra preta* (black earth) site on the Negro River (Heckenberger et al. 1998, 1999, 2001). Notably, the "elite/ceremonial" ceramic ware is largely found in the core area at Açutuba, and it may be related to feasting in or near the putative plaza. Less-decorated, less-elaborate ceramics are spread all across Açutuba in the core and in all outlying areas, the latter of which lack the "elite/ceremonial" ware. The nonelaborate pottery is scattered over an area much larger than that of the polychrome ware, stretching for about 3 km cumulatively across the high bluffs that constitute the Açutuba site. The nonelaborate ceramics are demonstrably contemporaneous with the "elite/ceremonial" ceramics through stratigraphic associations and direct dating of the

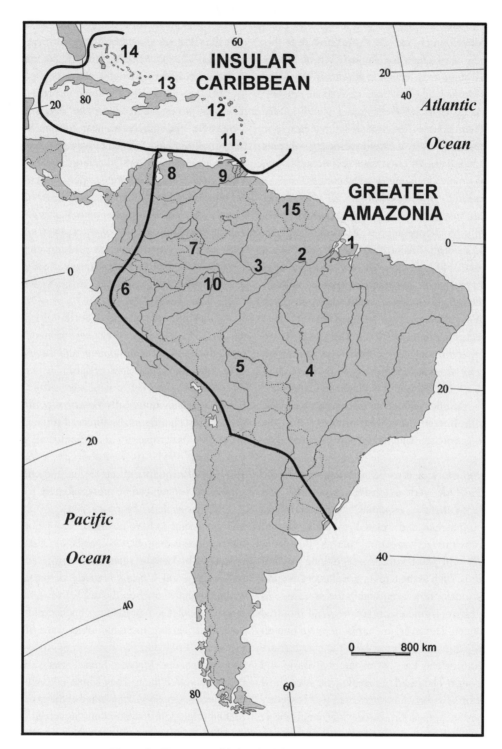

Figure 34. Key geographic locales in lowland South America,
including Greater Amazonia and the Insular Caribbean.

Key: (1) Marajo Island, (2) Tapajos area, (3) Central Amazonia, (4) Upper Xingu, (5) Llanos de Mojos,
(6) Sangay area, (7) Northwest Amazonia, (8) Venezuelan Llanos, (9) Middle/Lower Orinoco, (10)
Omagua area, (11) Southern Lesser Antilles, (12) Northern Lesser Antilles, (13) Hispaniola/Greater
Antilles, (14) Bahamas and Turks & Caicos, (15) Guyana coast.

organic temper in both assemblages. At least 1,000 years of antecedent development can be demonstrated at this and other nearby sites identified through recent survey work in the CAP study area, including the earlier "Modeled and Incised"/ "Barrancoid" tradition, ca. 300 BC–AD 800 (Heckenberger et al. 1998, 1999; Petersen et al. 2001). We feel that local Guarita phase sites after AD 800 represent one socially complex polity, likely a chiefdom society, whereas the earlier Barrancoid sites represent lesser social complexity, possibly a set of simple chiefdoms or tribal polities.

Recent research by Heckenberger in the Upper Xingu has demonstrated comparably extensive sites that are roughly contemporaneous with and perhaps later than those in central Amazonia. The Upper Xingu is situated about 1,400 km southeast of the CAP area at the southeastern margin of Amazonia. Abundant evidence of huge settlements, 30–50 hectares and larger, has been identified in this upland riverine setting (Heckenberger 1996, 1998; Heckenberger et al. 1999). The Upper Xingu sites conclusively represent large, complex groups, which are quite different from but connected to the surviving, smaller and less complex populations of Xinguano Amerindians. Varzea does not occur anywhere near these sites, since fertile floodplains are not represented in the Upper Xingu, nor were settlements necessarily situated on bluffs per se.

Multiple prehistoric and early historical sites in the Upper Xingu include very extensive earthworks that cover several kilometers, including outer perimeter or "defensive" trenches and related mounds, curbed roadways, and obvious, curbed central "plazas." The latter trait, the open central plaza, still persists among modern Xinguano cultures, such as the Kuikuru, Kalapalo, Waura, and others, and today plazas are roughly the same size as the prehistoric/early historic examples—several hundred meters in diameter. However, in terms of their overall extent, modern Xinguano settlements at their largest are perhaps one-tenth or less the size of the prehistoric and early historical sites. The dated archaeological sites show a radical reduction in settlement size over time, apparently reflecting severe depopulation before sustained direct contact with nonindigenous Brazilians began, ca. AD 1700–1800 (Heckenberger 1996).

Beyond these examples from our own research showing different degrees of social complexity, other unequivocal evidence of prehistoric complex polities is selectively represented all across Amazonia. Notable examples include one or more polities on the very large island of Marajo at the mouth of the Amazon, and the Tapajos and their ancestors on the Tapajos and Amazon rivers. Still others were present in the Llanos de Mojos near the Amazonian headwaters in Bolivia and at Sangay on other headwaters near the Ecuadorian Andes, for example. Adjacent lowland areas beyond the Amazon proper also witnessed chiefdoms in prehistoric and early historical times, such as in the llanos of non-coastal Venezuela and others in near-coastal Venezuela, and perhaps in Guyana, French Guyana, and Surinam, among others. Extensive earthworks, large settlements, extensive trade, and/or fine, elaborate, often polychrome ceramics are represented in most of these cases. All of these, except Marajo and Sangay, apparently collapsed during the early contact period as a result of external pressures (Denevan 1966, 1992, 1996; Denevan and Zucchi 1978; Oliver 1989; Redmond et al. 1999; Roosevelt 1993, 1999:23–27; Rostain 1991, 1999; Spencer 1998; Versteeg and Rostain 1997; Whitehead 1998, 1999).

At Marajo, the late prehistoric Polychrome tradition residents built extensive earthen mounds to raise their residences above the floodplain, and these mounds, along with other structural and ceramic evidence much like that from the CAP study area, suggest the presence of at least several unequivocally complex polities. They were presumably chiefdoms, but there is some argument about the degree of complexity and what to call them (Meggers and Evans 1957, 1983; Roosevelt 1989, 1991, 1993, 1994, 1999). Interpretations differ, and only a very brief, simplified version can be presented here.

The so-called Marajoara phase of the Polychrome tradition seems to have collapsed well before the arrival of the Europeans and other colonials, at least in the scenario postulated by Betty Meggers and Cliff Evans (1957, 1983). In Meggers and Evans's scenario of repeated prehistoric migrations into the region, the large earthworks are considered quite anomalous, representing unexpected complexity in Amazonia. In fact, these and other traits of the Marajoara phase are attributed to a migration of Andean peoples who came down the Amazon prehistorically, bringing social complexity with them. They supposedly set up a derivative complex society on Marajo Island at the extreme eastern end of their migration, and later they "devolved."

The Marajoara more likely represent a chiefdom society in the reasoned view of Anna Roosevelt (1989, 1991, 1993, 1994; cf. 1999:20–23) on the basis of her own more recent research at Marajo, and she does not recognize any migration from the Andes. Instead, Roosevelt postulates the internal development of social complexity for the Marajoara by about 1,800–2,000 years ago, or ca. AD 1–200. The Marajoara phase flourished for many centuries until it collapsed by ca. 1300, owing in part to new migrants of the Arua phase, or so the original Meggers and Evans (1957, 1983) hypothesis suggests. The non-mound-building Arua lived in smaller, simpler settlements and showed other forms of "devolution" relative to their predecessors. It is not entirely clear, however, if the Arua phase really represents another migration. Roosevelt's research at Marajo presents strong alternatives to some of the ideas of Meggers and Evans, but it too seems to show some sort of (not fully addressed) collapse during late prehistory (e.g., Roosevelt 1991:64–66).

Stephen Rostain (1999) has conducted recent research at the opposite extreme of Amazonia from Marajo, studying at Sangay one of the largest known sites in the region, and it too shows the apparent collapse of social complexity, most likely from a local "chiefdom" to a "tribe." Social complexity may have appeared there by 700 BC or somewhat later, and it lasted until about AD 400 or so, during the time of "Upano culture" as present at the Huapula site at Sangay, covering an area of about 72 hectares. The Upano culture, presumably representing a chiefdom society, built very extensive earthworks over and beyond this large site, including mounds centered on plazas and sunken "roadways" and "canals" (or trenches). The Upano culture was also involved in unequivocal long-distance trade.

The later, Huapula culture followed the Upano culture at ca. AD 700–1200, with evidence of a dramatic eruption of the Sangay volcano separating them stratigraphically. Members of the Huapula culture resided on the preexisting mounds, but they apparently did not build any mounds themselves, nor did they participate in long-distance trade, unlike their predecessors. In fact, the Huapula culture seems much like the ethnographically known Achuar, or Jivaroan Amerindians, a tribal people who reside in the area today. In this case, eruption of the nearby Sangay volcano somehow apparently contributed to the collapse of the socially complex Upano culture, along with other disruptive factors (Rostain 1999).

Regardless of the precise dating, these examples show that complex societies were widespread along substantial and lesser rivers in Amazonia (and beyond) by late prehistory. Also, although we may be accused of heresy here, it should be obvious that complex societies were not necessarily associated with fertile riverine floodplains. Diverse complex societies developed beyond the area of varzea floodplains. Based more on conjecture than fact, we believe that a combination of terra firme, non-floodplain horticulture and extensive aquatic resources supported these polities, although floodplain horticulture directly contributed to Amerindian economies in some settings.

Social Complexity in the Insular Caribbean

The origins of the known chiefdoms, or *cacicazgos,* of the Taino in the insular Caribbean are less obscure than most cases from Amazonia. The socially complex Taino, or Arawaks, as they have often been called because of their language family, lived in the Greater Antilles, the Bahamas, and Turks & Caicos. We believe that they also lived in the northern Lesser Antilles. In any case, the Taino were almost certainly derived from the late prehistoric peoples in the South America lowlands, specifically the Orinoco River of Venezuela and likely elsewhere (Allaire 1999; Rouse 1962, 1992).

The culture history of the insular Caribbean includes two of the three periods represented in Amazonia, the late Preceramic period (regionally subdivided into the Lithic and Archaic), ca. 5000/4000 BC to 500 BC/AD 600, and the Ceramic period, ca. 500 BC/AD 600 to AD 1500. The Ceramic period is often subdivided into the Early Ceramic (or Saladoid), ca. 500 BC–AD 600, and Late Ceramic (or Post-Saladoid/Ostionoid), ca. AD 600–1500. The Taino emerged archaeologically some time before AD 1000–1200 during the Post-Saladoid/Ostionoid period, and they were certainly chiefdoms in some or all manifestations (e.g., Allaire 1999; Crock 2000; Keegan 1997; Petersen 1997; Redmond et al. 1999:109–110; Redmond and Spencer 1994; Rouse 1962, 1992; Wilson 1990).

The earliest settlement of the insular Caribbean began well before the primary ancestors of the Taino arrived. Preceramic hunter-gatherers were present on some Caribbean islands by 5000–4000 BC, as in Trinidad and some of the Greater Antilles. These initial colonists originated in the lowlands of Central and/or South America (we favor the latter), and their precise origins are poorly known. We do know that they were dependent on relatively rare terrestrial foods on the islands and more so on marine resources once they spread into the insular Caribbean (Petersen 1997; Rouse 1986, 1992).

Much more clearly, a second human colonization brought farming, pottery-making, and various other lowland-derived customs into the eastern Caribbean islands by ca. 500 BC near the onset of the Saladoid period (Allaire 1999; Heckenberger and Petersen 1999; Petersen 1996; Rouse 1962, 1986, 1992; Siegel 1999; Watters 1997). These people likely were the main (or sole?) ancestors of the historical Amerindians all across the oceanic, offshore Caribbean. Spreading from the middle-lower Orinoco River in Venezuela northward all the way to Puerto Rico, pottery-making farmers replaced or in some cases coexisted with the preceramic hunter-gatherers, until the hunter-gatherers were largely or completely absorbed. Farming practices could have spread to the insular Caribbean from South America without a mass migration, but the available evidence strongly supports an actual migration (Rouse 1962, 1986, 1992).

During Saladoid times, the first pottery-making farmers exhibited much of what would ultimately characterize the Taino two thousand years later at the time of European contact. Relatively little distinguishes the Saladoid from the Taino archaeologically in our view, with the exception of large public/ceremonial courts among the Taino in the Greater Antilles and a few other related traits. Even the public/ceremonial spaces of the Taino evolved from the open central plazas characteristic of Saladoid settlements, a feature that came with them from South America, as still seen among the Xinguanos in Brazil (Heckenberger and Petersen 1999; Petersen 1996; Siegel 1999). Numerous continuities exist between the Saladoid and the Taino, which suggests that the seeds of social complexity likely arrived with the Saladoid from South America. This may not be coincidental; rather, it has been suggested that social complexity was inherent within Arawakan cultures generally (Heckenberger 2001).

In any case, the socially complex Taino were most thoroughly (if still incompletely) recorded in Hispaniola, along with a smaller amount of historical information from Cuba, Puerto Rico, and the Bahamas and Turks & Caicos (Allaire 1999; Curet 1992; Keegan 1997; Rouse 1992; Sued Badillo 1995; Wilson 1990). Representatives in most of Hispaniola, Puerto Rico, and perhaps easternmost Cuba have been designated as the Classic Taino (for whom of all the Taino the only substantial historical records exist); the Lucayan Taino lived in the Bahamas and Turks & Caicos. The Western Taino were in southwestern Hispaniola, Jamaica, and most, if not all, of central and western Cuba. The Western Taino are less well known historically than the Classic Taino. Some researchers have also hypothesized the existence of an eastern branch of the Taino in the northern Lesser Antilles, based solely on archaeological data (Rouse 1992). The Eastern Taino are poorly known in general, and they directly concern us here because they may have experienced collapse before European contact.

Notably, the stereotypically complex Classic Taino have been recognized only in those areas where historical records exist. The complexity of contemporary Taino peoples nearby to the west and the east has been often downplayed, regardless of apparent close relationships. Ethnohistory may well have colored our recognition of social complexity in this case, and we suspect that all of these people were much more alike than different and were somehow Taino-related.

The first Amerindians who met Columbus and gave him scant gold and other "treasures" in 1492 were representatives of the Taino (Alegria 1980; Keegan 1997; Rouse 1992; Wilson 1990). When he returned to the Caribbean with other Europeans in 1493, Columbus met the Island Carib in Guadeloupe and elsewhere, but few useful details were recorded about them. Island Caribs generally lived in the southern portion of the Lesser Antilles, or "Windward Islands," all the way to South America at the time of contact (Allaire 1999; Hulme and Whitehead 1992; Whitehead 1999; Whitehead, ed. 1995). The Island Carib were historically represented in the northern Lesser Antilles, or "Leeward Islands," but not substantially.

The Island Carib are poorly known before ca. 1620–1630. When European colonization of the Lesser Antilles got underway, the Island Carib had already undergone long-term contact and disruption, and this has likely biased our appreciation of the cultures and perhaps their complexity. Traditionally (and perhaps falsely), the Island Carib have been labeled as "cannibal" aggressors who preyed on their neighbors, such as the Taino, at the time of Columbus. This conflict likely included the Eastern Taino of the Leeward Islands (who were sometimes labeled as "Carib" by the Spanish) and, more definitively, the Classic Taino of the Greater Antilles. However, closer analysis of the ethnohistoric data suggests that this interaction may have included other, less violent forms, along with warfare (Allaire 1980, 1999; Sued Badillo 1995).

The Island Carib were culturally much closer to the Taino than past researchers have generally recognized, and the Island Carib likewise may well be descendants of the Arawakan-speaking migrants who came during the Saladoid period. Unlike the Taino, the Island Carib managed to survive as a distinct culture historically, and they still reside on a few islands of the Lesser Antilles, with others now on the Caribbean coast of Central America. In contrast, the Taino were quickly lost as a discrete culture (or set of cultures) as a result of enslavement, warfare, disease, and mistreatment brought by the Spanish colonists and other slaves in the Greater Antilles and elsewhere. Some scholars have speculated that the Island Carib contributed to the demise of the Eastern Taino, possibly depopulating the Leeward Islands of all Eastern Taino by ca. 1300–1450—that is, before European contact. In effect, this would have caused the complete collapse of the Eastern Taino, from Anguilla and St. Martin in the north to Antigua and Montserrat in the south (Crock 2000; Rouse 1992).

Alternatively, though much less definitively, it is possible that the Eastern Taino persisted locally in the Leeward Islands until the time of European contact and that it was the forces of contact that decimated them. In this scenario, the Eastern Taino were effaced during the contact period of the 1500s, but before they could be recorded by the Spanish—perhaps finishing off a process of destabilization begun by the Island Carib, prehistorically or historically (Crock 2000; Hofman 1993:211–212, 222; Petersen and Crock 2001). However, this late-survival scenario for the Amerindians in the Leeward Islands has yet to be clearly supported by local archaeological evidence, and it seems more likely that traumatic forces, perhaps the Island Carib, had indeed disrupted the Eastern Taino before European contact. This is the second focal issue addressed in this paper, and the strongest case for the collapse of a complex society in the insular Caribbean prehistorically.

COLLAPSE IN AMAZONIA AND THE CARIBBEAN

The archaeological record in Amazonia is still poorly known, and the case is only slightly better in the insular Caribbean. Nonetheless, archaeological evidence of social complexity has been recognized in both regions—specifically, chiefdoms, in some or all cases—and these occurrences suggest that chiefdoms were more widespread than is known through ethnohistory alone. At least several examples of potential prehistoric and postcontact collapse have been recognized as well, as briefly introduced above. In the case of Marajo Island, the example of "collapse" at ca. 1300 predates European contact by several centuries. At Sangay, collapse may have occurred prehistorically at least 1,000 years before European contact, and it was seemingly due to a natural catastrophe, at least in part. In the insular Caribbean, collapse also may have predated European contact, at least in the northern Lesser Antilles. Thus, two of these examples, Marajo and the northern Lesser Antilles, by necessity may be attributable to prehistoric endogenous and indigenous dynamics, rather than exogenous factors; the other, Sangay, is a form of prehistoric exogenous collapse, perhaps with unknown endogenous, indigenous factors involved as well.

Collapse in Amazonia

The best known example of endogenous collapse in Amazonia has been reconstructed on Marajo Island, but others can be suggested as well. Beginning with Marajo, in their original formulation Meggers and Evans (1957, 1983)

agreed that the mound-building people of the Marajoara phase of the Polychrome tradition were superceded by non-mound-building people of the Arua phase, along with other changes. All evidence clearly suggests that this was an endogenous collapse, or "devolution," as they called it, on the basis of archaeological variables, although recent research may show the Marajoara surviving into the contact period (D. Schaan, personal communication 2001). Setting this possibility aside, after the collapse of the Marajoara and replacement by the Arua phase, all Amerindians in Marajo ultimately became extinct relatively quickly during the historical period, probably by 1650 or so.

In this case, the critical variables are *when* and *why* did indigenous collapse *first* occur? Quite possibly, the Marajoara collapse occurred because of invasion by new Amerindians of the Arua phase, with a population replacement. Alternatively, perhaps the Marajoara people persisted in the face of prehistoric collapse that occurred for some other reason(s), without population replacement. European artifacts are found in Arua phase sites, but precisely how old is this phase? When did it begin, and when did the Marajoara phase "collapse" locally? Unfortunately, we cannot be absolutely certain about the dates, but the collapse at Marajo seemingly predated contact by several hundred years, occurring by ca. 1300.

It is possible that the same circumstance of late prehistoric endogenous collapse pertains to the present authors' joint research in the CAP study area near the confluence of the Negro and Solimoes rivers. Several large (even huge) settlements and dozens of smaller but contemporaneous ones are now known in this area, seemingly producing a bimodal, two-tiered settlement hierarchy, as would pertain to a chiefdom society according to one classic definition (Carneiro 1981). Also, probable elite and nonelite ceramics and various types of earthworks occur at the larger sites, largely defensive features. These remains are assigned to the Guarita phase of the Polychrome tradition and perhaps earlier. Thus, they are at least partially contemporaneous with the generally similar Marajoara phase.

One or more central Amazonian polities may have collapsed in the CAP area before European contact owing to indigenous factors such as intergroup warfare; we have no evidence of contact between Amerindians and Europeans at any of these sites, but this remains unclear. Ethnohistoric data certainly suggest that large riverine areas were locally abandoned on the main Solimoes River upstream from the CAP area before the arrival of Europeans—that is, by at least ca. 1540–1560—owing to intergroup hostilities, leaving very large "buffer zones" between different polities. Other discrete, sometimes large areas were still occupied in central and western Amazonia at this time, such as those of the historical Omagua and the Tapajos, as mentioned above. These polities collapsed rather quickly after direct contact (DeBoer 1981; Denevan 1996; Myers 1976, 1992; Nimuendajú 1952; Roosevelt 1999).

In the case of the Upper Xingu, collapse only occurred *after* the arrival of Europeans in South America, even though only distantly, as is more typically known in the historical record of Amazonia. Collapse in the Upper Xingu occurred well before sustained direct contact with Europeans, however, making this a rare documented case where exogenous collapse can be established owing to indirect or infrequent direct contact (Heckenberger 1996; Heckenberger et al. 1999). Given the likelihood that other indigenous factors were involved, collapse in the Upper Xingu may have had an endogenous component too. At least several of us believe that the Upper Xingu transformation represents a shift from "chiefdom"-level societies to more egalitarian, "tribal" ones after the arrival of Europeans in Brazil. Xinguano groups made extensive earthworks for several hundred years prehistorically. However, earthwork building was abandoned well before the 1880s, and group sizes dropped drastically. They became what are today small, autonomous "tribal" groups, probably by ca. 1700–1800. Here we suspect that epidemics and other diseases were spread from Europeans and others to the Xinguanos via intermediary Amerindian groups, along with the possibility of other intervening factors. For example, a few slave raiders may have reached the Upper Xingu by 1700–1750 based on local oral history, perhaps also helping to introduce disease at this time.

For the Xinguanos, the first documented nonindigenous, direct contact occurred during the 1880s when Karl von den Steinen, a German explorer and budding anthropologist, arrived along with others. By this time the Xinguanos very much resembled the present-day societies (Heckenberger 1996). This was well after many other Amerindians in Amazonia had been destroyed by nonindigenous contact. Many examples of dramatic and devastating contact are known from Amazonia and nearby, such as along the coast of Brazil, the main stem of the Amazon River, and elsewhere. Although complete destruction did not occur in all cases, collapse or severe disruption ultimately faced (or faces) each indigenous society in Amazonia owing to exogenous factors, with some groups undergoing this same dreadful process today—the Yanomamo on the border of Brazil and Venezuela, for example.

Collapse in the Insular Caribbean

In the insular Caribbean, the rate of exogenous collapse was even more dramatic than in Amazonia shortly after contact, with the population plunging from perhaps several million or more Taino in Hispaniola in 1492 to essentially none by 1540, a period of less than 50 years. The Taino culture, or set of cultures, was made extinct in terms of its independent functioning, although its genetic heritage lives on to verying extents in the Greater Antilles and elsewhere.

Perhaps of more interest in the present case is the possibility of prehistoric endogenous collapse in at least one portion of the Lesser Antilles before contact. This is the most plausible case of endogenous collapse of a complex society in the insular Caribbean known to date, although collapse of less-complex and non-complex societies may have occurred multiple times before then. The Lesser Antillean case may be analogous to the example from Marajo Island since some researchers say that it represents indigenous depopulation caused by other Amerindians. In this scenario, the northern Lesser Antilles became a "no man's land" as a result of Island Carib attacks against the Eastern Taino. For example, Rouse (1992) and others have noted the complete lack of evidence of European contact at late Amerindian sites across the Leeward Islands between Guadeloupe and the Virgin Islands. These islands were perhaps effectively depopulated by 1300–1450 for some reason. Historical records suggest that the Island Carib were present on a few of the Leeward Islands for brief periods historically (e.g., St. Kitts), but they did not leave much, if any, of an archaeological signature.

If this reconstruction of late prehistoric depopulation is correct for the northeastern Caribbean, the Eastern Taino were the local losers well before meeting any Europeans. The Eastern Taino, living in several or more polities, may have been completely lost in this process, having perhaps fled to join other Taino to the west in the Greater Antilles. Alternatively, they may have been forcibly (or peacefully?) absorbed by the Island Carib farther south in the Lesser Antilles before the arrival of Europeans. Island Carib oral history related to Carib ethnogenesis may support the latter scenario, but even if so, it remains unclear just when this occurred—was it, in fact, prehistoric?

Alternatively, it is possible that some or all Eastern Taino inhabitants were still present historically in the Leeward Islands during the early-mid 1500s, but they were lost before they were recorded in any detail. If so, either the Eastern Taino were soon driven to the west and/

or south, they were killed by European diseases, and/or they were lost through enslavement.

Enslavement would have been particularly traumatic, potentially disrupting a whole group instantaneously, as we know happened during Spanish slave raids in the Bahamas, various islands in the Lesser Antilles, and Aruba, for example (e.g., Oliver 1989; Sued Badillo 1995:66). Perhaps some Eastern Taino were absorbed by their apparent brethren, the Classic Taino, just prior to overall collapse and destruction of all Taino, ca. 1520–1540. Alternatively, perhaps the Eastern Taino were absorbed by the "enemy" Island Carib at this early date and thereby lost to recorded history.

Besides this late case of either late prehistoric or early historical collapse, other collapses may have occurred in the insular Caribbean well before 1400–1500. However, they would not necessarily have involved the collapse of complex societies per se. For example, local polities of a relatively noncomplex sort may have collapsed when preceramic hunter-gatherers first faced pottery-making farmer migrants between ca. 500 BC and AD 600 during the Saladoid period. This episodic process may also have occurred in the early portion of the Post-Saladoid (or Ostionoid) period—ca. 600–900, for example, when pottery-making farmers spread further, colonizing additional, previously inhabited islands, such as Hispaniola and Cuba, where preceramic groups were still living. Regardless of these possibilities, none of these hypothetical endogenous transformations came close to the exogenous crash that occurred after European contact.

POSSIBLE FACTORS BEHIND COLLAPSE

While obviously speculative, the foregoing summary of pre-contact and contact-induced collapse is important for a broad understanding of the mechanisms behind collapse as an outgrowth of factors internal and external to Amerindian polities in the South American lowlands. These hypotheses have been proposed to provoke further research, rather than ignoring the possibility of social complexity and its collapse, as some regional researchers have been prone to do. Many skeptics only trust ethnohistorically documented examples of social complexity, and even then they typically mistrust many of the relevant details. Others, still more skeptical, dismiss social complexity in some or all of these cases altogether. Alternatively, among the cases where social complexity is archaeologically recognizable, the collapse and demise of these polities is often ascribed to colonial events related to European contact, given the obvious correlation

(e.g., Roosevelt 1993; Wilson 1990). Although colonial contact obviously was very devastating in many, many cases, we should not let the scale and devastation of the exogenous historical examples completely overshadow the probability of endogenous collapse due to internal factors, prehistorically and perhaps historically as well.

If indeed the Marajoara and Eastern Taino, for example, suffered collapse before the arrival of colonial peoples, we need to explore just which factors were responsible for these endogenous transformations. Of course, multiple factors may well be relevant rather than just one, and all hypotheses are likely gross simplifications of reality. The broad model of collapse proposed by Tainter (1988), recognizing that diminishing returns may lead to collapse among complex societies, is potentially relevant for both areas. That is, we can hypothesize that some factor(s) made the maintenance of social complexity in the Marajo area impossible during late prehistory, and we suggest that it was most likely political/ideological rather than strictly economic and/or environmental in origin. In particular, it may have been due to external pressure from other Amerindians.

Our best understanding of the internal affairs of socially complex chiefdoms in Amazonia suggests that some, if not all, were inherently unstable. Initially, they represented temporary and shifting political alliances that brought particular individuals, "big men"/"chieftains," into positions of power, sometimes for quite short periods. Such polities are difficult to isolate archaeologically owing to their localized and short-term nature, and few, if any, have been recognized thus far. In other cases, local polities were less fleeting, and they became more secure across larger areas with attendant settlement hierarchies based on the intensification of non-floodplain crops, such as manioc. As such, they were represented for long enough periods to be archaeologically recognizable, as at Marajo, central Amazonia, Upper Xingu, Sangay, and the Leeward Islands. Political power would have been secured across individual and even multiple lifetimes in these cases, as seems to be represented archaeologically in both Amazonia and the insular Caribbean, but the seeds of instability were also long-lasting.

Tribes led by "big men"/"chieftains" evolved into chiefdoms led by "chiefs" in such cases, and these socially complex polities persisted for varying lengths of time. For example, in the CAP study area in central Amazonia, one or more possible chiefdoms postdate ca. AD 800 and seemingly lasted for as long as 600–700 years. Comparable developments likely date considerably earlier at Marajo, as early as AD 200, and lasted about 1,100 years in that case. Social complexity at Sangay may have been present as early as 700 BC, and it lasted somewhere between 700 and 1,100 years, depending on when it began. This early development may be due to the rich volcanic soils in the Selva Alta of Ecuador and/or direct Andean influences, as trade between the two areas is obvious in the archaeological record.

In the Upper Xingu, probable chiefdoms arose by AD 1000–1200, which was later than on the central and lower Amazon and at Sangay, and they persisted for about 500–600 years in the Upper Xingu. In the insular Caribbean, chiefdoms began no later than AD 900–1000, if not earlier, and lasted for about 600 years at a minimum, at least in the Greater Antilles and probably in the Lesser Antilles as well. This may even have occurred during the late prehistoric Post-Saladoid/Ostionoid period, after ca. AD 600–900. However, several of us see the origins of prehistoric Caribbean chiefdoms as early as the preceding Saladoid period, ca. 500 BC–AD 600. We also see the Eastern Taino in the northern Lesser Antilles, like the Classic Taino, as ultimately socially complex, and as participants in chiefdoms parallel to and/or directly connected with the Greater Antilles.

With the passage of time, the mix of the costs and benefits shifted adversely for some reason under the conditions of inherent political instability that contributed to the rise of these chiefdoms in the first place. Again following Tainter (1988), we believe that historical contingencies generated by the relationships and power of individual leaders as well as broader political linkages were responsible for the initial development of some, if not many, complex societies. Such factors led to the later collapse of these polities, if it was not due to European contact in the case of the northern Lesser Antilles and central Amazonia. Indirect contact with nonindigenous people was almost certainly responsible for collapse in the Upper Xingu.

Given the limitations of the archaeological record in both regions, we cannot be certain which nonidiosyncratic factors pertained to the origins, maintenance, and collapse of different complex polities in the broad South American lowlands. Nonetheless, it seems highly unlikely that environmental factors constrained these societies very much. Thus, the environment alone was likely not responsible for any case of endogenous collapse and only for some cases of catastrophic exogenous collapse. In fact, local aquatic environments in various portions of Amazonia and the insular Caribbean almost surely provided very rich and diverse resources sufficient for supporting social complexity. Ecologically rich settings were widespread over broad areas along the rivers and the seacoast, based on the location of extensive settlements, as is now known with varying degrees of certainty. Virtually inexhaustible food resources were available in the rivers and sea across lowland South America. However, the Amerindians surely combined rich aquatic resources with intensive and extensive non-floodplain horticulture in all portions of these regions, and this farming was almost certainly centered on manioc.

Modeling the development and collapse of social complexity in Amazonia and the insular Caribbean is obviously difficult at this point. In Amazonia, past researchers have suggested that supposedly unlimited territory made it possible for groups under population and/or environmental pressure to relocate themselves to start anew. In reality, however, if environmental richness is confined to the interface between non-floodplain farming and aquatic resources in Amazonia, then optimum settings were confined to the margins of the waterways, or the "bluff" zone, throughout the region (Denevan 1996). These settings are not as limited as the area of the varzea per se, but such locations are not ubiquitous either. Farmers who lived in such optimum settings along Amazonian waterways may have been pushed and pulled by their neighbors, farmers and non-farmers alike. Thus, the nature of local resources and population growth in Amazonia may have generally structured the development and collapse of complex societies.

In the case of the Leeward Islands in the northeastern Caribbean, environmental heterogeneity structured local economies and, by extension, local sociopolitical developments to a degree. Again, some may believe that environmental conditions restricted the evolution of social complexity there. However, island analogues from the Pacific demonstrate that the presence of complex societies is not necessarily confined to environmentally rich islands in the first place, especially when trade and long-distance interaction are characteristic. In Micronesia and Polynesia, for example, social complexity transcended "rich" and "poor" environments, especially where the individual polities included diverse island settings and/ or were interconnected with other polities. In the insular Caribbean, the sea also provided very rich resources more or less everywhere, and lowland-derived horticulture, again manioc-based, was an important complement to seafood. Local environments may have structured specific inter-island linkages, especially on the smaller, more depauperate islands. Nonetheless, political factors were critical in the definition of the character and extent of the polities beyond general environmental conditions.

Such inter-island linkages have been recognized across the Caribbean region. In fact, among the large islands, cross-channel archaeological connections *between* islands have long been recognized as sometimes more relevant than connections *within* individual islands, specifically among the large islands of the Greater Antilles (Rouse 1992). This scenario seems anomalous at first, but under closer scrutiny it reflects the high value placed on and even the necessity of inter-island linkages. These linkages pertained between local, nearby islands, and also between broader portions of the Lesser Antilles and Greater Antilles, as reflected by the distribution of raw materials and artifact styles, among other evidence (Crock 2000; Hofman 1993; Watters 1997).

For example, soil fertility and aridity vary greatly among different Caribbean islands. Rather different wet-volcanic and dry-carbonate islands were joined in common economic systems within the Leeward Islands. This inter-island dependence is especially evident on the relatively inhospitable, low-lying carbonate islands, where rich soils are rare and aridity is characteristic. Moreover, broader linkages between the local area and other islands southward in the Lesser Antilles and westward to the Greater Antilles are also evident, probably for trade and local group security, as in times of local devastation from hurricanes, for example. We know of comparable examples from Micronesia, as in the case of Yap, Ulithi, Lamotrek, and other islands up to 1,000 km distant from one another (Crock 2000; Petersen and Crock 2001).

Substantial occupation of the arid carbonate islands in the Lesser Antilles and the Bahamas (and Turks & Caicos) only began during late prehistory, as was the case in Jamaica, where its relative remoteness apparently delayed settlement, rather than its aridity and poor soils. All of this late colonization may be directly attributable to the elaboration of social complexity that developed regionally by AD 900–1000 or earlier. These examples of late colonization must be at least partially attributable to the nature of the complex societies that spawned them. Long-distance economic systems came along with and fostered colonization of these new islands, where farming was sometimes very difficult and the only constant was food from the sea. Much later, when individual islands were put under stress for some reason and their local and distant polity connections were truncated, these settings were no longer habitable. Thus, at least some islands may have been voluntarily abandoned as being too costly or unsafe, as possibly happened prehistorically in the northern Lesser Antilles (Sued Badillo 1995).

We hypothesize that under late prehistoric political stresses and strains, whether due to internal political conditions and/or to Island Carib warfare, the Leeward Islands were abandoned before the Europeans and other colonials arrived. This occurred when the costs of staying exceeded the benefits. Most Caribbean islands are also subject to natural disasters, such as droughts, hurricanes, storm surges, and earthquakes. Consequently, it is even possible that one or more disasters led to abandonment of some settlements on some islands before late prehistory and thus collapse in those locations was environmentally based, at least in part. For example, disasters may have occurred in late Saladoid times, as at Trants in Montserrat at ca. AD 400–500, and during Post-Saladoid/Ostionoid times, as at Sandy Ground and perhaps Shoal Bay in Anguilla. However, natural catastrophes likely were not of sufficient magnitude to cause the synchronous abandonment of the Leeward Islands. Again, if such widespread abandonment occurred during late prehistory, before the arrival of Europeans and others, it was much more likely a product of inter-regional political/ideological and warfare factors rather than strictly environmental ones.

Once we establish social complexity, by whatever means, we need to rigorously pursue its developmental trajectories wherever possible, as we have tentatively done here. In particular, evidence of collapse is important for understanding these trajectories and the settings where it has and has not occurred. However, we readily admit that the collapse of complex (and other) societies is not easy to address, especially where some continuity pertained over the period of collapse without causing recognizable abandonment or some other equally dramatic signature in the archaeological record.

SUMMARY AND CONCLUSIONS

In summary, this necessarily brief chapter raises many more questions than it can answer about the collapse of late prehistoric and early historical social complexity in Amazonia and the insular Caribbean. In the case of the Caribbean, it is not absolutely clear if any collapse occurred prior to the arrival of European and other colonial peoples, but this now seems likely. However, in at least one or more cases from Amazonia discussed here it seems that the collapse of social complexity, almost surely representing chiefdoms, occurred prehistorically. This must have been the case at Marajo and Sangay, and perhaps central Amazonia too, but it was not the case in the Upper Xingu.

142 / JAMES B. PETERSEN, MICHAEL J. HECKENBERGER, EDUARDO GOES NEVES, JOHN G. CROCK, AND ROBERT N. BARTONE

In the case of Marajo Island, the Amerindians did not completely disappear after their "collapse"; instead their system seemingly "devolved," or became less complex. In rough terms, they probably went from a chiefdom-level society to a tribal one, with or without an influx of new people, before being ultimately destroyed by contact with nonindigenous people several hundred years later. Although for a different reason and much earlier, the Sangay collapse may have been comparable to Marajo in broad terms, especially if other native polities contributed to the effects of the volcanic disaster which apparently caused the collapse.

In contrast, the residents of the Leeward Islands in the Caribbean, known to some as the Eastern Taino, may have been completely destroyed, or perhaps one and all voluntarily picked up and left the region during late prehistory under conditions of endogenous collapse. If the latter scenario is the case, endogenous factors must have caused their initial collapse even though exogenous, nonindigenous factors were responsible for the ultimate demise of the Taino in general and many of the Island Carib after contact.

How might we test these propositions in the archaeological record? First, we need to acquire more carefully collected survey and excavation data and then look carefully to find archaeological signatures therein. More specifically, we need to continue looking for evidence of stratigraphic sequences; settlement patterns; social interaction, such as trade and warfare; corporate constructions, such as earthworks; equality and inequality in burials; and differential artifact distributions, among other avenues. This will help us demonstrate social complexity in the first place and its internal chronology. We also need to build models to evaluate varying taxonomies of social complexity and its representation in the archaeological record. Paleoenvironmental data also would help us assess potential effects under changing environmental conditions. As we have said above, we do not believe that environments alone could have caused collapse on anything other than the local level, but the Sangay example suggests that environmental factors may well be relevant to understanding collapse.

Use of ethnohistoric and archaeological data to enable broad comparison of social complexity in Amazonia and the insular Caribbean remains to be done, but rich analogues useful for comparative analysis are known elsewhere, especially through archaeology. The Hopewellian and Mississippian mound builders and the Anasazi, Mogollon, and Hohokam of North America, for example, would provide useful points of comparison for the scale of the Marajo and Upper Xingu earthworks. These examples and others from elsewhere suggest that people of varying social complexity have been responsible for monumental earthworks. However, in nearly all cases, the mound builders were socially complex on some level. Through ethnology we can certainly see that not all people who are socially complex represent themselves through earth moving, at least not as is evident through conventional archaeology, nor is all earth moving necessarily reflective of social complexity.

Concerted research in Amazonia and the insular Caribbean is necessary to refine our sense of chronology, settlement patterns and site hierarchy, and social interaction of different forms, along with various other archaeological issues. Better resolution of these issues, in turn, will help us determine when and where the collapse of social complexity is demonstrable in prehistoric and historical contexts. In addition, continued assessment of theoretical models should help us develop criteria by which we can evaluate the dimensions of collapse in particular locales. In this manner we should be able to more fully understand collapse as part and parcel of Amerindian cultural evolution in the lowlands of Social America.

Our collective years of research in Amazonia and the Caribbean reflect the assistance and support of many people who have helped us along the way. Although we cannot acknowledge all of them here, we are certainly thankful for help from many people. Many colleagues have kindly provided reference materials used herein, including (but not limited to) Louis Allaire, Robert Carneiro, Warren DeBoer, Bill Denevan, Corinne Hofman, Betty Meggers, Tom Myers, Jim Richardson, Anna Roosevelt, Stephen Rostain, Ben Rouse, Peter Siegel, Aad Versteeg, Dave Watters, Sam Wilson, Bill Woods, and Alberta Zucchi. We thank Jimmy Railey and Rick Reycraft for their invitation to participate in the symposium in which this paper was presented. In addition, Jim drafted the map that accompanies this article. Likewise, we thank the two symposium discussants, Joseph Tainter and Antonio Gilman, for their patience awaiting the first draft of this paper and their useful critique of it.

what are the problem
w/ previous research
↳ simplistic models

lo page de Piater
Carnal
Towney

succession is problem for
chiefly cycling
↳ Anderson

REFERENCES CITED

Alegria, Ricardo E.
1980 *Cristobal Colon y el tesoro de los Indios Tainos de la Espanola.* Santo Domingo: Fundacion Garcia-Arevalo.

Allaire, Louis
1980 On the Historicity of Carib Migrations in the Lesser Antilles. *American Antiquity* 45:238–245.
1999 Archaeology of the Caribbean Region. In *The Cambridge History of the Native Peoples of the Americas,* Vol. III: South America, edited by Frank Salomon and Stuart B. Schwartz, pp. 668–733. Cambridge: Cambridge University Press.

Arnold, Jeanne E., ed.
1996 *Emergent Complexity: The Evolution of Intermediate Societies.* International Monographs in Prehistory 9. Ann Arbor.

Boomert, Arie
1987 Gifts of the Amazons: "Green" Stone Pendants and Beads as Items of Ceremonial Exchange in Amazonia and the Caribbean. *Antropológica* 67:33–54.

Carneiro, Robert L.
1981 The Chiefdom: Precursor of the State. In *The Transition to Statehood in the New World*, edited by Grant D. Jones and Robert R. Kautz, pp. 37–79. Cambridge: Cambridge University Press.
1998 What Happened at the Flashpoint? Conjectures on Chiefdom Formation at the Very Moment of Conception. In *Chiefdoms and Chieftaincy in the Americas*, edited by Elsa M. Redmond, pp. 18–42. Gainesville: University of Florida Press.

Crock, John G.
2000 *Interisland Interaction and the Development of Chiefdoms in the Eastern Caribbean.* Unpublished Ph.D. dissertation, Department of Anthropology, University of Pittsburgh.

Curet, Antonio L.
1992 *The Development of Chiefdoms in the Greater Antilles: A Regional Study of the Valley of Maunabo, Puerto Rico.* Unpublished Ph.D. dissertation, Department of Anthropology, Arizona State University, Tempe.

DeBoer, Warren R.
1981 Buffer Zones in the Cultural Ecology of Aboriginal Amazonia: An Ethnohistorical Approach. *American Antiquity* 46:364–377.

Denevan, William M.
1966 *The Aboriginal Cultural Geography of the Llanos de Mojos of Bolivia.* Berkeley: University of California Press.
1992 The Aboriginal Population of Amazonia. In *The Native Population of the Americas in 1492*, second ed., edited by William M. Denevan, pp. 205–234. Madison: University of Wisconsin Press.

1996 A Bluff Model of Riverine Settlement in Prehistoric Amazonia. *Annals of the Association of American Geographers* 86:654–681.

Denevan, William M., and Alberta Zucchi
1978 Ridged-Field Excavations in the Central Orinoco Llanos, Venezuela. In *Advances in Andean Archaeology*, edited by David Browman, pp. 235–245. The Hague: Mouton.

Earle, Timothy K.
1987 Chiefdoms in Archaeological and Ethnohistorical Perspective. *Annual Review of Anthropology* 16:279–308.
1997 *How Chiefs Come to Power: The Political Economy in Prehistory.* Stanford: Stanford University Press.

Heckenberger, Michael J.
1996 *War and Peace in the Shadow of Empire: Sociocultural Change in the Upper Xingu of Southeastern Amazonia, ca. A.D. 1400–2000.* Unpublished Ph.D. dissertation, Department of Anthropology, University of Pittsburgh.
1998 Manioc Agriculture and Sedentism in Amazonia: The Upper Xingu Example. *Antiquity* 72:633–648.
2001 Rethinking the Arawak Diaspora: Hierarchy, Regionality, and the Amazonian "Formative." Ms. in preparation.

Heckenberger, Michael J., and James B. Petersen
1999 Concentric Circular Village patterns in the Caribbean: Comparisons from Amazonia. In *Proceedings of the 16th International Congress for Caribbean Archaeology*, edited by Gerard Richard, pp. 379–390. Basse Terre: Conseil Regional de la Guadeloupe.

Heckenberger, Michael J., Eduardo Goes Neves, and James B. Petersen
1998 De onde surgem os modelos? As origens e expansoes Tupi na Amazonia Central. *Revista de Antropologia* 41:69–96.

Heckenberger, Michael J., James B. Petersen, and Eduardo Goes Neves
1999 Village Size and Permanence in Amazonia: Two Archaeological Examples from Brazil. *Latin American Antiquity* 10:353–376.
2001 Of Lost Civilizations and Primitive Tribes, Amazonia: Reply to Meggers. *Latin American Antiquity* 12:328–333.

Hofman, Corrine
1993 *In Search of the Native Population of Pre-Columbian Saba (400–1450 A.D.), Part One: Pottery Styles and Their Interpretations.* Ph.D. dissertation, Leiden University, Leiden.

Hulme, Peter, and Neil L. Whitehead, eds.
1992 *Wild Majesty: Encounters with Caribs from Columbus to the Present Day, an Anthology.* Oxford: Oxford University Press.

Johnson, Allen W., and Timothy Earle

1987 *The Evolution of Human Societies: From Foraging Group to Agrarian State*. Stanford: Stanford University Press.

Kaufman, Herbert
1988 The Collapse of Ancient States and Civilizations as an Organizational Problem. In *The Collapse of Ancient States and Civilizations*, edited by Norman Yoffee and George L. Cowgill, pp. 219–235.·Tucson: University of Arizona Press.

Keegan, William F.
1997 *Bahamian Archaeology: Life in the Bahamas and Turks & Caicos before Columbus*. Nassau, The Bahamas: Media Publishing.

Lathrap, Donald W.
1970 *The Upper Amazon*. New York: Praeger.
1973 The Antiquity and Importance of Long Distance Trade Relationships in the Moist Tropics of Pre-Columbian South America. *World Archaeology* 5:170–186.

Meggers, Betty
1971 *Amazonia: Man and Culture in a Counterfeit Paradise*. Arlington Heights, Chicago: AHM Publishing.
2001 The Continuing Quest for El Dorado: Round Two. *Latin American Antiquity* 12:304–325.

Meggers, Betty, and Clifford Evans
1957 *Archeological Investigations at the Mouth of the Amazon*. Bureau of American Ethnology Bulletin 167. Washington, DC: Smithsonian Institution.
1983 Lowland South American and the Antilles. In *Ancient South Americans*, edited by Jesse D. Jennings, pp. 287–335. San Francisco: W.H. Freeman.

Metraux, Alfred
1948 Tribes of the Middle and Upper Amazon. In *The Tropical Forest Tribes*, edited by Julian H. Steward, pp. 687–712. Handbook of South American Indians, Vol. 3. Bureau of American Ethnology 143. Washington, DC: Smithsonian Institution.

Monteiro, John M.
1999 The Crises and Transformations of Invaded Societies: Coastal Brazil in the Sixteenth Century. In *The Cambridge History of the Native Peoples of the Americas*, Vol. III: South America, edited by Frank Salomon and Stuart B. Schwartz, pp. 973–1023. Cambridge: Cambridge University Press.

Moran, Emilio F.
1993 *Through Amazonian Eyes: The Human Ecology of Amazonian Populations*. Iowa City: University of Iowa Press.

Morey, Robert V.
1979 A Joyful Harvest of Souls: Disease and the Destruction of the Llanos Indians. *Antropologica* 52:77–108.

Myers, Thomas P.
1976 Defended Territories and No-Man's-Lands. *American Anthropologist* 78:354–355.

1982 Aboriginal Trade Networks in Amazonia. In *Networks of the Past: Regional Interaction in Archaeology*, edited by Peter D. Francis, F. J. Kense and P. G. Duke, pp. 19–30. Calgary: University of Calgary Archaeological Association.
1992 The Expansion and Collapse of the Omagua. *Journal of the Steward Anthropological Society* 20:129–152.

Neves, Eduardo Goes
1998 *Paths through Dark Waters: Archaeology as Indigenous History in the Upper Rio Negro, Northwest Amazon*. Unpublished Ph.D. dissertation. Department of Anthropology, Indiana University, Bloomington.
1999 Changing Perspectives in Amazonian Archaeology. In *Archaeology in Latin America*, edited by Gustavo G. Politis and Benjamin Alberti, pp. 216–242. London: Routledge.
2001 Indigenous Historical Trajectories in the Upper Rio Negro Basin. In *The Unknown Amazon*, edited by Colin McEwan, Cristiana Barreto, and Eduardo Neves, pp. 266–286. London: British Museum Press.

Nimuendajú, Curt
1952 The Tapajó. *Kroeber Anthropological Society Papers* 6:1–25. Berkeley.

Oberg, Kalervo
1955 Types of Social Structure among the Lowland Tribes of South and Central America. *American Anthropologist* 57:472–487.

Oliver, Jose R.
1989 *The Archaeological, Linguisitic and Ethnohistorical Evidence for the Expansion of Arawakans into Northwestern Venezuela and Northwestern Columbia*. Unpublished Ph.D. dissertation, Department of Anthropology, University of Illinois, Champaign-Urbana.
2001 The Archaeology of Forest Foraging and Agricultural Production in Amazonia. In *The Unknown Amazon*, edited by Colin McEwan, Cristiana Barreto and Eduardo Neves, pp. 50–85. London: British Museum Press.

Petersen, James B.
1996 The Archaeology of Trants, Montserrat, Part 3: Chronological and Settlement Data. *Annals of Carnegie Museum* 65:323–361.
1997 Taino, Island Carib, and Prehistoric Amerindian Economies in the West Indies: Tropical Forest Adaptations to Island Environments. In *The Indigenous People of the Caribbean*, edited by Samuel M. Wilson, pp. 118–130. Gainesville: University of Florida Press.

Petersen, James B., and John G. Crock
2001 Late Saladoid to Late Prehistoric Occupation in Anguilla: Site Setting, Chronology and Settlement Hierarchy. In *Proceedings of the 18ᵗʰ International Congress for Caribbean Archaeology*, edited by Gerard Richard, pp. 124–135. Guadeloupe: Region Conseil.

Petersen, James B., Michael J. Heckenberger, and Eduardo Goes Neves

2001 Gift from the Past: *Terra Preta* and Prehistoric Amerindian Occupation in Amazonia. In *The Unknown Amazon*, edited by Colin McEwan, Cristiana Barreto, and Eduardo Neves, pp. 86–105. London: British Museum Press.

Porro, Antonio

1992 Historia indigena do alto e medio Amazonas: Seculos XVI a XVIII. In *Historia dos Indios no Brasil*, edited by Manuela Carneiro da Cunha, pp. 175–196. São Paolo: Companhia das Letras.

1994 Social Organization and Political Power in the Amazon Floodplain: The Ethnohistorical Sources. In *Amazonian Indians from Prehistory to the Present: Anthropological Perspectives*, edited by Anna Roosevelt, pp. 79–94. Tucson: University of Arizona Press.

Redmond, Elsa M., and Charles S. Spencer

1994 The *Cacicazgo*: An Indigenous Design. In *Caciques and Their People: A Volume in Honour of Ronald Spores*, edited by Joyce Marcus and Judith Francis Zeitlin, pp. 189–225. Anthropological Papers 89. Ann Arbor: Museum of Anthropology, University of Michigan.

Redmond, Elsa M., Rafael A. Gasson, and Charles S. Spencer

1999 A Macroregional View of Cycling Chiefdoms in the Western Venezuelan Llanos. In *Complex Polities in the Ancient Tropical World*, edited by Elisabeth A. Bacus and Lisa J. Lucero, pp. 109–129. Archeological Papers of the American Anthropological Association 9. Washington, D.C.

Roosevelt, Anna C.

1980 *Parmana: Prehistoric Maize and Manioc Subsistence along the Amazon and Orinoco*. New York: Academic Press.

1987 Chiefdoms in the Amazon and Orinoco. In *Chiefdoms in the Americas*, edited by Robert D. Drennan and Carlos A. Uribe, pp. 153–185. Lanham, MD: University Press of America.

1989 Resource Management in Amazonia before the Conquest: Beyond Ethnographic Projection. In *Resource Management in Amazonia: Folk and Indigenous Strategies*, edited by Darrel A. Posey and William Balee, pp. 30–62. Advances in Economic Botany 7. New York Botanical Garden.

1991 *Moundbuilders of the Amazon: Geophysical Archaeology on Marajo Island, Brazil*. New York: Academic Press.

1993 The Rise and Fall of the Amazon Chiefdoms. *L'Homme* 33:255–283.

1994 Amazonian Anthropology: Strategy for a New Synthesis. In *Amazonian Indians from Prehistory to the Present: Anthropological Perspectives*, edited by Anna Roosevelt, pp. 1–29. Tucson: University of Arizona Press.

1999 The Development of Prehistoric Complex Societies: Amazonia, a Tropical Forest. In *Complex Polities in the Ancient Tropical World*, edited by Elisabeth A. Bacus and Lisa J. Lucero, pp. 13–33. Archeological Papers of the American Anthropological Association 9. Washington, D.C.

Rostain, Stephen

1991 *Les champs surleves amerindiens de la Guyanne*. Paris: Centre ORSTOM de Cayenne, University de Paris.

1999 Secuencia arquologica en monticulos del valle del Upano en la Amazonia Ecuatoriana. *Bulletin de l'institut francais d'etudes andines* 28(1):53–89.

Rouse, Irving

1962 The Intermediate Area, Amazonia, and the Caribbean Area. In *Courses Toward Urban Life: Archeological Considerations of Some Cultural Alternates*, edited by Robert J. Braidwood and Gordon R. Willey, pp. 34–59. Chicago: Aldine.

1986 *Migrations in Prehistory: Inferring Population Movement from Cultural Remains*. New Haven: Yale University Press.

1992 *The Taino: Rise and Decline of the People Who Greeted Columbus*. New Haven: Yale University Press.

Siegel, Peter E.

1999 Contested Places and Places of Contest: The Evolution of Social Power and Ceremonial Space in Prehistoric Puerto Rico. *Latin American Antiquity* 10:209–238.

Spencer, Charles S.

1998 Investigating the Development of Venezuelan Chiefdoms. In *Chiefdoms and Chieftaincy in the Americas*, edited by Elsa M. Redmond, pp. 104–137. Gainesville: University of Florida Press.

Steward, Julian H.

1948 Culture Areas of the Tropical Forests. In *The Tropical Forest Tribes*, edited by Julian H. Steward, pp. 883–899. Handbook of South American Indians, vol. 3. Bureau of American Ethnology 143. Washington, DC: Smithsonian Institution.

Steward, Julian H., and Louis C. Faron

1959 *Native Peoples of South America*. New York: McGraw-Hill.

Sued Badillo, Jalil

1995 The Island Caribs: New Approaches to the Question of Ethnicity in the Early Colonial Caribbean. In *Wolves from the Sea: Readings in the Anthropology of the Native Caribbean*, edited by Neil L. Whitehead, pp. 61–89. Leiden: KITLV Press.

Tainter, Joseph A.

1988 *The Collapse of Complex Societies*. Cambridge: Cambridge University Press.

Versteeg, Aad H., and Stephen Rostain, eds.

1997 *The Archaeology of Aruba: The Tanki Flip Site*. Publication of the Archaeological Museum of Aruba 8. Publication of the Foundation for Scientific Research in the Caribbean Region 141. Aruba and Amsterdam.

Vidal, Sylvia, and Alberta Zucchi

1996 Impacto de la colonizacion hispanolusitana en las organizacioness sociopoliticas y economicas de los Maipures-Arawakos del Alto Orinoco–Rio Negro (Siglos XVII–XVIII). *America Negra* 11:107–129.

Watters, David R.

1997 Maritime Trade in the Prehistoric Eastern Caribbean. In *The Indigenous People of the Caribbean,* edited by Samuel M. Wilson, pp. 88–99. Gainesville: University Press of Florida.

Whitehead, Neil L.

1996 Amazonian Archaeology: Searching for Pardise? A Review of Recent Literature and Fieldwork. *Journal of Archaeological Research* 4:241–264.

1998 Colonial Chiefdoms of the Lower Orinoco and Guayana Coast. In *Chiefdoms and Chieftaincy in the Americas,* edited by Elsa M. Redmond, pp. 150–163. Gainesville: University Press of Florida.

1999 The Crises and Transformations of Invaded Societies: The Caribbean (1492–1580). In *The Cambridge History of the Native Peoples of the Americas,* Vol. III: South America, edited by Frank Salomon and Stuart B. Schwartz, pp. 864–903. Cambridge: Cambridge University Press.

Whitehead, Neil L., ed.

1995 *Wolves from the Sea: Readings in the Anthropology of the Native Caribbean.* Leiden: KITLV Press.

Wilson, Samuel M.

1990 *Hispaniola: Caribbean Chiefdoms in the Age of Columbus.* Tuscaloosa: University of Alabama Press.

Woods, William I., and Joseph M. McCann

1999 The Anthropogenic Origin and Persistence of Amazonian Dark Earths. *Yearbook of the Conference of Latin Americanist Geographers* 25:7–14.

Wright, Robin M.

1999 Destruction, Resistance, and Transformation— Southern, Coastal, and Northern Brazil (1580–1890). In *The Cambridge History of the Native Peoples of the Americas,* Vol. III: South America, edited by Frank Salomon and Stuart B. Schwartz, pp. 287–381. Cambridge: Cambridge University Press.

Yoffee, Norman

1988 Orienting Collapse. In *The Collapse of Ancient States and Civilizations,* edited by Norman Yoffe and George L. Cowgill, pp. 1–19. Tucson: University of Arizona Press.

10

Contemplating Cahokia's Collapse

John E. Kelly

T HE EMERGENCE OF SOCIAL INEQUALITY DURING THE COURSE OF human social evolution is a widespread phenomenon that has numerous and diverse roots with an array of different outcomes. A variety of elements relating to hierarchical control and horizontal specialization and differentiation within relatively large populations is used to delineate kin-based societies featuring ranked and inherited social positions, often referred to as chiefdoms. Understanding the cyclical nature of these rather fragile yet complex entities in terms of their development, florescence, and decline is a daunting task. While a considerable amount of literature has been devoted to the origins of chiefdoms and states (e.g., Beck 2003; Carneiro 1981; Earle 1997; Feinman and Marcus 1998), less effort has been dedicated to the "collapse" of these complex societies. Over the past century a number of different causes, ranging from catastrophic to the subtle nuances of the mystic, have been discussed in the historical, social, and political literature. Within recent years a number of archaeologists (e.g., Tainter 1988; Yoffee and Cowgill 1988) have undertaken the task of systematically examining the collapse of complex societies.

Certainly the notion of collapse conveys a certain level of meltdown within any system, especially as it pertains to social and political institutions. Whether this breakdown results in the ultimate demise of the polity is another consideration. Or perhaps the ability of these cultural systems to adapt to and rebound from the underlying causes reflects the flexibility of reorganization at much simpler levels, socially and politically. As Tainter (1988:37–38) notes, complex societies are "problem-solving organizations," and their ability to deal with such changes reinforces this role.

The Mississippian cultural tradition at the onset of the second millennium within eastern North America marks the climax of societal complexity some five hundred years before the collision of these societies with colonizing European states. This cultural tradition consists of, by definition, a polythetic set of attributes. When viewed in societal terms Mississippian chiefdoms are political entities that vary in size and duration and have their own historical sequences. In his research on the Mississippian, especially those complexes known as South Appalachian Mississippian, David Anderson (1994, 1996a, 1996b) has discussed the cycling of these systems. Basically, most Mississippian systems go through a historical cycle of emergence, florescence, and decline. Hally (1996a:120), for example, has documented 14 to 41 collapses among the numerous chiefdoms spanning nearly five centuries in northern Georgia. Anderson (1996b:236–237) has proposed that factional competition for the office of chief is often the primary cause of political instability within chiefdoms; hence it is one possible factor leading to their decline or collapse. More recently, Blitz (1999) has discussed the endemic nature of the fusion-fission processes within the various South Appalachian Mississippian chiefdoms.

CAHOKIA: A BRIEF PERSPECTIVE

Within the broader Mississippian cultural tradition are embedded multiple smaller traditions. One of the earliest regional traditions to emerge on the northern edge of the Mississippian world was Cahokia. This site and its satellite settlements are located within the central Mississippi River valley opposite modern-day St. Louis (Figure 35). As with its other Mississippian kindred, Cahokia exhibits the classic cycle of emergence, florescence, decline, and then abandonment (Milner 1990, 1998, 2006).

The Cahokia chiefdom is at the high end of the Mississippian spectrum in terms of its political complexity. Within the past three decades research has been primarily focused on Cahokia's emergence (e.g., Kelly 1980; Pauketat 1994). As noted by Milner (2006: xx–xxi) researchers in the 1980s recognized the abrupt change in settlement patterns and material culture between the Emergent and Early Mississippian complexes of the American Bottom. Pauketat (1994) has characterized the change from the relatively simple chiefdoms of the

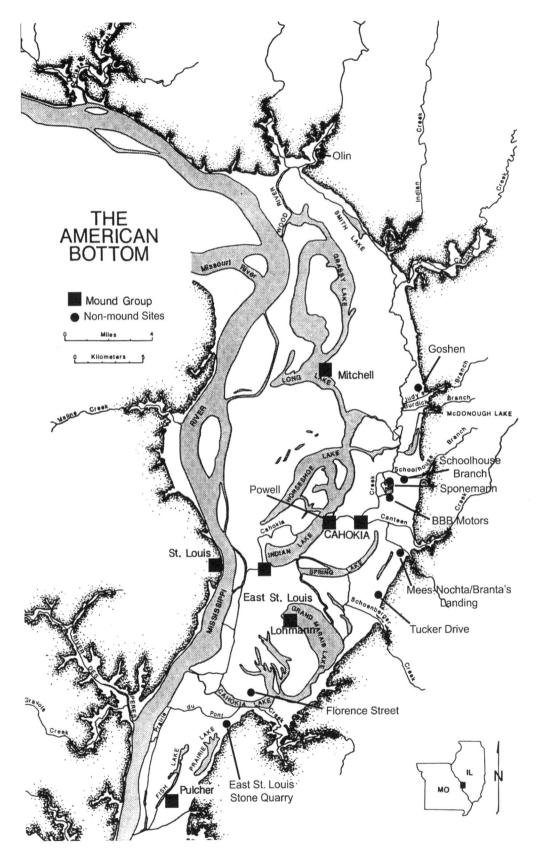

Figure 35. Distribution of Mississippian mound centers and selected sites within the northern American Bottom. Baseline data for map reflects rivers, floodplain, and topography ca. 1800.

indigenous late Emergent Mississippian period to the sudden consolidation of populations into an extraregional ritual capital (Kelly 1996) at Cahokia as the "Big Bang" (Pauketat 1993a). Pauketat (1998) has persistently and incorrectly critiqued prevailing notions about Cahokia's emergence by characterizing them as being gradual in nature. His position is clearly anti-evolutionary and posits an abrupt creation centered on agency. His "Big Bang" is an example of "punctated equilibrium." This comparison is disingenuous because rates of change in archaeologically visible measures of sociopolitical complexity in the American Bottom and elsewhere vary greatly over time (e.g., Milner 2006). More recently, this early stage in Cahokia's development has been characterized as *hypercentralization* (Pauketat and Emerson 1999).

While a considerable amount of debate has been generated about its level of complexity, especially the role of agency in the overt dominance and power of a centralized elite, there is no questioning Cahokia's uniqueness. It is important to emphasize, as Milner (1990) did more than a decade ago, that Cahokia and the other mound complexes in the region have unique histories as communities (Figure 36), and many of these centers were quasi-autonomous. It is also important to note the rapid nature of change within the Cahokia chiefdom, especially in regard to the material remains as well as the organization of communities. Such changes make it possible to clearly delimit relatively short episodes of time (Figure 37) and thus monitor the context of the change, even though the precise dates for these intervals are matters of debate. Although space limitations do not permit a detailing of these changes here, one can readily note another major discontinuity in the site's and region's history at ca. AD 1200, characterized by Brown (2001) as the "Moorehead Moment." (All dates in this chapter are AD.) In fact, one can perhaps best describe these later changes as also abrupt and punctuated and not gradual. Clearly there are threads of continuity in certain aspects of the Cahokia tradition, and the level of abruptness is also quite variable, as are the rates of change. In comparing Moundville and Cahokia, Beck (2006) has argued for variability within these chiefdoms focusing on constituent versus apical hierarchies and the development of the latter out the former, in the case of Cahokia.

Over the years researchers have considered Cahokia's collapse and abandonment, but not in a rigorous and systematic manner. In fact, in his volume on collapse, Tainter (1988) briefly discusses Cahokia and the perspectives as they were then known. Basically, any discussion of Cahokia at the time was, to a large extent, based on Melvin Fowler's (1975; Young and Fowler 2000)

research. One topic of interest to Fowler was the impact that Cahokia had on the "exhaustion of local resources (timber, game, fertile soil), and the rise of competitive political centers" (Tainter 1988:47). Pfeiffer, an anthropological synthesizer of information on Cahokia, suggested that it was a case of "population pressure on a technology unable to feed both the populace and the bureaucracy" (Tainter 1988:57). In many respects the work of Fowler and his students resulted in the perception of Cahokia as a monolithic hierarchy that focused on the Stirling phase (1100–1200) peak. That perspective stemmed largely from the proposed tightly integrated, four-tiered hierarchy of sites, with Cahokia at the top. At the time Gregg (1975) estimated that the population at Cahokia was at least 20,000, but in an editorial footnote in the same article he doubled this figure. This estimate became embedded in the popular and professional literature of the time and is still thought by some researchers to be reliable (see Young and Fowler 2000:310–311).

As new data poured in from the highway projects around Cahokia during the several years on either side of 1980, the complexity surrounding Cahokia's rise and eventual abandonment was beginning to become a little clearer and more focused. The first synthetic treatment of this work in the 1984 American Bottom summary volume (Bareis and Porter 1984), however, did not address the issue of collapse. The Mississippian authors in that volume (Milner et al. 1984) did note that during the mid-fourteenth century Cahokia ceased to be a significant regional capitol.

One of the initial outgrowths of these investigations resulted in George Milner's (1986) population studies which highlighted some of the demographic trends, such as a peak in the rural population during the Stirling phase, and a significant decrease thereafter (Figure 38). Milner's study was restricted to a small segment of the floodplain south of Cahokia and did not take into account the two mound centers, Pulcher and Lohmann, located within the study area. Nor did he consider the dispersal of populations into the adjacent uplands during the Late Mississippian because systematically collected data on such areas were not available in the early 1980s (Koldehoff 1989; Woods and Holley 1991). The inclusion of the aforementioned two mound centers would only have accentuated the population levels of the early phases, Lohmann and Stirling. The addition of the uplands, if at all possible to estimate, would not have significantly altered the Late Mississippian levels. In fact, recent investigations (Pauketat 2003; Powell and Kelly 2001) in the uplands have documented Early Mississippian use of the area,

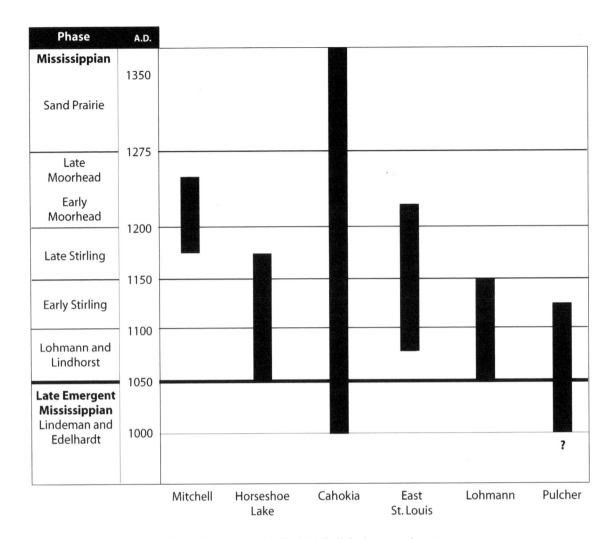

Figure 36. Duration of selected Mississippian mound centers.

especially during the Lohmann and early Stirling phases where such evidence is not easily recognized from surface surveys. Nonetheless, Milner's work is an important methodological benchmark, and he has recently (Milner 1998, 2006) extended his efforts to include Cahokia and the region as a whole (Figure 38).

Milner (1984) has also been responsible for several studies examining the health of Mississippian populations. Most of the work has focused on the Late Mississippian cemeteries surrounding Cahokia, largely because of the nature of available skeletal collections. The results suggest a relatively healthy adult population, with children under greater stress. Thus, disease does not appear to be an issue at this point in Cahokia's demise.

Nearly two decades ago Hall (1991:33) suggested that Cahokia's decline can be "attributed to improved techno-environmental adaptations that reduced the advantages

of large Mississippian population centers in major river bottoms and permitted smaller scattered populations to live in a greater variety of locations at a tribal level of organization." He further notes the use of eight-row Northern Flint corn and the attraction to bison hunting on the plains to the west and thus a westward movement of Missouri and Illinois populations, reducing the "population circumscription" in the "greater Cahokia area."

One exception to the lack of focused research into Cahokia's demise is the Lopinot and Woods (1993) study on environmental degradation as a contributing factor. Other researchers have issued some insightful comments and perspectives that are worth noting. Most of the investigators are in agreement that the peak at Cahokia occurred during the Stirling phase, and most, such as Pauketat (1994, 2004), indicate its gradual demise after that time. Pauketat and others believe the source of this

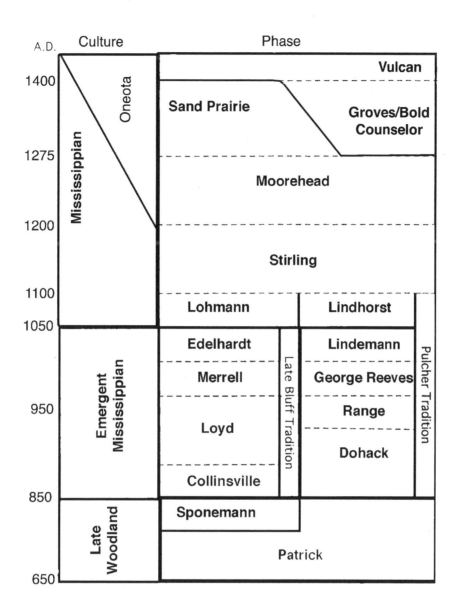

Figure 37. American Bottom chronology (calibrated dates).

decline can be readily traced back to Cahokia's political beginnings and, like Anderson, attribute the primary source of Cahokia's demise to political fragmentation (see Young and Fowler 2000:314). More recently, Emerson (1997; Emerson and Hargrave 2000) has posited, based on the reexamination of cemetery data outside the site, an abrupt change at the end of the Moorehead and beginning of the Sand Prairie phase, and that the "final Cahokian decline, when it came during the early Sand Prairie phase, was total" (Emerson 1997:260). It is not clear what Emerson means by "total." Emerson and Hargrave (2000) argue that the Florence and East St. Louis Stone Quarry cemeteries are not Sand Prairie, as originally posited by Milner and

colleagues (1984), but instead are late Moorehead based on the radiocarbon assays. This reassessment is incorrect since the American Bottom sequence relies primarily on the ceramic assemblages, and the two assemblages in question can be attributed to the Sand Prairie phase. Radiocarbon dates, as has been argued elsewhere (Kelly 1980), are not suitable for these types of nuanced details.

It is the contention here that the demise of Cahokia has to be viewed within the context of its history and at a number of concentric levels: intrasite, intersite, and extra-regional, including a consideration of the environmental setting. Plotting the dynamic nature of these interactions at multiple levels through time is crucial, as is an

152 / JOHN E. KELLY

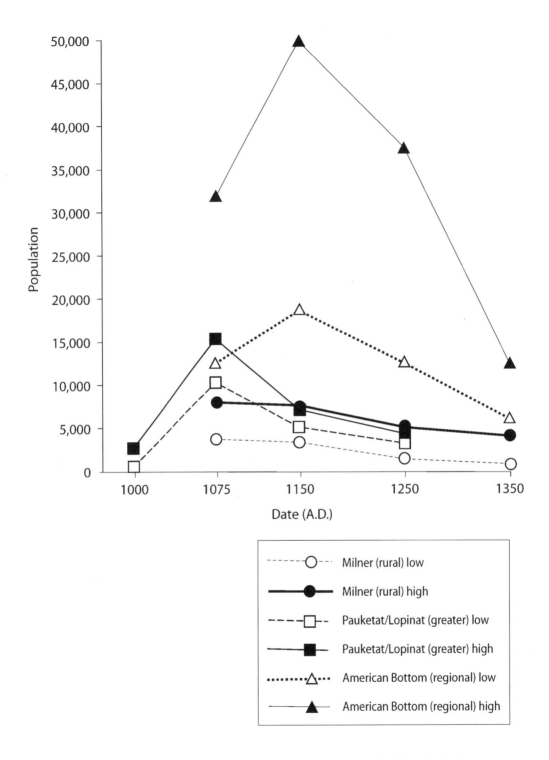

Figure 38. Population estimates for rural (Milner) and Greater (Pauketat/Lopinot)
Cahokia and the American Bottom Mississippian.

understanding of the manner in which society is segmented and specialized. The purpose here is to sketch the outlines of what we know at this point in time. Ongoing research by the author, Jim Brown of Northwestern University, and Mary Beth Trubitt of the Arkansas Archaeological Survey will help provide some resolution, if not a viable explanation for Cahokia's demise.

A HISTORICAL OVERVIEW

In order to understand the collapse of Cahokia, I will begin with a brief history of the Cahokia chiefdom. Throughout its history, Cahokia served as the capital of this polity. There is no apparent disruption in its history as a center, although a major social-political discontinuity is evident at the end of the Stirling phase (Figure 37). In effect there are two separate epochs in the site's history, and this brings into question the possibility of two distinct and significant changes within the Cahokia tradition. Early Cahokia is centered around Cahokia as a supraregional ritual center (Kelly 1997) that is unique for the Mississippian in terms of its overall scale, number of mounds, and plazas. The second epoch is more in line, and coeval, with the classic manifestations of what archaeologists have characterized as Middle Mississippian, based in part on Holmes's (1903) delineation of the "Middle Mississippi" ceramic provenance.

The initial shift represents a transformation that involves internal factionalization, shortly after the Stirling peak. Some marked changes are evident in material culture, the symbolic milieu, mound construction, community organization, and site and regional demography. However, a reorganization of society at a number of different levels still does not diminish the overall importance of Cahokia as a regional as well as a supraregional capital. In her recent article on the Moorehead phase, Trubitt (2000) discusses the dichotomy as one entailing a shift in elite strategy from a corporate level to a network level (Blanton 1998; Blanton et al. 1996; Feinman 1995, 1998, 2000), especially as it pertains to prestige goods. The second change, which might be characterized as a collapse, entails an abandonment of Cahokia as a Mississippian "mound center," and it does appear to have been abrupt and final.

In the Beginning

At the onset, Cahokia represents a uniquely constituted ritual center characterized by a community plan of four plazas distributed about a smaller Monks Mound (Kelly 1996) (Figure 39). Cahokia's founding has to be examined, however, within the context of the extraregional landscape. The boundaries of this chiefdom, if in fact there were any, are for the most part confined to within 20 km of the center (Kelly 2002). Attempts have been made to establish a dichotomous pattern of resistance on the part of some of Cahokia's rural inhabitants (Wilson 1998; Emerson and Pauketat 2002); however, this perspective is tightly melded with the notion of power and dominance on the part of the Cahokia elite. A number of researchers, such as Pauketat and Emerson, have focused on a top-down approach, whereas others, such as Mehrer (1995), Milner (1990, 1998, 2006), and Muller (1997), have argued that, although complex, Cahokia did not dominate the surrounding landscape. Instead, a more middle course has been proposed (L. Kelly 2000), with Cahokia the primary focus of ritual activities in which the regional population participated.

The Early Stirling Apogee

The Stirling phase, in essence, represents the success of Cahokia's initial political consolidation as a ritual capital. Ramey Incised jars serve as the hallmark of Cahokia during its peak and, as discussed by Pauketat and Emerson (1991), serve to mark rites of intensification. The rapid decline in population observed during the Stirling phase reflects the replacement of residential precincts by areas of monumental architecture, such as the Woodhenge monument. New centers such as East St. Louis emerge; smaller centers such as Lohmann, Horseshoe Lake, and Powell continue; and the small, non-mound, ritually specialized nodal centers (Emerson 1997; Mehrer 1995; Milner 1990) become distinct yet short-lived elements on the rural landscape surrounding the center. The resulting process of remaking the social landscape at this time and during the preceding decades to a large extent reflects the success of a dominate lineage, its agents, and an ideology that is shared with communities that extend from Wisconsin to the Ohio and from the Great Plains to the Great Lakes (Kelly 1991). Although the geographic extent of this chiefdom was perhaps greater than during the previous political episode, Cahokia was not a paramount chiefdom controlling multiple smaller, complex polities spread over a large geographic region. The Midwestern Mississippian world during the middle of the twelfth century was a small one. Small chiefdoms were beginning to take root in the area of the Ohio-Mississippi confluence (Cobb and Butler 2006; Muller 1997) as well along the Mississippi River to the south (Morse and Morse 1983) (Figure 40).

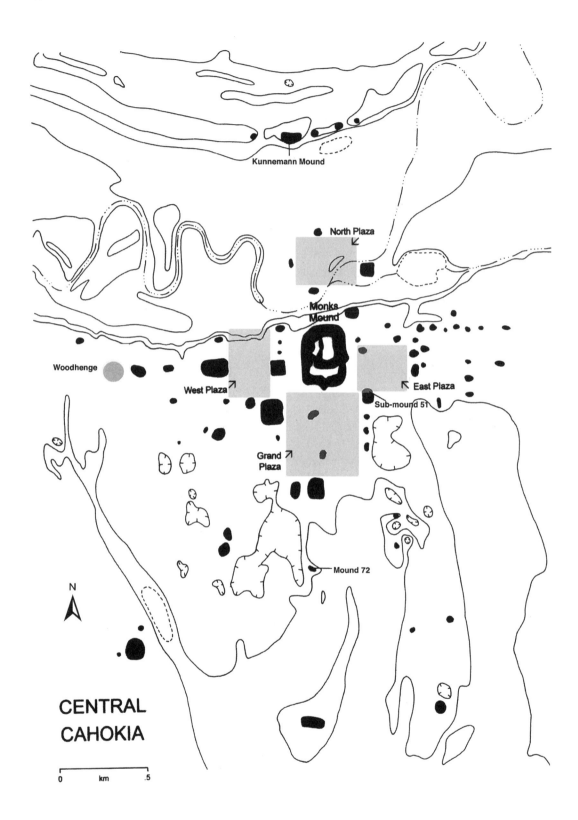

Figure 39. Central Cahokia site plan, Lohmann/Stirling phases.

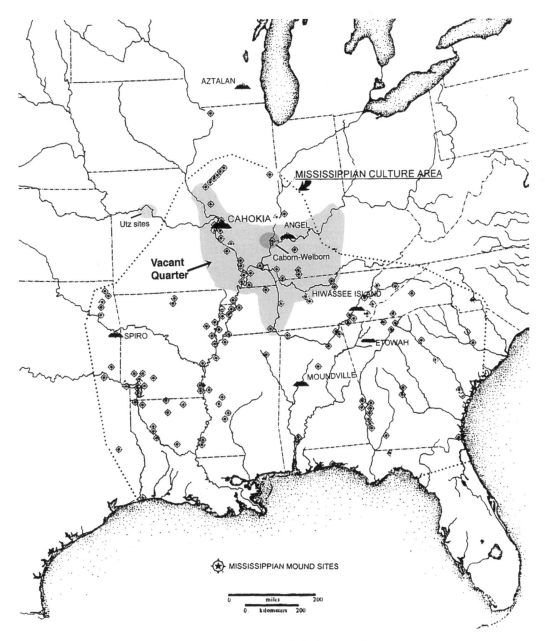

Figure 40. Distribution of Mississippian mound centers.

The seeming success of Cahokia's ruling lineage and its successive chiefs most likely came under assault upon their deaths. It was then that a number of events set into motion the dispersal of the population locally and regionally. One of the events described by Anderson (1996b) is the selection of a new ruler. Rules of inheritance are often an important element of chiefdoms, and any ambiguities would have resulted in competition for the residence on the top of Monks Mound, which would have been divisive. This process of internal factionalization appears to have effected the overall change in the geopolitical landscape of the American Bottom and, for that matter, the entire

Midwest sometime during the latter half of the twelfth century. The outcome was a new regime with attenuated ties to the past. In fact, by the beginning of the thirteenth century Cahokia was still the dominant community locally and beyond—however, on a much smaller scale. Numerous small polities emerged throughout the Midwest at this time. The seeds of Cahokia's reorganization as a center had been sown and were dispersed throughout the Midwestern prairies. The dominance of a much smaller Cahokia persisted for another century, when again there was a scaling back (Milner 1998). Although mounds at the site continued to be used and an occasional stage added, evidence for the construction of new mounds is lacking. This may signal a significant change in ritual activity at the site and regionwide. Cahokia was the only center within a relatively large area, but by the end of the fourteenth century, Cahokia was abandoned. Recent survey and excavation data indicate a subsequent Oneota occupation in a restricted area of the region that dates to the fifteenth century (Booth and Koldehoff 1999).

MODELS OF CHANGE

In order to understand these changes I examine the previous models of Cahokia's collapse. The most popular model on environmental degradation relies heavily on the large populations present at Cahokia and the region during the twelfth century, and the demand placed on wood (e.g., Iseminger 1997).

Environmental Degradation

The types of environmental changes that might have contributed to Cahokia's abandonment as a mound center include resource depletions, climatic change, hydrologic change, and earthquakes. The latter has come to the forefront of archaeological research as a result of seismologists (Tuttle et al. 2002) documenting the periodicity and frequency of earthquakes in the Mississippi Valley related to the New Madrid fault. Interestingly, two of the most severe earthquakes occurred in the early tenth century, nearly a century before the site's emergence as a mound center, and in the early fifteenth century, nearly a century after Cahokia's abandonment. Although evidence of earthquake activity has been found in the Meramec Valley southwest of Cahokia, to my knowledge none has been identified in the American Bottom.

Throughout the Mississippian occupation of the American Bottom a number of environmental changes have been noted. Perhaps the most obvious was the settlement shift to higher landforms during the Moorehead and Sand Prairie phases (Milner et al. 1984). Beyond this change in settlement location we have no independent evidence to suggest the level of water tables changed or that there were more frequent floods from upland streams. Woods (1996) has suggested that more frequent flash floods resulted in increased erosion of deforested uplands and exacerbated an existing problem of wood overexploitation.

Perhaps one of the earliest discussions of change related to Cahokia was the climatic change described by David Baerreis, Reid Bryson, and Wayne Wendland in the late 1960s and early 1970s (Bryson et al. 1970). Their

efforts to document climatic change, especially in northwest Iowa, utilizing proxy data, such as pollen, mollusks, and microfauna, from archaeological contexts did suggest that a drought in the late twelfth century may have been critical in terms of cultural changes at Cahokia. Efforts currently underway by Scott Meeks (2006) at the University of Tennessee have provided some new and significant data for the Southeast as far north as Williams's (1990) "Vacant Quarter," including evidence for a mega-drought covering much of the Vacant Quarter between 1344 and potentially as late as 1372 (Meeks 2006:12). These dates coincide with recent dates for the Sand Prairie occupation on the Merrell Tract/Tract 15B west of Monks Mound (Figure 41). If this evidence is indeed accurate and does cover the area of the Vacant Quarter, we may have identified at least one major factor in Cahokia's abandonment. Meek (2006:14) argues "sustained drought resulted in catastrophic crop failure and promoted political instability which in turn fostered the demise of Mississippian chiefly authority."

As a result of analysis of wood from archaeological contexts in conjunction with a soils study, Lopinot and Woods (1993) proposed that Cahokians had a significant impact on the local environment, especially the possible deforestation of the adjacent uplands. The underlying premise was that given a population size of 15,000–20,000 at Cahokia and the demand for trees for buildings, such as the central palisade (Iseminger 1997), and fuel, the impact on the environment was unavoidable. This deforestation, in turn, resulted in increased soil erosion. Investigations at the Goshen site, located on a fan northeast of Cahokia, have provided evidence for upland erosion during the Mississippian period. This formed the basis for Woods's (1996) proposal that the large Stirling phase population consumed wood in such quantities that upland areas were exposed to significant erosion, which ultimately impacted the agricultural fields on the alluvial fans around Cahokia. More recent evidence collected by this author from other excavated Mississippian sites situated on similar fans throughout the region, on the other hand, indicates more stable landscapes (Table 2). The precontact deposits are capped by extensive erosion from clearing and coal mining during the nineteenth century. It is the contention here that, although Cahokians had an impact on the environment, it was localized. One aspect not taken into account in the deforestation model is the rate of recovery and regeneration of forested areas. An understanding of ecological succession in terms of tree species is critical for modeling the impact. Many of the slope forests are now composed of species not suitable for building materials or fuel, and presumably that was the case in the past.

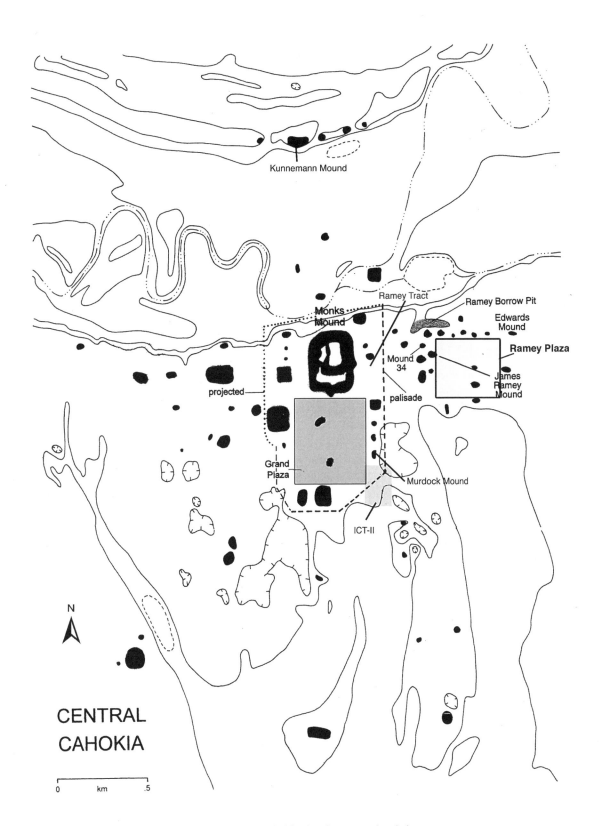

Figure 41. Central Cahokia site plan, Moorehead phase.

Table 2. Summary of buried Mississippian sites on alluvial fans

Site Name	Drainage	Approx. Depth of Recent Alluvial Deposits (m)	Component	Source
Goshen	Judy's Branch	0.90	Early Mississipian	Holley and Brown 1989
Schoolhouse Branch	Schoolhouse Branch	0.50	Moorehead phase	Notes on file at Powell Archaeological Research Center (PARC)
Branta's Landing	Little Canteen Creek	0.50–0.95	Stirling phase	Notes on file at Powell Archaeological Research Center (PARC)
Mees-Nochta	Little Canteen Creek	0.40	Lohmann phase	Notes on file at Powell Archaeological Research Center (PARC)
Tucker Drive	Unnamed Tributary	0.70	Sand Prairie phase	Notes on file at Powell Archaeological Research Center (PARC)
Needle-in-a Haystack	Schoenberger Creek	0.6–1.0 m	Mississippian	Kelly 1998

Evidence for upland cultivation and occupation remains quite limited, although the amount of survey coverage is finally increasing (e.g., Pauketat 2003).

The evidence from the Goshen site, located 7.5 km east of the Mississippian center of Mitchell, in all likelihood represents an example of some type of deforestation. However, I would argue that it could represent the localized clearing of an area for building materials, such as poles for a palisade at the Mitchell mound center (Porter 1974). Clearly the model proposed by Lopinot and Woods is testable from the available archaeological evidence, and it is important that we continue to build on their efforts.

Internal Causes: Factionalization

Many Mississippian researchers are now addressing the endemic nature of political factionalization as the basis for the demise, collapse, and abandonment of Mississippian chiefdoms. The successes of leaders would result in others wanting to be in that enviable position. The eagerness of others to replicate and further extend such achievements led to a situation of competition for the single, exalted position of chief (Anderson 1996b). This is certainly an important cause of the initial transformation at Cahokia, which began during the latter part of the Stirling phase.

Several lines of evidence for such changes exist. Perhaps the most visible and dramatic is the erection of the central palisade. The palisade's construction resulted in the reorganization of the central community, which involved the abandonment of the North, West, and East Plazas (Figure 39). The East Plaza was reconstituted as the Ramey Plaza outside the central palisade (Figure 41) to the east. Not only was a palisade erected at Cahokia, but also at the nearby East St. Louis mound group (Kelly 1994, 1997) (Figure 42); the small upland hamlet of Olin, north of Cahokia; and possibly the Mitchell mound center (Porter 1974) 10 km to the north (Kelly et al. n.d.).

The most dramatic case is associated with the East St. Louis mound center, where a double line of posts with an external ditch was erected around the central precinct (Figure 42). Within this enclosure, a series of smaller structures was erected, many of which burned and were found to contain intact materials, including deposits of maize. These "houses" are tightly packed and are considerably smaller (mean floor area ca. 6.7 m^2) than the typical late Stirling phase structures (mean floor area ca. 22.2 m^2) in the region (Figure 43). Although the burning could be a ritualized act, the unusual array of large stone tools left behind, such as hoes, celts, gouges, and large bifaces known as Ramey knives, could have been used as weapons to fend off an attack. The ceramic assemblage is similar to other late Stirling assemblages except for some notable differences evident in the Ramey Incised jars associated with these hovels. As discussed by Pauketat and Emerson (1991), Ramey Incised jars are considered to be the product of centralized production. Stoltman (1991) has documented the distinctive nature of the paste, reinforcing the argument for restricted production of this ware. While Ramey Incised jars are ubiquitous in the East St. Louis houses, what is of interest is that they do not conform in terms of paste, form, and decorative methods to others in the regional sample. Presumably the production of these copies was not under the control of Cahokia, and thus their production and display at the East St. Louis mound center may represent a form of symbolic defiance of central authority (Kelly 1999).

Other changes evident at this time include the abandonment of the late Stirling residential area of ICT-II (Interpretive Center Tract II) within central Cahokia immediately outside the palisade to the southeast (Collins 1997; Mehrer and Collins 1995). The area was later reoccupied during the Moorehead phase. Of specific interest in the Late Stirling residential area was a catastrophically burned structure similar to a burned Late Stirling phase house on the Ramey Tract 800 m to the north (Pauketat 1987). The latter structure was cut

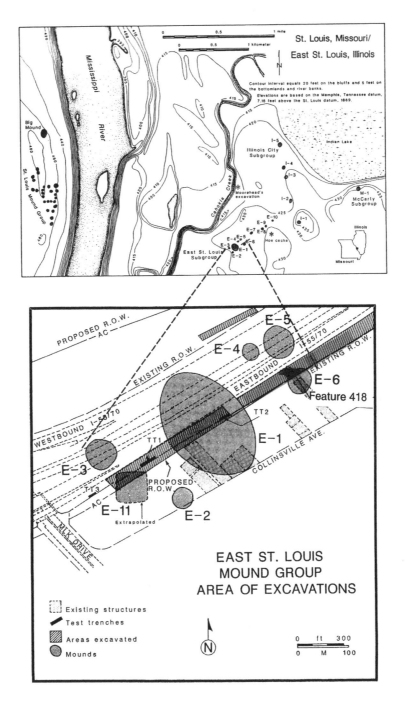

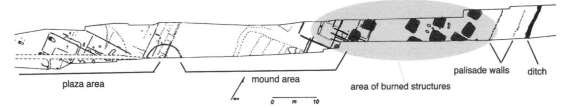

East St. Louis Mound Group
1991-2 Excavations
Plaza-Joshway Mound-Palisade Area

Figure 42. East St. Louis Mound Group palisade.

Size Distribution of Late Stirling House Basins

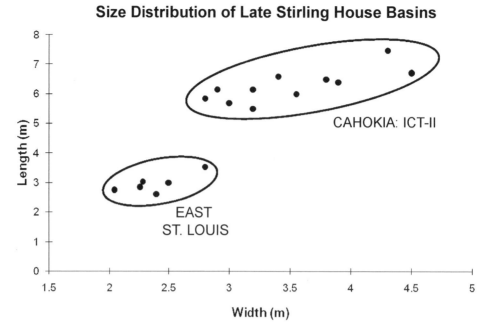

Figure 43. Distribution of Late Stirling house widths vs. lengths from East St. Louis and Cahokia.

through by one of the palisade walls. Again, whether these burned facilities described by Pauketat as catastrophic reflect ritualized acts associated with a specific case of abandonment or some type of other symbolic statement relating to the presumed political fragmentation at this time needs careful consideration.

Three kilometers to the east of central Cahokia we see a similar destructive event with several fertility figurines. The initial discovery of two fireclay figurines from Stirling phase contexts at the BBB Motor site during the course of the FAI-270 project (Emerson 1982) was an important first step in the differentiation and delineation of nodal communities as part of Cahokia's settlement system. For early Cahokia, these unique sculptures symbolically embody the role of fertility as a dominant ideological theme, and the individuals portrayed may represent specific "spirits" or goddesses (Reilly 2004). Ultimately this focus on fertility as a theme has its roots in the Emergent Mississippian societies of the region (Kelly 2002). A kilometer to the north at the Sponemann site (Fortier 1992), at least three additional, elaborately carved statuettes were recovered from slightly later Stirling phase contexts. They also reify this universal theme of fertility and the dominant role of women in Cahokian society. Unlike the two earlier "goddesses," the Sponemann figurines were purposely broken, burned, and dispersed within the settlement. Again, whether this represents a ritual act or a symbolic statement on the failure of the existing institutions remains an intriguing question. What is important is the timing

of this destructive performance with the aforementioned events at East St. Louis and Cahokia.

One final episode that caps the end of the Stirling phase was the abandonment of Monks Mound's fourth terrace and the placement of a meter of fill over the remains of the summit's large (800 m^2) building (Fischer 1972). Similar capping of other mounds, such as Kunnemann (Pauketat 1993b), Murdock (Kelly 1997; Trubitt 2000), and the Powell mound (Kelly 1997), serve to symbolically mark the end of the reign of Cahokia's early elite. They are in effect buried and then memorialized. These mounds, like their earlier inhabitants, continue to silently dominate the landscape.

When one looks beyond the bluffs of the Mississippi surrounding Cahokia, there is a dispersal of the population not only into the adjacent uplands but also into the river valleys, such as the Kaskaskia (Moffat 1985) to the east, where new, smaller polities were established. These people, whose ancestors presumably traveled to Cahokia more than 150 years before to celebrate its creation as a World Center shrine (Hall 1996), were now leaving to establish their own domains. Their ties to Cahokia, however, were not fully severed. We see that these communities continued to be linked to Cahokia because of similar symbolic expressions on ceramic vessels and a strong degree of similarity in the composition of their ceramic assemblages. Like Cahokia, some of these new centers are fortified (O'Brien et al. 1982), emphasizing the concerns of overt threats of aggression, whether real or perceived. Symbolically this concern with what we would call warfare is also evident in the iconography of the Southeastern Ceremonial Complex, especially in the form of falcon impersonators; decapitated heads; and various implements and emblems of warfare (Brown and Dye 2007; Dye 2004). As Jim Brown (2007) has recently discussed, it is not the warfare per se that is important, but an attempt to grapple with the forces of dark and evil and the rebirth of ancestral figures, symbolized by the "rise" of the planet Venus in the pre-dawn morning.

Although Emerson (1997; Emerson and Hargrave 2000) has attempted to convey in his studies a strong dichotomy in the relationship between the Moorehead and Sand Prairie phases, the continuity is stronger than that observed between the Stirling and Moorehead phases. Nonetheless, the demographic changes at the site and in the surrounding area reflect an acceleration of cultural atrophy of the Cahokia chiefdom during the fourteenth century (Milner 1998). In addition to a much smaller population, the mound construction, especially the creation of new mounds, so important to what was Cahokia is no longer evident. This in turn may be linked to the process of creating new public or specialized buildings in which their burial and rebirth were part of the process of mound construction. These changes seen at Cahokia were also occurring over a much broader geographic area. Williams's (1990, 2001) formulation of the Vacant Quarter reflects the abandonment of numerous Mississippian centers from Memphis to St. Louis and thus represents factors that extend beyond the internal dynamics of individual polities. Although the area was probably never completely depopulated, mound centers ceased to exist as viable communities and centers of political and ritual activity, and they became silent monuments to a once dynamic past.

What then? One of the patterns of eastern North American societies since the Middle Archaic is a tradition of creating new World Center shrines (Hall 1996). Cahokia was certainly one such shrine at its inception. During the fifteenth century a number of new "centers" emerged in the Prairie Peninsula of the Midwest. These are characterized not by large mounds, but by extensive areas of occupation. One such area is centered on the Utz site in central Missouri (Yelton 1998); another, known as Caborn-Welborn, emerged at the mouth of the Wabash River where it meets the Ohio (Green and Munson 1978; Pollack 2004). Recent work in the American Bottom has documented Oneota settlement in a portion of the Cahokia site (Figure 44) and along the bluffs south of Cahokia (Figure 45). Presumably it was at these locations that the remaining inhabitants of Cahokia congregated.

dated

SUMMARY

Mississippian chiefdoms included numerous polities that covered the southeastern quarter of the Eastern Woodlands from the eleventh century well into the sixteenth century and beyond in a few instances. These polities represented the most complex non-state entities north of Mexico encountered by Europeans in the early sixteenth century. Societies categorized as chiefdoms based on numerous global ethnographic examples are often perceived as a necessary precursor to state formation. They are dynamic yet fragile entities that seem to endure for varying periods of time before disappearing. Whether one characterizes their abandonment as "collapse" is certainly debatable. A brief perusal of the Mississippian literature indicates that only a few researchers (Hally 1996a; Pollack 2004) actually use the term to characterize what happens to many chiefdoms at the end of their existence. Others use terms such as abandonment and demise. Clearly what is important is to identify those factors that contributed to this process of dissolution. In particular, Anderson (1994, 1996a, 1996b) has addressed some of these issues in his research, and more recently Blitz (1999) has argued that these polities were not only subject to the cycling identified by Anderson but also were able to expand and contract in a variety of ways. To a large extent the political fragility of the Mississippian chiefdom rests on the authority invested in those leaders designated as chiefs (see Payne 2002). While one can look at such issues in terms of the internal dynamics of these polities, issues relating to interaction with other chiefdoms and the more mundane aspects of population health and disease, resources, and environmental change are important considerations. There is no simple answer to the question of chiefdom collapse, word and each polity needs to be examined within the context of all possibilities.

Perhaps the earliest Mississippian chiefdom to emerge was Cahokia. At the outset in the late Emergent Mississippian of the early tenth century, numerous smaller communities consolidated into a much larger community. The sudden transformation of the landscape both within this ritualized center and the surrounding region produced an unusual phenomenon. A number of individuals (Saitta 1994; Trubitt 2000) have emphasized the corporate nature of early Cahokia. Outside the Coles Creek mound groups in the lower Mississippi Valley, Cahokia stood out from the few mound centers that were scattered throughout the Southeast and Midwest. The rapid development of Oneota complexes to the north and the formulation of other Mississippian

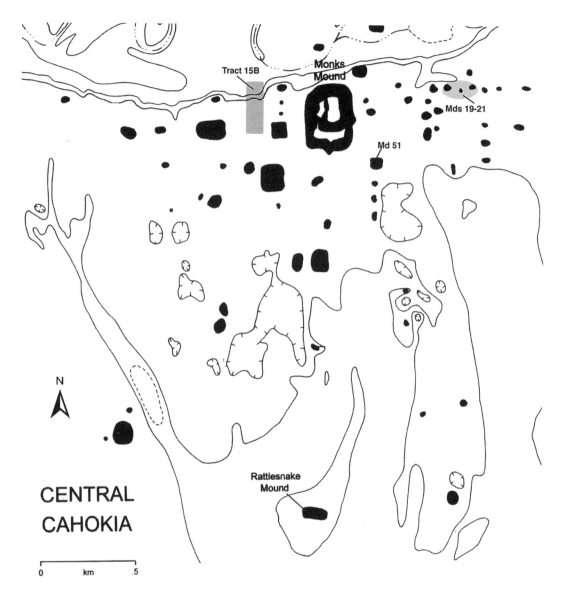

Figure 44. Oneota Sites in central Cahokia.

polities in the Eastern Woodlands during the twelfth century coincided with a number of significant changes at Cahokia which are described by Trubitt as a shift to a network type of political strategy by its chiefs. Also of note was a noticeable depopulation of the site and region (Milner 2006). This is an example of the process of fissioning characterized by Blitz (1999) that resulted in the appearance of other smaller polities just beyond Cahokia's effective reach. There is substantial evidence for intergroup conflict in the form of palisaded centers and villages throughout much of the Southeast and Midwest by the onset of the thirteenth century (Milner 1999). This is a pattern that spreads across the Eastern Woodlands and onto the Plains and is also evident in the ethnohistoric records of European encounters.

The abandonment of Cahokia as a viable center by the end of the fourteenth century can be seen as a political collapse. This event is not unique to this center but is evident throughout much of the mid-south as part Williams's Vacant Quarter. While there has been a focus on the impact of Cahokian populations on the local environment, there is insufficient evidence to see it as a sole cause of the site's abandonment. With Meeks's (2006) recent work to the south and the identification of a mega-drought during the mid to late fourteenth century, however, we can began to examine in greater detail how

John Winger volume

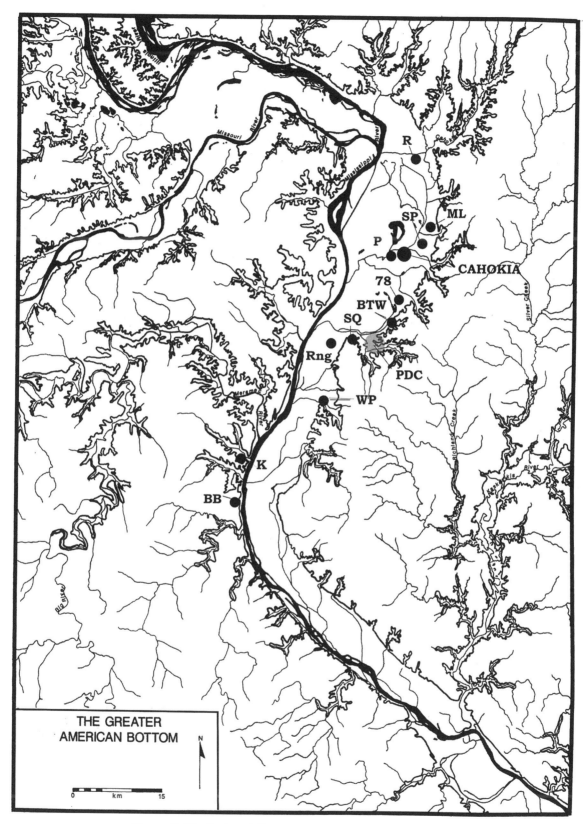

Figure 45. Distribution of Oneota Sites within the American Bottom.

Key: 78, 78th Street; BB, Bushberg Beach; BTW, Booker T. Washington; K, Kimmswick; ML, McDonough Lake; P, Powell; PDC, Prairie du Pont Creek site complex; R, Ringering; Rng, Range; SP, Sponemann; SQ, Stolle Quarry; WP, Westpark.

such a change impacted these polities. With the apparent cessation of mound construction at Cahokia after the Moorehead phase, which was a key component of its original ritual constitution, it is clear that changes had been set in motion that led to the amalgamation of the population with societies we classify archaeologically as Oneota. Although the site's abandonment may signal its end as a Mississippian polity, this did not preclude its continued use as a sacred place on the landscape by its descendants.

In summary, while the most popular explanation of Cahokia's collapse has centered on environmental degradation, others have posited that the basis for collapse is inherently fixed within the political structures of Mississippian chiefdoms. In reviewing the evidence from Cahokia and its satellites it is evident that there were two episodes of significant and rather abrupt change at Cahokia. The earliest was a transformation in the existing hegemony, one that can be readily related to internal factionalization. The subsequent demise of the Cahokia chiefdom is one of political collapse, which resulted in the abandonment of Cahokia as a Mississippian center. This later collapse, although involving internal social and political dynamics, relates more to the dynamics outside the region and the establishment of new centers linked to the upper Midwestern Oneota traditions. For the American Bottom, such a concentration occurs some 14 km south of Cahokia and is part of the broader Oneota utilization of the area. In the end our understanding of the interaction between the Oneota societies to the north of Cahokia and the indigenous populations within the American Bottom are critical to the composition of post-Cahokia American Bottom populations. The negotiation of these social and political relationships coupled with an understanding of how the natural landscape has changed vis-a-vis climatic change and the human impact on that environment will contribute to a more accurate perspective on the collapse of Mississippian polities.

The author would like to extend his appreciation to the editors of this volume first for including me in the symposium at the 2000 SAAs in Philadelphia and second for extending an invitation to be part of this volume. A number of individuals have taken the time to provide comments on the paper, including James Brown, Lucretia Kelly, and George Milner. Their efforts are greatly appreciated. In the early stages of preparing this chapter, Ronda Sackett helped immensely in compiling the bibliography and carefully cross-checking it with the text. Finally, I would like to thank June-el Piper and Jim Railey for the time they spent editing both the text and especially the figures, and Donna Carpio for drafting the edited figures.

REFERENCES

Anderson, David G.
  1994 *The Savannah River Chiefdoms: Political Change in the Late Prehistoric Southeast.* Tuscaloosa: University of Alabama Press.
  1996a Chiefly Cycling and Large-Scale Abandonments as Viewed from the Savannah River Basin. In *Political Structure and Change in the Prehistoric Southeastern United States,* edited by John F. Scarry, pp. 150–191. Gainesville: University Press of Florida.
  1996b Fluctuations between Simple and Complex Chiefdoms: Cycling in the Late Prehistoric Southeast. In *Political Structure and Change in the Prehistoric Southeastern United States,* edited by John F. Scarry, pp. 231–252. Gainesville: University Press of Florida.
Baries, Charles J., and James W. Porter
  1984 *American Bottom Archaeology: A Summary of the FAI-270 Project.* Urbana: University of Illinois Press.
Beck, Robert
  2003 Consolidation and Hierarchy: Chiefdom Variability in the Mississippian Southeast. *American Antiquity* 68:641–661.

  2006 Persuasive Politics and Domination at Cahokia and Moundville. In *Leadership and Polity in Mississippian Society,* edited by Brian M. Butler and Paul D. Welch, pp. 19–42. Center for Archaeological Investigations, Occasional Paper 33. Carbondale: Southern Illinois University.
Blanton, Richard E.
  1998 Beyond Centralization: Steps towards Egalitarian Behavior in Archaic States. In *Archaic States,* edited by Gary M. Feinman and Joyce Marcus, pp. 135–172. Santa Fe: School of American Research.
Blanton, Richard E., Gary M. Feinman, Stephan A. Kowalewski, and Peter N. Peregrine
  1996 A Dual-Processual Theory for the Evolution of Meso-american Civilization. *Current Anthropology* 37:1–31.
Blitz, John H.
  1999 Mississippian Chiefdoms and the Fission-Fusion Process. *American Antiquity* 64:577–592.
Booth, Donald L., and Brad Koldehoff
  1999 *The Emergency Watershed Protection Archaeological Survey Project.* Illinois Transportation Archaeological

Research Program Research Reports 62. University of Illinois Urbana-Champaign.

Brown, James A.

2001 The Invention of an Art Style as an Instrument of Elite Control in the Mississippian Southeast. Paper presented at the 58th annual meeting of the Southeastern Archaeological Conference, November 16, Chattanooga.

2007 On the Identity of the Birdman within Mississippian Period Art and Iconography. In *Ancient Objects and Sacred Realms: Interpretations of Mississippian Iconography,* edited by F. Kent Reilly III and James F. Garber, pp. 56–106. Austin: University of Texas Press.

Brown, James A., and David Dye

2007 Severed Heads and Sacred Scalplocks: Mississippian Iconographic Trophies. In *The Taking and Displaying of Human Trophies by Amerindians,* edited by Richard J. Chacon and David H. Dye, pp. 274–294. New York: Springer.

Bryson, Reid A., David A. Barreis, and Wayne M. Wendland

1970 The Character of Late-Glacial and Post-Glacial Climatic Changes. In *Pleistocene and Recent Environments of the Central Great Plains,* edited by Jr. and J. Knox Jones Wakefield Port, Jr., pp. 53–74. Lawrence: University Press of Kansas.

Carneiro, Robert L.

1981 The Chiefdom: Precursor to the State. In *The Transition to Statehood in the New World,* edited by Grant D. Jones and Robert R. Kantz, pp. 37–79. New York: Cambridge University Press.

Cobb, Charles, and Brian Butler

2006 Mississippian Migration and Emplacement in the Lower Ohio Valley. In *Leadership and Polity in Mississippian Society,* edited by Brian M. Butler and Paul D. Welch, pp. 328–347. Center for Archaeological Investigations, Occasional Paper 33. Carbondale: Southern Illinois University.

Collins, James M.

1997 Cahokia Settlement and Social Structures as Viewed from the ICT-II. In *Cahokia: Domination and Ideology in the Mississippian World,* edited by T. R. Pauketat and T. E. Emerson, pp. 124–140. Lincoln: University of Nebraska Press.

Dye, David

2004 Art, Ritual, and Chiefly Warfare in the Mississippian World. In *Hero, Hawk, and Open Hand: American Indian Art of the Ancient Midwest and South,* edited by Richard F. Townsend, pp. 191–205. Art Institute of Chicago, in association with Yale University Press, New Haven.

Earle, Timothy

1997 *How Chiefs Come to Power: The Political Economy in Prehistory.* Palo Alto: Stanford University Press.

Emerson, Thomas E.

1982 *Mississippian Stone Images in Illinois.* Illinois Archaeological Survey Circular 6. Urbana.

1997 *Cahokia and the Archaeology of Power.* Tuscaloosa: University of Alabama Press.

Emerson, Thomas E., and Eve Hargrave

2000 Strangers in Paradise? Recognizing Ethnic Mortuary Diversity on the Fringes of Cahokia. *Southeastern Archaeology* 19:1–23.

Emerson, Thomas E., and Timothy R. Pauketat

2002 Embodying Power and Resistance at Cahokia. In *The Dynamics of Power,* edited by M. O'Donovan, pp. 102–125. Center for Archaeological Investigations, Occasional Paper 30. Carbondale: Southern Illinois University.

Emerson, Thomas E., Eve Hargrave, and Kristin Hedman

2003 Death and Ritual in Early Rural Cahokia. In *Theory, Method, and Technique in Modern Archaeology,* edited by R. J. Jeske and D. K. Charles, pp. 163–181. Westport CT: Bergin and Garvey.

Feinman, Gary M.

1995 The Emergence of Inequality: A Focus on Strategies and Processes. In *Foundations of Social Inequality,* edited by T. D. Price and G. M. Feinman, pp. 255–280. New York: Plenum Press.

1998 Corporate/Network; A New Perspective on Leadership in the American Southwest. In *Hierarchies in Action: Who Benefits?* edited by M. A. Diehl, pp. 152–180. Center for Archaeological Investigations, Occasional Paper 27. Carbondale: Southern Illinois University.

2000 Dual-Processual Theory and Social Formations in the Southwest. In *Alternative Leadership Strategies in the Prehispanic Southwest,* edited by Barbara J. Mills, pp. 207–224. Tucson: University of Arizona Press.

Feinman, Gary M., and Joyce Marcus, eds.

1998 *Archaic States.* Santa Fe: School of American Research Press.

Fischer, Fred W.

1972 Recent Archaeological Investigations on the Fourth Elevation of Monks Mound, Madison County, Illinois. Unpublished ms. on file, Department of Anthropology, Washington University, St. Louis.

Fortier, Andrew C.

1992 Stone Figurines. In *The Sponemann Site 2 (11-Ms-517): The Mississippian and Oneota Occupations*, by Douglas K. Jackson, Andrew C. Fortier, and Joyce A. Williams, pp. 276–303. American Bottom Archaeology FAI-270 Site Reports, Vol 24. Urbana: University of Illinois Press.

Fowler, Melvin L.

1975 A Pre-Columbian Urban Center on the Mississippi. *Scientific American* 233:92–101.

Green, Thomas J., and Cheryl A. Munson

1978 Mississippian Settlement Patterns in Southwestern Indiana. In *Mississippian Settlement Patterns,* edited by Bruce D. Smith, pp. 292–330. New York: Academic Press.

Gregg, Michael L.

1975 A Population Estimate for Cahokia. In *Perspectives in Cahokia Archaeology*, pp. 126–136. Urbana: Illinois Archaeological Survey, Bulletin 10.

Hall, Robert L.

1991 Cahokia Identity and Interaction Models of Cahokia Mississippian. In *Cahokia and the Hinterlands: Middle Mississippian Cultures of the Midwest*, edited by T. E. Emerson and R. B. Lewis, pp. 3–34. Urbana: University of Illinois Press.

1996 American Indian Worlds, World Quarters, World Centers, and their Shrines. In *The Ancient Skies and Sky Watchers of Cahokia: Woodhenges, Eclipses, and Cahokian Cosmology*, edited by Melvin Fowler. *Wisconsin Archeologist* 77(3/4):120–127.

Hally, David J.

1993 The Territorial Size of Mississippian Chiefdoms. In *Archaeology of Eastern North America: Papers in Honor of S. Williams*, edited by J. B. Stoltman, pp. 143–168. Jackson: Mississippi Department of Archives and History, Archaeological Report No. 25.

1996 Platform-Mound Construction and the Instability of Mississippian Chiefdoms. In *Political Structure and Change in the Prehistoric Southeastern United States*, edited by John F. Scarry, pp. 92–127. Gainesville: University Press of Florida.

Holmes, William H.

1903 Aboriginal Pottery of the Eastern United States. In *Twentieth Annual Report of the Bureau of American Ethnology*, pp. 1–201. Washington DC: Smithsonian Institution.

Iseminger, William R.

1997 Culture and Environment in the American Bottom: The Rise and Fall of Cahokia Mounds. In *Common Fields: An Environmental History of St. Louis*, edited by Andrew Hurley, pp. 38–57. St. Louis: Missouri Historical Society Press.

Kelly, John E.

1980 *Formative Developments at Cahokia and the Adjacent American Bottom: A Merrell Tract Perspective*. Unpublished Ph.D. dissertation, University of Wisconsin, Madison.

1991 Cahokia and Its Role as a Gateway Center in Interregional Exchange. In *Cahokia and the Hinterlands: Middle Mississippian Cultures of the Midwest*, edited by T. E. Emerson and R. B. Lewis, pp. 61–82. Urbana: University of Illinois Press.

1994 The Archaeology of the East St. Louis Mound Center: Past and Present. *Illinois Archaeology* 6:1–57.

1996 Redefining Cahokia: Prince(ples) and Elements of Community Organization. In *The Ancient Skies and Sky Watchers of Cahokia: Woodhenges, Eclipses,*

and Cahokian Cosmology, edited by Melvin Fowler. *Wisconsin Archeologist* 77(3/4):97–119.

1997 Stirling-Phase Sociopolitical Activity at East St. Louis and Cahokia. In *Cahokia: Domination and Ideology in the Mississippian World*, edited by T. R. Pauketat and T. E. Emerson, pp. 141–166. Lincoln: University of Nebraska Press.

1999 The Context of the East St. Louis Palisade: Run! The Giants are Coming. Paper presented at the 56th annual meeting of the Southeastern Archaeological Conference, November 12, Pensacola.

2002 The Pulcher Tradition and the Ritualization of Cahokia: A Perspective from Cahokia's Southern Neighbor. *Southeastern Archaeology* 21:136–48.

Kelly, John E., Mary Beth Trubitt, William Iseminger, and Sidney Denny

n.d. In Defense of Cahokia: Defining the Central Palisade. Unpublished ms. in the authors' possession.

Kelly, Lucretia S.

2000 *Social Implications of Faunal Provisioning of the Cahokia Site: Initial Mississippian, Lohmann Phase*. Unpublished Ph.D. dissertation, Washington University, St. Louis.

Koldehoff, Brad

1989 Cahokia's Immediate Hinterland: The Mississippian Occupation of Douglas Creek. *Illinois Archaeology* 1:39–68.

Lopinot, Neal H., and William I. Woods

1993 Wood Overexploitation and the Collapse of Cahokia. In *Foraging and Farming in the Eastern Woodlands*, edited by C. M. Scarry, pp. 206–231. Gainesville: University Press of Florida.

Meeks, Scott

2006 Drought, Subsistence Stress, and Political Instability: Late Prehistoric Abandonment in the Tennessee River Valley. Paper presented at the 63rd annual meeting of the Southeastern Archaeological Conference, November 21, Little Rock.

Mehrer, Mark M.

1995 *Cahokia's Countryside: Household Archaeology, Settlement Patterns, and Social Power*. DeKalb: Northern Illinois University Press.

Mehrer, Mark W., and James M. Collins

1995 Household Archaeology at Cahokia and in Its Hinterlands. In *Mississippian Communities and Households*, edited by J. D. Rogers and B. D. Smith, pp. 32–57. Tuscaloosa: University of Alabama Press.

Milner, George R.

1984 Social and Temporal Implications of Variation among American Bottom Mississippian Cemeteries. *American Antiquity* 49:468–488.

1986 Mississippian Period Population Density in a Segment of the Central Mississippi Valley. *American Antiquity* 51:227–238.

1990 The Late Prehistoric Cahokia Cultural System of the Mississippi River Valley: Foundations, Florescence, and Fragmentation. *Journal of World Prehistory* 4:1–43.

1996 Development and Dissolution of a Mississippian Society in the American Bottom. In *Political Structure and Change in the Prehistoric Southeastern United States,* edited by John F. Scarry, pp. 27–52. Gainesville: University Press of Florida.

1998 *The Cahokia Chiefdom: The Archaeology of a Mississippian Society.* Washington, DC: Smithsonian Institution Press.

1999 Warfare in Prehistoric and Early Historic Eastern North America. *Journal of Archaeological Research* 7:105–151.

2006 *The Cahokia Chiefdom: The Archaeology of a Mississippian Society.* Gainesville: University of Florida Press.

Milner, George R., T. E. Emerson, M. W. Mehrer, J. A. Williams, and D. Esarey

1984 Mississippian and Oneota Period. In *American Bottom Archaeology,* edited by C. J. Bareis and J. W. Porter, pp. 158–186. Urbana: University of Illinois Press.

Moffat, Charles

1985 *The Mississippian Occupation of the Upper Kaskaskia Valley: Problems in Culture History and Economic Organization.* Unpublished Ph.D. Dissertation, Department of Anthropology, University of Illinois Urbana-Champaign.

Morse, Dan F., and Phyllis A. Morse

1983 *Archaeology of the Central Mississippi Valley.* New York: Academic Press.

Muller, Jon

1997 *Mississippian Political Economy.* Plenum Press, New York and London.

O'Brien, Michael J., John L. Beets, Robert E. Warren, Tachpong Hotrabhavananda, Terry W. Barney, and Eric Voight

1982 Digital Enhancement and Grey-leveling Slicing of Aerial Photographs: Techniques for Archaeological Analysis of Intrasite Variability. *World Archaeology* 14:173–190.

Pauketat, Timothy R.

1987 A Burned Domestic Building at Cahokia. *Wisconsin Archeologist* 68:212–327.

1993a Big Bang in the Bottom: Political Consolidation and Mississippian at Cahokia. Paper presented at the 58th annual meeting of the Society for American Archaeology, St. Louis.

1993b *Temples for Cahokia's Lords: Preston Holder's 1955–1956 Excavations of the Kunnemann Mound.* Memoirs of the Museum of Anthropology, University of Michigan, 26. Ann Arbor.

1994 *The Ascent of Chief: Cahokia and Mississippian Politics in Native North America.* Tuscaloosa: University of Alabama Press.

1998 Refiguring the Archaeology of Greater Cahokia. *Journal of Archaeological Research* 6:45–89.

2003 Resettled Farmers and the Making of a Mississippian Polity. *American Antiquity* 68:39–66.

2004 *Ancient Cahokia and the Mississippians.* Cambridge: Cambridge University Press.

Pauketat, Timothy R., and Thomas E. Emerson

1991 The Ideology of Authority and the Power of the Pot. *American Anthropologist* 93:919–941.

1999 The Representation of Hegemony as Community at Cahokia. In *Material Symbols: Culture and Economy in Prehistory,* edited by J. Robb, pp. 302–317. Center for Archaeological Investigations, Occasional Paper 26. Carbondale: Southern Illinois University.

Payne, Claudine

2002 Architectural Reflections of Power and Authority in Mississippian Towns. In *The Dynamics of Power,* edited by Maria O'Donovan, pp. 188–213. Center for Archaeological Investigations, Occasional Paper 30. Carbondale: Southern Illinois University.

2006 The Foundations of Leadership in Mississippian Chiefdoms: Perspectives from Lake Jackson and Upper Nodena. In *Leadership and Polity in Mississippian Society,* edited by Brian M. Butler and Paul D. Welch, pp. 91–111. Center for Archaeological Investigations, Occasional Paper 33. Carbondale: Southern Illinois University.

Pollack, David

2004 *Caborn-Welborn: Constructing a New Society after the Angel Chiefdom Collapse.* Tuscaloosa: University of Alabama Press.

2006 Late Mississippian Caborn-Welborn Social and Political Relationships. In *Leadership and Polity in Mississippian Society,* edited by Brian M. Butler and Paul D. Welch, pp. 309–327. Center for Archaeological Investigations, Occasional Paper 33. Carbondale: Southern Illinois University.

Porter, James W.

1974 *Cahokia Archaeology as Viewed from the Mitchell Site: A Satellite Community at 1150–1200.* Ph.D. dissertation, University of Wisconsin. University Microfilms, Ann Arbor.

Powell, Gina, and John E. Kelly

2001 The Lehman-Sommers Site: Implications of Settlement Organization and Process as Regards Cahokia Domination and Resistance. Paper presented at the 66th annual meeting of the Society for American Archaeology, April 21, New Orleans.

Reilly, Kent F., III

2004 People of Earth, People of Sky. In *Hero, Hawk, and Open Hand: American Indian Art of the Ancient Midwest and South,* edited by Richard F. Townsend, pp. 125–137. Art Institute of Chicago, in association with Yale University Press, New Haven.

Saitta, Dean J.

1994 Agency, Class, and Archaeological Interpretation. *Journal of Anthropological Archaeology* 13:201–227.

Stoltman, James B.

1991 Ceramic Petrography as a Technique for Documenting Cultural Interaction: An Example from the Upper Mississippi Valley. *American Antiquity* 56:103–120.

Tainter, Joseph A.

1988 *The Collapse of Complex Societies.* Cambridge: Cambridge University Press.

Trubitt, Mary Beth D.

2000 Mound Building and Prestige Goods Exchange; Changing Strategies in the Cahokia Chiefdom. *American Antiquity* 675:669–690.

Tuttle, Martitia P. and Eugene S. Schweig, John D. Sims, Robert H. Lafferty, Lorraine W. Wolf, and Marion L. Haynes

2002 The Earthquake Potential of the New Madrid Seismic Zone. *Bulletin of the Seismological Society of America* (92):2080–2089.

Williams, Stephen

1990 The Vacant Quarter and Other Late Events in the Lower Valley. In *Towns and Temples along the Mississippi,* edited by David H. Dye and Cheryl A. Cox., pp. 170–180. Tuscaloosa: University of Alabama Press.

2001 The Vacant Quarter Hypothesis and the Yazoo Delta. In *Societies in Eclipse: Archaeology of the Eastern Woodlands Indians, A.D. 1400–1700,* edited by David S. Brose, C. Wesley Cowan, and Robert C. Mainfort Jr, pp. 191–203. Washington, DC: Smithsonian Institution Press.

Wilson, Gregory D.

1998 A Case Study of Mississippian Resistance in the American Bottom. Unpublished Master's thesis, Department of Anthropology, University of Oklahoma, Norman.

Woods, William I.

1996 The Fall of Cahokia: An Unintended Suicide. Paper presented at the Illinois History Symposium, December 1, Springfield.

Woods, William I., and George R. Holley

1991 Upland Mississippian Settlement in the American Bottom Region. In *Cahokia and the Hinterlands: Middle Mississippian Cultures of the Midwest,* edited by T. E. Emerson and R. B. Lewis, pp. 46–60. Urbana: University of Illinois Press.

Yelton, Jeffery K.

1998 A Different View of Oneota Taxonomy and Origins in the Lower Missouri Valley. In *Oneota Taxonomy: Papers from the Oneota Symposium of the 54th Plains Anthropological Conference,* edited by R. Eric Hollinger and David W. Benn. *Wisconsin Archeologist* 79(2):268–283.

Yoffee, Norman and George Cowgill

1988 *The Collapse of Ancient States and Civilizations.* Tucson: University of Arizona Press.

Young, Bilone W., and Melvin L. Fowler

2000 *Cahokia: The Great Native American Metropolis.* Urbana: University of Illinois Press.

Contributors

Mark W. Allen, Associate Professor of Anthropology, Department of Geography and Anthropology, California State Polytechnic University, Pomona CA. Email: mwallen@csupomonma.edu

Robert N. Bartone, Assistant Director for Archaeology, University of Maine, Farmington.

Garth Bawden, Professor (retired), Department of Anthropology, University of New Mexico. Email: gbawden@unm.edu

John G. Crock, Assistant Professor, Department of Anthropology, University of Vermont. Email: John.Crock@uvm.edu

Michael J. Heckenberger, Associate Professor, Department of Anthropology, University of Florida. Email: mheckenb@anthro.ufl.edu

John E. Kelly, Senior Lecturer in Archaeology, Department of Anthropology, Washington University in St. Louis. Email: jkelly@artsci.wustl.edu

Eduardo Goes Neves, Associate Professor, Museu de Arqueologia e Etnologia, Universidade de São Paulo, Brazil.

James B. Petersen (1954–2005), former Professor and Chair, Department of Anthropology, University of Vermont.

Jim A. Railey, Principal Investigator, SWCA Environmental Consultants, Albuquerque. Email: jrailey5715@msn.com

Richard Martin Reycraft, Chief of Preservation, New Mexico State Monuments. Email: richard.reycraft@state.nm.us

Helaine Silverman, Professor, Department of Anthropology, University of Illinois at Urbana-Champaign. Email: helaine@uiuc.edu

Peter S. Wells, Professor, Department of Anthropology, University of Minnesota. Email: Wells001@umn.edu

Allen Zagarell, Professor, Department of Anthropology, Western Michigan University. Email: allen.zagarell@wmich.edu

Index

Mid South Conference
June 21 on campus
due June 1st
a to whenever